VRIL AND GERMANIC MAGIC

BALDER
RISING
PUBLISHING

VRIL AND GERMANIC MAGIC:

HOW TO HARNESS VRIL AND USE IT ACCORDING TO THE PRINCIPLE OF GERMANIC MAGIC

by

Robert Blumetti

ISBN 978-1-67800-055-4

I would like to extend special thanks to Dr. Robert Goodman for his help in editing this book.

I dedicate this book to my old friend and mentor Robert Zoller who led me to the Rainbow Bridge.

Robert Zoller passed away on Jan 24, 2020 2:15pm one day before his 73th birthday, Robert E Zoller.

Bob Zoller was my mentor and friend. I met him in 1980, while we worked at Barnes and Nobles, located at Rockerfeller Center in NYC. His father was German-Lutherian, and his mother was Irish-Catholic. He told me he grew up in the 30 years war. He and his brother were not brought up in any faith. His parents wanted him to decide for their selves. He became a heathen. He was a world renown astrologer and wrote several books on the subject. I remember Bob telling me, in the year 2000 that there would be a major terrorist attack on the northeast coast of the United States, some where between Washington DC and Boston in either August or September 2001. A year later was the Islamic attack on New York and in Washington DC.

We became good friends and in 1984 he invited me to join his Norse Rune study group. It was a epiphany for me and changed my life. Ever since I have been a dedicated heathen. We used to get together often and spend hours talking and researching many subjects. He was a genius and a noble soul. Sometimes we would spend a whole day in Manhattan. Once we walked from 86 Street in the upper east side, down to Canal Street talking about every subject under the sun.

Bob suffered from Parkinson since 1989. And though the disease took its toll on his body, his mind remained sharp to the end.

Robert E Zoller
Born Jan. 25, 1947 -- Died Jan. 24, 2020

Other Books by Robert Blumetti

On Odinism:
Vril: the Secret to a Happy and Successful Life
Vrilology: the Secret Science of the Ancient Aryans
The Book of Balder Rising
The new Book of Balder Rising
The Complete Edda
The Elder Futhark
Yggdrasil Training Program
- Hel: Part One
- Jotunheim: Part Two
- Svartalfheim: Part Three
- Niflheim: Part Four
- Midgard: Part Five
- Muspellheim: Part Six
- Ljossalfheim: Part Seven
- Vanaheim: Part Eight
- Asgard: Part Nine

Fiction:
The Falin Crisis
Galactic Affairs Short Stories
What If?
More What Ifs?
New Earth Odyssey series:
- The Return of the White Stone: Part 1
- The Quest Begins: Part 2
- The Witch's Cauldron and the Dragon's Fir: Part 3
- Fire and Ice: Part 4
- The War of the Stones: Part 5
- Into the Darkness: Part 6

The Bully-High Lord of Uppsala-Hof
Happy Yule to You Too

The Table of Contents

Balder Rising!
How Do I Know I am a Vril Being?
Let Wunjo Control What You Think
The Vril is With You
Align Yourself With the Gods
You Have a Choice

Foreword

One day in 1984, one of my oldest and dearest friends, Robert Zoller, asked me to take part in a study group he was organizing on the Old Norse pagan religion. I was not very religious, but always enjoyed reading the myths and folklore of Europe, so I agreed. My motivation was threefold: I wanted to learn something about the pre-Christian customs of Europe, I thought it would be interesting to expand my knowledge of European history and civilization and I was accommodating a friend. I was not very religious or spiritual at this point in my life, but the folklore and mythology of Europe had always fascinated me, so I agreed. It was a decision that would change my life.

I grew up in a time when the American nation was undergoing political and cultural transformations that could only be described as a "culture war." The political left in America was challenging everything that I held dear about America and Western Civilization. I never was a part of the "Sixties generation," and remained something of an outcast of my generation. When I graduated from high school in 1971, I joined the United States Army in my desire to find a world of tradition and order, and I even volunteered to fight in Vietnam. The three years in the Army was an awakening, for I discovered that the Armed Forces was not a bastion of American traditions or a conservative refuge from the social conflict and changes taking place in America. I left the Army disillusioned and confused. When I returned to civilian life I plunged myself into politics.

My life was one of conflict. I was angry at the world and wanted to change it, or preserve it. For the next thirty years I threw myself into politics, undergoing many transformations—from a right-wing radical supporter of George Wallace to a Republican supporter of Ronald Reagan, then to a crusader for Patrick Buchanan, and joining both major parties and even third parties. I did not abandon politics, politics abandoned me. I came to the conclusion that all political movements in the 20th, and now the 21st centuries are based on what the historian Paul Johnson wrote in his book, *Modern Times: A History of the 20th Century,* that all political movements, whether its Libertarian, Consevative, Liberal, Progressive, Socialist, Communicst of Fascist are all based on an ideology that through social engineering, and through the power of the government, rooted in the believe that we can remake the human being into something "better," "noble," and even "perfect." I have come to realize that the quest for perfect cannot be through the politics of transforming the external world and think that perfect social conditions will create the perfected human being. Perfection or the quest to improve the human being into something better must come from within. It is a quest that each individual must take on his or her own. It is a solidary journey and it cannot be imposed on the collective by a dominating government, economic order, or religious zealism.

It was during the early stages of my realization that I joined Zoller's study group, which met every other Friday evening for three years, even as I was actively involved in the political world of confrontation. It was during these four years that the seeds of spiritual transformation were planted that would change my life many years later. I do not want this book to be about politics, but added this background to merely help you understand how profoundly I experienced the great transformation once I surrendered to the greater powers in the universe, and discovered the secret to change my life and the world around myself.

My "conversion" to Asatru was very different from most people that I have met over the last thirty-fives who join Asatru. Most people were invited to attend a gather or blot of an established kindred and found the sense of folk-community inviting. Many joined because Asatru was predominately "eightist" politically and they wanted to be part of a community or movement that reflected their political views without being a political organization. I did not find the religion or community aspect of an Asatru community inticing because there were very few Asatru kindreds or other Asatru groups around in the 1980s. When Zoller invited be to be a part of his "study group" I did so because as a historian I was always interested in the history and culture of Europe. I also was interested in mythology and Runes from an achidemic point of view because I was writing a novel that was similar to Tolkien's Lord of the Rings and wanted to know more about Runes.

Zoller gather each of us who attended his group a copy of Edred Thorsson's new book *Futhark*, and told us of a meeting he attended with Thorsson, David James and Garman Lord. Zoller organized his meetings by opening with a group chant of the twenty-four Runes of the Elder Futhark. He dedicated the meetings to Freyja, and we chant to the Seitherkona. We began by studying *Futherk* and reading from Snorri's Prose Edda. Little did I know that the next three years would be a epiphany that would change my life.

Order vs. Chaos–The Cosmic Struggle Between the Gods and the Giants

Studying the Old Norse tradition, we learned the fundamental governing principle in all ancient belief systems—that there are two forces at work in the universe: Order and Chaos! This struggle is personified by a pantheon of Gods who are engaged in a conflict with a pantheon of Giant (Jotun)s. The images of Gods—superior and noble beings who look and behave like us, but have great powers to control and tame the forces of nature, are archetypes in the human subconscious that all races and nations share. At the same time, all races and nations also visualize the forces of destruction and chaos as gigantic beings known by different names. These forces appear in our subconscious as great beings or beasts, huge and powerful, but frightening and terrible, because they represent storms, earthquakes, volcanos, plagues, droughts, and other forces that cause death and destruction.

Understanding the universe as an arena where the Gods competed to control the forces of chaos, the Giants, our ancestors wished to align themselves with the Gods. Doing so filled their lives with the divine powers of order and progress. This way they consciously worked toward forging bonds with the Gods, to lead lives filled with happiness, success, love and joy. They realized individuals who aligned themselves with the Giants, the forces of chaos, experienced a life filled with chaos, disorder and suffering. Our ancestors understood that we possessed the power to choose the type of life we want to lead. Whether one perceives these forces as Gods and Giants or not, the principle is the same. Chaos and Order—you have the free will to decide for yourself which one of these principles you will align yourself with.

The purpose of this book is to reveal a universal force we refer to as Vril, and the power you have to tap it to bring Order or Chaos into your life.

I Awaken

The period I was involved in Bob Zoller's study group, if my memory serves, was 1984 through 1987. I do not want to turn this into a history of our little group nut I feel I need to convey three incidents I experienced during that time, and how they affected me so profoundly. As I said, Bob Zoller's study group met every other Friday—the day dedicated to Freyja, the Goddess of Love and Joy—and Bob wanted our group filled with a harmonious Joy and Love of what we were trying to accomplish. We started out with about six people, but all very willing and interested in what Bob had to teach us. He began by having us read the Prose Edda and teaching us about the Runes of the Elder Futhark. He taught the proper way to meditate, which included the correct way to breathe, visualize and chant. He emphasized starting by the chanting of Wunjo, the Rune which stands for joy, harmony and happiness. We also chanted to Freyja, calling on her to fill us with love, joy and happiness. Several things I learned as we progressed:

First, there is a universal force at work throughout the universe that is a source of power that anyone can learn to tap into and use to improve their lives.

Second, there is a universal intelligence at work, known by many different names, that manifests itself to different people in different ways, according to their genetic-spiritual heritage.

Last, we have the tools available to help us tap into this force and intelligence. The tools have been presented to us in many different forms according to—once again—our genetic-spiritual heritage.

Now, I know this sounds very "New Ageist" but I also realized, and Bob enphaised this point, each folk developed a unique heathen tradition that could not and should not be mixed with other traditions. Bob was very folkist and this became apparent when we studied Orlog and our ancestral stream.

As we learned through meditation to apply what we were discovering, I discovered I was psychic. I soon realized that this discovery was not exclusive to me, but that all members of our little group were experiencing similar revelations about themselves. It dawned on us that we all have these abilities latent within us, waiting for us to discover how to develop and use them, and that they were not extrasensory, but a sixth sense alongside those of sight, taste, hearing, smell and touch.

My first profound experience during the first year of our meetings I discovered I could enter a trance-like state during our chanting, and even developed the ability to leave my physical body in what is referred to as *faring-forth*, more commonly called astral travel. In one out-of-body experience, I found myself standing on the bow of a ship. It appeared to be made of gold, and sailing through a black ocean, under a black sky with no stars, amidst huge golden icebergs. Then, before me appeared a beautiful woman encased in a golden halo. She told me she was the Goddess Freyja that I was one of her children and if I dedicated myself to her and to the Gods, I would be rewarded with the secret to a happy and successful life. She said she was sent by Odin and put the opportunity to follow Odin. She said not to answer but that he would appear to me for my answer.

And this is just what happened. My second experience also happened while I was in a trance several months later. This time I found myself standing before Odin, and he asked me if I had agreed to Freyja's proposal. When I answered yes, he impaled me on his spear. I could see Runes carved into the spear and felt no pain or fear, but reinvigorated as a current of energy flowed through me.

Before Zoller began holding his classes I had a nightmare. It happened on March 15, 1984. I found myself swimming under water. It was dark and I knew that something horrific was chasing me. I looked behind me and saw a great white shark with jaws wide open. The shark clamped his jaws down around my waste and I woke up screaming bloody murder. It was the worst nightmare I ever perience and for a long time I would have dreams involving sharks until I learned the master lucid dreaming and wake myself up whenever I found myself on a body of water or even near water.

In of the topics were discussed in Zoller's classes was that each of us was assigned an individual Norn when we are born who determines our life path. He said that if we ever saw our Norn it would be in the form of a terrible beast and it meant we would die. One year to the day I had that horrific dream, I was crossing Park Ave in New York City about 7:30 in the evening, after leaving work. It was raining and I waited for the red light to change to green before I crossed. Now Park Ave has an island running down the middle of the street dividing the traffic going in opposite direction. I reached the island and then began crossing when a van made a right turn and slammed into me, throwing me some fifteen feet through the air. Whe I opened my eyes I found myself lying on the street with about a half dozen people kneeling around. But when I saw the driver get out of van, I turned into a berker and tried to leap to my feet shouting that I was going to kill the driver. Well, the people held me down warning that I might have internal injuries.

I went to the hospital even though I appeared perfectly all right and after hours of x-rays and test I was released and told that I was very lucking to be alive. It was only later when I told everyone at the next meeting with Zoller that Bob remind me of my dream which happened exactly one year ago. By the way, it was on the Ives of March. Zoller explained he felt that This happened right after I told Odin I would dedicate myself to him and that I was meant to die, but Odin intervened because of my oath to him. On that day I was totally hooked.

The third and final incident occurred after my escape from "death by van," in the sanctuary of my bedroom. I was awakened one night to discover a beautiful young man standing at the foot of my bed. He was filled with a light that shined from within. He smiled and told me his name was Balder, the son of Odin. He asked me if I knew what his father had whispered into his ear on his funeral pyre. From my knowledge of the Edda, I had to say no. No one did. He told me Odin whispered three Runes: Dagaz, Nauthiz and Ansuz. Dagaz stood for enlightenment that comes with secret knowledge and the light that comes with the dawn of a new day. Nauthiz was need-fire that burned within us, necessary to survive and evolve beyond what we were. Ansuz stood for the Gods, and the secret knowledge that Odin possesses and bestows upon those he's chosen. It was not until many years later, after our little group dissolved, that I fully understood the meaning of the three Runes collectively: *Balder was telling me that the Gods dwelled within us, within our very DNA; that the same divine powers they possessed, we too possessed; and that we could discover how to tap into this source if we had the need to improve ourselves and evolve into a higher state.*

I know what must be going through your mind. You must think I am crazy. The Gods speaking to him? Ha! Well, it took even me about fifteen years before I fully accepted that these experiences were real. After my involvement in Bob's study group ended, I put my newfound spiritualism aside, though I practiced Rune magic and Seither privately. I became a solidtary practitioner of Germanic magic and heathenism. My fundamental outlook had changed, but I had not fully integrated it into my total being. It would be another fifteen years until I finally surrendered myself to those experiences of so long before.

A New Direction

During the fifteen years between my involvement in Bob's study group and my fully devoted myself to the Gods in 2002, I was still heavily involved in politics. I wanted to make this a better world for people, especially for young people. But after four years of George H. W. Bush and eight years of Clinton, I was ready to give up politics for good. I believe that the “coronation” of George W. Bush as president by his election in 2000 had convinced me finally that there is no way one can truly make a better world through the confrontation of politics. I saw that my many years in politics had achieved absolutely nothing. I realize, as I think many people today do, that no matter who gets elected, be they Democrats or Republicans, nothing ever changes except the pockets into which all the big money goes.

I first became involved in politics in 1968. I was in high school and the presidential race for president was exceptionally exciting considering what was taking place in the country. Demonstrations by the so-called "New Left," our major cities were being burnt to the ground by rioting blacks, we were still fighting the Vietnam War, Martin Luthar King and Robert Kenndy were both assassinated within months of each other. And there were three candidates running for president that year: Richard Nixon on the Republian Party, Hubert Humphrey on the Democrat Party and George Wallace on the American Independent Party.

When I discovered that all three candidates were scheduled to speak at the Madison Square Garden at different time, I convinced my father to take me to hear what each candidate had to say. And he did. My father was a great father and I deeply loved him.

When Nixon spoke, the Garden was packed and there attendees were respectful and enthuisactic but Nixon was a terrible speak, boring and bland. Humphrey's appearance was also to a packed Garden but about a third of the attendees were protesting. The Democrat Party was deeply divided between traditional working class Democrats and the New Left who were Marxists and revolutionaries. Humphrey quickly loss control of the event constantly shouting at the protestors to "shout up" and exchanging insults, pleading for the right to be heard. Lastly Wallace spoke at the Garden. The gardon was only half filled but the crowd eas fanatical. Though there were demonstrations outside, very few of the protestor found their way nside, and those who did did not last long. When they tried to disrupt Wallace's speech the attendees, who were primarily working class, white ehtnics set upon the leftists like wolves into a flock of deer and threw them out while Wallace cheered them on. I was deeply moved by Wallace's call to "Stand up for America" and his followers devotion. That night I dedicated myself to politics and believed that if the political situation had not fundamentally changed by the year 2000 the United States was doomed. I remained true to the oath I took to myself and, when the year 2000 arrived and nothing changed, I turned by mack on politics and devoted myself to heathenism.

The year 2000 was one of great reflection and deep soul-searching. I remembered the promise made by Freyja and decided to write a book on the Norse Gods. I reread and meditated on the Norse myths and soon completed *The Book of Balder Rising*. Things immediately began to happen. I had been trying to buy a condominium or co-op apartment for six months with no luck. Then, a week after I finished the book, my sister told me she had found a house for me. I told her I could not afford a house, but she said I could afford this one. She asked me to trust her and I did, buying the house unseen. It turned out to be a fixer-upper, and I purchased it for $250,000. I moved in and began fixing it up and after two years sold it for $380,000. I do believe that the Gods had rewarded me for fulfilling my part of the bargain I made with them long ago. But the story does not end here.

Before I sold the house in 2005 for that nice profit, I was having problems finding another house. My nephew asked me if I would go in with him and look to purchase a two-family house. I agreed on the condition that we could find something suitable. We thought we had found a house, but the deal fell through. Once again I turned to the Gods and over the Columbus Day weekend, I meditated on the problem. That Monday night I dreamed of my father, who had died in my arms in 1977, and who in 1982 had visited me from the beyond and told me everything would be all right and things would change for the better, but that I had to be patient. This had happened in broad daylight and he even touched me. It was one of the most beautiful experiences I had ever had.

On the Monday night of the 2005 Columbus holiday weekend, I had a dream that I was in heaven, visiting my father. He was living in the house we grew up in. He was born in the slums of New York City and worked two jobs so he could fulfill his lifelong dream of owning his own home, which, when he did, filled him with joy. He was a good man, a loving and responsible husband and father to us. He told me that the afterlife that awaits us is manifested by all our actions in this life, and this is why his afterlife was a duplication of the house he owned, because it was his idea of heaven. He told me he was happy and then promised me that he would find me another house.

When I woke the next morning, I was moved by the dream, which was so vivid and real. That afternoon, one of the realtors called me and told me that the house I was asking for had been sold, but that she had another that would be perfect. I asked and she immediately took me there. When we arrived I was amazed. It was a fantastic two-family house—everything I wanted. I was sure it would be too expensive, but she told me that it was owned by a widow who had been trying to sell it for nine months. Two prospective buyers had each backed out at the last minute. She originally had it on the market for $600,000, which was the going price for a house like this in that area, but she had come down to $500,000, and felt she would accept an offer of $475,000. I immediately asked to put in a bid for me, and she called the owner on her cell phone. I was overjoyed when my bid was accepted.

Leaving that house, I was taken aback when I noticed the address was 184. 1+8+4=13. My father was born on August 13, a Friday. He always considered it his lucky number and used to tell me and my sister stories about how lucky this number was throughout his life. A friend of mine pointed out that the date of my visit to this house was October 12. October was the 10th month. 1+0=1 and it was the twelfth day, 1+2=3—13!! I eventually purchased the house and everyone was happy, including the seller, who was pleased that the house she and her husband lived in for 45 years would be owned by people she approved of. The whole experience was moving and I knew that it was ordained by divine powers.

Many other things began to manifest themselves from 2002 on. I ran into some old friends and I began holding my own study group. Our little group has grown and established The Folk Faith of Balder Rising. My health has improved, my financial situation has improved, my social life has improved. I have never been happier. Our Folk Faith is growing and I am now doing what I never could before: help people and work to make this world a better place, even if only one person at a time. I have written a second book, *Vrilology*, which explores the historic background of the Life Force, which we refer to as Vril, and another simple book explaining just what Vril is and how it can help people improve their lives, filling them with happiness, joy and prosperity. That book is titled *Vril; The Secret to a Happy and Successful Life*.

I decided that this book was only an introduction to the basics of the science of Vril and another book was needed to further explain just what Vril is, how it works and how it is connected to the Northern tradition of Norse cosmology. That is why I wrote this book, *The Secret Power of Vril: Discovering How to Harness the Life Force of the Gods*.

Chapter One: What is Vril?

In a recent episode of the television series *Universe*, entitled *Extreme Energy*, it was explained that everything in the universe, all organic and inorganic matter, all forms of energy and even the space between planets, stars and galaxies is made up of energy. It also said that there is a fixed amount of energy that has its origin with the Big Bang, but later in the episode, it spoke of how the universe is expanding and that as it does, the density of energy between the heavenly bodies is constant. It further explained that the only way this constant state of energy could be maintained is if there were additional amounts of energy entering our universe from another universe. The program then continued and eventually revealed that the present-day scientific community had no idea just what is this universal source of energy. It was all a great big mystery. I must admit that I felt a certain sense of superiority knowing that Vrilology knew what this universal energy was: Vril.

To explore the question, "What is Vril," we will have to enter the realm of quantum physics. Though Vrilology is considered a form of esoteric discipline, which we might refer to as "magic," it might seem strange exploring a field dealing with science or physics, but it really isn't. Magic is actually a realm of science that traditional academia has not been able to mathematically prove, until now. With the discoveries and explorations into the realms of quantum physics, we are beginning to reveal the hidden truths to what has been referred to as "Magic," in the past.

We consider it necessary to give you a crash course on quantum physics because so much of what is being discovered in this field of science is relevant to what has been discarded by science as "hocus-pocus" or Magic in the past.

Up to now, science was able to trace its beliefs about the real world back to the teachings of Isaac Newton. It is the ideas and philosophical foundation that were laid down during the Seventeenth Century's "Age of Enlightenment" that still forms the basis for modern day science. These theories claim that everything in the universe is divisible, isolated from each other and self-contained. This train of thought considers our bodies mere biochemical machines that we discard after we die, and that our mind is the product of the brain's system of electrical impulses. The Enlightenment chased God and the supernatural from the universe, espically from the discipline of science. All consciousness was lacking in matter. Charles Darwin reduced all life to chance, and random selection, without purpose and consciousness. Humanity is nothing more than an evolutionary accident. But all this began to change with the exploration of quantum physics.

Quantum Physics and Vril

Despite the contemporary scientific community's refusal to accept the existence of a universal energy (Vril), many scientists have bucked the traditional scientific community and have begun exploring it. A very good examination of modern-day scientists investigating Vril is reported in Lynne McTaggart's book, *The Field: Quest for the Secret Force of the Universe*. If you don't already have a copy of Lynn McTaggart's book, you should run out and get it. It is an excellent book on the discussion of Vril, though the authoress never refers to the field of universal energy as Vril. She simply refers to it as "The Field." She tells us of the efforts by respected scientists in various disciplines who have discovered the existence of this mysterious field of energy over the last few decades, and have been conducting experiments to measure and identify it. She recounts many of these experiments in her remarkable book. Let us quote from the prologue of the book:

> *What they* (various scientists) *have discovered is nothing less than astonishing. At our most elemental level, we are not a chemical reaction, but an energetic charge. Human beings and all living things are a coalescence of energy in a field of energy connected to every other thing in the world. This pulsating energy field is the central engine of*

our being and our consciousness, the alpha and the omega of our existence.

McTaggart claims that there is no duality of existence in us (me and not-me), "but one underlying energy." This energy is Vril, and it is responsible for all our mental functions, even the most complicated functions. It provides power for all the functions of our body, and it is the source for the blueprint of our growth and development. It powers every aspect of our being—our organs, our brain, our mind, memory, consciousness and subconscious. "The field (Vril) is the force, rather than germs or genes, that finally determines whether we are healthy or ill, the force which must be tapped in order to heal." She quotes Einstein when he said, "The field is the only reality."

McTaggart explains that classical physics sees the universe as machine and man as survival machine. This, she says, leads humanity to the development of technology to master the natural environment, but has been deficient in its development of understanding the spiritual and metaphysical reality. *We might understand how the body works, but still lack any understanding of how life begins, what is the process behind thinking, why we get ill or even how a single cell can grow and develop into a fully developed human being.*

Pioneers of Quantum Physics

There have been many scientists studying the nature of quantum physics, but we will mention a few pioneers of the 20th Century: Erwin Schrodinger, Werner Heisenberg, Niels Bohr and Wolfgang Pauli. These pioneers of quantum physics explored the nature of matter and they were amazed at what they discovered. Matter, even the tiniest bits of matter (subatomic particles), or at least what we think of as matter when we touch something solid, is not solid at all. Matter as we know it is actually sometimes one thing, and at other times something else. *If fact, it can be many different things at the same time.* These subatomic particles have no meaning in isolation, but only in relationship with everything else. What this means is that to understand the universe, we must see it as a web of dynamic interaction of everything in it. This means time and space, as we understand these concepts, do not exist.

Many of these pioneers of quantum physics examined different esoteric traditions. Pauli studied the Kabbala; Bohr, the Tao and Chinese philosophy; Schrodinger, Hindu philosophy; and Heisenberg, the Platonic theory of ancient Greece. It is a pity no one examined their own Northern Tradition that included Vril, but all of these other traditions are different cultural variations of the study of Vril and the Life Force of the Gods.

To simplify Heisenberg, one might say that the *observer alters the observed by the simple act of observation.* What Heisenberg is saying is that consciousness does play a role in the so-called physical universe. It was an accepted and unchallenged truth that the laws of the physical universe did not change, and it did not matter which mind was observing, because the results would be the same, time after time. But quantum physics has concluded that it did matter what mind was doing the observing. The outcome of an experiment was no longer determined by the laws of the physical universe, but by the consciousness of the observer. According to Michael Talbot, in his book, *Mysticism and the New Physics*: "In simpler terms, all possible outcomes of an experiment exist, according to [one] interpretation, in an indefinite number of parallel realities. Aside from the dazzling implications of such a concept, the Everett-Wheeler metatheorem presents the same paradox encountered in the theologian's concept of an omnipotent God." Or, perhaps we should say...Gods!

These physicists never made the leap in their studies of quantum physics. They examined quantum theory in the laboratory, where they successfully demonstrated quantum effects with non-living subatomic particles. Unfortunately, they did not extend their work to include the consequences of their theory on living things. But others would carry on their work.

Ether and Vril

Scientists long considered the universe to be filled with a substance that was referred to as *ether*, which is another name for Vril. Let us quote from an Internet article written by a Professor A. Zielinski at the Web site www.viewzone.com/unified.field.html. He explains how two scientists by the names of Edward William Morley and Albert Michelson tried to prove that ether (Vril) was uniformly distributed throughout the universe. They used a special sensitive interferometer to measure the absolute motion of the Earth in space. They did this by directing the device in the various compass directions. But their experiments failed to show relative motion of the Earth to ether in any horizontal direction. This would mean the earth had no motion in space, which we know is false, but Michelson and Morley thought their experiment failed, and thus failed to prove the existence of ether. Science, including that of Einstein, afterward was convinced that ether did not exist. Zielinski wrote:

> *The assumption of Michelson and Morley that aether (ether or Vril) was uniform and at rest in space, was a fundamental error. Had Michelson and Morley pointed their interferometer in a vertical plane, they would have concluded that the earth is moving in a perpendicular direction to the surface of the earth into space. A worldwide verification of their experiment would have indicated that the earth is moving everywhere simultaneously in a vertical direction into space, which is, of course, not possible. The only conclusion therefore is: aether is constantly moving towards the earth in straight perpendicular lines, just like reversed rays of energy. . . . Consequent experiments and observations were so coherent that the existence of aether could not be ignored any longer, and the need of a concept or theory that would describe the essence, qualities and behavior of aether, was required for me to continue my own*

> *research in the field of quantum electrodynamics, which is my field of activity.*

Due to this one mistaken experiment, ether, or Vril, was ignored, and thus only today has science begun to accept the reality of a universal energy source that can be accounted for in quantum physics, often referred to as *Zero Point Field.*

Zero Point Field

The investigation into quantum physics has continued and physicists are delving into areas of research where the pioneers had left off. Some have explored a few equations abstracted from quantum physics which deal with a sea of microscopic vibrations in the space between objects. We refer to this region of research as the *Zero Point Field.* Once we include Zero Point Field in the equation, our concept of the universe is transformed into a heaving sea of energy—Vril. *This means that everything is united or connected with everything else in this one vast quantum field of Vril energy.*

A second point is also made obvious—*we are all made of the same substance.* On our most fundamental level of existence, everything, including human beings, along with all other living things, is pulsating with Vril energy, and we are exchanging this energy with the inexhaustible supply of Vril that fills the universe. Lynne McTaggart writes:

> *Living things emitted a weak radiation, and this was the most crucial aspect of biological processes. Information about all aspects of life, from cellular communication to the vast array of controls of DNA, was relayed through an information exchange on the quantum level. Even our minds, that other supposedly so outside of the laws of matter, operated according to quantum processes. Thinking, feeling—every higher cognitive function—had to do with quantum information pulsing simultaneously through our brains and body. Human perception occurred because of*

interactions between the subatomic particles of our brains and the quantum energy sea. We literally resonated with our world.

Now, I know you might be asking, what does all this have to do with Magic and the esoteric? The truth is—Magic and the esoteric is a form of science rooted in quantum physics. *We are truly living in remarkable times!*

There are many scientists working to verify preliminary evidence that there is a universal Life-Force, which we in the Folk Faith of Balder Rising refer to as Vril, and that this force can be demonstrated through scientific experiment.

James Clerk Maxwell proposed that space was ether that transmitted light electromagnetically. His view of the universe was the dominant one until Albert Michelson and Edward Morley failed to prove the existence of ether (Vril). In 1911, Max Planck, one of the founding fathers of quantum theory, showed that space was indeed an ocean of vibrating energy. Once again, let's see what McTaggart writes: "In the quantum world, quantum fields are not mediated by forces but by exchanges of energy, which is constantly redistributed in a dynamic pattern. This constant exchange is an intrinsic property of particles, so that even real particles are nothing more than a little knot of energy which briefly emerges and disappears back into the underlying field." She goes on to say that the only reality was the field (Vril) itself, and Zero Point Field is the repository of all fields of energy, or "the field of fields." Energy is constantly being radiated with the exchange of every virtual particle. The amount of zero-point energy in one transaction is unimaginably small. But, if you add up all the particles in the universe, all of them constantly popping in and out of being, you will discover a vast, limitless supply of energy, greater by far than the energy density in an atomic nucleus. This supply of energy, just sitting there in the background of space, is so great that the total energy of Zero Point Field is so vast that it is even greater than all energy in matter by a factor of 10 to the 40th, or 1 followed by 40 zeros. In fact, there is enough energy in a single cubic meter of space to boil all the oceans of the earth.

Classical physics described how the machine (the physical laws of the universe) worked, but said nothing about what powered it. Quantum physics is an exploration of the force (Vril) that powers the machine. Zero Point Field offers a scientific explanation of the Life-Force, or what we refer to as Vril. Laser physicist Hal Puthoff theorizes that Zero Point Field (Vril) is a "kind of self-regenerating grand ground state of the universe," that would mean everything, including us, along with all matter, are literally connected to everything else in the universe, even if it exists at the farthest reaches of the other side of the universe. It is through the waves of Vril energy, or Zero Point Field, that everything is connected to everything.

Quantum Physics and Quantum Evolution

Quantum physics is a new field that permits us to explore new realities that are being discovered, which conflict with what we thought was reality, including Einsteinian physics. It is also challenging the concepts of Darwinian evolution. What was once considered "Magic" is now being explained according to quantum mechanics. This is especially true of the idea that our minds have the power to change and shape the material world around us. This takes us into the question of *Intelligent Design and evolution.*

According to Darwinian evolution, one species is transformed into another species as a result of natural selection. This process is the result of pure chance due to changes in the environment. Pressures from the changing environment weed out detrimental characteristics or genes and permits only better-suited genes to dominate and determine the nature of an organism. As a result, those individuals with the best-suited genes survive to pass their genes to the next generation. Thus, those individuals within an organism will survive in the competition to dominate and thrive, eliminating all other competitors. This theory is known as survival of the fittest.

This process of natural selection should take a very long time. It is painfully slow, but if we examine the biological and fossil records, what we discover does not conform to the theory of natural selection. What we find in fossil and genetic records conflict with the Darwinian theory of natural selection. There are occasional spurts of evolution when changes take place very suddenly and rapidly. An example of this is the Cambrian explosion. This took place during the Cambrian Period, which encompassed a mere fifteen million years. This may sound like a long time to us, but it is actually a very short period in evolutionary time. During the Cambrian Period we can see the evidence of an enormous explosion of new life suddenly appearing. This rapid appearance of new life forms was far too fast and rapid to be explained by Darwinian evolution. But even this period of rapid evolution can't explain what is referred to as *purposeful evolution.*

To explain this process better, we will examine a more recent situation that took place in Manchester, England. It involves the peppered moth, which lived on birch trees and was speckled white. This color pattern permitted the moth to blend into with the bark of the birch trees and avoid being eaten by birds. But their environment was transformed with the opening of a coal plant in Manchester. The soot produced by the plant blackened the trees. This left the white moths defenseless against the birds, which could easily spot them. But in just a few generations, the moth population underwent a transformation in its color pattern from its predominant color of white to a solid black. This proved better suited as camouflage against the soot-covered trees.

This quick transformation to all black does not fit into the randomness and gradualness of Darwinian evolution. The black coloration appeared too quickly. If the theory of Darwinian evolution holds true, there should have been moths with many different color patterns. Moths with blue, red, and green coloration patterns should have also appeared and gradually died out as their coloration failed to protect them from the birds. This would have fit in with the randomness of Darwinian evolution. But there were no green, red and blue moths. There should have been a variety of different colored moths appearing and dying out in a random fashion. Even if we say that a black moth gene was already present and with each generation only the moths that possessed this gene survived to pass it on to the next generation until it dominated the species, there still should have been other colors appearing. Even for moths, the transformation into the color necessary for successful protection was too quick a transformation to be explained by Darwinian evolution. But if this example does not convince you, we can examine another example.

Now let's look at an even more recent example of purposeful evolution that is taking place right now. In Africa the number of African elephants born without tusks is increasing. Why? Because poachers are killing elphants for their tusks, something is happening at the quantum level within the elephants' DNA causing elephants to be born without tusks. Once tusks were an advantage for the survival of elephants, but now, because of poaching, it is a detirment to their survival. Thus purposeful evolution is causing a change within the genetics of African elephants. I would hypothesis that at some point when poaching come to an end because there will be no more African elephants with tusk, elephants will once again give birth to baby elephants with tusks, just as the spoted moths in England once again became spotted when trees were no longer covered with the black pollutiants.

To prove this point we can turn our attention an experiment conducted in a controlled laboratory, involving a strain produced by a researcher of *E. coli* bacteria that could not digest lactose. The researcher spread the bacteria onto a plate that contained lactose. Since the bacteria could not digest lactose, it starved and died out, or at least 98 percent of the bacteria starved. The other 2 percent not only survived, but continued to thrive. Somehow, the other 2 percent spontaneously mutated a gene, permitting it to digest lactose in one generation. *One generation!* This is not only astonishing it is supposed to be *impossible* according to Darwinian evolution. It conflicts with all known laws of randomness. Of all the genes in an *E. coli*'s DNA and the rarity of mutation, how did this 2 percent mutate the one gene necessary to survive? IT DEFIES RANDOMNESS.

And it did not happen once, but every time the experiment has conducted. What are the chances of it happening over and over? According to Darwinian evolution, it should not have happened at all, but it did, every time it was performed.

The Origin of Life

We're going to have to journey back to the very beginning. Yet's get back to the primordial soup to a time when the engine of evolution first switched on. This is a time before the first cell appeared.

According to the theory of Darwinian evolution, everything has to evolve from a simpler, less complex form. If this is so, then what was there before there was the single cell? If we go back still farther, before the first cell, we are going to be confronted with questions that need to be answered. Where does the border between chemistry and life exist? How far can we reduce life and still call it life? Can we consider DNA alive? What about a chromosome, or a protein or an enzyme? Can anyone truly state for sure when life made the leap from the chemical primordial soup to the first cell?

50 years ago it was believed that hydrogen, methane, and water existed in the Earth's early atmosphere. And if lightning struck those gases, it would have been possible for simple organic compounds to form, heating up the proverbial primordial soup from which the first molecules of life were created. Researchers produced this process in the lab. They were able to produce the building blocks of proteins—a slurry of amino acids—in a bottle full of such gases after submitting them to electrical discharges, but is this life?

So you can see the problem that we face if we accept the Darwinian theory of evolution to explain the creation of life. How do we go from a slurry of amino acids and produce the first bit of life? That's an evolutionary gap that cannot be explained by Darwinian evolution.

So how do we explain it?

Easy---*Intelligent design!!!*

Intelligent Design and Quantum Evolution

When we say intelligent design, we are not talking about the Christian concept of God creating the universe in seven days a little over six thousand years ago. What we are saying is that *consciousness plays a role in creation.* Not just the original creation, but ALL CREATION! The essence of quantum physics, or evolution, is that reality is changeable based on intelligent observation. When atoms or subatomic particles are observed or measured, their nature changes. Now, if one consciously measures what can be changed through observation or measurement, then we have to ask the question: Is it possible to will something to change? Not only does this new field of quantum evolution offer the strongest support for this notion—intelligent design—but it also answers the fundamental question of who the designer is.

IT IS US!!!!

We have the power within us to change the nature of reality through those principles laid down in quantum physics.

To understand Vrilology, you must first understand quantum theory. We don't have time for a full Ph.D. program here, but we need to make clear three simple principles.

We must understand that once matter is broken down to the subatomic level—the world of electrons, protons and neutrons—the classical laws of the universe begin to erode. German physicist Max Planck discovered long ago that electrons, protons and neutrons act as both particles and waves. This might seem contradictory because particles are thought to have distinct orbits and paths, while waves lack any specific coordinates, and can be more diffuse.

The fact is, subatomic particles possess the dual potential to be either a wave or a particle. This of course, is contradictory to classical physics, for it means that matter is not set in solidified form but can be shaped and molded into different realities. The question is how can this be done? This question brings us face to face with the Heisenberg Uncertainty Principle.

German physicist Werner Heisenberg claimed, on the basis of experiments with subatomic particles, that nothing's state is certain until it is observed. This is easy enough for us to accept in the world of subatomic particles, whose condition is already far removed from our everyday observations. But Schrodinger posed a problem that might sound more philosophic than scientific: If you put a cat in an opaque closed box, hooked to a device that may kill the cat at any moment depending on the state of an atom's nucleus that behaves according to the uncertainty principle, then the cat's *being* alive or dead would likewise be in suspense until you open the box. Your action to *look* inside the box would cause reality to choose one state or the other for the cat.

Let us give you an example of what we are talking about. It is referred to as the classic double-slit test.

Let's say you have two walls, one in front of the other with a space between them. Now, let's also say that the first wall has two slits in it.

Shrodinger's Cat

If you took a gun and sprayed a bullet at both slits, you'd get a certain pattern on the wall on the far side that would look like two bullet riddled patterns. Let's call the bullet riddled wall Pattern A. It is the illustration you would get if you sprayed bullets or particles through the two slits.

Now, instead of bullets, we'll shine a big spotlight on the first wall. The light will pass through both slits, but because light travels in waves, we'll get a different pattern on the far wall that would look like two sets of three bars.

This patterning is caused by the light waves passing through the right and left windows interfering with each other. So let's call the pattern caused by the waves passing through the slits Pattern B.

Next, we're going to take an electron gun and shoot a single line of electrons at the twin slits. Can you guess what pattern we would get? You would probably guess that we would get the pattern that looks like what we got when we fired bullets through the slits, which would be Pattern A. But when this experiment is conducted in laboratory tests you *always* get Pattern B. That's right, the wave pattern. Does this mean that electrons shoot out of the gun like light out of a flashlight, traveling in waves and creating Pattern B? Like waves?

Yes, but only when no one is actually witnessing the electrons passing through the slits.

The scientists conducting the experiment placed a little clicker at one of the slits to beep whenever it sensed an electron passing through the slit, so it could count or observe the passage of an electron passing the detector. Now, can you guess what was the pattern?

You would think it wouldn't change, right?

In the larger world, we would be correct, but not in the subatomic world. Once the device was switched on, it immediately changed into Pattern A.

We can see that the simple act of measuring is going to change the pattern. Though it may seem impossible, *it is true*. This is what we mean when we say that electrons exist in a constant state of both wave and particle. They always possess this duality until SOMETHING COUNTS THE ELECTRONS. That simple act of counting the electron will cause it to collapse into one or the other reality.

The next question we have got to ask is: If the world we live in, and everything we touch, feel and know, is made up of atoms, and if atoms are made up of subatomic particles, then where is the line between the phantom world of quantum mechanics and our world of real objects?

The simple act of measuring changes to the very nature of reality which will cause subatomic particles to collapse, which means that such measuring devices must be present everywhere in the universe. And they are. The environment is constantly measuring the subatomic world, collapsing potential into hard reality. You have only to look at your hands. Go ahead and hold them up before you and take a good look at them. Clasp them together and feel how solid they are, but are they as solid as they feel? At the quantum level, the subatomic particles that make up atoms in your hands operate according to fuzzy quantum rules. They are mostly energy. Billions of atoms that make up your hands are more energy than subatomic particles. But those atoms are bumping, jostling, and interacting with each other. In this way, they are constantly measuring one another—forcing potential into one fixed reality.

I know it sounds bizarre, but we've hardly scratched the surface of this fuzzy world of quantum physics. But for now, all you need to know to understand Vrilology, and our relationship with the Gods, are these three points:

1) Subatomic particles exist in a quantum state of potential.

2) It takes a measuring tool to collapse that potential.

3) It is the environment that constantly performs those measurements to fix our reality.

Now, what does all this have to do with quantum evolution?

We have to ask ourselves, what is DNA? Is it nothing but a molecular machine, producing all the basic building blocks of cells, of bodies? Is DNA not merely genetic codes locked in chemical bonds? And what breaks these bonds, turning genes on and off? Is it the movement of electrons and protons? If it is, then do subatomic particles obey the rules of classical or quantum physics?

THE ANSWER IS QUANTUM!

Thus, a proton can be in two places at once—A and B—turning a gene on or off. This means the gene is both on and off until something measures it.

And what measures it?

The environment.

And the environment of the gene is the DNA molecule itself.

And where do the Gods dwell?

IN YOUR DNA!

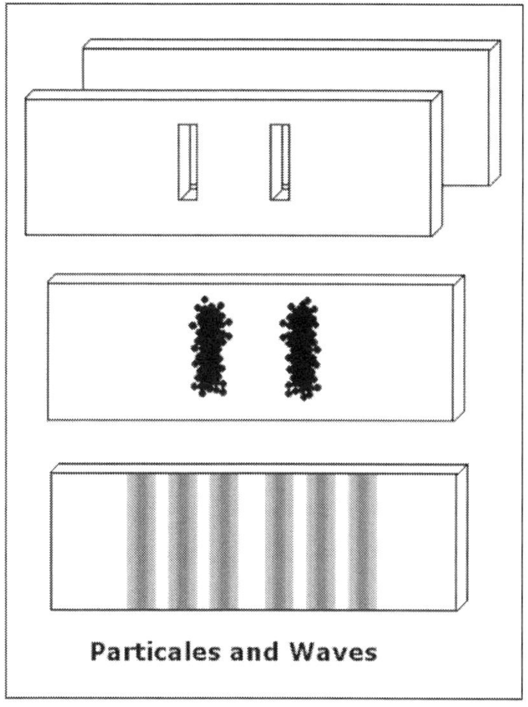

Particales and Waves

At the most fundamental level, the living cell acts as its own quantum measuring device and it is this constant cellular measurement device that is the true engine of evolution, because it is the realm of the Gods. It explains how mutations are not random and why evolution occurs at a pace faster than attributable to random chance—because the Gods, at some point, decide certain changes are necessary to fit into their grand scheme of maintaining order in the universe, in their eternal struggle with the Giants—the forces of chaos.

Why is all this so Important to Understanding Metaphysics?

If you are asking yourself this question, you can pat yourself on the back, because it is a very important question. But if you still cannot answer the question, then let us answer it for you. It can be summed up in several short principles that you need to understand.

1) The physical universe is not something separate from us, and our minds.

2) Quantum physics states that reality can be changed through observation or measurement.

3) By training our minds, through Vrilology (the science of Vril), we can change our reality.

4) The Gods determine the laws of the physical universe.

5) We can align ourselves with the Gods, and thus, in this way, integrate what we desire into their work to maintain order in the universe.

6) We have the power to harness Vril, and use it to create pathways into the future that will be filled with what we desire. *This means we have the means to control our Wyrd!*

Everything Vibrates

Because everything in the universe is made of energy, it is important to grasp the concept that everything in the universe vibrates. This is true throughout the universe on the macrocosmic level and on the microcosmic level as well. Every atom in our body, in every speck of dust on every planet is constantly vibrating. In fact, our reality is a vibratory reality, and vibrations are really sounds of different frequencies. We respond to these sounds or frequencies, though we might not realize it, because most vibrations cannot be heard, but all vibrations can be felt! Atoms are tiny little oscillators, pulsating with energy. These oscillators in nature, though, might be vibrating *out of phase*, but will sometimes form a rhythmic synchrony by vibrating in phase with each other. There are many examples, but one of the more obvious examples of this phenomenon is a school of fish swimming in synchrony. Science refers to this as *rhythm entrainment*. Nature finds it more economical to synchronize phases of similar frequencies.

If you pick any solid object and hold it—glass, or a rock, or a dish—anything solid, and touch it, feel it. It feels pretty solid—right? Well, the truth of the matter is that the solid object you are holding is not solid at all, but is more than 99 percent energy. It is made up of *trillions and trillions* of atoms. And atoms, as we have said before, are actually more than 99 percent energy. That's right—*pulsating and vibrating frequencies!* Each atom is made up of a nucleus surrounded by electrons and protons whirling about it in orbit. The parts of the atom are referred to as subatomic particles, and they make up less than 1 percent of the atoms. The rest is energy---VRIL ENERGY! The reason they rotate around the nucleus is vibrations. Since you are made up of trillions and trillions of atoms vibrating, *you are actually made up of Vril energy—more than 99 percent Vril energy.* Along with everything else in the universe, you are constantly vibrating. Therefore, when physical matter is magnified, we discover that we are really made up of void permeated by oscillating fields of Vril energy. This is what we mean by *objective physical reality*.

Now that we have established that our bodies are really matrixes of oscillating fields of Vril energy, we need to understand that the human body can easily be influenced by fields of energy from outside the body. There are various kinds of external frequencies of vibratory energy fields that affect us that include changing low-frequency electromagnetic fields generated by different weather patterns or by changing magnetic and gravitational fields of the earth, which is constantly being affected by the Moon and the Sun. We know that birds and other animals rely on such external energy fields for their migratory behavior. Our bodies can even be influenced by artificial fields produced by radio and television networks. But the human body also generates electrostatic fields of its own. When in the meditative state, our bodies go into resonance with the electric fields surrounding the planet. The human mind also resonates at different frequencies, which we have explored in previous lessons.

Four thousands of years, philosophers and occultists have been experimenting with different techniques, which permit them to develop the ability to manifest an expanding harmonious resonant state of meditation. These techniques involve the ability to use one's mind to slow down the metabolic rate of the body, until less oxygen is required to keep the body functioning. Eventually, one becomes more proficient in the methods of meditation. When you reach this level of proficiency your breathing becomes so gentle as not to disturb the resonant state of the aorta. There develops an automatic process in which the lungs and the diaphragm regulate the heart-aorta system. In this state, the lungs, diaphragm and the heart-aorta system are tuned to the same resonant behavior. This state of synchrony happens in spite of occasional shallow breathing, which will naturally extend to the entire body. Every part of the inner body, including the skeleton, muscles, as well as the inner organs, eventually begin to move coherently at about 7 cycles per second. This level of cycles happens to lie within the range of the natural frequency of the normal, healthy body. *Because this is the normal and natural range of frequency of the body*, it takes very little effort on behalf of the heart-aorta system to keep the body functioning at this rate. The destructive interference that would normally affect the body, when it is functioning at unnatural cycles, ceases. The body then begins to act in an increasingly coherent fashion.

The resonance of the body falls into a very restful and beneficial state, once this state is achieved. Scientific studies have confirmed that meditation can affect the body, not just subjectively, but also causing a very marked physiological transformation by soothing jagged nerves, eliminating anxiety, relieving stress, lowering blood pressure, helping to prevent the buildup of cholesterol, and ensuring the proper distribution of oxygen to the body. Mentally, it slowly raises the "elevation of levels of consciousness," with continued practice. These effects on the human body and mind usually are felt at different rates for different individuals. People who naturally possess highly developed, psychic abilities, will feel these effects sooner than others. *But this state of higher consciousness will eventually manifest itself in a large percentage of the practitioners who continually work at meditation.* They will soon discover new and broader horizons opening up to them, which will fill their lives to a degree they could not have imagined before.

When this state of higher consciousness is achieved, the vibrating body and the mind begin to vibrate in synchrony with the electrostatic field of the planet. This vibration causes a regular repetitive signal or wave to propagate within this field, permitting you to move upward or downward within higher and lower vibratory zones. Your vibration will entrain any other body vibrating at the same frequencies close to it. This means that other people who are also meditating, whether in close vicinity, or on the other side of the planet, who reach this resonant frequency will be drawn and locked into the frequency. This means that the nucleus of a meditating body or bodies will emit a simple harmonic motion or a "sound" of approximately 7 Hz., causing them to be synchronized through the electrostatic field of the planet. This emission will entrain others and help them in their effort to achieve the resonant state. *The more bodies that become locked in, the stronger the signal becomes.*

Remember, when we meditate, we consciously control our spirito-physical bodies to the point where we become locked into a particular frequency, which then hooks up with other spirito-physical bodies functioning at the same frequency, just as it does with a school of swimming fish.

By now you should understand that our physical bodies, as well as all matter, are not as solid as they appear, but are made up of interacting energy fields vibrating at tremendous frequencies.

All matter is made up of atoms, and atoms are made up of Vril, or more than 99 percent of each atom is. At room temperature an atom will vibrate at a rate of 10 to the 15th power Hz. This number is 1,000,000,000,000,000 times-a-second. But if you think this is fast, then check out the rate of vibration of the nucleus of the atom, which vibrates at 10 to the 22th power or 10,000,000,000,000,000,000,000 per second. UGH!!!! These numbers can give you a headache just thinking about such speeds! Because these are inconceivably fast rates, the Gods, as they created live systems, had to manufacture a sensory organ that will allow these living things to interact with the environment. In order for the Gods to communicate with our slow minds, they had to largely abandon the enormous information-processing capacity that is inherent in matter itself. The act of vibrating means something is moving between two different states, and if that something—in this case an atom—is vibrating a million billion times a second, that means it is occupying two distinct states, so many times a second. But how can our slow-processing mind comprehend such tremendously rapid vibrations?

The solution that the Gods provided was to bind atoms into molecules, which have much lower vibratory rates, due to their much larger mass. Now, we have to remember that these molecules still vibrate at very fast rates—Gigahertz (10 to the 9th power Hz – 1,000,000,000 per second) rates. But they too are bound up within larger units—living cells, which are the building blocks of all organisms. And the living cells are bound up within the specialized nerve cells, or neurons. They vibrate at a reasonable rate of just 10 to the third power Hz (1,000 per second). Because our atoms are vibrating at such rapid rates, a million billion times a second, they must be vibrating between two realities. *Those realities are action and rest at the same time.* This state of possessing two different realities at once is what we refer to as our *subjective reality*, (fields of energy vibrating at incredibly fast speeds) as opposed to our *objective reality* (solid matter). Itchak Bentov compares this action-and-rest language, in his book, *Stalking the Wild Pendulum*, to the motion of a pendulum or an oscillator. Bentov writes: "Like a pendulum, which swings out, it reaches a point of rest before swinging back in the other direction. For a split second it has to become nonmaterial for a very short period of time and expand into space at an almost infinite velocity. Without this vibration (swinging back and forth) there is no objective or subjective reality."

The Universal Sea of Energy

Modern science has made great strides in understanding the universe in the last one hundred years, but it still has a long way to go to fully realize the true nature of the cosmos. It has come to recognize that matter and energy make for only about 5 percent of the universe, which is governed by the "four forces," known as electromagnetism, gravity, strong nuclear force and weak nuclear force. Another 20 percent is composed of "Dark Matter," while the other 75 percent is filled with "Dark Energy." The former is a force that holds the universe together while the latter causes it to expand. Since there is more than three times as much Dark Energy as Dark Matter, the universe is expanding outward. Recently, cosmologists had come to the conclusion that Dark Energy is an all-elusive power source that appears to "blink" in and out of the universe. Its density in the ever-expanding distances between planets, stars, and galaxies remains constant, so there must be additional amounts of Dark Energy entering our universe from another universe or dimension. Unconventional scientists refer to this power source as zero-point energy or gravity. *This mysterious source of infinite power is what we might refer to as Vril.* But we know that Vril is within everything in the universe. It fills every atom in the universe. Once we understand this, then we can accept the fact that we live within a universal sea of energy (Vril energy), just as the ancient philosophers wrote about. Combine this fact with the knowledge that the universe is like a hologram, and we can then begin to understand how we possess the ability to change our future life pathways through the application of sufficient mental concentration by developing an illuminated will. This illuminated will can reach into our unconscious mind with the assistance of such tools as the Runes.

Now that we realize that we are living within a sea of universal energy, called Vril, we can recognize that this force is the substance that makes up everything in the universe. Everything is made of Vril, including us. This force is everywhere, in everything and in you. Accept the truth that this force gives form to all things in the universe, including your physical body. Vril is the same life force that sets a galaxy spinning in the universe, and causes a flower to blossom. It is the same force that causes volcanos to explode, and breathes life into a newborn baby. *Know also that this force gives substance to your mind.* Like your thoughts, feelings, dreams and imagination, it has no limits. Its dimensions are without limitation. It is eternal, and cannot be destroyed. It is the tool both of the Gods, who use it to maintain order in the universe, and of the Giants, who cause chaos to ripple throughout the cosmos. Know that you are almost entirely made up of Vril, and that this force is divine, and it is a divine power within you that you can learn to harness, control and shape to create the future you desire. Trust in your powers to harness Vril, and learn how to use it to change the physical world around you.

The trillions of atoms that make up our bodies are tiny little oscillators. Working together, they are all parts of one great oscillator, which is your body. This means that each second of every day, we are constantly expanding into a space-like dimension, thousands, no, millions of times a second, that rapidly and then collapsing back just as rapidly, at the rate of atomic vibration. However, *in an altered state of consciousness we can expand our subjective time greatly.*

Controlling Time with Our Minds

Research has shown that when we observe time, we can change its passage. Have you ever heard the expression, "Time stood still for me." Well, during incidents when your life is on the line, or you are facing some great trauma, your perception of time actually changes. A test was conducted where an individual was fitted with a device made up of many small flashing lights. It was placed on his arm and it was programed to flash a number so fast that the subject could not see the number, just flashing lights. Then, he was dropped from 12 stories, hooked to a device. As he fell, he observed the flashing lights, and was able to see the number flashing. This was done over and over, and each time, the mind was able to adjust the flow of time, slowing it down so that he could see the number flashing. Thus, his state of consciousness was altered by the drop and thus *was able to control the flow of time*. This proves that we have within us the ability to tap into the universal mind—the consciousness of the Gods—and draw from their divine consciousness useful information. This consciousness exists on a much higher state of reality. This is done without using up much objective time. So our reality is made up of a constant rapid back-and-forth shuttling between our solid reality and the way-out realities, which we share with everybody else. An expanded or higher state of consciousness implies an expansion of our psyche into space. We are able to do this because we exist within a sea of energy, Vril energy, and this energy is used by the Gods to hold the universe together, keeping it functioning according to the physical laws that govern the objective universe. Through our minds, we can rise to a higher state of consciousness, and tap into this energy, harness it and transform our sense of reality.

We know that sound travels faster under water than it does through the air. The universe is like a vast and infinite sea, filled with Vril energy. This energy is quantum in nature, blinking in and out of the universe, and can collapse on itself, becoming whatever the conscious mind desires it to be. We will get into the different levels of consciousness shortly, but for now, we can refer to two levels of consciousness: humanity and the Gods. Both are affecting change throughout the universe through vibrations. The mind of the Gods is resonating thought throughout the universe, shaping and giving form to Vril energy, thus, supporting the physical laws that hold the universe together. Humanity has the same potential, though on a lesser scale, because our level of consciousness is lower then that which the Gods occupy. But we can raise our consciousness so that we can forge a link, a rainbow bridge, through the development of our Bifrost Gland (Third Eye). This will permit our minds to resonate more effectively, giving shape and form to the currents of Vril energy.

This brings us now to the understanding that everything in the universe is interconnected through the vast ocean of Vril energy. Since all matter is made up of atoms, and all atoms in almost entirely Vril, everything thus is interconnected, just as all the oceans of the Earth are interconnected by the same supply of water. Theoretically, one can put a message in a bottle, and throw it into the ocean in New York. In time, it can circle the entire globe and be found anywhere in the world. The same is true of the Vrilic nature of the universe. You can also send out a thought, and with the proper level of consciousness, *that thought can instantly resonate across the entire universe.* This process also works in reverse. By projecting one's consciousness into the universal sea of Vril while in a heightened state of consciousness, one can obtain information or knowledge about any subject from anywhere in the universe. Thus, thought waves, fed by Vrilic energy, can interconnect and affect other human beings.

All Matter is Energy—Vril Energy

You now understand that the universe is a sea of Vril energy, all interconnected. Currents of Vril energy are flowing in all directions, and as these currents spread through the vastness of the universal sea, like waves, they are constantly entering everything in the universe. Thus, all matter and energy is made up of Vril energy waves or currents. Let us discuss the realm of physical law for a moment. The waves or currents of Vril energy can manifest in the form of electromagnetic fields. When these currents of wiggling waves of energy interact with the retina of the eye, it can appear as a particle of light, or a photon. What is a photon? It is a tiny piece of vibrating Vril or electromagnetic field. Now, if the Vrilic field is wiggled even faster, it transforms into X rays. X rays are more powerful than ordinary light. But if we wiggle the currents of Vril even faster, the X rays will change into gamma rays. Gamma rays have the potential to break up into electrons and positrons, which are subatomic particles and building blocks of matter. What we are saying is this: *The vibrating consciousness, whether the consciousness that exists on a higher or lower level, is producing physical matter.*

All matter is made from rapidly vibrating Vrilic energy. Everything around, including ourselves, is made from atoms, which are mostly Vril, vibrating at different frequencies. The atom is made of a shell of orbiting electrons with a nucleus in the center. We can understand the nature of the composition of the atom better if we try to visualize the nucleus as being the size of a grain of sand. The orbiting shell of electrons would be approximately 300 feet in diameter, or the length of a football field. The electrons orbiting the nucleus would be much smaller than the nucleus. The rest of the huge sphere would appear to be empty space, but in reality it is filled with Vril energy. It is the Vril energy that is being shaped by the electrons rotating around the nucleus. Different amounts of electrons, rotating at different speeds, create different types of matter.

If we are largely empty space we should be able to pass through each other, but atoms either attach themselves together or repel each other. The reason solid objects can't pass through each is something known in the world of physics as "the Pauli exclusion principle,' which states that no two electrons can exist in the same quantum state. This means that when two nearly identical elctrons get too close the repel each other. This is the reason solid objects appear solid. But if we can somehow neutralize the exlusion principle we should be able to pass through solid objects.

But quantum theory also can cause electrons to bind together into molecules. When two atons get close together they either bounce off each other or bind together. This happens when two or more atons chare their electrons. The result is that quantum theory has some mind-bending principles such as: you cannot know the exact velocity and location of any particle; particles can in some sense be in two places at the same time; all particles exist as mixtures of different states simultaneously; you can disappear and reappear somewhere else; spinning particles can be a mixture of particles moving spinning both up and down simultaneously. But we know that observation can cause particles to act in different ways. We need to ask ourselves—is magic the prcess of the mind acting on particles on the quantum level of reality?

Now, remember that consciousness fills the universe, interacting with Vril everywhere, and thus has the potential to change and affect the structure of the atom. Thus, atoms, and hence matter, can be shaped and formed into anything at will, by

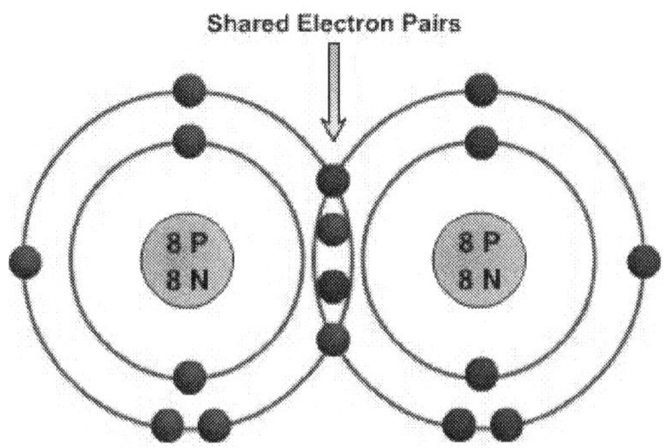

Oxygen (O_2) Molecule

the will of the Gods, because of their possession of a consciousness on a higher plane of existence.

Before we leave this subject, think of yourself as a thin, filmy sponge. Your sponge body is immersed in the infinite sea of Vril energy. Vril energy passes through you just as water would pass through a sponge as the sponge passes through the water. Like the water that passes through the sponge, the Vril energy flows into the body, filling it, and then passes out once again. So too does our body, as it moves through the universe, act like a sponge passing through the water. *Vril energy flows into our body, filling it, providing sustenance and animation—hence, life.* We are inseparable from it, so, just as to a sponge in a sea of water, a ripple of Vril energy passing through that universal sea will pass through your body, affecting it. And if the ripple is caused by thoughts, then we can see that the mind has the potential to affect change in the physical universe.

Different Levels of Consciousness

Let's begin by defining *consciousness*. This requires that we explore the nature of both the *quantity* and *quality* of

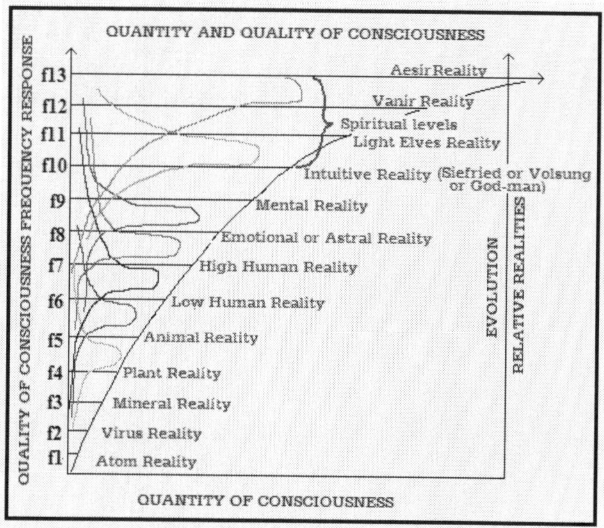

Different Levels of Consciousness

consciousness. Now, let's see if we can explain just what is consciousness in the simplest possible terms. *First, it is the capacity of our minds to respond to stimuli.* If we expose an atom to ultraviolet light, it will naturally respond to it, until we remove the light...in which case, it stops. We can say that an atom has a very simple form of consciousness, because different responses can be elicited from it by placing it under different forms of stimuli. This can also be done with a virus or bacterium. When we do the same with animals and humans, the number of types of response increases, because their consciousness is more developed. This is what we will refer to as the quantity of consciousness. *Consciousness is associated with the ability to respond to external stimuli.* Therefore, we must conclude that an atom has a very primitive form of consciousness. If we accept this, *then it means that all matter, which is made up of atoms, has consciousness.* Now, we might find it hard to believe that a rock has consciousness, and can be considered a living thing, but this is due to our human limitations. There are stones in Death Valley that move by themselves. We don't know how it is done, but they do move, very slowly, but move nonetheless. Our most ancient ancestors believed all Nature, including rocks, was alive and possessed consciousness.

Modern science has reduced what is "alive" to that which can reproduce. But this is quite arbitrary. We have a very hard time trying to perceive different forms of systems that might actually function differently from the way humans do, so we naturally tend to project our own behavior onto other systems. This results in modern science saying that life is that which possesses all the characteristics that we possess. Thus we assume that the atom cannot be alive because it does not function *exactly* the way we do. We then project this preconceived notion of what is "alive" onto each larger aggregate, assuming there is no life until we reach an aggregate of atoms that has reached a certain stage of organization, where "life," as we understand it, appears. *We assume that life exists only at the stage of aggregate where we can recognize our own behavior in it.*

The basic premise of Vrilology is that consciousness resides in matter; put another way, all mass (matter) contains consciousness (or life) to a greater or lesser extent. It may be more refined than human consciousness (the Gods) or more primitive.

But Vrilology teaches that humans have within us the ability to communicate with the levels of higher consciousness. These levels of higher consciousness represent the Gods, and the gods dwell within us. Thus, when properly trained we can interact with anything that has consciousness on whatever level, including the Gods!!!

As we said, there are two aspects to the nature of consciousness, the quantity and quality of consciousness. We are providing a diagram to help you better understand the relationship of the two aspects of the different levels of consciousness. On the horizontal line we plot the quantity of consciousness and on the vertical line its quality. We will use the atom as a basic unit of consciousness. We are assigning an arbitrary scale of numbers to the various categories of beings. The frequency response of the atom will be designated as f1; next comes a virus, f2; then a rock, f3; a plant, f4; an animal, f5. A human actually has two levels of consciousness, high and low, designated as f6 and f7. The most highly developed intelligence of human beings is designated as f7. The band between f6 and f7 represents the responses of the human nervous system to all possible stimuli delivered to it by our senses. This includes instruments that we use as extensions of our senses.

Now, we mean to explore the meaning of lower and higher levels of consciousness. We might be able to make this clearer by providing a simple example. Let us say we show a man a painting of a village and ask him to describe it. The probable answer will be "a village scene." Let us show the same picture to a second man. The second man might describe the picture in great detail, exploring the style, the composition, and the color scheme, describing the features of the scene in great detail, the type of architecture, what country the village might be located in. He might have to be told to stop talking too much about the picture. It is obvious that the second man has a broader range and refinement of responses. He will describe the picture with greater fidelity due to his more developed perception. This is the difference across the human band of f6 and f7. The human occupying the higher band, f7, can perceive the nature of his environment and reality of the universe through his more heightened senses; these go beyond the normal five senses, which all humans naturally possess and occupy a position on level f6. Your ability to perceive the environment around you is an indication of your capacity to utilize your senses, not just the five senses, but your extra sensory perceptions, with great efficiency. There exists a spectrum of realities in Nature, each occupied by a population having a certain level of consciousness.

We are suggesting that a mineral or a vegetable has some consciousness and forms a reality of its own. This was a common belief among our ancestors, who believed that everything in the universe–all matter–possessed some degree of consciousness. We can see this belief system in Tolkien's great literary work, *The Lord of the Rings*. He describes a race of giants that he calls "Ents," which are tree giants, who care for the forest. In fact, even trees have a degree of consciousness far beyond what natural science would attribute to them, for the Ents are able to "herd" the tree, proving that even trees possess the power of mobility. It was also believed that the druids of the Celts could speak with animals, trees and even rocks. There is even a reference to the nature of consciousness in all things in the Norse myths.

In Norse mythology, in the tale of Balder's death, his mother, Frigga, asked everything in the universe, even every plant and rock, to take an oath never to harm her son, Balder.

Well, this is indication that our ancestors understood that everything has consciousness, even those things that can't reproduce or move about on their own power.

Let us examine the diagram. The curved line that stretches across the chart diagonally represents the relationship between quantity and the quality of consciousness. We draw your attention to the fact that the curved line becomes almost parallel with the horizontal line at the top which we relate to the Aesir. Note how the difference between each level of reality gets progressively larger as we progress higher on the scale. We can conclude that the realm or reality of the Aesir, which is where Odin resides, contains all consciousness there is in the universe. *It is the source of all consciousness—which is the Gods!!!*

Next, look at the little bell-shaped curves on the left vertical line. These curves are the *"energy-exchange curves."* At the bottom of the chart, you will notice that they are smaller, but the higher we move vertically, the greater the energy-exchange curves grow in height. This means that the higher the realm of reality, the greater is the interaction with the surrounding environment. At the highest levels, one possesses absolute control over the environment. At this point, we can ask the question: How does our reality differ from other realities? The answer is: Our nervous system, which interprets reality for us, interacts strongly within the band of frequencies from f6 to f7. We have evolved to the level of exchanging maximum energy with our present environment or level of reality, and are in resonance with it. This is the meaning of the energy-exchange curve.

Vril Energy Powers Our Consciousness

If you examine the diagram, you will notice the energy-exchange curve extends into realities above and below its normal range of reality. This is true for every reality, including the human reality. You will notice that the human reality curve extends upward into the astral reality range, which is a dream state. You should also note that the astral reality's energy curve reaches down to the mineral level. This means that beings within the astral reality can reach down and interact with levels below it. Just as we can enter the astral level when we sleep or while we are in a meditative state, so too can beings in the astral level travel down into the lower levels. We need to look into the differences between the *relative* and *absolute* components of creation, and how they affect us.

We know that everything in the universe, including humans, is made up of atoms, and the atom is vibrating with energy—Vril energy—as electrons quickly rotate about its nucleus, causing a pulsation. This pulsation is the result of the electrons rotating about the nucleus, capturing and holding Vril. This pulsation transforms Vril, changing the property of the atom and giving the object that the atom is a part of its nature. The pulsation acts like a pendulum, just as Itzhak Bentov explains in his book, *Stalking the Wild Pendulum*. The atom pulsates between the ***relative*** and ***absolute***.

Itzhak Bentov uses the illustration of a deep sea to explain the nature of the absolute and the relative:

Let us represent the absolute by the image of a boundless deep sea. The surface of the sea is very calm and so smooth as to be invisible. The absolute is the reference against which we compare everything else. Now let us ripple the surface of this sea. We watch the waves appear and break up the smooth surface. This rippling makes the surface suddenly visible. By analogy, when motion or vibration appears in the absolute, it becomes visible or manifest, and we call it the relative, or physical reality.

Bentov is saying that the sea represents an *all-pervading component*, and that this all-pervading component is the totality of the different realities. It is what Bentov refers to as the *absolute* or *pure consciousness*. If we produce ripples in this sea, they will not manifest themselves at the lower layers of the sea, where a state of eternal rest will exist. Remember that the different sizes of the ripples are in proportion to the different realities that we show to exist in the chart. The larger waves are associated with the lower spectrum of realities. Here there are lower-frequency responses, manifesting lower quantities of consciousness, while the very fine, higher frequencies will manifest themselves in the higher realm of realities, and correspond to the higher levels just below the absolute.

If we go to the very lowest level, which is a quantum of electricity, a single electron, we must understand that this electron is a wave packet possessing a certain frequency of vibration, which determines the energy of the electron. But physical science will not be able to explain just what causes the electron to vibrate. Bentov provides an explanation: "But if we were to use the analogy of the sea of the absolute, we would visualize the quantum as a packet of ripples on the surface of that sea. It vibrates relative to the calm layers of the infinite sea of pure consciousness, and now we may answer the question as to 'what it is that vibrates within the quantum.'" It is a unit of pure consciousness that vibrates there.

All matter vibrates because it is made up of quanta of energy, and thus it is the changing component of pure energy—Vril. We divide creation into two components, the absolute and the relative. The absolute is fixed, eternal, and invisible, while the relative is the visible, manifest, and changing aspect, symbolized by the Rune Isa. Isa is the Rune of contraction, cessation of all movement. The relative is then symbolized by the Rune Fehu, the Rune of directed, expansive force, like the pendulum swinging. Here we have the opposing forces of Ginnungagap—fire and ice. As we explore the nature of the Runes, and their role as tools to harness and shape Vril, this will become clearer.

Now that we see that reality is made up of two components—one, an immutable, the cessation of motion defined by the Rune Isa, and the other, the dynamic, vibrating, expansive aspect of the same thing, defined by the Rune Fehu, which generates formation of life, or the power of creation—we can understand how both mind and matter are made of the same basic stuff. The difference between the two is that we may see solid matter as made up of larger, slower waves or ripples, which implies that it possesses less energy of the absolute, or it is sending off its energy, losing it as it sends it forth, and the mind, which is made up of much finer ripples, pulling them inward and absorbing them, thus building up its source of energy in its contraction, which implies that it possesses more of Vril. But then the contraction releases its energy, sending it forth as Fehu, only to be absorbed and contracted once more in the principle of Isa. The process is repeated infinitely.

The different higher and lower realities, as shown on our chart, can be scaled according to the refinement or coarseness of the frequencies. The lower realities would be defined by how large and coarse a frequency might be, while the higher levels of reality would be defined by the refinement of the higher frequencies. The same scale could be used to define people. Everything, and everyone, is made up of relative and absolute components. *Not every person has the same frequency.* Some individuals might vibrate at higher rates of resolution then others. Such individuals would possess greater psychic powers. But the rate of vibration is not fixed. *Vrilology teaches that we have the means to potentially increase our absolute, and thus increase our powers.*

The Human Body Is a Living Vril Oscillator

We might ask the question: What was the nature of our reality before the vibratory motion started? Clearly the non-vibratory state was the basis of that reality before the vibratory motion arose and became our physical manifest reality. We may refer to this non-vibratory base as the absolute proto-space—the time before the formation of Ymir (which can be considered the Norse cosmological equivalent to the Big Bang). We can also define the absolute as being an infinitely fine relative, that is, where the waves are so minute and their frequency so high that they are invisible. When this happens, we have a surface that appears calm and smooth but contains a tremendous energy and is full of creative potential. This is the actual definition of the absolute to the extent that it can be defined); it is *a high-energy creative potential* (Ymir), plus *intelligence* (the Gods). The intelligence (the Gods) adds self-organizing capability to any entity in creation. Thus we have the birth of Ymir (the Big Bang), Ymir (Chaotic proto-universe that existed right after the Big Bang) and the slaughter of Ymir (which is the reorganization of his parts to fashion the universe by the Gods, thus giving it order or physical laws). *The absolute is thus a state in which the contrasting concepts became reconciled and fused. Movement and rest fuse into one.*

This absolute proto-space is then a state, before Ymir, when the contrasting force of Isa (Ice) and Fehu (Fire), or Niflhem and Musspellheim, become reconciled and fused. Expansion and contraction, or movement and rest, are fused into one, resulting in the first reality, the first age of the universe, which was one of chaos, until the Gods' intelligence appeared to give it order, shape and form. If we accept the fact that everything is a vibratory reality, from the micro-levels to the macro-levels, then we have to accept that everything oscillates between two states of rest (Isa-

Fehu-Isa). Everything is producing sound. This is true not only of our bodies, but also of our minds.

If we refer back to the chart dealing with different realities,

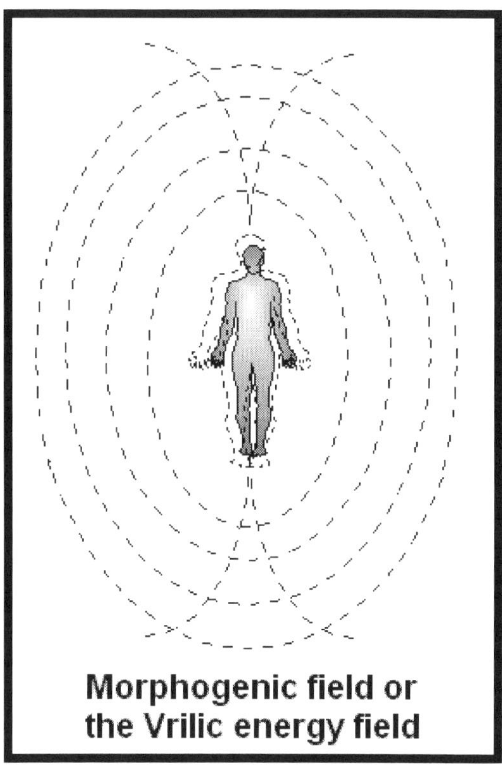

Morphogenic field or the Vrilic energy field

we can examine some of the differences to help us understand how vibrations can affect our minds and bodies. First, let us examine the *Mineral Reality*. If you were to imagine yourself being a rock, you would probably have a dim perception of the differences between hot and cold, light and dark. There might even be some form of communication with other rocks, but your perception of anything else would be extremely limited. But the most i mportant thing to understand about this level of reality is that there is no growth, just attrition. The energy exchange curve extends into the plant reality and never goes down to zero.

Let us now explore the next level of reality, the *Plant Reality*. Unlike the Rock Reality, there is growth and reproduction on this level of reality. This is what we traditionally referred to as "life." The quantity of consciousness is higher than that of a rock. Plants have a developed response to stimuli. There is an acute awareness of light and dark, difference in the season and weather, a lively social life, and even sex. They can react to attacks by insects and animals. Plants even respond to human emotions as well as music.

The next reality to examine is *Animal Reality*. Here you will find a broader span of emotions, a freedom of movement in three dimensions, and greater communications; and when domesticated, animals can acquire the ability to communicate with humans. There is social consciousness in the form of herd instinct, and some animals are highly inventive and intelligent. You probably have begun to notice from the diagram that each reality does not reach down to zero but does extend to the higher and lower realities. It is through this bridging of different realities that all things are connected.

The next reality is *Human Reality*. The interesting thing about human consciousness is that it can be developed to expand and learn how to interact with the whole spectrum of realities. This is the real meaning of "expansion of consciousness." *This means that our nervous system is capable of being developed to such a point that we can tune in on any of these realities, from the very lowest mineral to the very highest spiritual levels.*

What is important to understand is that Vril is disseminated throughout your body to different Hvel, or energy centers, and from these points to different areas of your body, by way of your spine and the nervous system. In fact, you have two nervous systems: the *sensori-motor* and the *autonomic* nervous systems. The sensori-motor system is connected to your spine and the twenty-four vertebrae, which correspond to the twenty-four Runes of the Elder Futhark. It then branches off at each vertebra to connect with every part of your body. It signals various muscles to exert themselves as directed by the brain, and receives impressions of sensations from every part of the body to the brain as feedback data on how the various regions of the body are functioning. This system will send orders for various parts of the body to react, such as reacting to external sensations that could cause pain.

The autonomic nervous system is in charge of those tasks that are unconscious, such as regulating your heartbeat or the movement of materials in your stomach and intestines. What is important to know is that Vril energy is constantly being channeled to every part of the body through both nervous systems. It is reacting to mental vibrations from the brain, received from the mind, both consciously and unconsciously.

Vril energy is constantly flowing into our bodies, replenishing the source of energy that holds the atoms together. The atoms are vibrating at different frequencies, causing matter to take on different forms, shapes and textures. Vril energy is moving throughout our bodies, reinforcing and replenishing the energy source of each atom, and thus ensuring life. Vril enters the body and coalesces within the solar plexus. From there it moves through the spinal cord by way of our nervous systems, directed by the resonances of the command of the mind, which disseminates it throughout the body. This ensures that our physical bodies can interact with our physical environment. But our bodies can also vibrate at rates lower and higher than that of our physical reality, and thus our bodies are connected to different realities possessing higher and lower rates of vibration. When our consciousness extends to higher realities, we enter the realms of the clairvoyants, with such powers as the perception of auras, telepathy, astral projection, remote viewing, and other abilities associated with psychic abilities.

Through the development of our minds to control our rates of vibration by chanting, and using the Runes, we can learn to resonate on the higher levels of reality. Thus, we can strengthen our extra-physical bodies, or those parts of our multi-dimensional souls. This will permit us to function on the higher levels of reality, including the astral, the mental, the causal and the intuitive.

We will later explain the nature of your multi-dimensional soul and the astral or auric body that extends beyond your physical body. This auric body can be developed to expand itself into the higher realms of the mental and causal realities.

Harnessing Vril for Reality-transference of Consciousness

As we stated before, the universe is a sea of Vril energy. So let us think of it as a pond with a surface that is very still. Now, if we throw in a pebble, it will cause ripples to expand outward. The ripples will continue to expand, growing wider and wider in every direction. You should visualize the pebble as an individual mind, and the ripples on the surface as mental vibration, or thought waves, expanding outward on the surface of the sea of Vril energy. Every time we think or express some deep feelings, we are sending out ripples into the Vrilic sea. Now, what if we drop several pebbles into the pond? Each will cause ripples to expand outward in all directions. As the ripples expand, they will interconnect. Now visualize each pebble as an individual sending out thought or mental waves, causing ripples in the sea of Vril. You can understand from this example how our thoughts connect with each other, touching everyone around us. Like the ripples transforming the surface of the pound from a calm surface to one of interconnecting and interlocking expanding ripples, so too our thoughts and feelings are sending out ripples or waves of thought and emotions, transforming or affecting the environment around each of us, and even affecting each other.

We can explore how thoughts and feelings can affect our surrounding environment by examining the development of a Nature Spirit. Imagine that there is a valley with a large rock formation protruding from the valley floor. Remember that we said that matter is consciousness, or contains consciousness? The consciousness of the rock, if there is enough of it (a critical mass), will develop a dim awareness of self. Over millions of years this dim awareness may grow into a sharpened identity, possibly through interaction with other creatures. Animals have much more highly developed consciousness than a rock. If animals find the rock formation a suitable place to find cover from the elements, and can make crevices within the rock their home for breeding and as a hiding place, the animals will feel grateful to the rock. *The collective cumulative sense of gratitude over time will cause an evolution in the rock's consciousness.* And its ego will be boosted if birds come and make nests and lay eggs in it. The evolving life and consciousness of the birds and animals, which are higher than that of the rock, *will give its consciousness a push upward.* Sooner or later the consciousness of the rock will evolve into a *"spirit of the rock."* By now the rock has learned that if it extends protection to these creatures, they respond with grateful feelings. Slowly, therefore, it begins to understand that its business is to protect them. Soon the rock becomes quite adept at this. Its evolved consciousness will attract more creatures over time. *Being in close contact with live beings, over a very long period of time, the less developed consciousness of the rock will slowly evolve into a higher range of consciousness, and widen his range of responses.* It will have a relatively low-frequency response, corresponding to that of the mineral level of consciousness, but in this case it will be at the very top of the band delineating the mineral consciousness. It will border on the plant consciousness, and its energy-exchange curve will reach into that of the astral region.

Now, let's say human beings discover this rock. If one of the humans is sensitive to Nature, he will *feel* that there is *something special about the rock.* Have you ever been out walking and found a rock, and stopped to pick it up for no other reason than *it felt right?* You would hold it in your hand and for no particular reason, *you just feel something about the rock that feels right.* Most likely, you will pocket it and take it home, and you might even take to carrying it with you wherever you go as a *Good Luck Rock.* The reason is simple. There is something about the energy, or consciousness of the rock that *speaks to you.* The consciousness of the rock can communicate with your higher consciousness without your fully understanding it. Well, the same is true with our example. The rock will produce some particular feeling in him, either of protection or repulsion. A spirit such as this might want to impress man by producing some type of trick. When this happens, the man, if he notices it, will become duly impressed. He might tell others of his tribe that there is great power at the site of the rock. Some other people will come around who have heard about the happenings around the rock. They will also witness the tricks, and pretty soon there is a cult centered around the rock. This boosts the ego of the spirit of the rock immensely because the thoughts of the people who concentrate on it add to its power. As more and more people worship it, its power continues to increase. It is now hob-nobbing with royalty as more and more people concentrate on the rock. This adds to its ability to perform more and more tricks because its ability to do so is stimulated by the level of energy produced by the human nervous system. Eventually, the primitive people will bring it sacrifices to draw it to their side. It is known that miners in copper mines of Peru sacrifice llamas to the spirit of the mine every year with great pomp and ceremony. According to the miners, this spirit, who is the individuated consciousness of a vein of copper, will be appeased by this sacrifice and not harm or cause accidents to the people working in the mine, who, in effect, are digging up and diminishing his body. The people of ancient Iceland began holding their assemblies at a site just like this rock that came to be known as the All-Thing, and today it still is considered a sacred site in Iceland, and holds a special place in the culture of the country. And there are literally thousands of examples of this throughout the world.

Now let's think about how this process works out between a human and his pet animal. If the human truly desires a pet, as opposed to "keeping" an animal for practical reasons such as security, the pet and the human will develop a close, symbiotic relationship. The love, care, and affection that the human displays toward the pet will help to develop and evolve the animal's soul. It will take on human characteristics. Its energy curve will rise. It will become more than an animal. At the same time, the human's soul will also be transformed, taking on the responsibility of showing affection toward a "wild" creature, whose natural instincts will help in his improved health physically and his spiritual evolution, causing his energy-curve to increase greatly.

This fact addresses the subject of the process or effect that mental thought waves have on things and people. Every thought you have is Vril energy that causes the neurons in the brain to fire in a certain pattern. This process naturally produces tiny Vrilic currents along definite paths in the brain cortex. The activity in the cortex can be picked up by sensitive instruments through electrodes on the surface of the skull. In other words, a thought that starts out as a tiny stir eventually develops into a full-fledged thought producing at least a 70 millivolt potential somewhere in the cortex. The first neuron is charged up and this in turn causes other neutrons to fire in a certain sequence. Remember that no energy is ever lost in the universe. If we pick up the currents produced by the thought outside the head, it means that the energy of the thought was broadcast in the form of electromagnetic waves at the velocity of light into the environment, and finally into the cosmos filled with Vril. These electromagnetic waves are the ripples on the surface of the pond.

We should point out the difference between *focused thought,* and typical, normal thinking processes that produce typical, normal thoughts. Your mind is constantly thinking; even when you are sleeping, your mind is still thinking. But these thoughts are just random, typical thoughts about problems and situations that we encounter every day of our lives. As long we are just producing idle thoughts, the thought energy is diffuse, and it eventually spreads out, weakens, and disappears. *However, when we consciously concentrate and send coherent thoughts, that thought energy or thought form will impinge on the person for whom the thought was meant.* The difference between idle thought and focused thought is likened to the difference between light produced by a flashlight and the beam of light produced by a laser. The former is diffused, spreads out and weakens, but a laser is concentrated and focused so that it can travel effectively over greater distances, than normal light.

Now, all these minor gods and Nature spirits rely on the energy they get from others to keep themselves powerful. Just like the politicians and celebrities, who elicit life energies from their constituencies, their power and influence remains dependent on the size and strength of their constituencies. Eventually, as their constituency diminishes, they fade from the scene, as did the Gods of our ancestors. Like everything in Nature, including the relationship between the mortal and the divine, the principle of *as above, so below*, and the reverse, *as below, so above*, is fundamental.

The Gods have great power because their energy curve is so far above ours. When we celebrate and concentrate on them, we are providing them with a means to increase their influence in Midgard. We are opening a path across the Rainbow Bridge for the Gods in Asgard to ride down and influence events here, in Midgard. At the same time, the flow of energy is two-way. Our energy curves are also increasing and we are causing a generated and engineered evolution of ourselves upward into the astral level of consciousness, and hopefully beyond into the mental and intuitive levels. *This is what is meant by a Vril Being or God-man.*

Chapter Two: Creation Myth in Norse Cosmology

Understanding the Nature of the Gods

As we move into the Twenty-First Century, modern science is revealing that human beings possess the potential for capabilities that are quite beyond anything we previously even imagined possible. This revelation presents new challenges and discoveries that have elicited from every field of scientific research and discipline the collective efforts of researchers to provide a new picture of human existence, along with a new understanding of the nature of human consciousness.

Newtonian World View of the Universe as Machine

Prior to the discoveries of the Twentieth Century, Western science held fast to the firm conviction that the universe was composed of solid matter. Einstein's theory of relativity and quantum physics would begin to cause us to challenge this preconception. Atoms were considered the basic building blocks of this material universe. They were thought of as tiny, compact and indestructible solid matter. Their existence was limited according to fixed laws within a three dimensional space. The evolution of matter progressed in a linear and orderly progression, moving from the past, through the present, and into the future. Western science held fast to a determinist viewpoint that viewed the universe as a gigantic machine. Scientists, philosophers and political theorists held fast to this determinist world view, confident that some day they would discover all the rules governing this machine, so they could play God in discovering everything that had happened in the past and predicting everything that would happen in the future. They were confident that once they discovered the rules, they would be masters over all they beheld. They even believed they could create life through a process of simply mixing certain chemicals in a test tube.

Within this Newtonian world view, life, consciousness, human beings, and creative intelligence were reduced to simple accidental by-products that evolved from an astonishing series of circumstances of matter interacting with matter. This materialistic model lends itself to a logic that hypothesizes that human consciousness, intelligence, morality, ethics, art, religion, and science itself are all simply by-products of material processes that occur within the brain.

We know that consciousness has its origins in the brain, but this is entirely arbitrary. Endless clinical and experimental observations have shown a correlation between states of consciousness and various neurophysiological and pathological conditions that include infections, traumas, intoxications, tumors, and strokes, that prove beyond a shadow of a doubt that our mental performance and health are linked to biological processes in our brains. But this is not proof that consciousness is simply a biological reaction to workings of a biological organ, in this case the brain. It means that the brain is the seat of our consciousness, but does not necessarily mean that consciousness originates in or is produced by our brains. This assumption by Western science is a metaphysical rather than a scientific fact. We can make an analogy by stating that an expert television repair man can tell us what is wrong with a defective television set and how to repair it so that it will work once more, but this is not proof that the set itself was responsible for producing the programs we see when we turn it on. But when we discuss the brain, it is the exact logic that is employed by mechanistic science as "proof" that consciousness is produced by the brain.

Consciousness and Cosmos: Science Discovers Mind in Nature

By thc mid-Twentieth Century, the Newtonian view of physics had given way to new theories about the nature of the atom. Newton's idea that the indestructible atom was the most elementary building block of matter gave way to a new theory of physics that contained notions of even smaller and more elementary parts–protons, neutrons, and electrons.

Newton's principles were challenged by the discovery of literally hundreds of new subatomic particles that possessed strange behavior that did not fit nicely into Newtonian theory. The very nature of these subatomic particles proved to be paradoxical. When examined, these subatomic particles behaved like material entities, but in other experiments they displayed a very different property that appeared wavelike. This came to be known as the "wave-particle paradox."

The old view of the universe made up of solid, discrete objects was replaced by one of a microworld that was actually a complex web of unified events and relationships. Exploration of this microworld showed that consciousness is not a passive reflection the objective material world, but *that it actively participates in the creation of reality*.

Everything that we thought we knew according to Einstein's theory of relativity — that space is three-dimensional, that time is linear, and that space and time are separate entities — has been proven false. We now view them as an integrated, four-dimensional continuum known as "space-time." The new theory of quantum physics has challenged the old perspective of the universe laid down by Newton. It has replaced the old Newtonian principles regarding the boundaries between objects and the distinctions between matter and empty space. The universe is now seen as one continuous field of varying density instead of there being discrete objects separated by empty spaces. Matter and energy are now viewed as interchangeable. Consciousness is no longer something that exists within our brains, but rather an active and integral part of the universal fabric. The old Newtonian notion of the universe as a super-machine has been replaced by the idea that it is now one vast thought, as expressed by the British astronomer James Jeans.

Holography and the Implicate Order

A three-dimensional image can be created in space by use of a laser's coherent light of the same wave-length. This process is referred to as *Holography*. Like a picture projected from a photographic slide, a holograph is a record of an interference pattern of two halves of a laser beam. By using a partially silvered mirror, a beam of light can be split. Half of it is directed to the emulsion of the hologram that we can refer to as a reference beam. The other is reflected to the film from the object being holographed, and that half is referred to as the working beam. By enfolding the information in the two beams, a three dimensional image is created that is distributed throughout the hologram. When the hologram illuminated by the laser, its entirety can be reproduced or "unfolded" from a tiny section of the hologram. What this means is that if we could cut the hologram into a million pieces, each piece is still capable of reproducing the entire holographic image. If you can grasp this principle then you can understand how the God exist simultaneously in each atom within an individual, while at the same time existing in each atom in every one of us, just like the whole of a hologram exists in each piece of the hologram.

The world-renowned theoretical physicist, and formerly one of Einstein's coworkers, David Bohm, suggested that we could only perceive a tiny fragment of reality through our senses and nervous systems, even when we employ the most advanced scientific instruments. The reality of the world around is referred to by Bohm as "unfolded" or "explicate" order. He claims that what we perceive through our five senses emerges as special forms from a much larger matrix, which he refers to as the "enfolded" or "implicate" order. This larger matrix, or the enfolded or implicate order, is the actual hologram, and what we perceive through our five senses is a mere holographic image of the greater matrix. *What Bohm is saying is that there is a level of reality, which he describes as the implicate order, that is not accessible by our five senses or direct scientific scrutiny.* This is the level of reality in which the Gods dwell.

In Bohm's book *Wholeness and the Implicate Order*, two whole chapters are devoted to the relationship between consciousness and matter as seen through the eyes of modern physicists. *He explores the nature of this reality as an unbroken, coherent whole that is involved in an infinite process of transformation that he refers to as holomovement. The holomovement is the process by which the Gods are constantly seeking to transform chaos into order — thus, their ongoing struggle with the Giants.* This is an ongoing process, never ending, for the Gods are in a constant state of resisting the destructive forces of the Giants. The Giants' efforts to spread chaos in the universe is relentless and thus the Gods must ever work to hold back their influence.

Thus structures in the universe are nothing but abstractions. No matter how much time and effort we might invest in describing objects, entities, or events, we must ultimately concede that they are all derived from an indefinable and unknowable whole that is the struggle between the Gods and the Giants. Since the Gods must continuously work to maintain the ordered universe against the relentless efforts of the Giants to spread chaos, everything is in flux, always moving, so the use of nouns to describe what is happening can only mislead us.

The perception of life in terms of inanimate matter as described in Newtonian physics is outdated. Each part of energy and matter represents a microcosm that enfolds the whole. What we perceive as matter and life are mere absorptions, abstracted from the holomovement, that is, the undivided whole, but neither can be separated from the whole. Thus matter and life are what our five senses permit us to perceive in our limited ability to recognize the greater matrix of higher reality which exists on a level of existence where the struggle between the Gods and Giants, or Order and Chaos, is unfolding. This is also true of matter and consciousness, which are both aspects of the same undivided whole, because Vril exists in everything, in every atom, and can be controlled and transformed by the mind. The mind can control Vril, which is the fundamental essence of everything, by changing the frequency of vibration of matter. Remember from the previous chapter that the number of protons in the nucleus of an atom determines its chemical properties, and that the mass of the nucleus determines its resonant frequencies of vibration. Change the atom's vibration and you change its properties — mind over matter.

Bohm reminds us that even the process of abstraction, by which we create our illusions of separation from the whole, is itself an expression of the same struggle between the Gods and Giants and our willing alignment with the Gods in this struggle, which he refers to as holomovement. Once we accept this train of logic, we ultimately come to the realization that all perceptions and knowledge, which includes scientific work, are not objective reconstructions of reality. They are instead likened to artistic expressions, similar to what a painter will put on canvas when he is painting the image his mind processes when viewing a wildlife scene. What he paints might not be what is real, but reflects his perception of reality. We cannot measure true reality; in fact, the very essence of reality is its immeasurability.

Since true reality results from the struggle between the Gods and Giants, two forces that flow from a higher dimension of reality that exist on a higher plane of consciousness, we can never truly grasp the totality of reality; there are dimensions to it that exist beyond our three-dimensional perception of physical existence. This is also true of the nature of the Gods themselves, and it is true of the multiverse of the Yggdrasill, which is the structured form of reality that the Gods have created and struggle to maintain against the relentless forces of decay that are personified by the Giants.

Gregory Bateson, one of the most original theoreticians of our time, explains that the mind and nature form an indivisible unity. He challenges traditional thinking by demonstrating that in the world, all boundaries are illusory. He does not attribute the process of mental functioning exclusively to humans, but also to animals, plants, and even inorganic systems.

The Gods as beings of a higher plane of reality

A friend of mine told me she had trouble believing that there is a guy riding through the sky in a chariot pulled by two goats and that he throws a big hammer that unleashes thunderbolts.

She was referring to Thor, of course. I listened to her and had to admit that if I never heard of Thor and someone told me that this was the description of God, or a God, I would have trouble believing it also. That is, if I did not understand just what is a God.

The Gods are superior beings, with supernatural powers. They exists in a dimension of existence that can be described as a higher level of consciousness or existence. As we described in Chapter One about levels of consciousness and different realms or planes of existence that exist alongside our dimensions, but that we could not see or experience because their frequency of vibration was different, thus rendering them out of sync with our reality, the Gods exist on such a plane of reality. They exist within a dimension or level of reality that might very well possess more than three physical dimensions. If this is so, then we would never be able to comprehend their totality of reality because our mind or consciousness is unable to register and perceive physical dimensions beyond our own. But what would happen if a being–a God–from a dimension with more than three physical dimensions entered our three-dimensional reality? We would only be able to perceive three of their physical dimensions, and thus would never be able to fully comprehend what they really are like. Let me give you an example of what I am talking about by referring to a book by Edwin A. Abbot known as *Flatland.*

In the book, the author describes a reality with only two physical dimensions. Forward and backwards, and sideways. There is no height or depth. Everything exist within a reality that is physical like a sheet of paper. If a three dimension being from our dimension were to enter or pass through Flatland, the citizens of their reality would only be able to see that part of the three-dimensional being that is within this sheet of paper reality. Thus, the citizens of Flatland would never truly know the total physical description of the three dimension entity. He could only perceive two of his three physical dimensions. Secondly, the citizens of Flatland would then try and describe what they did perceive within the cultural context of their existence.

Now, if a being with more than three physical realities entered our three physical dimensional reality, we would only be able to perceive three of his dimensions. Then, what we did see, we could only describe within the cultural context of our reality. If

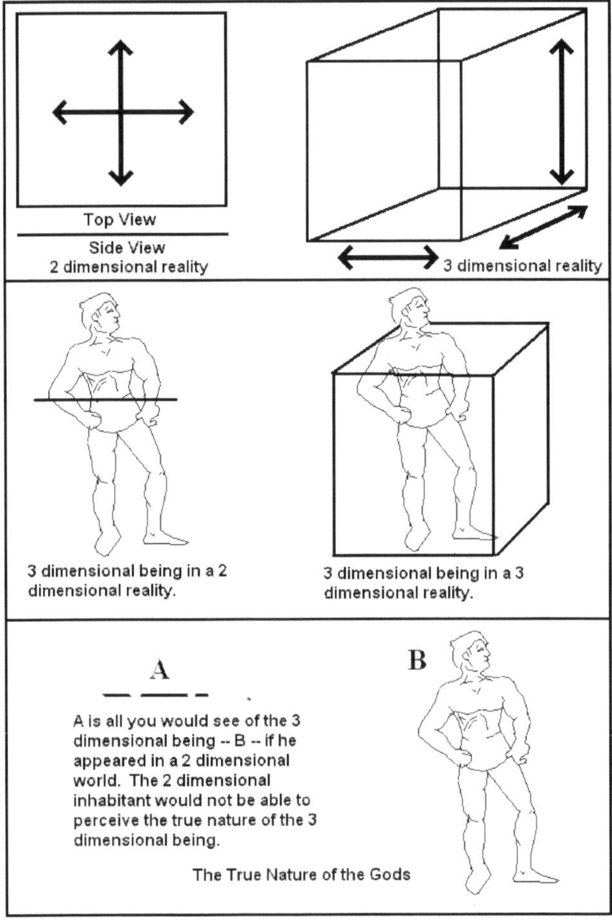

you are a man who comes into contact with a being who has great powers that stimulate our sexual senses, your brain would download the data and turn it into images that exist within your brain that have similar characteristics. Thus, your brain would transform the images into something familiar within your consciousness, and the entity would appear as a seductive woman of extraordinary beauty and sexuality. You would think of her as a Goddess of love and sexuality.

Let me give you another example of what I am talking about. If we come into contact with one of the Gods, we might perceive him as a great man, riding a chariot pulled by two goats and swinging a hammer that we call Thor. But, is this really what Thor looks like? Perhaps not, but when we perceive his existence through visions, meditation or trance, our three-dimensional senses cannot perceive the extra-dimensional reality of the nature of Thor. What our three-dimensional senses can pick up creates an image of what he is based on our limited perception of reality. If he possesses an energy that can be projected and can break barriers and stop the destructiveness of chaotic principles, restoring order, our limited ability to comprehend this power, which exists on a plane of existence beyond our three-dimensional perception, causes our brain to conjure up the image of something with these characteristics, which in this case would be a hammer. He also moves with great force and thus he is perceived as riding a chariot pulled by two great goats, who are beasts known for battering down opponents with their mighty horns. Thus we conceive Thor as owning a hammer as a weapon to combat the forces of chaos and riding a chariot pulled by goats. But this is the perception of Thor that we inherited from our ancestors because the images of him were objects that they could conjure in their minds to give substance to the entity of Thor as they understood reality. What if Thor never appeared to our ancestors? What if he made his first appearance to us in the 21st Century? Our imagery of him would be based upon objects that we are familiar with in our century. We would probably perceive him as a soldier riding a tank, which is an armored vehicle that can crash through any barrier and shoot projectiles from its barrel.

Journeys into Mythic Realities

When people think of myths they consider them fictitious, made-up fairy tales or adventure stories experienced by imaginary heroes in non-existent countries which are products of fantasy and imagination. Both C. G. Jung, the famous psychologist, and the world-renowned mythologist Joseph Campbell have explored the meaning of myths and mythologies, and have shown that this interpretation of mythology is superficial and incorrect. Both men came to the conclusion that myths are manifestations of fundamental organizing principles that exist within the cosmos that affect our lives on deeply personal and cultural levels. Jung called them archetypes.

These archetypes are not the creations of human imagination, though they express themselves through our individual psyches. These archetypes represent universal governing principles that are superordinated to our psyches and affect our individual lives on many levels. Jung believed these archetypes exerted a powerful influence on our individual lives, as well as on cultural and historical events. They represent universal principles that transcend historical, cultural and geographical boundaries, though they will take on various manifestations within each individual culture. But what is vitally important to understand is that archetypes are autonomous by nature, not dependent on us for their creation. We can tap into their existence by tapping into the great collective unconscious, or racial soul, which in Norse mythology is referred to as Mimir's Well. Their existence is independent and sovereign within what Jung as referred to as the collective unconscious.

Gods are beings that exist on a level of consciousness where Jung's archetypes exist, higher than the three-dimensional reality which we call existence. They are intelligent beings who have the capacity to affect our lives and human existence. They can communicate with us through our collective consciousness or kin-fetch. We can perceive them through altered states of consciousncss, when our minds transcend our reality and glimpse into other-worldly realities. But because our minds are conditioned to perceive data and process this data through a consciousness that is designed for three physical dimensions, we can only perceive three of the many dimensions of these beings–Gods–and according to images that are familiar to us within our reality, and thus we do not process or see those extra-dimensional features of these beings that exist beyond the three physical dimensions that we are familiar with.

Many of Jung's ideas about archetypes have been proven true by modern research into the field of non-ordinary states of consciousness. The boundaries we ordinarily see between myths and the material world tend to dissolve in non-ordinary states of consciousness, causing the world of archetypal realities to become increasingly real and palpable, even when the solid material world disintegrates into dynamic patterns of energy. In such circumstances, mythological figures literally come alive as Gods, with real consciousness and intelligence and assume independent states of existence within our reality. The same is true about landscapes that make up the mythic world, becoming as concrete and convincing as our everyday reality.

In their most elemental and profound forms, the Gods might appear to us as archetypes or cosmic principles that are completely abstract and beyond the capacities of human perception, because they possess dimensions to their nature that we are incapable of comprehending. However, in non-ordinary states, they may also appear in forms that we perceive through sight, hearing, smell, taste, touch, or the virtually palpable sense of a presence, and thus our consciousness gives them form and personality that we see as Gods. And yet, they exist in their extra-dimensional reality independently of our consciousness, for they are real, independent and intelligent beings, though existing in a realm of reality of such high consciousness that we cannot ordinarily perceive them without entering into a state of meditation or trance.

Ginnungagap

Northern scalds or learned men wrote extensive poems describing the adventures of the Gods and Goddesses worshiped by the people of Northern Europe. Some of these have been preserved in the Eddas and Sagas. These sagas or myths include the Norse perception of the origin of the universe or what might be referred to as "The Norse Creation Myth." They declared that in the beginning, when there was no earth, nor seas, nor air, nor anything in the universe there was an all-powerful being referred to as the *Allfather*, whom they dimly conceived as uncreated as well as unseen, and that whatever he willed came to pass. Who this being is, is unknown, but we speculate he was the consciousness of the Ginnic reality, the time before the creation of the *Yggdrasill*, which is the structured, orderly cosmos. This Allfather, which we can refer to as the Odin consciousness, was the consciousness of Odin before he was born into the form of Odin, Vili and Ve, a triplet divinity or Holy Divinity–three Gods in one.

Before the existence of our reality with three physical dimensions there existed what best can be described as this Ginnic reality, which took the form of a great abyss known as *Ginnungagap*, which means the "cleft of clefts," or "the yawning gulf." Its depth was bottomless, which means its dimension was infinite, and it was enveloped in perpetual twilight or darkness, meaning that it lacked substance, or three physical dimensions, as we comprehend reality. There were only two forces in existence in this Ginnic reality. They were the Force of Expansion and the Force of Contraction.

In the northern region of this vast void there existed the realm known as Niflheim, the home of ice, mist and darkness, of great cold in which all movement ceased in what might be referred to as a *zero point field*. This is the seat of the Form of Contraction. Like a black hole that sucks everything into it, even light, there is an infinite source of energy that is released. Thus, *in the center of Niflheim is a bubbling and exhaustless spring known as Hvergelmir, the seething cauldron, whose waters supplied twelve rivers known as the Elivagar.* As the waters of these streams flowed swiftly away from its source and encountered the cold blast of Niflehim they were transformed into huge blocks of ice, which rolled downward into the immeasurable depths of the great abyss with a continual roar like thunder.

What we can deduce from this description of Niflheim is that it was a realm of Form, where everything is pulled into the zero point field only to be released in an endless source of Vril energy that flows into the abyss of Ginnungagap, taking on the form of what might be considered what physicists today refer to as *dark matter.* Like the icy energies of Niflheim, dark matter pulls inward on itself and acts as a force of contraction or order within the present universe. If it dominated the universe, the entire universe would be pulled inward by its icy forces until everything would be compressed into an infinitesimally small point. The compression would result in heat beyond imagination, due to the fusion of everything, causing a release of an infinite supply of free energy that is described in the myths as the well of Hvergelmir (as described in Griminsmal 26), sending an infinite supply of Vril throughout the abyss in currents of energy that are described as rivers or streams.

In the Norse poem, Gylfaginning, stanza 51, we read about the existence of a terrible dragon or serpent by the name Nidhogg, who lives in this spring or well. Nidhogg is also reputed to exist in Hel (the Netherworld) and sucks on the life blood or life force of the dead, devouring their corpse (genetic essence), as he also gnaws on the roots of the Yggdrasill. Perhaps Nidhogg exists not in the well of Hvergelmir, but in one of its streams that flow down into Hel. The name Hvelgelmir is similar to many Giants', who have in their names the same root world gelmir, which means "water," which is symbolic for the currents of Vril energy that flow throughout the cosmos like "currents of water."

In nature, all things will eventually succumb to the forces of decay and collapse if abandoned. We must constantly work to maintain a house, repairing cracks, clearing away overgrowth of vegetation, applying new paint, preventing water damage, and performing the hundreds of small and great chores necessary to keep the house in good condition. If we do not, it will eventually succumb to chaos. The effects of nature, when unchecked, represent the Giants as agents of chaos and they will overtake the structure. Rain, snow, heat and wind, as well as animals and vegetation, will all gradually destroy the house. Water will fill any and all cracks, turning to ice when the weather turns cold, causing the cracks to get larger until the structure falls apart. Vegetation will have the same effect. Roots and branches will grow into any small crack, no matter how tiny, and gradually tear the structure apart as it grows. The cracks will increase until the entire structure falls apart.

These forces of nature are the *Nidhogg Principle* at work within the currents of natural forces; like the dragon in the stream of Vril flowing out of Hvelgelmir, it will eternally gnaw at the structure of the Yggdrasill, causing decay and eventual collapse. Nidhogg is the universal principle of Chaos and Decay, and these forces work also within the human body, both physically and spiritually, causing the process of cellular reproduction to break down, leading to illness, aging and eventual death, just as will wrong types of living, engaging in activities that will cause moral decline, spiritual decay and eventually, self-destructive behavior.

South of the dark chasm, and directly opposite Niflheim, is the realm known as *Musspellheim,* the home of elemental fire, where all is hot and bright, and whose frontiers are constantly guarded by the flaming Giant known as Surtur. He fiercely guards his realm with his flashing sword, which sends forth great showers of sparks that fall with a hissing sound upon the ice-blocks in the middle of the abyss.

There is no explanation of the origin of Surtur in the Norse myths. His origin is probably lost in time. Where did he come from? Has he always been? Or was his creation the result of the forces of heat and fire, the expansive energy of the Male Force that builds up within Musspellheim? We can make a case for Surtur being the personification of this Male Force of reproduction–expansive fire–within the Fehu Rune, and like Audhumla forming in Niflheim from the cold, he too probably came into existence in the same manner from the fire and heat of Musspellheim.

At the end of Ragnarok, Surtur lays waste to everything with his fiery sword, but out of the ashes, new life is born, and out of a new ocean (water-Laguz which is melted ice) is born a New Earth. Is this sea the principle of Female Form created from the impregnation of ice, causing it to melt and thus create life in the form of Audhumla? We will look into Audhumla shortly.

The expansive Force of Heat or sparks out of Musspellheim rises into the middle of Ginnungagap, causing the ice of Niflheim to melt, releasing the life-energy. This force is what physicists today refer to as **dark energy**. Dark energy is presently causing the universe to expand, because it makes up about 74 percent of the universe, while dark matter makes up about 22 percent. The rest of the universe is what we can refer to as the "physical universe," which includes all the gases (3.5 percent) and the stars, planets, etc...(0.5 percent). *This small 4 percent is governed by the four fundamental forces known as gravitational force, electromagnetic force, weak nuclear force and strong nuclear force.* Because dark energy, which is fire from Musspellheim, is three times as great as dark matter, ice from Niflheim, the fiery energy is causing the universe to expand until it grows so great that there will be nothing but a dark, icy infinity. If dark matter predominated in the universe, everything would be pulled inward by its icy energy, causing everything to fuse into the infinitely small point that would then explode in an unimaginable fiery force like the Big Bang. We have here the opposites acting in synchrony. Icy dark matter results in a fiery end, and fiery dark energy results in a icy death.

All-Father Or All-Orderer

Odin was the All-Father before he became Odin. In Old Norse, "All-Father" was spelled "Alfothr" which actually should be translated as "All-Orderer." He is the creator of the Cosmos, and the nine worlds. He was reborn into the Holy Trinity of Odin, Vili and Ve, and thus became one with his creation. This trinity was the creative force that gave shape to the universe, creating order out of chaos by slaying Ymir, who personifies chaos. Therefore, Odin is not only the All-Father, but the All-Orderer. In the Myths, Odin is described as a seeker of knowledge. He undergoes at least three ordeals in his quest for knowledge: hanging on the Yggdrasill; surrendering his eye for the right to drink form Mimir's well of knowledge, and his quest to retrieve the Mead of Inspiration. But if Odin is the All-Father and is all-knowing, why must he undergo such ordeals?

The Myths tell us that Odin and his two brothers, Vili and

ALL-FATHER -- ALFOTHR--ALL-ORDERED

Ve, were born from the union of God Borr and the Giantess Bestla. It was these three Gods who killed Ymir (Chaos) and from his parts, fashioned an ordered reality. But beforc Odin birth himself into his creation he was the All-Father. As the All-Father, he was pure consciousness. In this state he can be referred to as the "Odinic Consciousness." As pure consciousness, Odin can probably be considered androgynous, much like Ymir and Buri, the first God. In fact, if we examined the matrix of Ginnungagap, we will discover that it is a blueprint for the mind of the All-Father.

In the section on Ginnungagap, we discovered that it was a yawning void with two polarities: Muspellheim, the realm of fire and Niflheim, the realm of ice. Muspellheim is at the southern end of Ginnungagap. Fire is associated with the male principle of fire, and ruled over by the Fire Giant, Surtur, who possesses a fiery sward, which is an obvious phallic symbol. At the other end of the void is Niflheim, the realm of ice, which represents the female principle of ice. The two realms represent the two halves of the brain. Muspellheim is the left brain, and the seat of consciousness. Consciousness is thought and thoughts represent the active might of thinking. It is represented by one of Odin's ravens, Huginn, who is thought. The other realm, Niflheim, represents memory. Memories are thoughts that are no longer active. They are in a state of inertia, frozen in time until they are melt by the fiery sparks of thought that rise up from Muspellheim. Niflehim, the right brain, is the seat of the subconscious. Odin's second raven, Muninn represents memory. The description of how heat from Muspellheim melts the ice of Niflheim is likened to what happens when one meditates. In a meditative state, we cause the two halves of our mind—consciousness and subconsciousness---to work together. This is the mechanism that the Erulian employs to work magic, since magic is the act of the mind controlling and manipulating energy.

Odin is the force that holds the universe together and sets it on its path. He is the evolutionary momentum from which all things originated, and the progression that sets the seasons on their cycles. He is the giver of life and death, because both are necessary for the evolutionary process to continue. From his consciousness all the Gods were born. Every God and Goddess is a part of the All-Father, just as we are all a part of him. He gave life to our people and to all things. He is the source of divine consciousness and gave us self-awareness that distinguishes us from the animals. He gave us the will to grow and strive to make ourselves better, so that we might be more like him. He does not want worshipers on bent knees, but men and women standing upright celebrating his name and all the names of the Gods and Goddesses. Through him we look inward so that we might seek to deify the Self. The All-Father is the unity of the many aspects of the pantheon of Gods and Goddesses.

Odin is the All-Father, the Great God. He is unseen, but can be felt, especially in the natural surroundings of the forest. If you want to feel the presence of Odin, withdraw into the forest and wait there. Remain still and listen. You will feel his presence in the thousands of mysterious sounds and breaths of the forest. The wind that blows through the leaves and branches of the trees is the very essence of his spirit, and when the storm-winds blow through the forest you can feel him on his wild hunt. But most of all, you'll feel his essence in the strange and awful stillness that dwells in the forest, broken only by the forest murmurings. Odin's presence is especially felt in the sacred groves within the forest. Through meditation and chanting, this essence of Odin, which can more easily be felt within the forest, can be evoked in any place, but it will take a great deal of effort and work over a long period of time.

Ymir and Audhumla

Where the fire and ice mixed, steam formed and was changed into rime or hoar-frost, forming layer upon layer, until all the great central space was filled. The mixing of fire and ice caused the Life Force that we call Vril to form into an infinite energy source that filled the universe until it came to crystalize into the form of a great gigantic creature that we call *Ymir*, or *Orgelmir* (seething clay). Since he was formed from the rime, he was known by the name of Hrim-thurs, or ice-giant.

Ymir is the personification of unordered Vril. The universe was still in a chaotic state. Ymir, who was androgynous, embodying both the male and female principles, though these principles did not yet work in harmony according to the runic principle of Jera, thus creating an imbalance that caused a chaotic state of spirituality. Thus, Ymir was unbalanced and chaotic and the personification of uncontrolled Vril that caused destruction. But there was also another force coming into play, for Vril is a life force, and so was formed a nurturing force in the form a gigantic cow called Audhumla (the nourisher). Ymir sought out Audhumla, which was formed out of the same material as Ymir, but unlike the

Audhumla licks yeast in Niflheim as Ymir drinks from her udders

mixing of fire and ice, she was formed from the twelve streams of Vril that flowed out of Hvergelmir. Perhaps in the same way that Surtur was formed from the fiery Force of Musspellheim, Audhumla was formed from the icy form of Niflehim. Ymir noticed that from under her, four great streams of Vril flowed like streams of milk (Could they be the embodiment of the four forces of gravitational, electromagnetic, strong nuclear and weak nuclear?) and he began to suckle from her, taking nourishment from these four streams of Vril energy.

While all Ymir's nourishment was met, Audhumla looked about for nourishment for herself and began licking the salt from the ice of Niflheim. As she licked, her warm, rough tongue wore down the ice, revealing first hair, then the entire head of a God. Eventually he was free from the ice and he was born whole, androgynous like Ymir, but the male and female principles were balanced within this being, with the runic energy of Jera and Mannaz. This first of the Gods was called *Buri* (the producer).

There is no real explanation of the origin of Audhumla. She is the heating force within the Female Form of Niflheim. Niflheim is the realm where form takes place. It is the Female principle of nourishment. We can speculate that Audhumla has existed within Niflheim just as Surtur has within Musspellheim. Audhumla is described as licking the salt off the ice. The warmth of her tongue melts the ice and eventually the first God is born– Buri. It is this same principle that is symbolized by her tongue melting the ice to form the Well of Hvelgelmir and causing water to stream outward throughout the universe, which we can interpret as unleashing the Vrilic energies as currents that fill the universe.

Odin, Vili and Ve

ODIN-VILI-VE

Buri, who was androgynous, gave birth to a son by the name of *Borr* (born). The race of Giants born from the line of Thrudgelmir immediately began waging war against Buri and

Borr. Borr took a wife of a second race of Giants born from under Ymir's arms. Her name was Bestla, daughter of Bolthorn (the thorn of evil), and she gave birth to triplets named Odin (spirit), Vili (will) and Ve (holy), also known as Odin, Hoenir (Ve) and Lodur (Vili). They joined their father in his war against the Giants and killed Ymir. As Ymir sank down lifeless, his blood flowed from his body in such a deluge that it produced a great flood in which all his race perished, with the exception of Bergelmir and his wife, who escaped in a boat.

Bergelmir set up a new domain in a land that he called Jotunheim for himself and his progeny, who eventually grew into a new race of Frost Giants.

In the meantime, according Viktor Ryeberg, Odin, Vili and Ve each fathered a new race of divine beings. Odin was father to the race of Gods known as the Aesir, who settled in the heavenly realm of Asgard. Ve fathered the race of Gods known as the Vanir, who settled the earthly realm of Vanaheim, and Vili fathered the race of Light Elves in the airy realm of Ljossalfheim.

Creation of the Earth and the Universe

The Gods Odin, Vili and Ve attacked Ymir, killed him and created Midgard out of his remains. The meaning of this saga is simple: The Gods took Ymir, or chaotic Vril energy, reshaping its chaotic form, and giving order to the universe. *Some have interpreted Midgard as the planet Earth, but in reality it is the physical universe itself.* The saga describes how they formed the earth from Ymir's flesh and placed it within a grand bulwark made from his eyebrows, which can be interpreted as the magnetic field that holds the earth in orbit around the sun. Upon the earth, seas were created from Ymir's blood and sweat, while his bones were used to create the hills and mountains. His flat teeth were turned into cliffs, and his curly hair was transformed into the vegetation that grew upon the earth.

The Gods set to work now constructing the heavens by hoisting the Giant's skull to form the heavenly universe. They took Ymir's brains and created the clouds and atmosphere from them. They then took sparks from Musspellheim, and placed them in the heavens, turning them into the stars and other heavenly bodies, including our sun and moon.

The Giant Mundilfari had two beautiful children. His son was named *Mani* (the moon) and his daughter was *Sol* (the sun). He was very proud of their beauty, so when the Gods approached him, he was more than pleased when they asked his permission to transform them into the sky where they became the guardians of the Moon and the Sun, assuring that these celestial bodies continued on their course, giving light and warmth to the world. The sun was held in place by the gravitational force or steed known as Arvakr, the early walker, and the moon was held in orbit by the gravitational force known as the steed Alsvin, the rapid goer. They were harnessed to chariots in which the Sun and the Moon were carried across the heavenly expanse. The chariot that held the Sun in orbit had a shield. It was known as Svalin, the cooler, and protected the earth from its burning rays. We know this shield as the earth's magnetic shield (Made from Ymir's eyebrows?). The moon-car was similarly provided for, and called Alsvider, the all-swift, but no shield was required for this cart. The earth needed no protection from the moon's rays for they were a mere reflection of the sun's light.

The Gods then summoned the Giantess by the name of *Nott* (the night or eternal darkness of space), who was black and dark and the daughter of *Norvi.* She rode through the universal darkness that we think of as nighttime in a chariot pulled by the horse named *Hrimfaxi* (frost mane–which is interesting because the darkness of the universal space is freezing cold). The goddess of night thrice married. Her first husband was a Giant named *Naglfari,* and they had a son named *Aud* (strange, because in Iceland Aud is a girl's name). By her second husband, the Giant *Annar*, she had a daughter named *Jord* (earth–Thor's mother). But by her third husband, the God *Dellinger*, she had a son by the name of Dag or Day. He too was given a chariot and rode through the sky, following his mother.

But as chaos always waits for order to let down its guard, close upon the footsteps of Order, two wolves by the name of *Skoll* (repulsion) and *Hati* (hatred), symbolizing the chaotic forces, pursue the Sun and the Moon, and their sole aim is to try and overtake and swallow the Sun and the Moon.

Then the Gods placed four Dwarfs who worked endlessly to create four forces that hold the universe together and support the heavens. Our ancient ancestors referred to them as *North, South, East* and *West*, but today, physicists recognize them as the four forces of the universe known as gravitational force, electromagnetic forces, strong nuclear force and weak nuclear force. The Gods then took heat from Musspellheim and used it to transform Vril into the expansive force known as dark energy. Then they procured icy cold from Niflheim and used it to transform Vril into the force known as dark matter. In this way, the universe and everything in Midgard was held together by the physical laws created and supported by the Gods to hold the forces of Chaos, the Giants, in check.

Thus did the Gods transform Chaos into order, by slaying Ymir, the personification of Vril in a chaotic form and gave form and order to Midgard, which is the physical universe we live within.

The Dwarfs

While the Gods were occupied in the creation of the earth and providing for its illumination, they discovered a host of maggot-like creatures breeding within Ymir's flesh. The Gods took them and endowed them with superhuman intelligence. They then divided them into two classes. The first, known as the Black Dwarfs, were treacherous and cunning by nature and banished to a subterranean existence where they lived their lives never to walk in the sunlight, for the rays of the sun would turn them into stone. They are known by many names, some of which are trolls, ogres, gnomes and Kobolds. The rest were turned into Dark Dwarfs, who also lived underground and were endowed with great skills, turning the riches of the earth into great treasures and weapons and other devices empowered with magical powers from the magic taught to them by the Gods. All the races of Dwarfs lived in their subterranean realm known as Svarfalfheim.

The Three Divine Races

The Lore is confusing on whether another race of beings is counted among the races Dwarfs or not. They are known as the Elves. They vary in description and sometimes they are referred to as Fairies, which as tiny beings of light appeared to be a jovial folk who, when not spending their time nursing Nature and tending to the seasonal changes, come together in great Fairy Mounts and engage in joyous merriment. But other times they appear to be great beings of light and beauty, tall, strong and fair to look upon, possessing great magical powers and wisdom, and manifest themselves as a great host of warriors. They are reputed to live in Ljossalfheim, realm of the Light Elves, and their homeland is ruled by Frey.

The 19th Century "Germanist" from Sweden, Vicktor Ryeberg, claimed that there are three divine races who are related by birth and fathered by Odin, Vili and Ve. Odin, Vili and Ve are also known as Odin, Lodur and Hoenir. Odin fathered the race of Gods known as the Aesir and lived in the realm of Asgard. Lodur, or Ve, fathered another race of Gods known as the Vanir, who settled in the realm of Vanaheim. Hoenir, or Vili, is reputed by Ryeberg to have sired the race of Light Elves who live in Ljossalfehim.

The Giants

In most Indo-European mythologies there existed a race of beings who existed before the Gods. In the Norse cosmology they are known as *Giants*. The first Giant was Ymir, an androgynous being that represented Vril in an unorganized, unordered and chaotic form. From Ymir were born several races of Giants who represent the Force of Chaos, and constantly wage war the Gods, who are the agents of Order. The Gods must constantly work toward keeping the power of the Giants in check, or they would transform the universe into a realm of utter destruction. It is the power of the Gods that give order and structure to the universe by keeping the Giants under control.

While Ymir slept, from under his feet was born a race of Giants. The father of this race of Giants was known as *Thrudgelmir*, who was a terrible monster with six heads. It is not stated whether Thrudgelmir was androgynous or not, but his descendants would be terrible monsters and beasts. At the same time as Thrudgelmir was born, another Giant was born from the perspiration from under Ymir's arms. His name was *Bergelmir*, and after Ymir was killed by the Divine Trinity (Odin, Vili and Ve), his blood poured out of him in such force that it flooded the known universe. Legend tells us that Bergelmir and his wife survived the flood in a great boat they constructed, and set up residence in a realm known as Jotunheim and became the parents to all the races of Giants who survived the flood.

Some of the sagas tell us that in time the Giants born of Belgelmir separated into two very different races of Giants. The first were known as the *Thurs*, representing the forces of destruction, such as storms, volcanos and earthquakes, which devoured everything in their destructive rampages. The Thurs were reputed to be dull-witted and hated the Divine races, and represented the forces of Chaos. Some believe they might be descendants of Thrudgelmir who survived the Blood Flood. They personified those forces of nature that are destructive to man, Gods and Elves. The second race of Giants came to be known as *Jotuns*. Members of the Jotuns often intermarried with the Gods and joined their ranks. One of them is Mimir, Odin's uncle by his mother, and was known to be the guardian of the Well of Knowledge.

Creation of Living Organisms

One day Odin, Vile and Ve, also known as Odin, Lodur and Hoenir, descended to Midgard and felt that this realm needed its own inhabitants. While they were out walking along the seashore they came across two trees. One was an ash, from which they created the first man and named him *Ask*. The other tree was an elm, and from it they created the first woman, whom they named *Embla*. The Gods gazed upon their creation, and though they were pleased, they realized that it was unfinished. Odin decided to give them a gift of *Ond*, the breath of Life, by causing Vril energy to flow into them, and thus bestowed them with souls. Hoenir

ODIN, LODURR, HOENIR CREATE MALE AND FEMALE GENDERS

bestowed upon them the ability to move and senses to feel and comprehend the world around them, while Lodur gave them blood, blooming complexions and emotions. With these gifts, the race of humans was endowed with the powers of speech and thought, and with the ability to love and to hope. With these gifts the newly created man and woman were given Midgard to rule as they pleased.

One way of explaining this tale is that the three Gods are not creating the first man and woman, but the male and female genders for all life, including the first proto-humans. Later, in the tale of Rig, Heimdal creates from the proto-humans the modern races of mankind.

What is interesting about this creation story is, unlike other creation myths, such as those in the Bible, Koran and Torah, in which the first man and woman were made from dirt, inanimate substance, in the Norse Creation Myth man and woman were fashioned from living things–trees. The tree, like that of Yggdrasill – the cosmic tree — is symbolic of the life force or structured Vril, and thus the first humans were created from Vril, the life force of the Gods, by the Gods. What is also interesting is that the creation takes place by the seashore. This is so important for two reasons: first, Vril is associated with water, symbolized by the Rune Laguz, and in the realm of physical science, we know that life first appeared within the salt waters of the oceans.

Every time we sample the lore of the myths we discover hidden truths of science that were lost, and today being rediscovered. This is further proof that there once existed a great antediluvial civilization that Europeans are descended from, that possessed great knowledge of the truth of reality that was vaguely retained, hidden in the mysteries of myth and lore.

The Yggdrasill

The Gods not only created the physical universe (Midgard) but gave order to the multiverse and its extra dimensional frontiers. They nurtured the infinite ocean of Vril and soon it was transformed into a huge yew tree, or winter ash, as the ancient Norse referred to the yew. This cosmic tree is known as Yggdrasill, which means the steed of Odin. It soon grew so large that one of its roots reached into Niflheim itself, and drew nourishment from the well of Vril energy, Hvergelmir. A second root reached into the loftiest regions and drew nourishment from the Well of Urd in Asgard, where the keepers of time and Wyrd, the three Norns, constantly poured water on the root. The third root reached into Niflheim where it drew nourishment from the Well of Mimir, the well of knowledge.

These three roots determine the nature of Yggdrasill, for it draws nourishment from both the realms of Order (Asgard) and Chaos (Jotunheim) which shape and form the Vril energy that is drawn from Niflheim. *One must understand something of the tree's nature for its form exists within a realm with more than three physical dimensions, which means that its true shape is impossible for mortals to conceptualize with our minds limited to three physical dimensions. This is true of our conceptualizing the true nature of the Gods and the Giants.* We will discuss this in greater detail shortly. Therefore our minds will process any data concerning the true shape of the Yggdrasill through references within our three-dimensional reality. This has caused problems in trying to understand the structure of the cosmic tree.

Midgard, our three-dimensional physical reality, exists within the center of Yggdrasill, which is unique because other traditions such as the Jewish Kabbalah, places Midgard at the bottom of its world tree or tree of life. The position of the physical universe at the center of Yggdrasill is our conceptualization of our relationship to the other realms that make up the Yggdrasill. For the other realms are either of higher or lower frequencies or consciousness in relationship to Midgard. Above Midgard is Ljossalfheim, the realm of the Light Elves, and above Ljossalfheim is Asgard, which is located in the loftiest regions of the tree. Just below Midgard is Svartalfheim, and below this realm is the Netherworld known as Hel. To the north of Midgard is located Niflheim and to the south is Musspellheim, while in the west is located Vanaheim and in the east is Jotunheim. If we try to conceptualize the structure, we will notice problems with the structure in relationship to the location of the realms mentioned in the myths. The foremost is the location of Jotunheim and its relationship with Asgard and Midgard. Midgard is connected to Asgard by a rainbow bridge, and on the same plane of reality as Jotunheim is located on, and yet Jotunheim is connected to Asgard with their borders separated by the river Ifing. We can speculate that this river is a sea of Vril currents so violent in nature, because it is located between the realms of Order and Chaos, that it cannot easily be crossed. Two of the Gods that easily make the crossing from Order to Chaos and back again are Odin and Thor. We can also guess that the plane of reality that includes Niflheim, Musspellheim, Jotunheim and Vanaheim is actually on an angle of some kind. The descriptions of geography as well as time in the myths often are confusing because the Gods and the realms of the

Yggdrasill have more than three physical dimensions, which means we will be presented with difficulties trying to conceptualize them within our three-physical-dimensions consciousness.

On the topmost branches, known as Lerod, sits an eagle (Question: is the eagle named Lerod also?), and in between the eyes of the eagle is perched a falcon by the name of Vedfolnir,

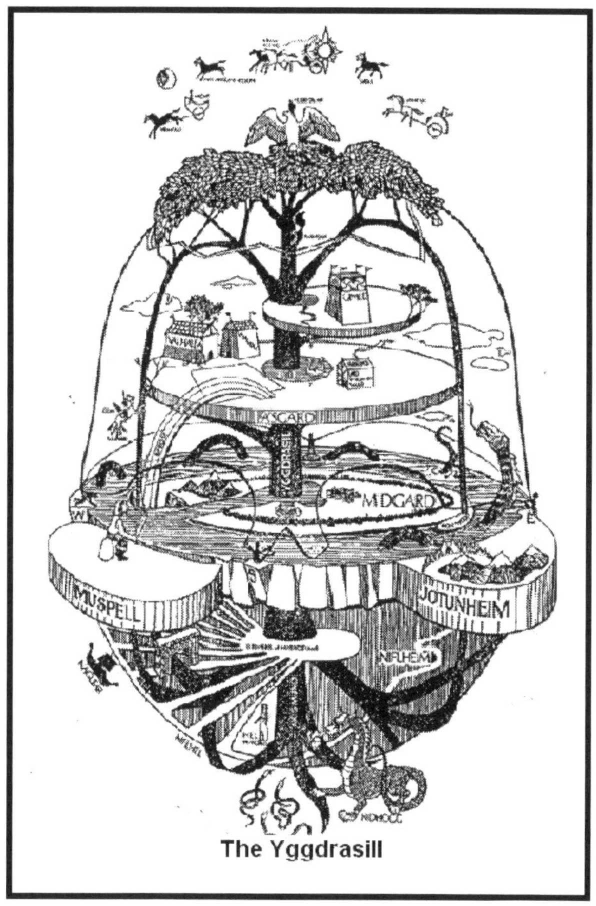

The Yggdrasill

who watched events unfolding in all the worlds of the Yggdrasill. Because the yew is an evergreen tree, its leaves never wither. Odin's goat, named Heidrun, feeds on the leaves, and produces a mead from its horns for the Gods to drink every day. There are also four stags by the names of Dain, Dvalin, Duneyr and Durathor (which are also the names of dwarfs) constantly feeding on the leaves, but from their horns a honey-dew is formed that drips down and furnishes water for all the rivers of the nine worlds. This could mean that the honey-dew is Vril and from their horns this life-giving energy is dispersed throughout the multiverse.

In Hel the terrible dragon exists by the name of Nidhogg, who swims down the stream from Hvergelmir and feeds on the souls of the dead, and then swims back up the stream to Niflehim and gnaws on Yggdrasill's root that grows out of the Well of Hvergelmir. We can see in the dragon the forces of Chaos always working to undermine the order of the multiverse. There is also a squirrel by the name of Ratatosk (branch-borer) who runs up and down the trunk, between the dragon in Hel and the Eagle in Asgard, spreading gossip between them, trying to create conflict between the dragon and eagle (Order and Chaos).

Odin Discovers The Elder Futhark

Odin conducted a quest for knowledge. One of the many feats he conducted to obtain this knowledge was to hang himself on the Yggdrasill as a sacrifice from himself to himself. He hung himself for nine days and nights from the sacred tree, gazing down into the immeasurable depths of Niflheim, plunged in deep thought, and self-wounded with his spear, before he won the knowledge he sought.

In Havamal we read:

138 I wot that I hung on the wind-tossed tree
all of nights nine,
wounded by spear, bespoken to Odin,
bespoken myself to myself,
upon that tree of which none will tell
from what roots it doth rise.

139 Neither horn they upheld nor handed me bread;

I looked below me—
aloud I cried—
caught the runes, caught them up wailing,
thence to the ground fell again.

140 From the son of Bolthorn, Bestla's father,
I mastered might songs nine,
and a drink I had of the dearest mead,
got from out of Othroerir.

141 Then began I to grow and gain in inisght,
to wax eke in wisdom:
one verse led on to another verse,
one poem led on to the other poem.

142 Runes wilt thou find, and rightly read,
of wondrous weight,
of might magic,
which that dyed the dread god,
which that made the holy hosts,
and were etched by Odin.

143 Odin among Aesir, for alfs, Dain,
Dvalin for the dwarfs,
Alsvith among etins, (but for earth-born men)
Wrought I some myself.

144 Know how to write,
know how to read,
know how to stain,
how to understand,
know how to ask,
know how to offer,
know how to supplicate,
know how to sacrifice?

145 Tis better unasked than offered overmuch;
for I doth a gift for gain;
tis better unasked than offered overmuch:
thus did Odin write before the earth began,
when up he rose in after time.

After Odin mastered the secrets of the Runes, he cut a piece of wood from the Yggdrasill tree and fashioned the spear, Gungnir,

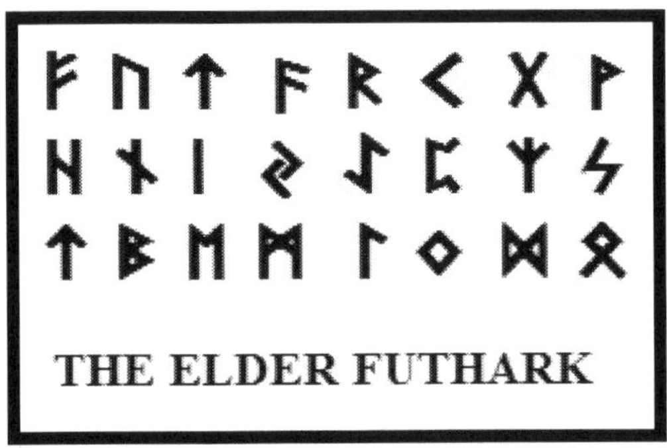

THE ELDER FUTHARK

and on the spear he carved the twenty-four Runes, and then, upon the teeth of his horse Sleipnir he carved the Runes, and upon the claws of the bear, and upon countless other animate and inanimate things. In this way Odin discovered that the energy of the runes existed in all things, in all nine worlds, in every atom and every subatomic particle. He obtained the gift of controlling the runic energies in all things, and thus gave him power over all things.

Odin passed these tools that he uses to harness Vril, to give order and structure to the multiverse, to us, his children, for our use to help us align ourselves with his great work. In this way, we can walk alongside the Gods and transform ourselves and the world we live within. We will begin to explore in great detail the Runes, their nature and how to use them as tools for transformation in our next class.

Chapter Three: Orlog, Wyrd and the Multi-dimensional Soul

A Secret Guarded Throughout Time

Many great thinkers throughout history believed there is a universal force that fills the universe with currents of energy, generating life, order and progress. Many different traditions and cultures across the world believed in this form of energy which was fundamental to all life. This infinite source of power is the essence of reality. This energy has been known by many names. In the Hindu tradition it is known as *prana*; the Greeks knew it as *pneuma*; Franz Anton Mesmer (1734-1815) referred to it as *animal magnetism*; in the Nineteenth Century Karl von Reichenbach called it the *Odic Force*; Whilhelm Reich labeled it *orgone*; in China it was known as *chi* or *qi*; the Japanese called it *Reiki*. The Asians use it as the foundation of their martial arts. Of the many names given it by sages over ages, I prefer "Vril," derived from the Sumerian "Vri-il", which means "like the gods," or "God-like." It has been used by several esoteric societies throughout history, including the Germanic magical order, Rosicrucians, the Illuminous Lodge and the Vril Society, as the foundation of their world-view. I will explain the runic principle behind the name Vril later in the book. Every atom in the universe is made of Vril. In fact, about 99.99% of each atom is Vril, which is harnessed and its natured shaped by the number of electrons rotating around its nucleus. Since everything and everyone is made of atoms, everything and everyone is made of Vril. Therefore we have it within us to tap into this universal force and control and shape it into whatever we desire, because quantum physics has determined that we have the power to change the nature of the subatomic particles within the atom. This means we have the ability to harness and shape this infinite energy and transform, not only the world around us, but ourselves. *This is the secret power of Vril.* The knowledge of controlling Vril is what we refer to as Vrilology—the science of Vril.

Through Vrilology, you will learn how to use to obtain everything you want: happiness, love, abundance and good health. Through the use of Vril you can do, have or be anything your heart desires. There is no limit to the things we can get through the use and understanding of Vril's potential. Ask yourself what you desire. Love, to find that special someone to share your journey through life? Wealth and riches? A big house or a fancy car? Do you want success? Freedom and independence? Through Vrilology, you have the ability to achieve whatever you want in life. There are no limits except those you create in your own mind. This is the great secret that has been guarded and protected by the powers in control.

Those powers that rule our society, which have ruled all societies and civilizations, know Vril by many names, and use different traditions to harness its power, but for the most part, these ruling elites have kept the great majority they rule ignorant of this great source of power. Yes, most religions, governments and ruling classes create false systems of belief for the masses while they practice privately and secretly to tap into and control this force. People go through their lives working, worshiping, raising families, struggling to succeed, hoping to provide a better life for themselves and their loved ones, exhausting themselves on a treadmill to nowhere while those who rule over them keep the secret of Vril to themselves. This is indeed what allows them to rule.

Many men and women who knew about Vril and its potential have expressed it in their poetry, music, novels, writings and paintings. Albert Einstein, Thomas Edison, William Shakespeare, William Blake, Ludwig van Beethoven, Richard Wagner, Ralph Waldo Emerson, Plato, Socrates, Leonardo da Vinci, Pythagoras, Sir Isaac Newton, Johann Wolfgang von Goethe, Wolfgang Amadeus Mozart, Jesus Christ and George Washington were just a few men and women who knew of Vril's existence and how to use its potential to transform our lives. They understood that what you weave in life will become your destiny.

They knew that you have the power to create your own destiny. This is The Law of Cause and Effect.

The Law of Cause and Effect

Everything that is manifested in your life, you have attracted through the law of cause and effect. It is drawn to you by whatever is going on in your mind: the images you have of yourself, your life and your situation in it. Those images and thoughts fill your mind and shape your destiny, creating your future. Every one of your thoughts is real and is creating a reality for you. This law was in existence at the beginning of time and is an eternal truth. It is this law that determines order in the universe, and thus serves the higher forces—the Gods. It was known to the people who lived during the Stone Age. This is why they painted images of hunters successfully hunting the wildlife of the time on the cave walls. Our Stone Age ancestors understood that if they could visualize themselves successfully hunting, their thoughts and feelings would come true. They understood there was a force our minds could tap into and use to manifest their desires in the real world.

Our ancestors thought of the Gods as the guardian who maintained order in the universe. To them, the Gods were in a constant struggle with the forces of chaos and destruction. They understood that the Gods shaped and formed this energy, Vril, into patterns that gave order and meaning to the universe, and they sought to align themselves with the Gods. What was true for them thousands of years ago is still true today. By aligning yourself with the Gods in the struggle that they are engaged in, maintaining order and progress, you can harness the power of Vril to shape every moment, so that your life will be filled with happiness, success, love and harmony. The alternative is aligning your self with chaos and disorder. Even if you are unaware of it, every day, with every action you take and with every thought and emotion, you are aligning yourself with one or the other. If your thoughts are drawing *disharmonic* feelings, then your life will be filled with chaos, but if your thoughts are in alignment with the forces of order and harmony, then you will draw on these attributes and make them the essence of your existence.

Why do more people not know of this simple Law of Cause and Effect? Those who know it guard it and keep it from becoming common knowledge, and keep the masses in the dark. While millions, even billions of people go to their church or temple, or support causes, or practice personal philosophies that all lead to failure, the ruling elite practice a separate set of beliefs. At the Bohemian Grove, a campsite outside of San Francisco, thousands of the most important, powerful and wealthy people from all over the globe gather for a weekend every summer to conduct a pagan ceremony. Among their members over the last one hundred years have been journalists, capitalists, professors, educators, philanthropists, scientists, politicians and even presidents of the United States, and they are constantly seeking new recruits. After watching a video on this subject with friends, one of them wondered, "If this is what the successful people believe, maybe we should believe it too." He hit the nail on the head. If you want to be successful, do what successful people do.

Around 96 percent of the world's wealth is controlled by one percent of the population. Why? How is this 1 percent able to obtain and keep 96 percent of the wealth (and power)? What do they know that we don't? The power of Vril. The secret of this source of power is known by such elites in all cultures. The elites teach each other this secret. Their children are brought up with a belief that they can do anything. This causes them to think differently than the rest of us. People who draw wealth and power into their lives use the Vril, consciously or unconsciously. They think of themselves as invincible, able to do anything. They know deep down that there is nothing they cannot accomplish. Their minds work differently from the rest of ours. They never waste time thinking of themselves as victims, failures, or inferior; they see themselves as capable of achieving anything they put their minds to. And their minds are disciplined, never permitting contradictory thoughts to invade. To them, wealth and power are natural, a normal part of their lives. They cannot even perceive life without wealth and power. It is the essence of their reality. Every action in their lives is toward achieving what they desire, which means their minds shaping Vril into what they desire–wealth and power.

This process is borne out in the lives of people who have made a fortune, only to lose it all, and then, within a short period of time, amass another. The reason is that at some point, something happens to cause them to change the way they think, and they temporarily fear something, and begin to see themselves as victims. But once they are able to recover control of their minds, their thoughts and feelings, they are able to go to work, thinking themselves wealthy and powerful again. Consciously or not, they are using their mind to harness Vril, shaping it to manifest their reality. Their predominant thoughts of wealth, success and power bring to them those things. This is The Law of Cause and Effect. You attract what you are preoccupied with most. If you obsess about being a victim, about failure and losing, then your life will be that of a victim, of failing and losing. People who have lost everything have lost it because they stopped thinking of themselves as successful, and permitted fears to invade their minds. But even once they seem to have lost everything, they retain knowledge of Vril and are able to turn their thoughts back to being successful, and tip the scales from negative to positive thinking. Wealth and power return.

What You Think, You Attract

Remember, what you think, you are manifesting in the material world around you. Your mind is a powerful transmitter of energy. Like a radio, it is sending thoughts, which are made of Vril energy, from your brain outward into the universe. These transmissions attract like thoughts and draw them in to shape and create your future. Have you ever become preoccupied with an unhappy thought, or a disturbing situation, and not been able to stop thinking about it? The thoughts soon affect your emotions. You become obsessed. If you continue to think one sustained thought long enough, your mind then acts like a magnet, attracting like thoughts to you. Eventually the negative, unhappy thoughts become a part of your Life Force, Vril, that powers every aspect about you—your body, your mind and the thoughts and feelings associated with it. And the more you think about it, the greater is the strength of the attraction. Soon these thoughts are affecting your life, creating a current that will guide you through your future pathway. In most cases, you eventually put it out of your thoughts, but without knowing it, you have stored those associated thoughts and feelings somewhere in your brain. This storehouse will continue to affect your life. We refer to this as your Orlog. It is the collection of past experiences that will help to create your future path through life. This future pathway is known as Wyrd.

Orlog, the Sum of Your Life, and Wyrd, Your Future Pathway

Your future is not predestined! Every action you took throughout your life, good and bad, was motivated by your thoughts and a result of your thinking process. Your thoughts create a pathway in the Vril energy fields in which you move through the future. This is cause and effect. The cause, your Orlog; the effect, your Wyrd. What you have experienced has been laid down for you to follow, by your dominant thoughts. Those thoughts that you obsessed over have paved the future path for you to follow. But this does not have to be this way any longer. You can begin to control the pathways of your future by controlling the way you think, and by thinking in a certain way that will assure that your future will be filled with what you desire. Remember, if you make what you want your dominant thoughts, you will bring them into your life in the future. Your future is created by your thoughts.

This principle can be summed up in five words: Your thoughts become your life. By dwelling on a thought, your mind is making it a part of your life. Let this principle seep into your consciousness until it dominates the way you think. Write it down and place it everywhere so that you will be continuously reminded of it.

Think of it as laying the pavement in the path to your future.

Think Positive Thoughts!

The law of cause and effect is impartial, not judgmental, and will give you exactly what you are thinking about. It does not care if you generate negative or positive thoughts; it will shape Vril in accordance. If you see yourself as a loser, one who does not have the ability to achieve what you want, you are sending out that signal. "I can't do anything right." By saying this over and over, you are affirming it to yourself. You feel this on every level. Your thoughts are shaping Vril that will create pathways into your future. So your future will be filled with events that will cause you to fail.

The law of cause and effect does not hear such words as "don't," "no," "not," or any other words of negation. Thus, if you say, "I don't want to fail," your mind is actually sending out, "I want to fail," because "don't" will not register with Vril. So, Vril will manifest those thoughts you focus on, even if you don't want them to manifest because they are negative. They will register and shape your future if you are thinking them. This is why it is so important to get into the habit of thinking about what you want to manifest in your life, and do it in a positive and affirming way. Thus, you have to arrange your thoughts for positive thinking. If you arrange your thoughts in negatives, they will be heard like this:

"I don't want to miss my bus."
"I don't want to get fired from my job."
"I don't want to be a victim."
"I don't want to catch a cold."

It will be heard like this:

"I want to miss my bus."
"I want to get fired."
"I want to be a victom."
"I want to catch a cold."

You must change the way you thinlg. Rearrange your thoughts:

> "I will catch my bus."
> "My boss is happy with my work."
> "I can overcome all obstacles."
> "I feel healthy and wonderful."

The World Was Not Created in the Beginning of Time, You are Creating it, Every Second.

We have to recondition ourselves into realizing that the universe was not created in one day or seven days, but is constantly being created. Every time an individual anywhere in the world has a thought, especially a prolonged and focused thought process, the act of creation takes place. You are creating your future by what you are concentrating on right now. And since our brains never truly rest, we are always thinking, and thus constantly creating. Those thoughts that you focus on the hardest and longest will manifest themselves in the most powerful way in your future. This is very important and cannot be stressed enough. Because if you are happy, your thoughts will create situations that will make you happier. But if you are always complaining about something and find fault in everything, then your thoughts will create situations in your future that will cause you to complain even more and be unhappy. This is true even if you spend time listening to others vent their complaints. You might think you are sympathizing and helping your friend who needs to get something off his or her chest, but in reality, you are drawing in their negative thoughts and assimilating them into your future. Vril will reflect back whatever thoughts you let fill you.

Your Bifrost Gland or Third Eye

In Norse cosmology, we mortals live in the realm of Midgard, which is the physical universe or the reality of three physical dimensions. The Gods live in the higher dimensional realm of Asgard. Communication between these two realms is by way of the "rainbow bridge" known as Bifrost. The Gods, with the exception of Thor who was too heavy, crossed Bifrost whenever they left Asgard to travel to Midgard (Earth) and other realms that

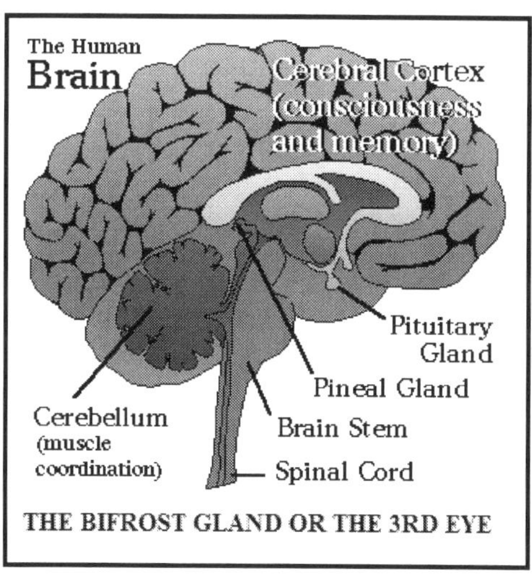

THE BIFROST GLAND OR THE 3RD EYE

existed in the cosmological cosmos known as Yggdrasill.

Most esoteric traditions claim we possess a "third eye" within our foreheads that permit communication with the higher and even lower realms that are extra-Midgardian, meaning they exist on a plane of reality that is different from our three-dimensional universe. In Vrilology we refer to this third eye as the Bifrost Gland, after the rainbow bridge.

The Bifrost Gland is a powerful conduit that helps us to channel Vril currents, harnessing its power in limitless quantities. This gland is actually the pineal and pituitary glands located in the brain, behind the forehead.

With the development of their Bifrost Gland, one can develop psychic powers, giving us a greater awareness of our relationships to the world we live in, both the Microcosm (Midgard) and the Macrocosm (Asgard) realms.

One of the fundamental goals of Vrilology is to provide exercises that will, in time, awaken your Bifrost Gland, so you can reconstruct the rainbow bridge, and through it reestablish a link between Midgard and Asgard. In this way, we are constructing lines of communication between ourselves and the Gods. We will explore how to use Runes to open the Third Eye or Bifrost Gland later in this book.

Left and Right Sides of Brain

Through Vrilology, we seek to reestablish this rainbow bridge and thus permit communication between ourselves, in Midgard, and the higher powers represented by the Gods, in Asgard. In thus way we can draw on the powers of the Gods, which exist within us, to transform us. This is accomplished by a consistent regimen of meditation, chanting and visualization.

To do this properly, we must first understand something of

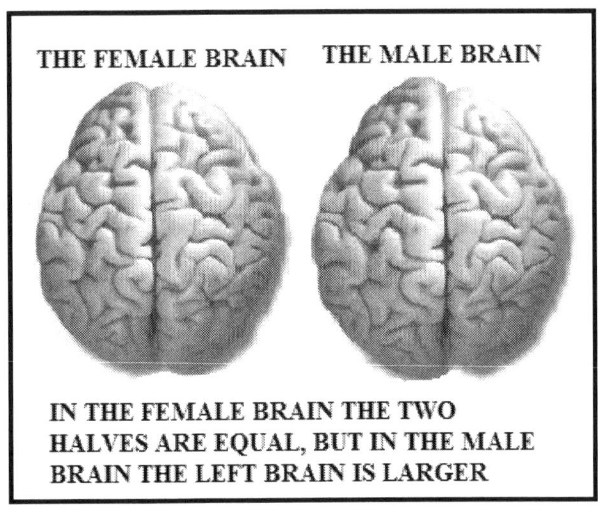

IN THE FEMALE BRAIN THE TWO HALVES ARE EQUAL, BUT IN THE MALE BRAIN THE LEFT BRAIN IS LARGER

the nature of our brain. It is within the brain that we can visualize and comprehend what we are doing and trying to accomplish. First of all, the human brain is designed differently in men and women. The brain is divided into two hemispheres—the right and the left sides. It is within the left side that we draw on our logical, analytical, mathematical, technical, problem solving, administrative, and organizational abilities. These characteristics are all part of the conscious mind. It is this side of the brain that controls our day-to-day actions and makes us feel guilty, and suspicious of things that we cannot explain within a scientific context. The right side of the brain houses our intuitive powers of imagination, inspiration, artistic creativity, and spirituality, as well as our psychic, artistic, holistic, conceptualizing, interpersonal, musical, verbal, and novel thought abilities. It is the spark of thought and idea. It is powered by emotions, but without the left side to balance it, it would cause us to act on whatever inspired us, for good or bad. Most importantly, our ability to contact the Gods, and draw on the endless reserve Vril, is rooted in the right side of the brain. We know that Midgard, the realm of man, and Asgard, the realm of the Gods, are connected by Bifrost, the rainbow bridge. These two halves of the brain speak different languages and communication between them is often murky and difficult at best. What we must do is construct a means of communication between these two halves so they can work together. This is done by constructing a bridge between them. This bridge is the rainbow bridge or Bifrost. Thus, the two halves of the brain, the left side being Midgard and the right side representing Asgard, can be taught to work together by the construction of this bridge that we refer to as the Bifrost Gland or Third Eye.

This is especially necessary for men, because the male brain is structured differently from the female brain. In the female brain, the two halves are the same size, but in the male brain, the left side is larger than the right side. This means that the left side dominates in the male brain. This is also the reason that throughout history, women have possessed greater psychic powers than men. In ancient times, the Romans looked to women known as Cybeles, to learn of future events and seek advice. The Greeks sought out their Oracle in Delphi, who was usually a woman, and the Germans and Norse considered women to possess the power to see into the future and were known as Volvas. This is where the term “woman’s intuition” comes from. The reason for this is simple—the female brain is in balance and is more dependent on the right side of the brain than the male brain.

Odin, the All-Father of the Gods, is known to have two ravens–Huginn and Muninn. They are the voices that speak to him, revealing to him knowledge of the universe. Each day they fly off and later return. Sitting on his shoulders, they whisper to him all they have learned. Huginn represents the left side of the brain, for he is the power of intellectual thought, while the right side of the brain is represented by Muninn, who is the power of reflective memory. The memory that Muninn represents is the sum total of past events, as well as future events. In the poetic Edda, Odin says:

Huginn and Muninn fly every day,
over the whole wide world;
I dread that Huginn will not come back,
but I fear even more for Muninn.

Reprogramming Our Brains

We must reprogram our brains to eliminate all doubts and feelings of failure, dissatisfaction, fear, anger and lack of belief. We obsess on these things which form barriers within our subconscious that create hesitation and cause us to fail. These obsessions will cause many to develop into "disharmonic beings" who are dominated by such feelings of depression, hatred for life, rebellion, and anger, which eventually leads them into chaotic, anarchistic behavior and self-destructive lifestyles. We need to rid ourselves of such influences.

We can also be influenced by the opinions of other people who ridicule us and accuse us of "wandering from the true path," or who readily share with us "their" fears and doubts. This is why it is so important that we be careful whom we choose as friends and associatc with. We don't need people to constantly dump their baggage on us.

Our Orlog is that part of the soul where all our past experiences, thoughts, feelings and actions are stored. They are constantly affecting us, the way we think and feel, and influencing the decisions that we make. We might not even be conscious of the way they are affecting us. What we have stored within the Orlog will cause us to obsess about certain things. If it happens to be something negative, it will cause whatever it is to appear in our lives. Your mind is constantly shaping the currents of Vril energy flowing into you, shaping them and giving them form. The things you obsess over will shape Vril into pathways that will attract these things and fill your future with them. *Like attracts like.* Your mind does this through the rhythms or vibrations that your brain emanates.

The physical reality of Midgard is interpreted for us by our conscious mind through our five senses. What we perceive through our five senses is recorded within the occipital cortex of the brain within a few seconds. There it is transformed into blips of electrical impulses that are transmitted through synapses, stored by the brain as a meaningless bundle. Your conscious mind will try to interpret that bundle of information through the totality of what is stored within your Orlog. Your conscious mind might not even be aware it received the information, but your subconscious mind will register the information, and process it for interpretation.

The most important part of the reception of information is its relevance to past experience. The totality of what is stored within the Orlog will color how we perceive the reality we come in contact with in the present. This means that all our memories might be false because information received by our senses is interpreted in a way that makes sense to the conscious mind.

Past experiences stored in our Orlog constantly color information being received by the brain. Those past experiences that we obsess on will have the greater influence in pre-coding new data received because our obsessions give them greater strength and influence.

Your interpretation of events and the world around you is based on what is filtered through your Orlog. This Orlog-colored perception will define how you view your opinion of yourself. Two people can view the same event, but they will have very different recollections of the event. The reason is that both of viewing the event through what is stored within their Orlog. What is stored there will cause them to see what is unfolding according to very different interpretations. This difference will have a continuing effect on their psyches and will cause us to see the objective world, in accordance with our individual subjective view of reality.

Be conscious of the words you use, for they are colored by what is stored within your Orlog and will determine your actions. If your thoughts are filled with doubts, those doubts will create a mind set that will cause you to fail. If your thoughts of yourself are filled with negative images of yourself and your life, those images will create a you that mimics the image you hold for yourself and it will be the image that everyone who comes into contact with you will see. You will become this negative person and your life will be filled with the negative things you obsess over. You are programing yourself to reflect the words you use. If you think you are unlucky, you will be unlucky. Once again, you are preprograming yourself to fail. .

You can change the world you live in by changing your language and the words you use on a daily basis. Consciously replace negative phrases with positive ones. Once you change your words, your thoughts will change and so will your energy. When we speak we are causing vibration. *Our words have vibrations and since everything in the universe vibrates, our words are constantly causing energy to change–Vril energy.* You will change the world around once you have changed the way you think, especially the way you think of yourself and the image you have of yourself. Like attracts like and you will draw beneficial situations into your life. You will replace bad luck with good luck. You will replace failure with success.

The Pituitary Gland

There is a space between the cortices, above the pituitary gland and above the hypothalamus, which was once a supercharged region of the brain in our ancient ancestors. All vertebrates possess the gland, but in some reptile species it actually evolved into a third eye. Because of this, it has often been referred to as the Third Eye. In humans it is believed to be the seat of telepathic and psychic powers. This gland has atrophied because of the degeneracy that has over taken humanity, resulting in the loss of psychic abilities which allowed our ancient ancestors to tap into Vril energy. What we are attempting to do through Vrilology is exercise this gland, and reawaken the innate potential, which still resides within the gland. In others words, we are trying to "jump-start" the gland.

Once the Bifrost Gland is developed to its full capacity, the individual will obtain knowledge stored in Mimir's Well, which is a universal source of information. The individual will develop the ability to see backward through time. This is often referred to as racial memory and is linked to the genetic ancestral stream, permitting us to see back even to the earliest time, when life first appeared in the biological soup, and follow the evolution of life through billions of years.

We must learn to control the body's ability to absorb Vril through the action of the mind in the form of controlled breathing, chanting, visualization, and the use of will power. To accomplish this we utilize the Runes, which are a powerful tool given to us by the Gods. Through their use we can learn to harness and shape Vril's power. Once we have learned these techniques, we can revive the Bifrost Gland, draw on increased amounts of Vril, and fill ourselves with its power. Then, through the proper use of the Runes, we can transform this Vrilic power into whatever purpose we wish.

The Three Norns: Past, Present and Future

In northern Europe, the Goddesses of Fate were known as Norns. They are represented by three sisters, the daughters of the Giant Norvi (Time), and descended from Nott (Night). In Norse cosmology, the Norns made their appearance right after the end of the Golden Age. They took up their place under one of the roots of the great world tree, Yggdrasill (which represents the ordered multi-dimensional cosmos), where the Urd Well is located. They were charged to warn the Gods of future evils, teach them to make good use of the present, and learn from the past.

Their names are Urd (Past), Verandi (Present), and Skuld (Future), and personify the past, present and future. It is their duty to weave the fate of all things, sprinkle the sacred world tree with water from the Urd Well every day, and place fresh earth around its roots so that it will continue to grow strong and hold together the entire universe. In this way, the Norns are working to maintain order in the cosmos by giving nourishment to the Yggdrasill. They

The three Norns: Urd, Verdandi and Skuld

are also charged with the duty to guard the precious golden apples that grow from the branches of the Yggdrasill, and permit no one except Idun, the Goddess of eternal youth and health, to pick them so that she could feed them to the Gods. The golden apples symbolize Vril's power to provide vitality and life itself. They also care for two swans, which swim on the mirror-like surface of the Urd Well. These swans are symbolic of the spirits of all living things, of rebirth and the evolutionary process that is part of the chain of life. The Norns adorn themselves with feathers from these swans and sometimes use the power of the feathers to appear as swans in Midgard, and bequeath to mortals knowledge of the future.

Two of the sisters, Urd and Verdandi, are considered very helpful. Urd appears as an old woman who is constantly looking backwards, while Verdandi is a mature woman, fearlessly looking directly ahead, not afraid to face the present. They have much to teach, and we should learn from them. But it is Skuld, who is a young and beautiful woman, and who often tears apart the web her two sisters weave, which means that nothing is "written in stone" and we still have the power, if we choose to develop it, to control our destiny; unfortunately, very few individuals develop such power. She looks forward and is usually veiled. She holds an unopen book and seldom lets anyone read from it.

The Norns are also mentioned in the Indo-European religion of the Vedic Aryans who settled in India. In their ancient language known as Sanskrit, they are called the *Lipikas*, which means "scribes" or "recorders." Just as the Norns record all that takes place, they set the stage for the future. This is also referred to as "Karma." Karma is the balancing act that is the natural law of consequences. You set your own future by your actions in the present, which are recorded in the past. Each individual's action will determine their future by the decisions the individual makes. Each individual has its own individual Norn that is called a Hamingja, which in Christian Theology is referred to as your guardian angel. The Norn weaves your destiny by recording your actions in the present, thus creating the future course in which you will travel. Thus, each of our lives is an interaction of our actions with the Life Force personified by the Norns.

Wyrd, the Norns' Web

The Norns spend most of their time weaving the web that is the destiny of all living things. This web is symbolic of the Wyrd, and fills the entire universe, appearing as black threads, and considered a bad omen if one should see them. The three Norns sing runic songs as they weave according to the wishes of Orlog.

Orlog is timeless and the eternal law of the universe, and is older than the beginning of time, and more powerful than the most powerful. It is the law of cause and effect—the substance from which the Norns weave their Web of Wyrd.

The net that the Norns weave holds the future, but a future that is filled with choices. Each of our destinies has been mapped for us, but the map is filled with crossroads. It is at these crossroads that we are expected to make choices. A crossroad is a point of great energy vortex and magical ceremonies are performed at such an intersection. The choices that we face in the future will be determined by our actions in the past. Thus, we are constantly weaving our future through the decisions that we make as we walk through life. The Wyrd is this process of making choices and moving forward until we come to another crossroad that is the creation of the decisions that we made in the past. *The decisions that we make will be colored by what has been stored in the Orlog.* "The past will come back to haunt us," is an old saying that is rooted in the understanding of the Wyrd. The Wyrd is that which has taken place and affects the present, which in turn will cause the future to unfold. In the old Roman religion, the Goddess of Luck, Fortuna, is the personification of the Wyrd.

Mind over Wyrd

Remember, what you obsess about, you are manifesting in the material world around you. Your mind is a powerful transmitter of energy. Like a radio, it is sending thoughts, shaped and molded currents of Vril energy emanating from your brain, outward into the vast universe. These mental transmissions attract like thoughts and draw them in to shape and create your future. Have you ever become preoccupied with an unhappy thought, or a disturbing situation, and could not stop thinking about it? The thoughts soon affect your emotions and you constantly find yourself thinking about the situation over and over. You eventually become obsessed with it, and if you continue to think this one sustained thought long enough, your mind uses the mental energy tainted by the obsession to shape and form pathways in your future designed according to the obsession. Eventually, the negative, unhappy thoughts shape the Vril currents that powers every aspect about you—your living body, your mind and the thoughts and feelings associated with it. And the more you think about it, the greater is the strength of the attraction. Soon, these thoughts are affecting your life, creating a current that will guide you through your future pathway.

In time your brain becomes programmed by these obsessions that are stored in that part of your soul that is your Orlog. As Vril energy is sent coursing through your spirito-physical body, it passes through you and becomes colored by what is stored there, and then is disseminated throughout you, affecting every atom within you by what is stored in your Orlog.

Your subconscious mind is always working and sending out Vril energy, not only affecting your spirito-physical body, but also coloring your conscious mind and the thoughts it generates that will affect your future actions. Your conscious mind might not even be aware of what your subconscious mind forces you to do or act out. You could actually do or say something that you are unaware of because your subconscious mind will make you blind and deaf to what you are doing, based on what is stored in your Orlog. It is the collection of past experiences that are stored in your Orlog that will create your future path through life. This future pathway is known as Wyrd.

Orlog and Your Future Pathways

Your entire life is a reflection of every one of your thoughts. Everything you have ever done, the good things and the bad things, has been a result of your thinking process. Your thoughts create a pathway in the Vril energy fields in which you move through the future. *This is cause and effect.* Your Orlog contains the total of all your past thoughts. *The future pathways have been set in motion by your Orlog, creating pathways into your future. This process is your Wyrd.* What you have experienced has been laid down for you to follow, by your dominant thoughts. Those thoughts you obsessed about have paved the future pathway (your Wyrd) for you to follow. *But you do not have to be a slave to this process. Your future is not predestined!* You can learn to control the pathways of your future by controlling the way you think, and by thinking in a certain way that will assure that your future will be filled with what you want and desire. There are Runes that you can use to cleanse your Orlog of all negativity. *Remember! If you make what you want your dominant thoughts, you will bring those things into your life in the future.*

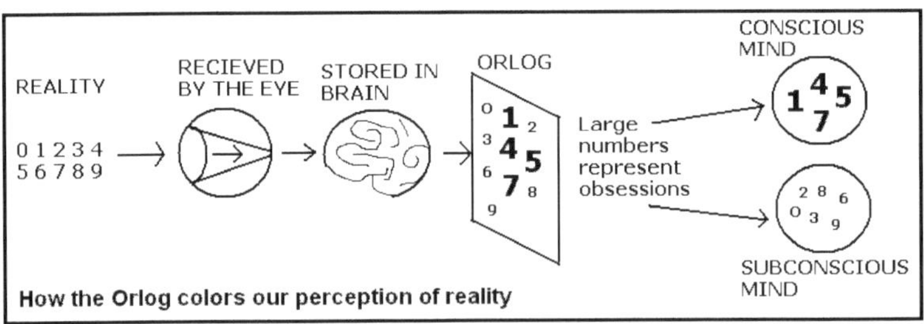

How the Orlog colors our perception of reality

Your Future Is Created by Your Thoughts

This guiding principle can be summed up in five words: *Your thoughts become your life.* By dwelling on a thought, your mind is making it a part of your life. Let this principle seep into your consciousness until it dominates the way you think. Write it down and place it everywhere so that you will be continuously reminded of it.

Think of it as laying the pavement in the pathway that leads into your future. You have to realize that your mind has a frequency. Your thoughts can be measured. We know what frequency is being sent out into the universe. If you are thinking a thought over and over, it will become fixed in your mind. *Your mind will soon be sending it out even when you are not consciously thinking about it.* The frequencies your mind sends out into the universe are in the form of thoughts, those things that you obsess over or dwell on. They can be measured, and are technically known as brain wave patterns. Your brain wave patterns, or thought frequencies, are the result of the electrical activity of your brain. Let us quickly review them for you.

Can we create a new future with the power of our thoughts?

At onetime the world of science was convinced that everything was separated from everything else. The great change in this out look began in 1995 when two Russian physicists at the Russian Academy of Sciences by the name of Vladimar Popomim and Peter Gariaev. They are considered the fathers of wave genetics. They researched the contents of DNA based on photons (light particles). In what has been dubbed *The Dna Phantom Effect* they showed they could remove the photons with a valve of air and a vacuum.

They conducted an experiment that conflicted with traditional science's claim that a void could not exist in a vacuum. They removed the photons from each space with a valve of air, but in each space some photons remained which could be measured. The photons separated as expected in the vacuum pipe in relatively unorganized patterns. The something amazing happened: the light particles organized themselves in various orders. The DNA had a direct impact of the photons, forming themselves into orderly patterns as if through an unseen power. Their Conclusion: *Human DNA Has a Direct Effect on the Physical World.*

This had never been observed before and it seemed to conflict with conventional physics. But when the DNA was removed from the pipe again, it was assumed that the sent order of the photons would dissolve and they would go back to the unordered distribution, but the oppsite happened. The photons behaved as if the DNA were still present and remained in that ordered division.

The conclusion was that the photons and DNA were still bound together even though they were separated from each other. It seemed as if they were bound together in a field that quantum physics referred to as *the quantum field. thus, so-called space is not empty. it is a field through which billions of information waves move and are interconnected.*

Since the discovery of this energy field there has been many names for iit: quantum field, Godly matrix, the field, quantum hologram, the source field, the torsion field. What is special about this energy field is that it is not like any other form of energy we know. *This energetic field that seems to function, lie a tightly woven net creates a type of bridge between the inner and outer worlds.*

In the same way that sound uses air, vibrating the air molecules pushing on other air molecules, until a wave is created, so too our released energy that holds our beliefs and thoughts also uses a medium which s the quantum field in order to be carried around the world.

This energy field makes it possible to be connected with everyone and everything, either consciously or unconsciously. The distance between the recipient of our thoughts and the person who sent it irrelvant. It does not matter if the person is standing next to you, lived down the block, in the next state or on the other side of the world. The energy generated and sent always finds the right person, even if that person isn't aware consciously.

Human feelings can affect our DNA. We now know that DNA is absolutely changeable and reacts to very subtle energetic vibrations. DNA actually changes its form based on our feelings. Researchers should how DNA responds to feelings of relaxation, drunkenness, approval, love or hate. When researchers felt negative emotions of anxiety, stress, anger or frustration the DNA strings shortened and actually stripped off many of its codes, but when they felt love, approval, or happiness the DNA grew longer.

People who are deeply in love can change the formation of their DNA. The key to good health is to practice feelings of joy, love, gratitude and respect because we can actually increase our resistancc to illncss 300,000 fold.

What we feel, think and believe is conllected in our DNA. This is called ORLOG.

The quantum field is actually the life-energy field that surrounds our physical bodies and within it is stored our Orlog. It is colored by our thoughts and feelings. That is why people will have a gut feeling when they come into contact with another person. A friend of mine complains that people tell him they feel intimidated by his very presence. He says he has not hostile feelings toward them and can't figure out why only one would feel like that around him. But he's the type to fixate on negative feelings, constantly dwelling on conspiracy theories and seeing enemies everywhere. He's always angry about his situation and the world around. His feelings of hostility has colored his life energy field (quantum field) and people can't help but feel what he feels.

What you are constantly affects your DNA.

DNA has a strong effect on its environmnet and leaves behind a lasting and permanent impression.

We can influence our DNA through our thoughts and feelings, that we can influence our own DNA.

Through the quantum field outside of the constraints of time and distance, we can connect t0o everything else in the world.

And is so doing we can draw anything we want into our lives' is a fantastic notion to many people.

This is the essence of the law of resonance–every thing is made of energy and everything vibrates!

That which we encounter in the outer world has an inner origin and this is our thoughts–the Law of Orlog!

Everything we think, feel or say intensifies our resonance field. This is why every thought of loss, and why every belief concerning gain brings about gain, knowing this, anything we want to change in our outer world can only be changed first through our thoughts.

Remember to use you inner most creativity to manifest that which you desire, and use it to become more aware of your well-being and to bring about the well-being of all.

How do our wishes become reality?

Our DNA is the carrier of our genetic code. DNA is occupied with the help of our genetic code, making protein bodies in the inner portions of the cell. Surprisingly, almost 90% of our DNA is ot needed for protein synthesis, but rather is essentially used for communication.

Poponin and Gariaev showed that DNA is really functions as a sender and receiver, proved that our DNA communicates not only with us, it also communicates with the DNA of other people. Our DNA is connected with everything that is.

Our DNA communicates with the DNA of other people, and it occurs on a higher dimension, outside of space and time, the term hyperspace is used to explain ths phenomena.

DNA uses worm holes in hyperspace to elimiate the distance of time and space to affect other people by our resonance. Our thoughts and feelings are sent through the energetic tunnels in hyperspace immediately affect their target and received by their DNA. This energy is noly only received by DNA, it is saved by it. DNA also serves as a data recorder. We have a huge data bank in our body, and it is known as Hamingja. It is the Hamingja that Orlog (data) is recorded and colors our life energy (Vril) to affect our health and well-being.

I have said time and again that all magic is the mind controlling and manipulating energy. What we dwell on, what we obsess over, affects us in totality, in every way. Therefore it is important to use affirmations to control our thoughts and feelings. This is why it is so important to meditate, because meditation is one of the surest ways to discipline your minds, especially your subconscious mind, to concentrate on the positive. Like attracts like. Our minds will bring more of what dwell on into our lives, and fill our future with more of what we obsess over.

Can we create a new future through the power of our minds? The answer is yes! Quantum physicists have discovered something very exciting, showing again that we can essentially change our lives at any time, and that we can make anything in life a reality. But it is up to you. If you act in ways that will bring great wealth into your lives there is no assurance you will succeed because you might be so full of doubt that you negative thoughts, even if they are within your subconscious mind, will cause you to fail. Successful people become billionaires because deep down in their subconscious minds they have an unshakable belief that it is their destiny to become a billionaire. This will cause them to make the correct decisions whenever they are confront with a choice.

Human beings harness and shape energy through their thoughts. Energy with a certain oscillation (caused by your Orlog) attracts reciprocal energy. Quantum physicists discovered that through the quantum wave our thoughts and beliefs space through space and time through what is called time waves. These are quantum waves that communicate through time, from the past toward the future that are known as *normal quantum waves (Orlog)*. At the same time there are quantum waves known as *conjugate complex waves* that communicate from the future to the past.

Normal Quantum Wave = Orlog
Conjugate Complex Waves = Wyrd.

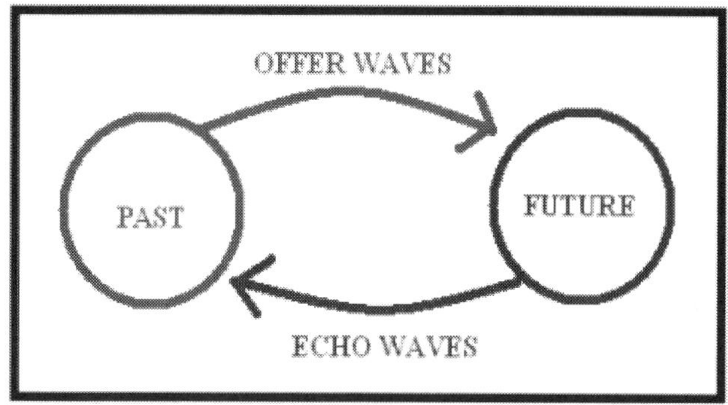

The waves that communicate toward the future are called by Poponon and Gariaev propositional waves of *Offer Waves*; and thise that communicate from the future toward the past are called *Echo Waves.*

When an echo wave out of the future encounters our offer wave from the past that we have put out there, one of the two waves shape the other bringing about what is known as an *event possibility.* The event possibility is when the past and the future communicate in similar ways with each and through the meeting of matching signals, create a concrete event of higher consciousness at the midpoint, which is an experienced present. *This mean that not only does the past influence the future, but the future also influence the past.* The truth of the nonlinearity of time means the future is not less real than the past.

The future already exist somewhere out there. Otherwise, it could not send any waves into the past, which is our present. And your future already exists, right now, in this very moment. But it I not predetermined because we each have different possibilities to chose from to create a different kind of future. In fact, science has shown that the probability exists that we can chose own future. *Our future already exists in countless versions.*

Our consciousness perceives only one time, the present, because our senses are limited. They take in only 8 percent of the entire light spectrum. Our senses cannot perceive 92 percent of our reality and that means it simply doesn't exist for us. And yet it is there. But we are our own measuring instrument, and because we cannot understand this we refuse to believe it. Nevertheless we are surrounded by a wealth of other energies, oscillations, waves, and information.

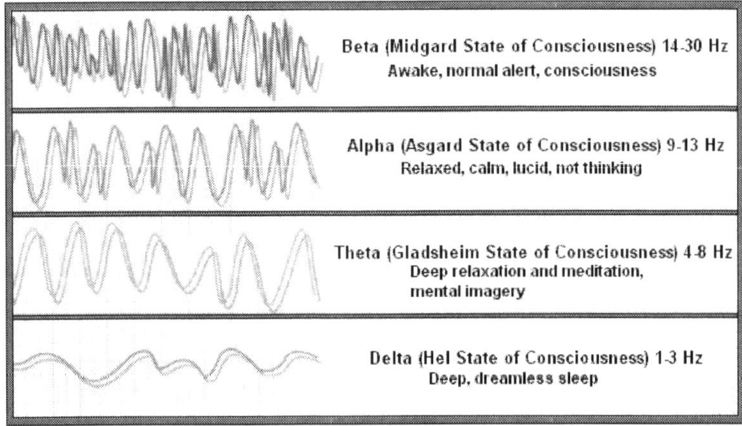

Mental Frequencies

Mental Frequencies

Beta- 13 to 26 Hertz. Beta is what your mind sends out in your normal "awake" state of mind. You cannot consciously manifest your thoughts into reality in this state, but what you are thinking in Beta eventually seeps into your higher states of mental consciousness. Beta is manifested by the left side of your brain, which will eventually implant thoughts into the right side of your brain, where your intuitive powers manifest themselves.

Alpha - 8 to 13 Hertz. Alpha is the state of mind that takes over when you are constantly thinking about something. It can be consciously induced through relaxation or meditation, but you will unconsciously slip into Alpha when you daydream, when you are driving, or just before you fall asleep or just after you wake up. In this state you have the ability to draw on the intuitive powers of the right side of your brain. Obsession works at the Alpha frequency, which is very effective in molding Vril energy into your future pathways or Wyrd. When your mind is functioning at Alpha, you send out currents of Vril energy even when you are not consciously thinking about it.

Theta - 4 to 8 Hertz. You will slip into this state of mind after you have passed through Alpha, just after you have awakened from sleep, or just as you are slipping off into dreamland. Your mind slips into Theta whenever you find your head bobbing on the edge of sleep — whenever you are in a situation that you find boring and you are having a hard time staying awake. Theta is your most meditative state of mind, and you can discover intuitive impulses during this time, when your mind is on the threshold of entering sleep. When you learn to consciously enter this state, your powers of mentally manifesting your future reality increase greatly.

Delta - 0 to 4 Hertz. Delta is the state of mind you enter when you are fully asleep. You become one with the Vril-filled universe in this state, but unfortunately it is very difficult to control your mind in this state. It is not impossible, but it does take a great deal of practice in preparing yourself before going to sleep to try to influence your mind while you are in Delta.

Your Mind Is like a Thought Magnet

As your mind dwells on certain thoughts, it is sending them out and shaping Vril that is coming into you. Your body and brain will be affected by this process. Your mind will receive Vril that has been shaped by your thoughts and it will create your physical reality. If you see yourself a victim all the time, Vril currents are drawn into you, programming your brain to create situations where you are victimized. If you see yourself living a life of abundance, Vril will manifest abundance in your life. If you see yourself famous, Vril will manifest situations that will bring you fame. If you see your life as one long struggle to survive in a cruel world, Vril will create roadblocks throughout your life that will prevent you from obtaining those things you want. Remember! In your Orlog is stored all your past thoughts, which shape your future pathway—your Wyrd. Your Orlog is creating a present state of mind, shaping Vril that you are drawing in, and creating things that will happen to you in your future.

This can be summed up in a simple thought: Your current dominant thoughts are creating things that will happen to you in your future. Hence—*your dominant thoughts are your future!* Your obsessions will manifest themselves in your future. But this is not necessarily a bad thing, *if* you can learn to control the way you think.

Holographic Universe

New discoveries in quantum physics have presented evidence that the universe is basically a holographic image. Through the power of the illuminated mind we can modify the universe, for the physical universe, according to quantum physics, is flexible and malleable. Everything solid is made up of subatomic particles, including atoms. Atoms are made up of neutrons, protons and electrons. But even these subatomic particles only makes up a tiny percentage of the atoms. The remainder is actually *Vril!* Therefore, if you continue to break apart an object into its subatomic components, they no longer resemble the original object. They are chameleon-like, able to change their form from wave to particle. In actuality, quantum physicists have discovered that electrons do not even possess dimensions, and do not even exist in our universe unless we are *consciously looking for them.* This means that unless your mind sends out thoughts about them, they do not exist. Their existence in this dimension is *dependent on* thoughts emanating from your mind! *And,* if this is not enough to convince you, quantum physics has shown evidence to support the theory that the behavior of the parts is dependent on the whole; which means they are not acting separately from the totality, but belong to an invisible, ordered system in the universe.

The English physicist David Bohm claimed that the physical reality that is the world in which we live is actually an illusion, similar to a holographic image, not unlike the "holograph deck" in the *Star Trek* television show. Bohm also postulates that there is a deeper order of reality that is the source for the appearance of all objects in the physical universe. He also claims that consciousness is a subtle form of matter, including things like rocks. Thus, all things possess a degree of life, or at the least a kind of animation, and possess some degree of intelligence. Therefore, life and intelligence can be found in everything—in matter, energy, space and time. The entire fabric of the universe is filled with an animated intelligence and consciousness. This is the ordered universe of the Gods. The Gods are constantly working to maintain order, holding back the relentless forces of decay and destruction that are the chaotic forces of the Giants. Just as the Gods are constantly shaping the universe on a grand scale, you can shape your tiny section of the universe in the same way by aligning yourself with the Gods. You can accomplish this the same way the Gods are doing it, by shaping the universal life force—Vril.

Once you become aware of this ultimate truth, you become aware of how powerful you really are: that your mind has the power to think thoughts, and then to transform those thoughts into physical reality.

Bending Your Wyrd

Remember that your life is like a mirror that reflects all your thoughts back at you. Every time you think of something, your mind creates a picture of the situation and sends it out. The flow of Vril energy that is pouring into you will be shaped by those thoughts and pictures and mold your future pathways. You must realize and accept that you are a powerful being, and you can shape and mold your future. *No one can stop you if you realize that you shape your destiny through your thoughts. If you think you are all-powerful, you will be all-powerful. But if you think of yourself as helpless, and a victim of the world and society around, you will be a helpless victim to the world and society around you. The choice is yours!*

Your collective thoughts create your life, and their effects upon you are still with you. You might not realize it, but even thoughts you had years ago, which you might not consciously be thinking about presently, are affecting your life. They create thinking patterns that are embedded within your brain and affect your subconscious. This is what we have been referring to as your *Orlog*. Orlog is that part of your Self, within your Aura, where your thoughts and memories of your past experiences congregate. They are creating your future pathways, which we refer to as *Wyrd*.

There is another aspect of your Orlog that remains to be mentioned. Your Orlog is the storehouse not only of your own thoughts, feelings and actions, it is the storehouse of the thoughts, feelings and actions also of your ancestors. The great or terrible things you do in your life will be passed down to your descendants. They will inherit not only your DNA, but part of your soul. The part of your soul that lives on after your death within the collective soul of your family (whose collective soul in turn lives on within the collective soul of your more distant genetic relatives) is known as your Kin-Fetch. It is the memories that people mistake for past lives and mistakenly attribute to reincarnation. In reality they are memories of your ancestors or others who are genetically related to you, even distantly. Your subconscious mind is able to tap into these memories because they represent powerful experiences —

experiences that in themselves have drawn on enormous amounts of Vril to keep themselves alive as memories within your ancestral line.

Normally we are helpless victims of our Orlog, because we don't know how to cleanse ourselves of what is collected within the Orlog. The combination of our obsessions and those ancestral memories causes us to become slaves to what is stored within our Orlog. *But you must know that you have the power to cleanse, or bend, your Orlog and change your thinking path, and thus control your destiny.*

You cannot erase your previous thoughts, but you can turn them into something useful and positive through simple runic meditation. By meditating, you are creating a state of calmness within your mind. Once you have achieved this, you have access to your Orlog and can literally flush out the negative energy attached to your old thoughts and replace them with new positive energy. Then you can begin the process of choosing your thoughts carefully. Every day, you can meditate for fifteen minutes and fill your Orlog with those positive thoughts that you want to go to work, shaping your Vril and molding your future. Since your mind will be focused during your meditative state, these thoughts will be all-powerful over your mundane, everyday thoughts.

We will not explain here how this is done, but later in this book we will give you a runic exercise on how to cleanse or bend your Orlog. But now we must explore the structure of the multidimensional soul.

What Is the Soul?

In Vrilology, which is rooted in the Northern conception, the soul is conceived of not as a single, undivided entity, but a variety of psychological constructs that blend together to make up the complete human being dwelling in Midgard. It is a composite of different parts, which make up a microcosm of the immense and varied macrocosm of the multi-verse in which we live. The soul constitutes a matrix of multi-layers and interrelated sections of your being, each with its own realm of influence, its own power, and its own impact on one's life.

What is important to understand is that the Northern soul is not the soul defined in Christian, Jewish, Muslim or other Middle Eastern traditions.

Let's begin by quickly examining the different parts that

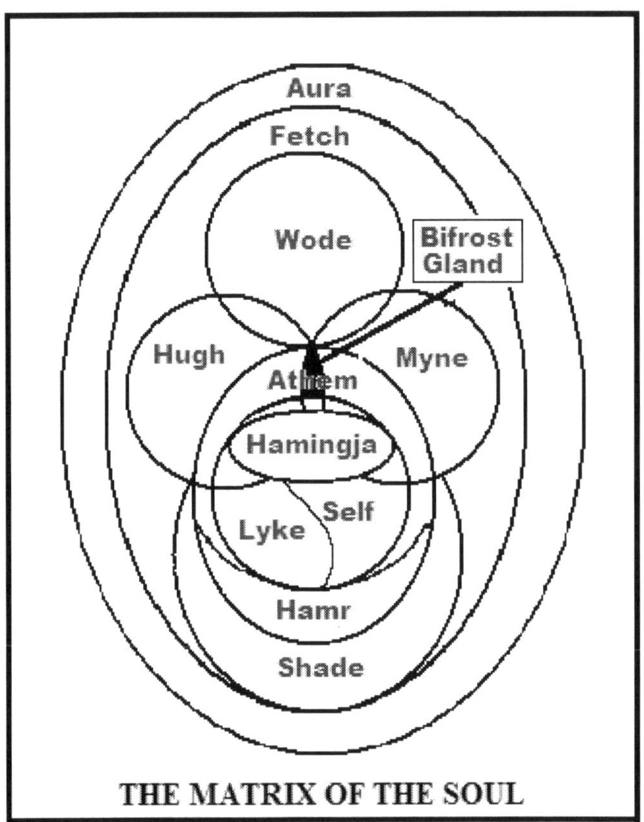

THE MATRIX OF THE SOUL

make up the Northern Concept of the Soul.

1) **SELF:** The Self, which is also referred to as *Mod*, is self-consciousness. It contains all that we are—our self-awareness, consciousness, and temporal being. It is a reflection of the "integrated self." It is situated at the center of our soul, and is the pillar that holds all the various aspects of the soul together. The

Self serves as a binding construct or faculty of synthesis and relationship for all other aspects of the Soul. We can describe this as the I-consciousness or Ego. It is the spiritual essence that the Christian tradition will refer to as the "soul," which is differentiated from the physical body. But in the Northern tradition, there is a strong recognition of unification of the body-soul referred to as the spirito-physical body.

The Self is the most important aspect of the Soul, for upon its maturation rests the spiritual advancement of the individuated human being. Edred Thorsson theorizes that upon death, the Self is that part of the Soul which survives into the hereafter or afterlife.

2) **LYKE:** The Lyke (Lik, Lich) is the physical body. Odin, Vili and Ve, also known as Odin, Hoenir and Lodhurr, are the Divine Trinity, which created humanity, and gave us three gifts. Lyke, which is our physical form, is the gift given to us by Lodhurr. Unlike the Jewish, Christian, and Islamic traditions, which claim the "soul" resides within the body, in Vrilology, the Body resides within the Soul. Surrounding the physical vehicle, or Lyke, is the aura, which is also part of the Soul. *AND unlike Middle Eastern cults, the body was NOT made of dirt, but from living trees, which personify the Life Force of the Gods—VRIL!!!*

The physical body is the most basic part of the Soul, because it is the vehicle of our incarnation in Midgard, through which our Wyrd plays out. Through it we are able to enact our will, the will of the Gods, and our destiny. We experience the physical world through it, and through it we leave our mark upon the world, or Midgard. *It is imperative that we honor the body as a vital part of maintaining a healthy soul.* It is the vessel of one's personal power. Maintaining a sense of mindfulness of eating healthily, exercising and keeping fit, pursuing self-discipline through martial arts, sports, dance, or yoga, and keeping the physical body free of toxic and hallucinatory substances, is vital.

We need to examine our attitudes toward every aspect of the world at large, and realize that every day we are bombarded by thousands of unconscious and subconscious messages, and very few of them reflect the values and ethics of our Heathen culture.

For the life we lead in Midgard will echo in eternity. There is no division between the spiritual and physical as reflected in other religions, including the three monotheistic religions as well as the religions of the Orient. In Vrilology, as in all European pagan traditions, the physical and spiritual flow effortlessly together and the holy is found as easily in one's daily life, work life, and romantic life as it is in the most moving of religious rites. *Because the physical body is part of the soul, if one's attitude toward the body is not healthy, then the soul itself cannot be healthy!!!*

3) **ATHEM:** The Athem is also referred to as *Ond*, and is the Vital Breath that Odin gives to all living things at birth. It animates the Soul, and keeps our whole being fed with Vril energy that sustains life itself. This is the gift given to us by Odin. It is our connection to the Gods—*the Breath of Odin.* Athem gives life and provides the ability for us to grow and evolve. Each breath we take calls to mind that sacred connection to the Gods, that part of our Soul that binds us to them and the cosmic unfolding of our spiritual evolution.

4) **HUGH**: Hugh is our intellect and rooted in the left side of the brain. Here is our capacity for intellectual thought, rational thinking and reasoning. It gives us cognitive functions and our ability to make sense of our experiences in Midgard. It enables us to learn, grow and process interactions with each other. Odin has two ravens. One is named *Huginn* and is the personification of Hugh, the left side of the brain.

5) **MYNE:** Myne is the right side of the brain. It is the root of memory, the subconscious mind, our racial memories. It is personified by Odin's other raven, *Muninn.* It was so precious to Odin that he worried more about the loss of Myne than about the loss of His ability to think cogently. Memory is that which conncets us to our tribe, Folk, self-definition, ancestors, and own evolution. It is our foundation, and it nourishes our growth and strength, much like a tree's roots ensure its survival. Many a philosopher has stated *that a people who have forgotten their history have no future.* Myne enables us to celebrate our uniqueness and our identity, and to learn from past experiences —

not just personal experiences, but those stored in our Orlog, the past experiences of our kinfolk.

The joining of Hugh and Myne is the forging of a bridge between us, in Midgard, and the Gods, in Asgard. In fact, we can use the Rune Mannaz as a tool to create this construction of the rainbow bridge, known in the Norse myths as the Bifrost bridge. It is the process of opening our Third Eye, which Vrilology refers to as the *Bifrost Gland.* By achieving this, we can reestablish a direct link between us and the Gods and draw on their powers to transform ourselves and the world around us. We teach how this is done in our Yggdrasill Training Program.

6) **WODE:** Sometimes referred to as *Odhr*, Wode is passion, ecstasy, inspiration and motivation. It can be associated with Odin (Odhr = Odin) or his Old English name, "Woden." It is the gift of Hoenir. It is by this power that magical force is manipulated through a high level of energy and enthusiasm, rising out of the normal state of consciousness. Just as intellect is part of the Soul, so to is our ability to feel passion to excel, to give exceptional devotion, inspiration and excellence to any endeavor. Wode is responsible for not only the creative inspiration of a poet or artist, but also the destructive force that empowers the berserker.

7) **HAMR:** Hamr is also known as *Hyde*, and it appears as a sort of mysterious, plasmic quasi-material usually having the rough shape of the body. It is sometimes referred to as a Ghost. It can be thought of as a form of soul-skin, which contains the various parts of the soul matrix that gives shape and direction to our will. The sorcerer sends forth his Hamr to work his will in astral form, to journey to other realms and in other states of being.

8) **SHADE:** The Shade or *Sal*, in Old Norse, is associated with Jung's Shadow concept, which contains the subliminal aspects of the psyche. What is important to understand is that the Shade is the continuum of the Shadow self after the disintegration of the various energy bodies upon death.

9) **FETCH:** The Fetch is also referred to as *Fylgia*. It is important to understand the nature of the Fetch, along with the next part of the Soul, the Hamingja, for the exercise we will teach you

in a later lesson. But let's not get ahead of ourselves. First the Fetch.

The Fetch is one of the most important psycho-spiritual aspects within the Soul. What is interesting is that most other esoteric traditions do not speak of the Fetch, and yet, it is one of the most significant constructs within you. There is a three-fold dimension of the Fetch that is not duplicated in other esoteric traditions, and it seems to be unique to the Norse tradition. It is a most beneficial aspect to your evolution into a Vril Being, and cannot be emphasized too highly when used properly.

When you have fully developed the powers of your Fetch, you can use it to provide you with:

1) new insights into the nature of the opposite sex; 2) improved relationships with your friends, family members, co-workers and other people in general; 3) help in balancing the polarities within your Soul; 4) assistance in the performance and development

of your psychic and esoteric abilities;

5) help to discover your animal totem; and

6) a connection with your ancestral Kin-Fetch and with higher intelligence in your Inner World.

The Fetch can manifest itself in three forms:

1) The first, always a human form of the opposite sex. This entity attaches itself to you for the duration of your life. This manifestation of your Fetch is one

of the reasons we emphasize the importance of

your DNA, because it will help you to connect with your ancestral stream.

2) Animal form, the most common form that you will probably call on for assistance. It normally takes the shape of your favorite animal, bird, fish or even insect. Sometimes the animal identity will surprise you because it will reflect the animal that best suits the character of your dominant personality. You can use your animal form for many different

3) Geometric forms, rare except for individuals with exceptional abilities who possess second sight. You

can increase your chances by strengthening your Hamingja reserves of Megin or Personal Luck.

Because the Fetch is attached to you throughout your life, part of it lives on beyond death in your ancestral stream that is referred to as your Racial Soul, Folk Soul or Kin-Fetch. It can be incarnated in future descendants and other individuals closely related to you genetically. Individuals who claim they have been reincarnated, and who have visions of past lives, are really tuning in to past life experiences that have been inherited from their ancestors, even the most distant ancestors and relatives, through the Kin-Fetch, or racial soul. These past experiences can influence your Orlog, which is actually part of your Aura, and will affect your Wyrd or future pathways.

10) **AURA/ORLOG:** Scientific progress has demonstrated that the human organism is not just a physical structure made up of molecules, but that we are also electrochemical and electromagnetic beings made up of energy fields. While science has paused at this threshold, there remain mysterious energy fields written about by the ancients that you can put to practical use for self-protection. One of these transpersonal fields is the Human Aura.

You auric energy bubble extends several feet beyond your physical body and is an extension of your Soul. This is what we mean when we say that your physical body is inside your Soul and not the other way around. It is the faculty by which you sense comfort or discomfort when in close proximity to another being, either seen or unseen. Few realize the tremendous range of potentials inherent in the aura as a tool of progress and protection. One of them has to do with your Personal Luck.

Within your Aura is located your Orlog. The Orlog is a trans-dimensional entity that is affected by your Soul, and thus affects your Wyrd — your future pathways or destiny. It is considered to be located within the Aura, or a part of it, from which the Norns weave your Wyrd. It stores your thoughts, feelings and those sensations that you have inherited from your ancestral stream. Thus it is directly affected by your Hugh, Myne and Kin-Fetch (which is a part of your Fetch).

11) **Hamingja:** Personal Luck is something that all European pagan traditions believed in. The Romans even had a Goddess to personify Luck by the name of *Fortuna*, who they believed chose mortals to be her favorites—Fortune's Favorites—who seemed to lead charmed lives. Caesar was believed to have been one of Fortune's favorites and lived a charmed life, achieving success in everything he did, *until his luck finally ran out!* Too bad he did not know how to recharge his Luck.

The Hamingja is that part of your personal aura/soul that harnesses Vril energy and transforms it into Luck, or Megin. Luck is then stored within the Hamingja, which acts as a reservoir for you to use. The Megin produced and stored there gives the entire auric field greater potency and much more flexibility for the workings of the human will.

Through study of the Northern mysteries, we know that:

1) the walls of the Hamingja can be strengthened using the Runes, Elhaz, Uruz and Laguz;

2) its capacity to hold energy can be increased using the Runes representing the five elements: **Fehu** (fire), **Uruz** (earth), **Laguz** (water) **Ansuz** (air) and **Isa** (ice), and the Rune **Elhaz**, used to strengthen your Hamingja so that it can hold additional amounts of Megin; and

3) it can be tasked to discharge its energy in a sending under the will of an illuminated mind using the Runes **Fehu, Raidho** and **Kenaz**, which are sending Runes.

Chapter Four: Using the Runes as Tools to Harness Vril

The Futhark

Collectively, the Runes are known as the Futhark. This name is taken from the first six Runes in the Futhark; Fehu (F), Uruz (U), Thurisaz (TH), Ansuz (A), Raidho (R) and Kenaz (K), just as the word "Alphabet" is taken from the first two letters of the Greek alphabet, alpha and beta. There are various Futharks: The Elder Futhark, the Younger Futhark, the Anglo-Saxon Futhark and the Armanen Futhark, but we will concern ourselves for now with the Elder Futhark. This is considered the oldest and most authentic of the Futharks.

The Runes are a collection of symbols that have been used for writing, and the ancient source for much of the early systems of writing, not only for Indo-Europeans in Europe and Asia, including the ancient Celts, Germans, the Italic people who eventually became the Romans, the ancient Iranians and Aryan invaders of India, but also for the various people of the Middle East, including the Sumers and the Phoenicians. But the Runes are more than just a script for writing. They were given to our ancestors by the Gods, probably in an original form that has been forgotten, but the present Elder Futhark grew out of our Folk's inner consciousness–the collective group soul—during the period of time after the great destruction (around 5600 B.C.) of the Ur-civilization. During that period of time known as the Great Trek (5600-1000 BCE), the refugees of the great destruction of that first civilization separated into the many different Indo-European tribes and spread out across the face of the old world. We have found hundreds of runic symbols that were used in the past, but only about forty or so symbols were ever organized into a working Futhark.

Phosphenes, Runes and Our Brains

Our brains are naturally programed to perceive geometric images in nature, the sounds we hear, and the sounds we make.

When you vocalize sounds, they resonate in your mind, which then

translates them into geometric images, which might result in lights appearing to flash on the insides of your eyelids when they are closed. These percepts are known as phosphenes. The receptors for light in our eyes are also sensitive to pressure, so one way to deliberately produce phosphenes is by pressing gently on a closed eye, especially moving a fingertip from place to place on the eyelid.

If you have ever suffered a trauma, or a hit to your head, you might remember "seeing stars." In times of stress, emotional and physical, especially when you suffer some kind of pain, it is not unusual for your mind to manifest images or flashes of light. Shamans explain that when they enter a deep state of meditation after undergoing a ritual of physical stress, or after they digested some mind-altering drug, they will see images after their consciousness leaves their bodies. This state can also be induced by less extreme methods.

The sounds we make with our voice have frequencies, and these frequencies resonate throughout our internal selves. We seldom take the time to really listen to the sound of our own voice. Only if you were to listen to yourself on a recording would you really know what your voice sounds like. We do not realize that there is great power in the sounds we articulate. The sound of our voice affects not only our entire body physically, but also our mind.

In Norse mythology there is a tale of Odin sacrificing himself to himself upon the Yggdrasrill—the World tree or Cosmic tree. Yggdrasill is the physical structure of the multiverse of the cosmos. It represents the totality of Vril energy given order by the Gods after they conquered chaos in the image of Ymir. Odin hung on the tree for nine days and nine nights, during which he ate no food nor drank any drink. He underwent a physical stress that induced a meditative state in which his mind was able to pierce the mysteries of the cosmos, which permitted him to discover how the Vril could be harnessed and shaped. While in this state he experienced the phenomenon that we described as phosphenes, which caused him to envision certain symbols. The experience caused a transformation within his Life-Force, causing him to evolve into a higher state of consciousness in which the secret knowledge of the Yggdrasill, or the Vril, was imparted into him. The nature of all existence appeared in his mind in the form of these symbols. He discovered that the Runes, or their energies, exist in all things, and by discovering the nature of the Runes and how to use them, he could gain control over all things. The Runes were given to us by Odin, to help us rebuild the bridge between us and the Gods and Goddesses. The God Heimdall taught our ancestors to use them. Their use helps to bring order and clarity to our lives.

Runes are symbolic of the power of Vril, endowed with a universal essence that cannot be manipulated and is unchangeable from generation to generation. The symbols appeared as geometric forms. By undergoing a similar process, we too can discover this secret knowledge of the universe. This is done through many hours of meditation, chanting and visualization. This process is known as Galdor Magic or Science. which triggers a neurological process that is an ingrained part of the way the brain functions, understood as phosphenes. In the brain's visual cortex, geometric shapes and images are processed. Every brain has phosphenes, naturally transforming the electric currents into these geometric shapes. With our eyes closed we can see evidence of phosphenes by the appearance of geometric shapes and images. They also can appear to us while we are in a trance-like state. This natural process is at the heart of the creation of the Runes, and how the Gods communicate with us, bestowing on us the encoded knowledge and understanding of the Vril.

We can learn to use these symbols as keys to unlock subconscious responses in the deepest recesses of our psyche. They form a bridge between the collective unconscious and your conscious mind, and awaken archetypes Carl Jung described as energy fields acting on your consciousness. Using them, your mind is more able to control and change the flow of Vril energy currents into patterns that you wish to manifest in your physical environment.

The Origin of the Runes

The explanation for the origin of the Runes can be examined in two different ways: one is historical and the other is mythological. The historical discipline of explaining where the Runes originated is a mere examination of the historical and archeological records. These sources do not tell us where the Runes originated, but merely how, how effectively, and where they were used in different periods of time. Though the historical and archeological records can enlighten us to the more recent (the last three thousand years) history of the use of the Runes, we need to turn to the mythological source for the origin of the Runes.

The earlicst historical or archeological record use of the Runes in Scandinavia appears around 250 BCE. It was a time of oral tradition. Almost nothing was written down, and when something was recorded, it was done by carving Runes into stone, bone, wood or metal. If we tried to discover some evidence from the historical and archeological records in Scandinavia, we would come up short. What explanations for the origin of the Runes existed in Scandinavia is purely mythological. It would be a mistake to assume that we must look to Scandinavia for the origin of the Runes, for the Runes did not originate there, nor did they originate with the Scandinavians, or even the greater variations of Germanic people, to which the Scandinavians belong. The Runes are Indo-European in Origin, but they have survived only in Scandinavia as both a form of script and magical devices used to control one's environment. This fact has only increased the mystery surrounding the origin of the Runes.

Vrilology teaches that there is just as much information from non-Scandinavian sources from this time period, as from millenniums before this period, that point to a much earlier origin of the Runes. There are actually hundreds of runic symbols that can be considered "Runes" but only about forty or so runic symbols have been organized into systematic sets that are referred to as Futharks. This has resulted in a confusion of the origin of the Runes and the origin of the Futharks. Is it possible that types of Futharks were in use long before the Elder Futhark came into existence between 1600 to 30 BCE? Or is the Elder Futhark much older, having undergone changes? Did other forms of writing which have characteristics similar to the Futhark Runes actually evolve or "degenerate" from the Futhark rather than the other way around?

Various forms of script from early Indo-European and possibility non-European writing has survived, and show a remarkable similarity with the Runes. Examples of this can be found in pre-Roman Italy. Etruscan, early Latin, Oscan, Umbrian and North Picene forms of writing have been found that all resemble runic symbols. Early Italic writing which pre-dates these types of runic script is also very similar to the Runes. In Asia Minor, what are known as the Hittite Runes date to 1600 BC and are almost identical to the Elder Futhark. Throughout central Asia, the early Turkish people used Runes very similar to the Elder Futhark known as Gokuturk, though the phonetic qualities and meanings are different because of the non-Indo-European origin of the Turkish language. These "Turkish Runes" date as far back as 300 BCE and were still in use around 20 CE.

All these example lead to the conclusion that the Runes were known by the original Indo-European people who originated in the Ukrainian-North Caucasian region. As they spread out across Europe, Asia and the Middle East, they brought the Runes with them, which eventually evolved into the many types of script that have been found in the archeological records.

Many historical and archeological scholars believe that the Runes in Scandinavia originated from the wanderings of the Germanic tribe known as the Heruli, who left Scandinavia some time around 100 BCE to 100 CE, and became mercenaries who traveled the mainland of Europe, only to return about 200 AD. The Greco-Roman historian Jordanes, wrote in 551 CE that the Herculi were expelled from their homeland in Denmark, but he does not record the exact date. As they traveled throughout Europe, they learned to read and write the Roman script from which they developed the system of Runes known as the Elder Futhark, and it spread to Scandinavia. There is recorded an increase in carving of Runes in Scandinavia about 250 AD, which is attributed to this theory of the origin of the Runes and the Elder Futhark. Some historians have speculated that the word *Erilaz*, which means "Rune Master," who were an order of magicians similar to the Druids of the Celts, is derived from the name Heruli. This theory ignores the many different runic symbols found throughout Europe, the Middle east and central Asia dating thousands of years before the Heruli.

If we examine the mythological source for the origin of the Runes then we can make the case for the Runes, and the Elder Futhark, being much older than the historical and archeological records would lead us to believe. Since we have evidence that the many different Indo-European peoples brought with them a form of script that seems to have originated in a type of runic writing, Vrilology makes the case that they all lead back to a single source which is the original homeland of the ancient Indo-European people. The primary mythological sources for their origin of the

Runes are two: the Poetic Edda and the Prose Edda, which are a collection of mythological tales. They were recorded in Iceland by Christian scholars during the Middle Ages, which means that even these sources are suspect of being changed for propaganda reasons. The Poetic Edda is a collection of thirty-five poems recorded by Saemund Sigfusson around 1100 AD. Around 1200 AD, a Christian scholar by the name of Snorri Sturlusson, who wished to preserve his heathen cultural heritage, composed these poems into two narratives dubbed the Prose Edda. Both authors were sincere in trying to preserve their cultural heritage, and though they might have had to compromise their story telling with modifications, these were probably kept to a minimum. We discover how the Gods learned about the Runes and how to use them in the Havamal, or "The Sayings of the High One" (Odin), when he hung himself on the Yggdrasill. In the Rigsthula, "The Song of Rig," we learn how Rig, or Heimdall, taught the sons of the Jarls (elite race of humans), Kon, who are a special order of magicians or Rune Masters, the use of the Runes.

A section of the Havamal is titled the *Runatals Thattr Odhni*, or "Odin's Song of the Runes." In it we read how Odin discovered the knowledge of the mastery of the Runes.

138 I wot that I hung on the wind-tossed tree
all of nights nine,
wounded by spear, bespoken to Odin,
bespoken myself to myself,
upon that tree of which none will tell
from what roots it doth rise.

139 Neither horn they upheld nor handed me bread;
I looked below me—
aloud I cried—
caught the runes, caught them up wailing,
thence to the ground fell again.

The wind-tossed tree or windy tree refers to the Vrilic currents of energy formed into the Yggdrasill, the Axis Mundi or cosmic pillar that holds the cosmos together, on which Odin sacrificed himself to himself by hanging on the tree, or immersed himself in Vril causing its Life Force to become his Life Force, for nine nights, thus assimilating the runic energies within himself. He develops the vision to see the Runes in the deepest levels of the cosmos. Through his mastery of Runic Magic, Odin becomes the chieftain among the Gods, possessing his wisdom, shamanistic abilities, poetic eloquence and leadership. This act of Odin hanging himself on the Yggdrasill permitted him to gain wisdom to master the use of the Runes. This is how he acquired the power to control Vril and give order to the universe.

142 Runes wilt thou find, and rightly read,
of wondrous weight,
of might magic,
which that dyed the dreaded god,
which that made the holy hosts,
and were etched by Odin.

143 Odin among Aesir, for alfs, Dain,
Dvalin for the dwarfs,
Alsvith among etins, (but for earth-born men)
Wrought I some myself.

What we have here is a mythological tale of the origin of the Runes cosmologically. The "holy host" is translated from the original word *Ginnregin*, who were the ancient rulers of Ginnungagap. They existed before the Gods were born and shaped or made the Runes. There could be two sources for this race of beings. The first could be Ymir and his Gigantic offspring, but a more likely older source for this term would be the Fire Giant, Surtur, and his sons, who live within Musspellheim and were said to exist before Ymir was born. The reference to the "dreaded god" is translated from *Fimblthular*. This could be Audhumla, the

Great Bovine or Cow, that gave nourishment to the Giants, and existed within Nifleim. Associating Fimblthular with Audhumla would make sense if we associate Ginnregin with Surtur and his sons. Both entities existed within the Ginnungingap before the formation of Ymir. Surtur is the Male Force, while Audhumla is the Female Form who is the great nurturing force of Vril that eventually gave birth to the Gods by mixing her saliva (nourishing potency) with the icy yeast of Niflheim. What it is interesting is how much the sounds we make when we chant the Runes sound like the way a cow moos. Fimblthular is translated as the "Great Singer" (*Fimbbul* means "great," and *thule* literally means "singer") and it is interesting how Rune chanting can be described as singing the Runes. We read how Finmblthular colored the Runes. The term "to color" meant to stain them by giving them lifeblood. Vril is referred to as the "Life Blood," and so Rune Masters would stain their set of Runes with their own blood, to endow them with their Life Blood. Since Vril energy is a vibratory energy, and vibrations are made when we sing or chant the Runes, Fimblthular instills the Runes with their vibratory essence. Finally we read that Odin (*Hropt*) gave the Runes their physical form by carving them.

What we are reading is how the Male Force from Musspellheim gave form to the Runes, while the female Form of Niflheim gave them color or life-giving and shaping energy, just as Aydhumla did when she licked the ice to give birth to the first God. Finally, Odin carved them, meaning he took these two principles, joining them together to create the Elder Futhark. If this all happened before Odin, Vili and Ve killed Ymir and gave order to the universe, it would mean that Yggdrasill existed in a chaotic form, not yet given structure and order by the Divine Trinity. This means that Odin had to learn of the Runes and discover how to master their use before he killed Ymir so that he could give order to the universe. This means that the Runes predate the creation process, and runic energy existed long before Odin, Vili and Ve were born, and even before Borr and Buri were born. But since the

Odinic Consciousness existed before Ginnungingap, Odin, in his pre-Odinic manifestation, created the Runes before Ginnungingap.

In the first stanza we learn how the living energy of the Runes, which is Vril, becomes a part of the Runes because of the staining process. Most Rune Masters who create their own set of Runes will mix some of their blood into red paint or ink when they stain the Runes. Even with store purchased sets of Rune one can perform a ritual where you take a few drops of your blood and mix it into water to consecrate the Runes so that you are "staining" them with your Life Force. In this way each Rune is like an individual human soul possessing its own unique, solitary focus, coloring its Vrilic energy with its own runic nature.

The second stanza explains that different beings in the nine worlds of the multiverse have learned to master the use of the Runes. It is believed that different species of beings—Gods, Elves, Dwarves and Giants (Etins)—have different sets of Runes. While there is no mention of humans, in another poem, The Song of Rig or the Rigsthula, we learn that Rig (Heimdall) teaches man how to use the Runes. Three races or divisions of mankind are created and to the descendants of the highest class, the Jarls, known as Kons, he gives knowledge of the Runes.

44. But Kon only, could carve Runes,
Runes lasting ay, life-keeping Runes;
to bring forth babes, birth Runes he knew,
to dull sword edges, and to calm the sea.

45. Fowls' speech he knew, and quenched fires,
could soothe sorrows, and the sick minds heal;
in his arms the strength, of eight men had.

46. In Runes he rivaled, Rig the Earl;
with wiles he warred, outwitting him;
thus got for himself, and gained to have,
the name of Rig, and Runic Lore.

It is to Kon, the son of Jarl, that Rig taught knowledge of Rune Magic. Kon is the descendants of the leadership class or highest race of man, born to rule or govern. From the way that these stanzas explain how the Runes are used, we can see that they are tools to help one control one's environment. They possess the power of transformation. They should be used to aid society, and for this reason, the leadership class must serve as well as lead. In ancient times only the ruling classes had the time to invest in the study of the deeper level of mysteries, to apply themselves to meditation and study of Runes.

I believe the truth of the origin of the Runes is more mythological and can be described as such:

1) Odin discovered the secret of the Runes while he hung on the World Tree.

2) His son, Heimdall, descended to Midgard (earth) and taught the Children of the Gods the secret of the Runes. (About 12,00 to 9,000 B.C. They lived on the shores of the Black Sea.)

3) These humans used the secret of the runes to harness Vril (life force of the Gods) to transform themselves and their world to create the Golden Age mentioned in the Norse Sagas, and described in most Indo-European mythologies.

4) This secret knowledge is referred to as Vrilology, and was corrupted, causing the Golden Age Civilization to decline and fall.

5) The descendants of this Golden Age Civilization became refugees after their civilization was destroyed when the Black Sea was flooded and became refugees who spread out across Eur-Asia, bringing the secret of the Runes, or what little they could preserve of it, with them.

6) This knowledge slowly evolved into the Indo-European languages and the scripts of most "alphabets" of peoples living across Europe, the Mediterranean, the Middle East and southern Asia.

Through our collective group soul, Odin transmits the knowledge of the Runes to us. It is through this process that we can once again assimilate the secret knowledge of the Runes into our consciousness through Vrilology. The Folk Faith of Balder Rising seeks the creation of a Vril Aristocracy, made up of men and women who are experts in the use of both Galdor and Seither Magic. The creation of this aristocracy of ruling Rune Masters is based on the Song of Rig's description of the ruling elite's requirement to be masters in Magic. Lords and Ladies within the Vril Aristocracy will discover what talents they have and then develop these talents. It is through the Yggdrasill Training Program that they can discover what abilities they have and then concentrate on fine-tuning them. Not every member of the Vril Aristocracy will possess the same abilities. Some will excel as warriors, others as healers, some as scholars and others in business.

The origin of the Runes is obscured by the darkness that has descended over the millenniums, as we try to look back in time to when our Folk had fallen from the heights of the vastly superior civilization that they created on the Black Sea plain, to the primitive state of refugees after their civilization was destroyed as a result of the flooding of the Black Sea around 5600 B.C. They took with them the rudiments of the superior technology of their civilizations—bits and pieces that they eventually lost the know-how to replicate and maintain—as they fell farther and farther into a state of "barbarism." As they traveled across regions of Europe, Asia and the Middle East, they took with them their memory of the Runes, but the knowledge of how to use them effectively to harness Vril was gradually lost until only a partial memory of the Lore was retailed and handed down through the generations. In many places the Runes evolved into script that was used for communication and record-keeping. In other places the Runes were retained as a system of magical tools, but the knowledge of how to use them was lost, except for a little know-how restricted to ruling, priestly orders. In the places the Runes were adopted and transformed into alien systems of magical working.

We can witness this historical process within the historical records that have been retained, or discovered by historians and archeologists. The earliest evidence of the Elder Futhark's being used in the form that we know today is with the Indo-European

Hittites in 1650 B.C. We can see for ourselves that they used a Futhark that is almost identical to the Elder Futhark that we use today. There a few variations such as Jera, which is rounded instead of sharply angled. Ansuz was used in both the right side and reverse form. This is also true of Berkano and Sowilo. Sowilo looks like the letter "M" on its side. Perthro was used as we use it today, but also as a form of broken Rune that formed two pieces in the way Jera does. Elhaz is also used in the traditional form but also in an upside-down Fehu with one arm. Mannaz has two variations: the traditional version, and a slightly altered variation. Lastly, Ingwaz appears not as a diamond, but as a square. But even with these variations, the Hittite Runes are very recognizable as the Elder Futhark that we use today.

Vrilology maintains that the Runes, in the form of the Elder Futhark, originates with Rig (Heimdall) descending to Earth, and teaching our ancestors who lived along the coast of the prehistorical Black Sea. The Futhark was a gift from the Gods. Contemporary historians and archeologists have debated three different theories to explain the origin of the Runes: the Latin/Greek theory, the Etruscan/North Italic theory, and the Native theory. We will quote from Freya Aswynn's book, *Northern Mysteries and Magic*.

"A Danish scientist, L. F. A. Wimmer, was of the opinion that the runes were an offspring of the Latin alphabet. He based his theory on the parallels that exist between various rune-signs and Latin letters, for example *F, R, H* and *B*. Furthermore, he also believed that the Futhark system was designed by a single individual. The date he suggested for the introduction of the Futhark was approximately 300 C.E. This assumption has been shown to be incorrect, because the first runic archaeological finds are dated earlier. The Swedish runologist O. Van Friesen put forward the theory that runic writing descended from the Greek cursive script and was carried northward by the Goths around the third century. Again, this date is too late. It is more likely that the Latin, Greek, and runic alphabets all descended from an older system of North italic origin. This is the opinion of two runologists, C. G. S. Marstrander and M. Hammarstrom."

The North Italic people were Indo-Europeans who settled in Italy and eventually fathered the Roman nation and other Latin nations of the Italian peninsula. The Runes introduced into Italy were probably in a state of degeneration. Their keepers had been refugees for several thousands of years, moving westward from what is today Ukraine, across Europe, until they crossed the Alps and settled in Italy between 2000 and 1500 BCE. We can see evidence of this in both the Latin alphabet and in Etruscan writing.

The evidence of runic writing and script in Italy is similar to the various runic-like inscriptions and sigils that have been found all across Europe. These symbols are evidence that the Indo-Europeans, as descendants of the parent civilization of the lost civilization of "Atlantis" (the original Aryans), created the Runes of the Elder Futhark from what the Gods taught them, and disseminated them throughout Europe, as well as Asia and the Middle East, in their wanderings after the parent civilization was destroyed around 5600 BCE.

An Short Introduction to the Runes

The first thing you need to do to become familiar with the Runes is to memorize their shapes and names. Write them down several times while saying their names, just like you did in the first grade and your teacher made you write the alphabet. You can break them down into three groups of eight. It is important that you memorize the entire Elder Futhark. Below we provide an illustration and the proper way to pronounce each Rune.

FEHU----fay-who
URUZ----ooo-rooze
THURISAZ----thoor-ee-sasz
ANSUZ----ahn-sooze
RAIDHO----rayd-hoe
KENAZ----kehn-ahsz
GEBO----gay-boe
WUNJO----woon-yoh

HAGALAZ----hah-gah-lahsz
NAUTHIZ----now-these
ISA----ee-sa
JERA----yeer-rah
EIHWAZ----eye-wahsz
PERTHRO----peer-throw
ELHAZ----ehl-hahsz
SOWILO----soe-wee-low
TIWAZ—tee-wahsz
BERKANO----beer-kahn-oh
EHWAZ----ay-wahsz
MANNAZ----mahn-nahsz
LAGUZ----lah-gooze
INGWAZ----eeng-wahsz
DAGAZ----dhah-gahsz
OTHALA----oh-tah-lah

Don't be discouraged if you cannot remember every one perfectly. With continuous use you will soon discover that they will become *a part of you*, and you will become as familiar with them as you are with the alphabet.

Three aspects of the Runes are:

1) their sound or vibratory frequency
2) the shape and form, and
3)the secret knowledge that is associated with each Rune.

A good Rune Master (Runester) is one who has mastered this threefold understanding of the Runes. Once have this threefold understanding of the nature of the Runes, you will, in time, enhance and broaden the inner essence of yourself as and individual through runic meditation. This process will ultimately enhance and strengthen the bond that joins you with our Gods, and the collective consciousness of your Folk. Through this process you will open yourself up, permitting the Folk Soul of your people to grow and guide you as an individual. This inner evolutionary process will assure the return of Balder within you, and cause the Gods who dwell within you to awaken, filling you with their divinity. *This is what we mean by Balder Rising.*

There are two ways in which we can study and come to understand the Runes, as well as making them a part of our lives. The first means is through individual study and meditation. This can be done in many ways. The way you wish to spend your time, and the amount of time you spend, in studying the Runes, will be determined by your need to commit to their study. I do not want to frighten you into thinking you must make a total commitment to the study of Runes. How much time and effort you do devote will be decided by you and your inner voice.

The second way to make the Runes a part of your daily life is to learn how to *think runically.* This does not mean simply memorizing the Futhark, nor studying the languages of the Runes and their lore. Runic thinking is the assimilation of the energy and spirit of the Runes, their lore, craft, ancient meanings, and their astral images until they become a part of you—they become your second nature. When you achieve this state, you automatically think runically. You will have achieved a level of spirituality in which the Runes have come to life within you. You will have absorbed their dynamic energies and they will become a part of you. The first step toward this goal is to familiarize your self with the Runes. We can begin this process by revering the nature of each individual Rune.

Right now you must be thinking, "What am I getting into?" Let me assure you that you need not spend a great deal of time absorbing the runes into your consciousness. There are twenty-four Runes, and you can completely memorize them all within twenty-four days, by taking one Rune a day and thinking about it and learning the simple meaning of it. It will probably take you fifteen minutes a day to remember enough of each Rune to memorize all twenty-four by the end of twenty-four days. Begin with Fehu. Write the name several times as you pronounce it. Then draw the image of Fehu, also pronouncing it. Then read the meaning of the

Rune that we provide in this chapter. The list of meanings is simple and direct. You need not trouble yourself with a deeper understanding of the Runes right now. The next day, do the same with the second Rune, Uruz. When you have completed the first Aett (eight Runes) review all eight of the first Aett until you can quickly and effortlessly recite them. Then continue with the second Aett (the next eight Runes, Hagalaz to Sowilo). Below is a list of the meaning of the Runes:

The First Aett

Fehu – Money, Fire – Used to increase your personal Luck and charisma, to increase your intake of Vril, and then send it outward.

Uruz – Wild Auroch – It has great healing powers, can harness the raw, untamed forces of the universe, especially those of the Earth, and strengthen the power of other Runes, as well as your thoughts and feelings.

Thurisaz – The God Thor, and the Giants – Possesses active, aggressive power used for defense, breaking down resistance, and the projection of power to crush, but also has secondary healing powers.

Ansuz – The Gods, Odin – The primary Rune of communication, wisdom, knowledge, speech, creativity, and psychic abilities.

Raidho – Wagon, Riding – The Rune of divine, or correct, order. It can be used to channel power onto the right road, or direction. Use on journeys, treks, or quests.

Kenaz – Torch or Light – The Rune of technology, harnessed fire, controlled energy used for creation and transformation.

Gebo – Gifts, Exchange – Representing the law of compensation, the exchange of powers, gifts, and the union of polarities to create balance.

Wunjo – Joy, Fellowship, Harmony – The Rune of harmony, joy and happiness. Helps to create harmony among people. The fulfiller of wishes. Strengthens and breaks bonds. Helps to maintain order.

The Second Aett:

Hagalaz – Hail – The force of devolution and evolution. Has the power to destroy what needs to be removed so that new life can grow, and helps one to start over. Can destroy what stands in your way of forward movement.

Nauthiz – Necessity, Need Fire – The force that drives you forward. "Necessity is the Mother of Invention." The force that is the drive behind determination. Primary counter-force to negative Orlog.

Isa – Ice – The power of concentration, contraction, stability, containment and confinement. Causes the cessation of all movement.

Jera – The Harvest – The fulfillment of good deeds planted. It represents the natural growth and development of the yearly and seasonal cycles of growth and turning. Powerful Fertility Rune.

Eihwaz – Yggdrasill (World Tree) – Connections among the nine realms of Norse cosmology. Its power, to help one travel astrally among the Nine Worlds of the Yggdrasill. It represents the Vril-ordered universe in the form of the World Tree, the Axis of Life.

Perthro – Lot Cup – It is the Rune representing the Law of Cause and Effect. One can use it to cleanse one's Orlog of negative influences. Can control your evolutionary development and growth. The Rune of Chance. Use to help you to learn to think runically.

Elhaz – Elk – represents the Life Force or Vril energy. You can use it to forge a link with the Valkyries, who communicate directly with the Gods. The Rune of Resurrection, representing Balder rising from the Netherworld. You can stand in this position when communicating with the Gods. Rune of Protection. Represents Bifrost, the rainbow bridge linking Midgard (the realm of humans) and Asgard (the realm of the Gods).

Sowilo – The Sun, the Lightning Bolt – The Rune of Balder, the Son of Odin reborn. The Rune of Success. It can be used to increase your psychic powers. Use it to help you become an enlightened and illuminated Being. The God-man.

The Third Aett:

Tiwaz – It personifies the God, Tyr, the God of Law, Government, Order and War. World Order. Helps to obtain Victory, justice and maintain social order. Can increase the powers of self-discipline, loyalty and honor.

Berkano – Birch Tree – Represents the Earth Mother, Frigga, the wife of Odin. This Rune deals with all affairs concerning birth, children, family, traditional marriage and traditional love. Use it to help with the creation of new ideas and concepts. Used in all matters dealing with female sexual potency.

Ehwaz – Horse – This Rune represents the harmonious team between horse and man, representing trust and loyalty. Can increase harmony in partnerships, marriage and all types of team work. Used to help with spiritual growth, development and journey. Use this Rune when dealing with all matters concerning the Fetch.

Mannaz – Mankind – The Rune of the God-man. Use to help with the evolution of superior or divine human. Used to open one's Bifrost Gland or Third Eye. Works toward the creation of a union of mortal and immortal. Deals with all affairs concerning marriage and love, traditional union between man and woman.

Laguz – Lake or Water – The Rune of the Life Force or Vril. Helps to explore the unconscious mind-states, as well as the unseen etheric patterns and fold of Vril energy fields. Development of your psychic abilities and Emotions.

Ingwaz – The God Ing – Personifies the Earth God, Frey or Ing. Rune of male fertility, and sexual potency. Used to manifest a sudden release of power or energy, as well as the transformation of power.

Dagaz – Day, Light – Used to create a union or cooperation between the right and left sides of the brain for the purpose of divine evolution and the development of your psychic powers. The Rune of Enlightenment and inspiration, growth and development. Spiritual awakening.

Othala – Homeland, land, property – This Rune deals with all matters concerning ancestral wealth, inheritance, genetics, DNA, blood and race, homeland, kind and nation. It is the Rune of Odin. Increase prosperity for the nation and family and all growth connected through blood and genetics. The Rune of the Erulians (the Wizards of Wotan).

Meditation and Chanting with Runes

By now, you have discovered that you have the power to conform your physical surroundings to your desires through your thoughts and feelings. You now understand that your thoughts and feelings are constantly shaping Vril flowing into you, which in turn creates future pathways that will determine the nature of your life as you move forward into the future. You understand that what you obsess over will be stored within your Orlog, and that its contents will color Vril as it creates your Wyrd (the nature of your future pathways).

Once you come to understand the nature of Vril, and your mind taps into and harnesses its power, using it to shape the nature of your reality, you can then begin to study methods of how to dynamically control it and expertly use it to make things happen. One way is through meditation and chanting. You can fine-tune your powers into instruments that can perform miracles.

Once you have made meditation a regular part of your daily activities, you will reach a level of mind control where your imagination will become a tool for solving problems, and you will discover that something beautiful will happen to you. You don't have to spend a great deal of time meditating. You can do it one to three times a day for about five to fifteen minutes, depending on your schedule. But the more you do meditate, the greater will become your command over your mental powers. You will not only be consciously sending thoughts into the Vril-filled universe, shaping the Vril flowing into you, but you will eventually create a direct bond between yourself and the Godly powers that are constantly forming and maintaining order throughout the universe.

Mental Frequencies

You have already explored how our minds work at different frequencies. For the sake of space and avoiding redundancy here, please reread that section dealing with the different frequencies of your mind. Your mind works normally at the frequency referred to as Beta, but it can also work in more advanced states of Alpha, Theta and Delta. It is at Alpha and Theta that we want to learn to meditate. We need to learn to quickly enter these states so that we can more effectively use the power of our minds to shape Vril into future pathways so that we can control the nature of our Wyrd. We explained that it is not always easy to control our thoughts, of which we average more than 60,000 a day. We cannot expect to control every one of these as they pop into our minds. But we can learn to enhance the power of certain consciously controlled thoughts. We can lend power to certain thoughts through meditation in both the Alpha and Theta states.

Your mind is more energetic in lower frequency states. Your brain can receive and store more information at the lower frequencies of Alpha and Theta. What we want to do is to help you enter both Alpha, (similar to daydreaming) and Theta (when you are halfway between awake and asleep).

First Exercise: Entering Alpha and Theta

You can follow these easy steps to enter the proper state of meditation. The best time of day to perform this simple exercise is just after you wake up, just before you go to bed, or in the late afternoon, in that order. You are naturally at Alpha when you wake up, or just before you fall asleep, or after you have had a big meal.

1) Sit in a comfortable position in a chair with your feet flat on the floor. Hold your head in a balanced position.

2) Next you need to completely relax. You can close your eyes if you wish. Begin with your head and concentrate on every part of your body: your head, face, jaw, neck, shoulders, arms, hands and fingers, upper body, lower body, hips, thighs, legs, and finally feet and toes. Concentrate on each part of your body, slowly feeling all your muscles relaxing. Let every part of you go limp. Take your time relaxing.

3) Once you have reached a state of total relaxation, you need to learn how to breathe properly. Most of the Vril we absorb is through the air we breathe. This is why breathing properly is very important. Take a long, deep breath, pulling the air deep into the lower part of your lungs, near the region of your solar plexus. Also, visualize or feel the Vril energy flowing deep into you and settling in your solar plexus. You can count to 9 as you inhale. As you do, your stomach should be expanding. Then hold your breath for 9 seconds. Finally, slowly exhale, counting to 9. You can repeat this breathing exercise 9 times. If you have trouble inhaling, holding your breath, and exhaling for 9 seconds at a time, don't worry. With a little practice it will come easier for you.

4) Now, if your eyes are closed, you can open them for a second and pick a spot on the ceiling or wall between 20 and 45 degrees above your eye level. Don't strain your eyes while doing this. Make sure you are comfortable. Continue to stare at the spot until your eyelids grow heavy. Keeping your eyes in that elevated position, let your eyes close. Your eyes in this position will trigger your mind, causing it to work in the lower frequency of Alpha.

5) After a few seconds, slowly begin counting from 100 backwards to 1, at one-second intervals. Later, as you practice more and more, you will be able to reduce the count, starting at 50, then 20, and eventually you will simply count from 10 to 1. As you count backwards, keep your mind focused on the numbers.

6) Once you have completed this 5 steps, you will be in Alpha, and you can then consciously reach the lower mental level of Theta. Just remain relaxed and concentrating on your inner peace. You say to yourself, "I will enter a deeper and more peaceful state of meditation by counting backwards from 5 to 1," and then do it and try and keep your mind concentrated on the stillness. You can do this as many times as you feel necessary to help you reach a deeper state of meditation. And though you will be in Alpha the very first time you perform this exercise, you should perform this routine every day for several weeks. Establish a routine of meditating two to three times a day if possible. If you do, in several weeks you will be able to enter Alpha and go into Theta immediately.

7) Once you have reached this level of meditation, simply keep your mind focused on one thought by saying to yourself: *Every day I am getting better and better.* In the beginning, keep everything simple. You can simply come out of this meditative state by counting from 1 to 5. As you reach the number 3, pause and say, *When I open my eyes, I will feel refreshed and recharged.* Then continue to count 4 and 5 and then open your eyes.

Second Exercise: Visualization

The next step in learning to meditate is visualization. Visualization is central to successful meditation. By mastering the routine of visualizing what you are thinking, your experience with meditation will be more powerful.

You can begin by creating a mental screen. Envision a movie screen while your eyes are closed. It should not be on the insides of your eyelids, but imagine it about six feet beyond your eyelids. Then project onto the screen whatever you wish to think about. You can begin with something easy. Imagine a banana, or apple or some other fruit that you like. See it in every detail. Examine its shape and color. Turn it around in your mind. Imagine the taste of the fruit as you bite into it. Feel its juice rolling down your chin. Feel yourself swallowing it. Make the experience as real as possible for yourself. Don't be surprised if in the next twenty-four hours the fruit you visualized appears unexpectedly in your daily routine. If it does, then you will have mastered the first step on the path of dynamically controlling your thought projection and shaping the Vril into a desired future pathway. You will have created the pathway into the future that you desired. You made the fruit appear in your life. This can be done with anything.

Next, you should visualize the Runes. You can begin with the first Rune, Fehu. Take a gray piece of paper. Use the standard size of 11 by 8.5 inches. Then, draw a red Fehu Rune in the center of the paper. The Rune should be about 9 inches high and about 5 inches wide.

Now, place it on the wall and then sit about 10 feet away from it. Stare at the Rune. Do not strain your eyes. Just keep them fixed on the Rune for about 5 minutes. Gradually you will notice the Rune moving, or appear to be moving. We want to learn how to see the energy that is behind the Runic forms. You will now begin to practice seeing through the form of each Rune and discover the Vrilic energy that lies behind them. By performing the following exercise you will discover the energy characteristic of each Rune and how it manifests itself in the objective universe. Once you have finished, you will have mastered the mental disciplines necessary to call on the divine powers of the Runes and use them in amazing ways.

Now, close your eyes and see the after-image on the inside of your eyelids. Use that image to create the image of the Rune, just as you saw it on the piece of paper before you. Soon you will be able to create the image of the Rune in your mind's eye without the help of the drawing of the Rune.

The next step is to sit before the blank wall without the drawing of the Rune. Concentrate on forming the Rune on the blank wall before you. Visualize the Rune forming before you See it take shape and grow. Do not close your eyes. It is important to keep your eyes open and concentrate on the Rune that you have visualized. Let the Rune pull you into it. Examine the shape of the Rune. Every feature of the Rune should be carefully examined, all its angles and segments.

As you continue to concentrate on the Rune, you might see it radiating, or changing shape, or glow. The Rune might even appear to be dancing, or change color. This means the Rune is filling your brain with its power and essence. Surrender yourself to the Rune, and imagine that you are connected to it. Once the Rune has filled your vision and your mind, you should be ready. Please make sure you have not looked away from the Rune. This is very important as you reach for the blank piece of paper and hold it up and cover the Rune without moving your head. Even though the paper is now blocking the Rune, you should still see the image of the Rune before you on the paper. You can then close your eyes and you should continue to see the Rune.

Third Exercise: Chanting the Rune

To chant the Runes properly, you should perform the steps to reach a proper relaxed state, and then perform the correct breathing exercise, enter your Alpha state, and finally move past Alpha and enter your Theta State. Once you have reached this deep level of meditation, remain in your position and keep your eyes closed, and visualize the Rune Fehu in your mind. Keep the image in your mind. See it materialize on the insides of your eyelids. Hold the image, take a deep breathe and then chant in a long, drawn out chant as you exhale:

Feeeeeeehhhhuuuuuuu.

Do this over and over as much as you want. You will feel its relaxing effects. As you do this, feel the Vril energy flowing through you, relaxing every muscle in your body and clearing your mind. Think of Fehu and what the Rune stands for as you chant its name and hold the image in your mind.

You can do one Rune a day until you have chanted all twenty-four Runes. Do not press yourself into trying to become proficient right away. With the information that has been provided to you in this book, you will have enough knowledge to pick and choose the appropriate Runes to use for manifesting whatever you wish to achieve through meditation. If you wish to buy a house, you can use Othala for immobile wealth and Raidho for the right path, which will help you do what you need to get the mortgage and find the right house. If you wish to create a loving relationship, you can use Gebo and Wunjo. Just read the meanings of the Runes provided in this chapter and meditate on them.

Chapter Five: Vril as Your Life Force

The Mechanism of Vril

We understand that the universe is filled with Vril, and Vril is not manufactured within the human body. It is a universal force which every atom in the universe is pulsating with. Is there a limit to the quantity of Vril? One might think that if there is a limit to the universe, then that is the limit to the amount of Vril, but some believe Vril, like subatomic particles, blinks in and out of our universe, which would mean there is no limit to the quantity of Vril.

Our bodies have the capacity to absorb Vril and store up a reserve supply, and use and transform Vril into various forms necessary for a variety of purposes in maintaining and ensuring the function of the many organs of the body. We also have the ability to increase the amount of Vril our bodies can store up, and use it for such purposes as increasing our supply of personal luck. But the Vril gathered, stored and transformed is never created by the human body, though it can be shaped and transformed. And just as Vril cannot be created, it cannot be destroyed.

The Nervous System

The mechanism by which Vril is passed throughout the body is the nervous system. The nervous system is divided **structurally** into two great systems:

1) the cerebro-spinal system and

2) the peripheral system.

The cerebro-spinal system consists of the brain and the spinal cord. The spinal cord runs down the trunk line of the spine, through the center of the twenty-four vertebrae of the spine (not counting the sacral region). The peripheral nervous system branches off it at each vertebra and also directly from the brain through the skull, to connect with every other part of the body.

The nervous system is also divided **functionally** into two systems. One functional system is called the autonomic nervous system, while the other has no good name but will be discussed here as the non-autonomic nervous system.

The functions of sensation, movement, consciousness,

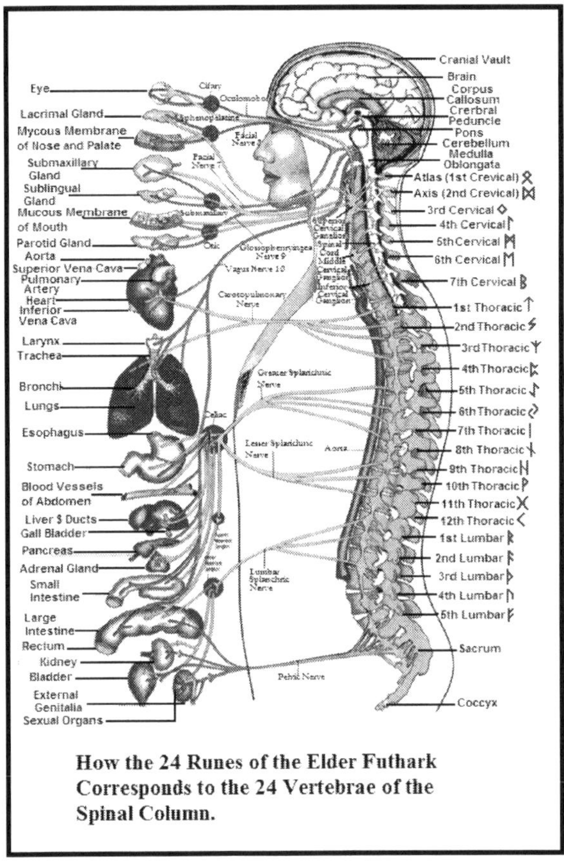

How the 24 Runes of the Elder Futhark Corresponds to the 24 Vertebrae of the Spinal Column.

volition, will, and all higher processes of thought and reason are the domains of the non-autonomic system. The five senses of feeling, taste, hearing, sight and smell are conveyed through it to the brain. Awareness of the outside world is received and transmitted to the brain and processed. The brain is divided into three parts: the medulla oblongata, the cerebellum, and the cerebrum. The medulla oblongata is situated at the base of the brain and considered the upper part of the spinal cord. It is often referred to as reptilian in nature, controlling certain functions of the autonomic nervous system, such as the activities of the heart, lungs, cardiovascular system, and abdominal organs. It also modulates some of the subconscious activities of the mind. The cerebellum, whose name means "little brain," is situated just above the medulla oblongata. It modulates muscular movements of the body. Without it we would not be able to smoothly walk, run, move our legs, arms, or fingers without conscious thought. These are actions that we learn, usually as an infant, and then perform without much thought, automatically and unconsciously. It is only when we desire to perform specific tasks of complexity that the cerebrum takes charge.

The cerebrum, or larger brain, comprises the greater part of the skull cavity. It is the seat of conscious thought, reason and reflection on new ideas, cognitive thought, memory and perception. It is the seat of intelligence and inspiration. The connection between the rest of the nervous system and the cerebrum must be maintained if sensation is to be felt throughout the body. This part of the brain is most important when dealing with consciousness and intelligence, and the seat of these functions rests in the cortex. The cerebrum sends out orders that control the motor functions. This is done by transmitting Vril to different parts of the body. It is done through the spinal cord, which occupies the spinal column or backbone. Spinal nerves spring from either side of the column, and then divide and subdivide, transmitting Vril to every part of the body. Without this complete system of nerves reaching into every tiny corner of the body, Vril would never reach out and fill every cell in the body. Parts of the body would be without connection to the brain and be cut off from the flow of Vril—the Life Force that animates the human body.

The spinal cord is actually a continuation of the brain. They two form two parts of the same system. The spinal cord is often referred to as the "backbone," and occupies the center of the spinal column running up and down the center of one's back. Though it is composed of both white and gray matter and separated into two parts by fissures, there always remains a ridge of connecting nerve matter, shaped like the letter "H." There are thirty-one pairs of spinal nerves emerging from either side of the cord. Each nerve has two roots, an anterior and a posterior. The way these two nerves work is simple. If one's foot was pricked, a sensory impulse would be transmitted to the spinal cord by way of the posterior root. A motor impulse would then be sent from the spinal ganglia to the foot by way of the anterior root causing a reaction. If the posterior root was cut, the foot would not feel any sensation if were pricked, but the foot could still move. If the anterior root was cut, the foot could still feel pain, but could not move. So, we can see that the spinal column and its nervous system is essential to both movement and sensation throughout the human body. If the spinal column was broken, it could cause paralysis and lack of all sensation through the body depending on where the spinal cord was severed.

The nerves emerging from the spinal column divide and subdivide until their "fingers" reach into every part of the human body. It functions like a great telephone system, with wires reaching into every point, no matter how important or insignificant. It is through this extensive system of expanding nerves that the brain is in contact with every part of the human body, and thus with every cell of the body. Through this extensive system of nerves, a supply of Vril is constantly sent to nourish every cell and every atom within each cell, just as blood is sent through the human body by way of the circulatory system of arteries, veins and capillaries. As mentioned before, these nerves convey sensations from every part of the body to the brain, and in return send orders for movement, and supply Vril from the brain. There are two classifications of nerves:

1) **The afferent nerves**, which carry a stimulus from a part of thc body to the brain's central nervous system.

2) **The efferent nerves**, which transmit motor impulses or incentives for movement to different parts of the body from the central nervous system in the brain.

The sensory nerves are afferent nerves while the efferent nerves are motor nerves. There are other nerves that do not fall into either category. The peripheral nervous system includes *ganglia*, which might be described as "little brains." They can be described as tiny knots of bunches of nerve matter, connected with nerve fibers.

The Sympathetic Nervous System

The autonomic nervous system is divided into the sympathetic and parasympathetic nervous systems. The sympathetic nervous system is connected to the spinal cord by ganglia that run down both sides of the spinal column of vertebrae, within the protective cusp of the vertebrae bone on both the right and left sides of the spinal cord. Unlike the non-autonomic nervous system, the sympathetic nervous system does not carry the objective intelligence from the brain to every part of the body, but instead, transmits the psychic or inner consciousness of the subconscious mind to all parts of the body. It is the sympathetic nervous system which connects with the psychic energy centers known as the Hvel, which will be discussed in another lesson in the training program.

Most of the involuntary processes of the human body are controlled by the autonomic system. Among them are processes dealing with nutrition, growth, repair, elimination of wastes, digestion, the immune defenses, respiration, circulation, and perspiration. The sympathetic nervous system has a double chain of ganglia, situated on both sides of the spinal column as described above. The parasympathetic nervous system has scattered ganglia in the head, neck, chest and abdomen, but situated principally in the area of the thoracic, abdominal and pelvic cavities, and as well as throughout the internal organs. Each ganglion helps to distribute Vril energy to various parts of the body. They increase and intensify Vril energy flowing through the sympathetic nervous system to whatever section of the body that has need of additional Vril. Some of the ganglia are related to the various hvel, or psychic centers in the body. A network, of very fine filaments connect the ganglia to the cerebro-spinal system and the sensory and motor nerves. From these ganglia, numerous fibers branch out throughout the body, reaching even the tiniest and most distant limbs, blood vessels, organs and muscles. Nerve-masses are formed throughout the body at various locations that are named *plexi*.

The plexi, or plexus for singular, are ever expanding networks of nerve endings that fan out through various parts of the body so that it can deliver Vril energy to every section of the body, even the most remote and tiniest regions. For instance, the sympathetic nerves that go to lungs will not just touch it, but from where they do touch it, spread out in ever multiplying fingers that spread into every section of the lungs, so that every cell within the lungs is able to receive Vril energy directly from the sympathetic nerve endings.

The principal and most important part plexus is the *solar plexus*.

It must be remembered that the autonomic nervous system acts on instinctual or subconscious instructions from the brain, but can be directed by the conscious mind if the conscious mind has been trained to properly send suggestions. Once the conscious mind has been trained to achieve this level of command over the body, the sympathetic nervous system can be utilized to direct Vril in ways that can be very beneficial to the health and well being of the body. Vril can even be sent to every cell in the body. Currents of Vril energy can be strengthened, directed and concentrated to help develop one's muscles as a form of internal exercise, to repair damaged tissues, to eliminate illness, foreign bacteria, disease, and other maladies harmful to the human body.

Paul Tice writes in *Vril or Vital Magnetism*: "The man or woman who understands the art of suggesting to the subconscious mind, and of directing currents of vril to the parts of the body, may keep his or her system in perfect condition and functioning power, and thus reach an old age of health, vigor, and vitality."

The Solar Plexus

The nervous system is very complex, and this is not the place to go into detailing the entire system, but there is a section of the system known as the solar plexus, which is a mat of sympathetic nerves that are situated at the epigastric region on either side of the spinal column, right behind what is sometimes known as "the pit of the stomach." It plays a very important part in the unconscious process of the body and contains both white and grey matter. It has been referred to as "the abdominal brain." It is this region where the body stores up Vril supplied for use throughout the body. It acts like a great storage battery used by the brain, drawing on the supply of Vril that is sent throughout the body to power its functions.

What is important to keep in mind is that the human mind unconsciously draws on the Vril to power the body. But we have to understand that it is possible to consciously draw on Vril and cause the flow to increase or decrease to all parts of the body, thus affecting the organs' abilities to perform properly. The conscious mind can be trained to affect the sympathetic nervous system, causing it to send supplies of Vril to different sections of the body through the use of thought and concentration. Thus, the trained individual can direct the flow of the Vril throughout the body, causing currents of Vril to strengthen and build up the body. We should not confuse the solar plexus with the Hamingja. The former is a physical organ of the body, which draws Vril into it and stores it before disseminating it up the spinal cord, to the brain and other parts of the body. The Hamingja is a part of your multi-dimensional soul, which draws on Vril from the solar plexus and transforms it into Megin, or Personal Luck.

Eihwaz and the Spinal Column

Eihwaz is the Rune associated with the Yggdrasill, the vertical cosmic axis and Kundalini fire, as well as the spinal cord. This Rune causes Vril energy to travel between the different worlds in the Yggdrasill, and between the different levels of consciousness. Like the Yggdrasill's position in the Cosmos, so is the role the spinal column plays within the human body. And as you can use Eihwaz to enhance your awareness of the framework of the Yggdrasill, so too can you use Eihwaz to develop your abilities to be more aware of the way Vril flows through your body and the effects it has on your physical well being. Through

Eihwaz you can discover mysteries, not only from deep within your inner perspectives, your microcosm, but also your outer perspectives, your macrocosm, and the relationship between these two different realities.

Eihwaz is also associated with the yew tree, which is a symbol of Yggdrasill and the spinal column. It is interesting to remember that in the Norse cosmology, Midgard is in the center of the World Tree diagram of the multi-verse. To rise upward is to enter the realms of higher consciousness, and to move downward is to enter the realms of lower consciousness. But we can also look at this from the perspective of macrocosm and microcosm. To rise higher is to explore the greater physical universe. We will learn how to do this through remote viewing and astral projection. But these disciplines can also help us to explore our microcosm. We can enter the human body and explore this mini-universe. It is possible to mentally travel through the veins and arteries into the different organs, and even enter the individual cells, or even go so far as explore individual atoms within the body. This discipline can be very useful in the art of healing. This ability is symbolized by the yew, which is a symbol of the mysteries of life and death.

The form of the Rune Eihwaz is very instructive of this mystery. If we examine the flow of Vrilic energy, we can discover a duality that is instrumental in the way we can explore either the macrocosm and microcosm, life and death, the outer and inner natures, and higher and lower consciousness.

The yew tree associated with Eihwaz is known as the tree of death because of its toxins. Yet it is a long-lived tree, and the most enduring of evergreens that live through winter. For these reasons it is associated with the Great Initiation of life, death and rebirth. It is the tree most affiliated with the shamanistic tradition of traveling to other realms, including the realm of the dead. Odin gained his power over life and death by hanging on the yew tree, the Yggdrasill. He sacrificed himself for himself as an initiation of death and rebirth.

Often water is the element associated with death. For this reason, the Goddess Ran, Aegir's wife, is, like Hel, the Queen of the Dead at sea. Those who die at sea are taken by her to her domain under the sea.

Eihwaz is also associated with fire, or the Kundalini Fire, because it is the Rune of the vertical axis, which corresponds to the human spine, which has twenty-four vertebrae, which in turn form a correspondence to the twenty-four Runes of the Elder Futhark. Kundalini fire is Vril energy that travels up and down the spinal column, and charges the different hvel with Vril or Megin energy.

Exercise Using the Spinal Column for Healing

If you study the diagram of the spinal column that we provide in this lesson, you will notice that there are twenty-four vertebrae. We make the association of twenty-four vertebrae with the twenty-four Runes of the Elder Futhark. As you also know, the Futhark is divided into three parts, or Aetts, which means eights. One of the associations you can make is with the musical harmonic scale from the movie *The Sound of Music*. Remember when Julie Andrews sings, "Doe, ray, me, fa, so, la, tee doe." Begin with Fehu located at the base of the spinal column, and then move up the spinal cord and associate each vertebrae with the sound of each musical note.

If you know anything about the structure of harmonics and nature, you will notice the equivalent to the progression in nature of three-to-one. This means there is a three-step development followed by a plateau or fourth step. This plateau is when either further development can be derailed or a metamorphosis can take place, permitting or ensuring further development and growth. Thus we have: doe, ray, me *fa*, so, la, tee *doe*. You can clearly see the 3-1, followed by another 3-1. Now, if we look at the spinal column, and begin to move up with the musical notes we have the runic association of:

Fehu–doe
Uruz-ray
Thurisaz-me
Ansuz-fa

Raidho-so
Kenaz-la
Gebo-tee
Wunjo-doe

We find this very interesting. The plateau is Ansuz. This is the rune of speech, communication, knowledge and the "release of mental fetters through an ecstatic state." It is the Odinic state of ecstasy.

This is followed by three more Runes and the next plateau is Wunjo–a state of joy and harmony among people. "The realization of truth!" Is this not the first step in the evolution toward a higher spiritual state?

But let's continue. We must begin again with the second aett.

Hagalaz–doe
Nauthiz–ray
Isa–me
Jera–fa
Eihwaz–so
Perthro–la
Elhaz–tee
Sowilo–doe

We can see that this second set of musical notes nicely corresponding to the second aetts. The first level is the first eight runes of Freyja's aett. Now this second level corresponds to Heimdall's aett. The first plateau of this level is Jera. This is the rune of evolution. "The turning of the year. Natural cycles. Fertility."

This is then followed by the further progression to the next plateau of Sowilo. "Strengthening of the psychic centers (Hvel). The individualization of the Being." The Sun! We refer to Sowilo as the Rune of Balder Risen. It is the state one achieves when the regenerative powers of Balder's resurrection and the beginning of acquiring a State of Gimli.

Now, for the final level, which looks like this:

Tiwaz-doe
Berkano–ray
Ehwaz–me
Mannaz–fa
Laguz–so
Ingwaz–la
Dagaz–tee
Othala–doe

The first plateau is Mannaz–the perfected human, which is the divine archetype structure, that is reached when opening of the third eye." This is part of the process of what the Folk Faith of Balder Rising refers to as *Balder Rising!*

And the final plateau is Othala. This is the Rune of the clan and inherited power, of the recreated bond between Asgard and Midgard.

So we have the following plateau Runes: Ansuz, Wunjo, Jera, Sowilo, Mannaz and Othala. Here we have a six-rune formula for spiritual rebirth and evolution.

We can use this process to help both with the healing process, but more importantly, use it as a Runic massage.

1) The patient can lie on his stomach. You should stand on the patient's left side. The patient should be naked from the waist up.

2) The masseuse then paints the Runes on each vertebrae, using a washable body paint. Give it a few minutes to dry.

3) Then the runic masseuse begins at the base of the spinal column, with Fehu, and harmonize the musical notes of doe, ray, me, fa, so, la, tee, doe. Remember, *me* and the second *doe* are the plateau notes.

4) The masseuse should place his left hand on Ansuz for *me (a plateau note)*, and his right hand on Fehu for *doe*. The left

hand connects with the right side of the brain while the left hand with the right brain. The masseuse should begin with his left hand on Ansuz and his right hand on Fehu, and chant the note doe, holding it as long as he can while holding both index fingers on the Rune-painted vertebrae. As he does, he should visualize the Rune Fehu.

5) He next places the index finger of the right hand on Uruz and does the same. Then he does the same with Thurisaz.

6) When he comes to Ansuz, he places the index fingers of both hands on it.

7) When he completes Ansuz, he places the left index finger on Wunjo and the right index finger on Raidho and continues in the same way.

8) He should continues up the spinal column until he finally completes it with Othala. This should help the flow of Vrilic energy to rise through the autonomic nervous system to the different parts of the body, ensuring the regenerative powers of Vril not only heal different parts of the body, but also help cause improvement, regeneration, and the expansion of all powers, physical and psychic, associated with different parts of the body.

To use this method to heal is very simple. The runic masseuse can locate the proper vertebra with a given part of the body or organ that is in need of healing, and direct the healing energies to it by concentrating on the vertebra, such as the 14th, Eihwaz, associated with the lungs. To understand how this process works, we should continue to examine the nervous system before leaving this lesson.

Ganglia and Plexus

The sympathetic nervous system is organized into two sets of ganglia extending down the thoracic and lumbar portions of the spinal column on both its right and left sides. The ganglia serve to distribute Vril throughout the body. The currents of Vril energy are increased and intensified as they pass through the sympathetic nervous system, providing the necessary Vril energy to ensure the maintenance and good health of the body. The ganglia also connect to the Hvels, or psychic centers. The nervous system eventually divides into what is referred to as a plexus, which is a wide fan of nerve endings spreading out everywhere. They serve to disseminate Vril from the nerves to a wide range of areas. Every part of the human body, no matter how distant or small, is connected to the sympathetic nervous system, including the cerebro-spinal system, which also requires a continuous supply of Vril to maintain its vitality.

A plexus provides a continuous supply of Vril energy to every muscle, every organ, every bone, every cell it is connected to. The energy that is transmitted through the plexus provides the needed Vril energy to give it power to move and carry back impressions of pain, injury or other sensations to the brain. Along with this plexus there is another means by which the sympathetic nervous system sends currents of Vril energy, which enables the body's various parts to continue to function properly under the directions of the will of the Cosmic Intelligence or the Gods.

The sympathetic nervous system actually ends at the top of the thoracic section of the spinal cord, with the vertebrae that equates with Tiwaz. The ganglia do not match up exactly with the top seven vertebrae of the spinal cord. Within this range of seven vertebrae, there are three parasympathetic ganglia: the Inferior Cervical Ganglion, the Middle Cervical ganglion and the Superior Cervical ganglion. The first vertebrae of the Cervical Cord is associated with Tiwaz, the Rune that is personified by Tyr. Tyr is the God of government, law and social order, and so we can use the vertebrae to channel Vril to the other ganglia that are not actually connected to the Cervical Cord, and thus send Vril to those parts of the body that are connected to the plexus at the nerve endings of these ganglia.

From the vertebrae associated with Tiwaz, the parasympathetic nervous system of ganglia moves up into the skull as the inferior, middle and superior ganglia. At the same time, the skull and cranium are balanced on the seven bone vertebrae within the cervical region. Here, the parasympathetic nervous system comes to an end in what is referred to as Ganglion of Ribes. The

Ganglion of Ribes happens to be located right near the pituitary gland. This is very significant for its function of transmitting Vril into the *Hamr* (etheric/astral) and the *Lik* (physical) bodies.

From this point, Vril energy continues to move into the sphenoid cavity which engulfs the pituitary gland. We must remember that the pituitary and pineal glands are what has been referred to as the Third Eye, and what the Folk Faith of Balder Rising refers to as the Bifrost Gland. Bifrost is the Rainbow Bridge that connects Midgard and Asgard, and permits communication and travel between the two realms. The Bifrost Gland, which is the united system of the pituitary and pineal glands, is the point from which the Life Force of the Gods (Vril) is received in Midgard. It is the lost link that we have with the Gods who created us, and can be regenerated. The Bifrost Gland (pituitary and pineal glands) is the beginning of the entire Vril transferral process from the Cosmic to Midgard realms. The pineal gland is at the Asgard end of the bridge, and the pituitary gland is on the Midgard end of the bridge.

Vril and the Well Being of the Human Body

Every activity within the physical body is caused by the flow of Vril into the body, and disseminated throughout it, into every cell, and even into every atom It is this mysterious force that is the origin of life within the body. From the inner activity within the tiniest cell, to the complex activities and workings of the organs of the body, Vril is the force that manifests activity and continues activity. It is through the subconscious mind that Vril is ever present as an active agent and power which ensures the continuous performance of every cell and organ in the body.

All life everywhere is dependent on Vril for its creation, continuation, and well being. From the tiniest bacteria to the giant Blue Whale, all life needs the continuous flow of Vril into it, and its dissemination throughout its physical and spiritual forms. It is this power that also ensures the working of the mind.

Every cell has its own tiny degree of consciousness, each powered with its own charge of Vril. Think of the billions of cells in the body as a bee hive or ant hill. Each cell is a member of the hive, like a tireless bee or ant, constantly working toward the maintenance and continuous well being of the collective. Every day and night, without rest, each cell is performing its assigned task until it finally wears itself out and dies. It is then replaced with another cell that takes its place and does the same. Each cell is actually an individual entity, but its individuality is submerged into the collective, working only for the well being of the whole, in a perfect communistic society.

There is no need to go into every task that is performed by the many different cells. There is not enough space. We have only to mention that every cell, no matter its task, possesses a consciousness that is submerged into the collective consciousness of the whole, and it is all powered by Vril energy. Every second of our lives, the vast army of cells that make up our bodies is working from birth to death, repairing, supporting, renovating, cleaning, replacing and defending every portion of the body. Every three weeks, we are entirely made over. It takes a great deal of power to ensure the continuation and survival of this vast and intricate system.

Physical science has never sufficiently explained the source of life. What is the energy that powers the human body, giving it life? This source of power is Vril. It is the Life Force of the Gods. It was Odin's gift, the gift of life, that he gave when Odin, Vili and Ve created the first man and woman. This three-gods-in-one gave shape, form and order to humans by causing Vril to fill the spirito-physical form of the first humans. And Vril is the same amazing source of power that gives shape, form and order to the galaxies that are spinning through the universe, just as it gives shape, form and order to the tiniest atom within us. The universe is filled with Vril, like a vast ocean. Its currents of energy are flowing everywhere, and especially into us, as it does with all forms of life. It is this constant flow of Vril energy that gives us life, and which needs a continuous replenishing of the store of Vril in the body to assure the continuation of life.

Vril is necessary for supporting life on all levels. Just as each cell and atom has a never-ending need to replenish its supply of Vril, so too do we have a need to replenish the supply of Vril to support the enormous expenditure of Vril necessary for our individual, voluntary activities. The human body has been rightly compared to a great and vastly complex machine, performing all sorts of activities. Every motion, even that of the tiniest cell, needs a supply of Vril energy to support it. Once again, let us read what Tice writes about this process: ". . . [E]ach expenditure must be paid for by a decrease in the store of Vril in the system. Each item of expenditure must be counterbalanced by a renewal of the supply, else there is physical deterioration and loss of energy to the individual."

Today, humanity as a whole is ignorant of the need to replenish their supply of Vril. We have lost the knowledge of how important it is to ensure the constant and steady flow of sufficient Vril to maintain the health and well being of our bodies and minds. Thus, over time, our bodies wear out due to a loss of vitality, virility and general nervous energy, and become physical wrecks, and subject to the many physical and mental illnesses that plague mankind today. This is due to the loss of Vril because of our obsessions that result in excessive emotional trauma. These emotional excesses consume enormous amounts of Vril, in portions greater then we can normally replenish, resulting in a decline in the amount of Vril harnessed to ensure our physical and mental well being. Even when we are sleeping, we can suffer a loss of vital Vril due to worry, anxiety and stress that can affect our sleep in the form of disturbing dreams and nightmares. When we do suffer from nervous breakdown or emotional stress, we need to learn how to calm ourselves and consciously replenish the supply of Vril. It is the purpose of Vrilology to teach us how we can not only ensure the continuous flow of necessary Vril energy, but also consciously increase the supply, store great amounts, and shape Vril for our needs.

It is of the utmost importance that we prevent wasting the supply of Vril needed to ensure good health and well being. This is second only in importance of knowing the proper methods of acquiring a greater supply of Vril that is necessary to meet the requirements of modern life. Life in contemporary society is filled with threats of ever greater conflicts and certain self-destruction that surely will result in greater emotional stress and trauma.

Life in today's modern, urbanized, mechanized, computerized civilization wastes great amounts of Vril, so we must learn to replenish the supply, to increase the amount of Vril that flows into us, and to shape and form whatever we might need to assure mental and physical well being. In the past, only a tiny group of people possessed this knowledge. This is why we read of individuals who lived healthy lives well into their nineties, while the rest of humanity suffered rapid deterioration and an early death, often before the age of forty. In the last century, physical science and medicine has been able to prolong life, but the quality of life is more often due to the way people live than to medicine. Medicine can ensure we live to one hundred years, but more often than not, it is merely existing, not living. When we hear tales of individuals like Benjamin Franklin living well into his nineties, not as an invalid, but filled with vitality, virility and energy that were unusual for a man half his age, we have to ask ourselves if he was privy to knowledge that was not accessible to the general public. Considering his activities in the occult sciences and esoteric mystery disciplines, and by reviewing his writings, we can conclude that Mr. Franklin was one of those select individuals that understood the methodology of Vril and how to use it to ensure his health and well being.

Thousands of years ago, when the Gods first descended to earth (Midgard) and bestowed on our ancestors the secret of harnessing Vril, our ancestors were able to use this knowledge to transform themselves physically into a race of God-men or supermen. The order that the Gods created ensures that nature adjusts the supply of Vril necessary to cause the process of evolution to work, by occasionally increasing the flow of Vril currents to create, through intelligent design, the mutation of those genetic traits needed for life to transform itself and adapt to the changing environment. The Gods decided, some ten thousand years ago, to give to mankind the knowledge necessary to control this process, and become masters of their own evolution. They were given the knowledge to prevent the unnatural waste of Vril, and also to increase the flow of Vril by methods that this training program is providing. This resulted in our ancestors' not only maintaining an equilibrium and balance needed to ensure good health and well being, but to go as far as changing themselves with this life-giving energy to increase the flow of Vril, harness it, and use it to transform themselves into a race of what can only be described as god-men. Thus they were able to set themselves up as a race apart from the rest of humanity. This is what we mean by transforming ourselves into Vril Beings. But to achieve this objective, we must discipline ourselves to a regimented schedule of training. The results will be increased efficiency in all that we do, increased physical, psychic and mental powers and increased success—and hopefully, increased happiness.

Visualizing the Flow of Vril into Your Body

We now know that Vril is inherent in all matter at the atomic and subatomic levels. The different nature of matter is the result of the various degrees of vibrations due to the relationships of the electrons and the neutrons, powered by Vril. Thus, we conclude that Vril is not only found in all matter, but *is more than 99 percent of all matter*. The amount of Vril in all matter is the same, whether it is a rock or air. But in its most usable form, Vril can be applied by man in precise combinations for various purposes, such as transforming his physical environment. The supply of Vril necessary for man to use to transform his reality, whether subjective or objective reality, is found in ample quantities in the food his eats, thc liquids he drinks, and the air he breaths. Whether or not we are conscious of the fact, we are constantly absorbing Vril. The amount of Vril that we take in to nourish us and maintain good health depends on how we breathe, what we eat, what we drink and also our behavior. Under normal conditions, the individual will take in the required amounts of Vril needed to maintain life, but under the conditions that we live in today, in the present urban environment, we live lives that waste our supply of

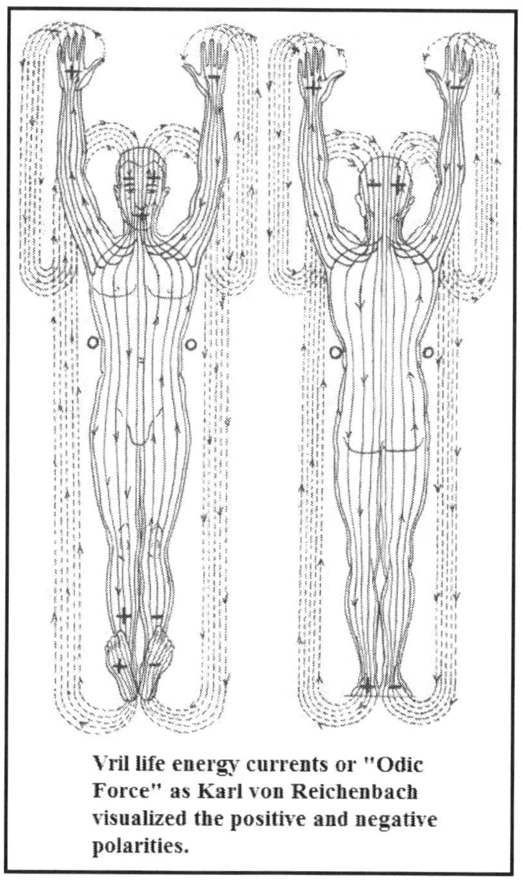

Vril life energy currents or "Odic Force" as Karl von Reichenbach visualized the positive and negative polarities.

Vril. Therefore, because of our wasteful practices, we must learn first, to consciously replenish our intake of Vril energy; second, to increase that supply; and third, to transform it into whatever it is we wish to manifest in our lives.

Try to visualize the process of absorbing Vril and channeling it throughout your body. Imagine you can *feel* the Vril's power coursing through your body, just as you might imagine your heart beating and pumping blood through your veins and arteries. The body will absorb Vril whether you visualize the process or not, but to do so will help the process increase the amount of Vril that is absorbed. What we want to do is to train our minds to master the process of Vril entering the body so that we can increase its flow when we desire it, send it to different parts of our bodies, where it might be needed, and finally to use it to transform the world around us. The mind can be used as the instrument of our salvation or the device by which we destroy ourselves. Its power can be used to evolve into a higher state of consciousness if we direct it properly, or it can be our bane, dragging us down into a life of chaos and self-destruction. Today in our commercially driven society, we are exploited every day by disharmonic forces of greed and avarice. We should always keep in mind that overindulgence is harmful and detrimental to good health. If we follow the rule to not overindulge, to eat and drink in moderation, and to be active and exercise regularly, most foods and drinks are basically good for us. To achieve and maintain good health it is important to eat balanced meals, and maintain wholeness, harmony, and rhythm in your habits and behavior. Though it might be necessary to use drugs and other medical assistance when you are stricken by illness, we must remember that these devices are remedies to assist in the healing process and not substitutes for proper behavior and maintenance of good health or recreation.

Good health requires balance in diet, exercise, behavior and thought. We must maintain a proper balance of good nutrition, physical activity and positive mental processes to ensure good health. The disruption of this balance will interfere with the natural vitality of the body and lead to a chemical imbalance—either acidic or alkaline. Both effects on the potential hydrogen, or pH, will affect the atomic orbits within each cell within the body, and can affect our health.

Through visualization, you can change any physical condition. Just make a mental image of what you think physical perfection is. Hold that image in your mind while you are meditating. Concentrate on it, and examine it in every detail. Let it sink into your consciousness. There are countless cases of people eliminating chronic conditions through this method in just weeks, in a few days, and even in just a few minutes. It is not easy, only because our minds are naturally undisciplined. You have to learn to concentrate and hold the image you are visualizing. This takes practice. It is not painful. You just have to develop patience and the ability to focus your thoughts on one image for as long as possible.

Remember that while you are focusing on a single thought, the image that you are focusing on is emanating vibrations that are resonating through the currents of Vril energy flowing into you. Vril flows into you, then spreads throughout your body, transforming it into the image you are concentrating on. We know that mental action is vibration. We also understand that all form is simply a mode of motion, a rate of vibration. This is quantum physics. You have within you the power to transform a subatomic particle by just observing it. You can transform it from a wave into a particle and back through the method of observing or measuring it. Therefore, any given vibration is immediately modified right down to its subatomic components through the power of your mind. This affects every cell in your body and changes the chemical composition in every group of living cells.

Charles Haanel wrote: "Everything in the Universe is what it is by virtue of its rate of vibration. Change the rate of vibration and you change the nature, quality and form. The vast panorama of nature, both visible and invisible, is being constantly changed by simply changing the rate of vibration, and as thought is a vibration we can also exercise this power. We can change the vibration and thus produce any condition which we desire to manifest in our bodies."

A Simple Exercise: Directing the Flow of Vril

While you are conducting your breathing exercises, imagine you can feel your body filling up with Vril as you inhale. Feel the currents of Vril flowing into you, not just through your mouth and nostrils, but into your Solar Plexus. Feel the power rushing into the Solar Plexus and then racing up your spine and into your brain. In the brain, your mind is transforming Vril into a healing power. You then send it back down the spine through the sympathetic nervous system into every part of your body. In this part of the process, you don't have to be specific as to where Vril is being sent, only that every part of your body is being filled with it. Later in your exercises, when you use the Runes in combination, you can be specific as to where you want Vril sent and for what purpose.

It is in your DNA that Vril will have the greatest effect, so, we want you to *will* Vril to enter your DNA:

1) Will it to enter your genes.
2) Will it to recharge every atom in your body.
3) Will it to fill your nervous system and spread out to every cell in your body.

What you are doing is creating a mental image, through visualization, and reinforcing it with the power of your mind. You are trying to create clear, strong mental images and then project them into the outer world through the use of the power of your will. This can be described as the one-point concentration of the will.

Either sit in a comfortable chair, or better, lie down on your bed. Then, proceed to use the relaxing exercises described earlier. Relax every muscle in your body. You might have discovered by now that this is actually a form of self hypnosis. Once you have achieved this state of relaxation, you can begin directing the flow of Vril throughout your body.

First: take a deep breath. As you do, visualize red-color Vril energy being pulled into your mouth and down into your lungs and finally reaching your Solar Plexus (the pit of your stomach). Make sure you take a deep breath. You can count to nine as you do. Then hold it within your Solar Plexus and slowly feel the air, void of Vril flowing out of you. Repeat this breathing exercise so that you have done it a total of nine times. Each time you take a breath, you are filling your Solar Plexus with more and more Vril.

Second: concentrate on your Solar Plexus, and tap into your stored supply of the Vril. You should then will this supply of power to every part of the body. Visualize Vril flowing through your nervous system. Feel Vril flowing through your nervous system. Feel the power flowing through your body like a current of water flowing through rivers, streams and channels.

Third: now that you have filled your body with Vril, concentrate on your feet and feel the energy within. Slowly more your concentration up your legs, across your hips through your body and arms and to the crown of your head. Now reverse the concentration back to your feet. Repeat this sweep of your body several times. Let each sweep take about five seconds. Each time you sweep you should feel a current of Vril sweep through your body. You will probably feel a tingling sensation as your mind passes through your body. Your skin will tingle as if ants are crawling over your and you will be inclined to scratch. Repeat the sweeps as much as you desire and slowly increase the speed. Each time you sweep you will feel more charged. Each sweep is cleansing your body of negative waste.

Fourth: once you feel charged, you can then concentrate on a certain part of your body and feel Vril moving toward this point. Feel the energy building there and know that you are channeling extra amounts of Vril there for whatever purpose you desire. This exercise is especially useful to help the healing process.

You can use this simple exercise to recharge yourself as often as you desire.

You need to understand that your health depends on your body's ability to make use of nutritional material that is needed to maintain the health of cells, and secondly to break down and excrete waste material from your body. All life requires that the body be able to perform these two basic functions. Food, water and air are the only things needed to ensure these constructive and destructive processes. Theoretically, your body should require just these three ingredients to continue functioning indefinitely. The lack of proper nutrition and the body's failure to break down and eject waste are the only causes for the cells in the body to lose their ability to receive enough Vril to maintain the health of the body. This is especially true of the destructive process from the body's failure to break down and eject toxins. Charles Haanel writes about this process: "However strange it may seem, it is the second or destructive activity that is, with rare exception, the cause of all disease. The waste material accumulates and saturates the tissues, which cause auto-intoxication. This may be partial or general. In the first case the disturbance will be local: in the second place it will affect the whole system."

Hvels and the Control of Vrilic Energy

As we have explained, Vril is constantly entering your body and is being channeled throughout your entire being, both spiritual and physical. Your soul is powered by the Vril currents. These currents are disseminated throughout you by way of your nervous system, to replenish Vril energy in every atom of your body. Your mind, both subconsciously and consciously, is working to channel this Vril energy in many different ways. How your mind channels Vril will depend on what is stored within your Orlog. You Orlog is part of your soul and acts like a filter which Vril passes through, and thus takes on the quality and nature of whatever is stored there. We have explored how you can cleanse your Orlog of negativity that might be stored there. This will cause you to bend your Wyrd and control your destiny. To do this effectively, you need to understand the nature of Hvels and their role in shaping Vril energy, and then you will be able to purify and change the nature of Vril currents by balancing the energy-shaping natures of your Hvels.

Hvel is old Norse for "wheel." Hvels are centers of Vril energy within the human body where Vril is concentrated, and correspond to the organization of the psychic powers of the mind that are powered by these currents of Vril flowing through your body. Throughout your body, you have points where Vril congregates, like pools where currents of water from merging rivers form whirlpools and vortexes. This happens at junctions where two or more rivers join. The flow of water then interacts and the force of movement will cause these whirlpools or vortexes containing powerful currents that can cause ships, boats and people to either sink or crash. The same is true of the flow of Vril energy throughout your body. The Chinese and Indians refer to them as Chakras (Sanskrit for "wheel") and claim that there are thousands (88,000) of such points of whirlpool energy. These points of energy, or whirlpools of energy, are the basis of the science of acupuncture. We refer to Chakras as Hvels, which are whirling centers of Vril energy. Though there are thousands of these points through your body, we will concentrate on the nine primary Hvels.

We have discussed how your Orlog is a storehouse of your thoughts, emotions and actions and acts collectively as a filtering agent of Vril energy, changing its nature and controlling its flow throughout your body and soul. What you think about, especially when you obsess on something, will control your emotional state, which in turn charges your Vril energy, causing it to take on its nature. In others words, the things you obsess on the most will affect your energy centers. Your obsessions will affect the Hvel energy centers.

Two Runes that are important to discuss in relationship to these Hvels are Sowilo and Eihwaz. Sowilo represents the Vril currents coursing through the body while Eihwaz represents the spinal column or cosmic axis (Yggdrasill). What is interesting is the shape of the two Runes. If you examine them you will discover that Eihwaz is a elongated version of Sowilo, tipped on its side.

The Asian traditions refer to seven primary Hvels or Chakras, though there are considered about eighty-eight thousand minor points of energy (Charras or Hvels) throughout the body. In Vrilology we consider there to be nine main psychic energy centers or Hvels. The eighth is above the feet and the ninth is below the feet.

The Nine Primary Hvels

Vrilology works with nine Hvels, which corresponds to the nine worlds of the Yggdrasill. Vril energy enters the human body through many avenues, but primarily through the head, being attracted to the power of the mind, represented as the "crown center" or the Asgard Hvel. It is then sent down the spinal cord by way of the sympathetic nervous system trunk channels that travel through the ganglia. As it travels down the spinal cord it is comparable the unorganized Vrilic energy that filled the universe at the beginning of time, that gave rise to the Ginnungagap. It passes down to the feet where it congregates in the two Hvels located below the feet, which correspond to Muspellheim, and just above the feet, which corresponds to Niflheim. Within these Hvels, Vril takes on the qualities of fire (expansive force) and ice (contractive form). It is here, where the two feet usually perform motion in the form of walking, that the forces mix and create the combustion of life in the formation of Ymir. Sparks rise from the Sole Hvel and mix with the Feet Hvel, causing a reaction similar to the Big Bang. Creation takes place. Thus, between the Feet Hvel (Niflheim) and the Sole Hvel (Musspellheim) we see the Ymir Factor take place. The Vrilic currents that now flow upward, back up the spinal cord (Yggdraill or Eihwaz Rune), will pass through the other seven Hvels corresponding to the other seven worlds of the Yggdrasill. As it does, it will be transformed, just as Ymir was transformed by Odin, Vili and Ve.

As Vril passes upward, it moves through each of the other Hvels, being transformed in different and specialized ways. It is this process of Vril moving upward, passing through each Hvel or world, that mirrors the reconstruction of Ymir by Odin, Vili and Ve, using his various parts, refashioning them in an orderly way, transforming formless and chaotic energy into a systematically organized cosmos.

1) Crown Hvel – Asgard – Othala (Dagaz)
2) Brow or Third Eye Hvel – Vanaheim – Dagaz (Elhaz, Mannaz, Othala)
3) Throat Hvel – Ljossalfheim – Ansuz
4) Heart Hvel – Midgard – Wunjo (Perthro, Sowilo)
5) Solar Plexus Hvel – Svartalfheim – Thuriaz (Jera, Uruz)

6) Spleen Hvel – Jotunheim – Laguz
7) Root Hvel – Hel – Kenaz (Fehu)
8) Feet Hvel – Niflheim – Isa (Hagalaz)
9) Sole Hvel – Muspellheim – Fehu

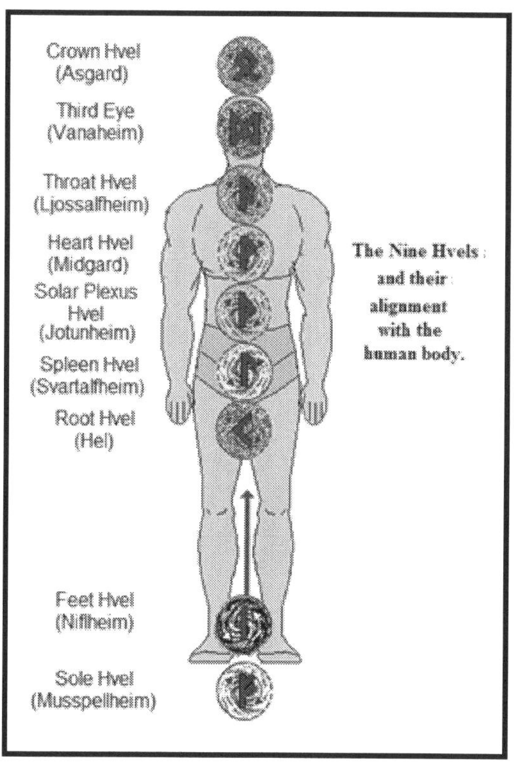

The Nine Hvels and their alignment with the human body.

At the Root Hvel, which represents Hel, the realm where the ego is asleep and unaware of its true esoteric heritage, Vrilic energy causes the inner Self, the awakening Ego-self human being, to regain consciousness of itself and its true heritage, and then rise from the Netherworld, much as Balder rises from the Netherworld and heralds in the Golden Age of Gimli.

Once Vril energy reaches your Mind, after passing through all the Hvels, it is then sent back down your spinal cord through the sympathetic nervous system to every part of your body, feeding Vril energy to every atom within your body and soul.

As Vril energy courses throughout your body, along your nervous system, it passes through the thousands of smaller points or Hvels where the nervous system branches off in different directions. It is at these Hvels that Vril energy coalesces into whirlpool-like vortexes. Every living creature has such points or Hvels, but for now we will concentrate on the nine most important Hvels, which are located deep within the center of your physical body, which is also part of the multi-dimensional extended Soul, and are aligned along the axis of your body that is aligned with your spine.

The Hvels in the lower regions of your body whirl at slower rates than those located in the higher areas of your body. They spin in a clockwise direction. If you were looking directly at a person, you could imagine them spinning on their side, like a ceiling fan suspended from a ceiling. The energy whirling within the Hvels spin faster in those Hvels located in the upper parts of the body and slower in the lower regions. The Feet and Sole Hvels have a different nature that we will explain shortly. The hues of the energy in each Hvel also appear to be of different colors, much as your aura can change color depending on the nature of the spirito-psychic make-up of your Soul. This change in the color of your aura is the result of what is going on in your Hvels — how Vril energy is transformed as it passes through your Hvels.

SOLE HVEL (Musspellheim): This Hvel is one of expansive power and represents the universal principle of Male Force. Here you can draw on the endless flow of Vril energy, increase its force and then release it. This is the center from which the force of pure energy constantly expands away from itself. The Sole Hvel is like a nuclear explosion, in which endless energy is released. This Hvel affects thoughts and feelings about all things dealing with expansion, growth and development, new adventures, increasing one's energy, strength and endurance. The Sole Hvel is actually the fastest spinning Hvel, even faster than the Crown. Because it spins so fast that its spinning is almost invisible, it appears like a white light. Here we have the paradox of opposites becoming one.

Vril energy that passes through the Sole Hvel will be charged and multiplied very rapidly, and quickly be drawn into the attracting force of the Feet Hvel.

If this Hvel is under-active, it will not be able to charge Vril so that it can expand enough to flow properly. If it is over active, you will have a tendency to be hyper and high strung. The Rune that governs this Hvel is Fehu.

FEET HVEL (Niflheim): The Feet Hvel is where energy is drawn into, like a black hole drawing in energy into its center, where it is compressed and compacted. The Feet Hvel represents the universal principle of Female Form. Force is mixed with Form and then released to create order. Within this Hvel, Force takes on shape and is transformed into matter. It deals with all matters concerning manifesting ideas, things and goals, and draws them into your life. The energy that is given expansive force in the Sole Hvel (Musspellheim) is drawn into this black hole and transformed into object-creating power that is then released upward toward the other seven Hvels. The Rune that governs this Hvel is Isa. This Hvel deals with all thoughts and feelings dealing with conservation, preserving, holding on to what one has, confinement, control, imprisonment, steadfastness. The Feet Hvel is the slowest spinning Hvel, and is almost motionless. Like a Black Hole, it appears Black.

Vril energy that has passed through the Sole Hvel is drawn into the Feet Hvel and compressed. The combined Form and Force of these two Hvels causes a chain reaction that sends Vril energy flowing back up the spinal column, causing it to pass through the upper seven Hvels. The Vril that is sent upward is now in balance, permitting it to be shaped by the other seven Hvels.

If this Hvel is dirty, you will find that you are unable to crystallize, or have trouble crystalizing, your thoughts and making things take form in your life. If it is over active, and out of balance, it will cause inertia and even paralysis, preventing you from taking action.

ROOT HVEL (Hel): Located at the base of the spinal column, the Root Hvel is the slowest spinning Hvel next to the Feet Hvel. Its slow rate causes it to appear like a brilliant red, like a red sun. When this Hvel is cleansed, there will appear sparkling white lights which mingle with the red color of the Root Hvel. But when it gets dirty, the reddish color turns a murky, dark red like that of dry blood.
ril energy that passes through the Root Hvel will affect the following things in your life:

- All financial issues dealing with money, investments, retirement, the economy, gambling, spending money, your career, your income, having the right job for you, promotions and advancements, employment and unemployment and your thoughts, plans and fears about your future financial well being.
- The home and where you will live, if you should move, how you maintain the upkeep of your home, its arrangement, and thoughts where you would love to live.
- Physical safety issues dealing with your sense of being safe or unsafe.
- Your needs, fear about having enough money to live on, enough food, sufficient clothing and other goods needed to maintain your well being.
- All issues dealing with possessions and material goods and things you need to survive.

The Rune that governs this Hvel is the Rune Kenaz.

Anxiety over the lack of material needs in your life can cause this Hvel to become dirty and shrink. Worrying about money will cause the energy-creating power of the Hvel to decline. Obsessions about money, career and possessions (the workaholic mind-set) causes this Hvel to slow and become "dirty" with the residue of such thoughts, much in the same way that slow-moving water will not be able to filter out the impurities within itself. Obsessions create imbalances, because when you obsess over things, the Hvels dealing with them will become under-active. This will affect the flow of Vril throughout your body, thus preventing some parts of your body from receiving the much-needed Vrilic energy, and thus permit decay, causing illness and aging.

SPLEEN HVEL (Svartalfheim): Sometimes referred as the Sacral Hvel, this Hvel is located midway between your navel and the base of your spine, and is connected to your spleen, the gland in your abdomen in which blood is modified. This Hvel spins slightly faster than the Root Hvel. It appears as a orangish-yellow color. A balanced Spleen Hvel appears more yellowish, while a dirty Hvel changes into a darker orange color.

The Spleen or Sacral Hvel governs those things dealing with cravings for physical pleasures such as eating, drinking, sex, or thrill-seeking. It deals with issues of addictions that includes drugs, gluttony, alcoholism, sexual perversions and promiscuity, and all things dealing with your body, such as exercise habits, sleeping patterns, weight problems, health habits, and obsessions about your physical appearance.

If you obsess over any of these issues, your Spleen Hvel will shrink and grow dirty, causing you to suffer from fatigue or listlessness. If you obsess on the appearance of your body, your Spleen Hvel will appear dirty and oversized. Having an over-sized or over-active Hvel is not a problem; it is only when there is extreme imbalance among the Hvels that problems get out of hand.

SOLAR PLEXUS HVEL (Jotunheim): The Solar Plexus Hvel is located just behind the navel. This Hvel spins at a slightly higher speed than the Spleen Hvel, and appears bright green in color. When clean it turns almost yellowish green, but when dirty it grows dark. The Solar Plexus is affected by obsessive thoughts and feelings dealing with issues of power relating to the fear of power and being out of control; fear of powerful people or authority figures; obsessions with power; concerns about people or nations that have too much power in the world; obsessions with past experiences of being overwhelmed or dominated by people with too much authority or power; issues dealing with fear of being controlled or losing control; the desire to control yourself, situation and others; or fear of being out of control.

Solar Plexus Hvel is governed by the Rune Thurisaz, but the Runes Uruz and Jera have lesser, secondary influences on this Hvel. If you obsess on fears of being controlled and manipulated, whether individually or by some grand conspiracy, your Hvel will grow dark and appear dirty. Fear of not having power will cause you to lose control over your life. If you obsess about having power over others, your Hvel will become over-active and if not balanced with the other Hvels, it will cause you to become intolerant or others, seeing everyone that does not agree with you 100% as your enemy or someone to be despised.

HEART HVEL (Midgard): The Heart Hvel is located in the center of the chest and represents Midgard, which is at the center of all things in relationship to human physical existence. It is the central point between the Root Hvel, representing Hel, and the Crown Hvel, representing Asgard. The Heart Hvel and all higher Hvels deal with spiritual issues. The Heart Hvel spins at a medium-fast rate and it is gold in color. A cleansed and balanced Heart Hvel shines a bright gold but a dirty or slow-moving Heart Hvel is tarnished and dirty-greenish.

The Heart Hvel is affected by thoughts and feelings dealing with issues of relationships with your parents, children, grandparents, your lovers or spouses, friends, co-workers, partners, employees, and just about everyonc you come into contact with. It deals with love, which includes Divine Love, your higher self, romantic love, platonic love and familial love. Personal attachments that include co-dependencies, dysfunctional relationships, and obsessions about a person are governed by this Hvel. Issues dealing with forgiveness or lack of forgiveness toward oneself, toward others, including both the living and the deceased, toward entities including countries, races, groups of people, governments and other organizations are also governed by the Heart Hvel. The Rune dealing with the Heart Hvel is Wunjo. Other, lesser Runes associated with the power of the Heart Hvel are Sowilo and Perthro.

Any fears about receiving love or giving love cause this Hvel to shrink and slow its rate of spinning. Relationship addictions cause it to grow dirty. This is also true of harmful love relationships. Distorted love, perverted love and misguided love will all badly affect the Heart Hvel. Love can be a source of great strength if it is not mistaken for ownership and possession, and instead we realize that the Love-Force gives us awareness that we have nothing to fear, like Balder who is invincible. His only weakness is the Mistletoe, which can be made into either a great love potion or a terrible poison.

The Heart Hvel is central to creating balance of the Hvels located throughout the Yggdrasill spinal column. It is here, in Midgard, that we can achieve the state of Balder Risen.

THROAT HVEL (Vanaheim): Located at the Adam's Apple is the Throat Hvel or Vanaheim. This Hvel is connected to the thyroid gland, and its color is blue. When it's clean it is a sparkling sky blue, but when it is dirty it looks greyish-blue.

The Throat Hvel governs those thoughts and feelings dealing with communication involving singing, writing, speaking, oratory, artistic projects, channeling, and teaching. It deals with the need to speak the truth to yourself and to others, especially those people who are close to you, who trust you, such as loved ones, family members and people who are dependent on you. It also deals with communication with the Gods and higher forces, with loved ones and others close to you in your life. If you lie and tell falsehoods you will cause your Throat Hvel to grow dirty and slow its rate of spinning. If you deliberately seek to cheat and harm others for your own benefit then this Hvel will grow very dark and appear like storm clouds in color.

Ansuz is the Rune that controls this Hvel.

THIRD EYE HVEL (Ljossalfheim): Above the Throat Hvel is the Third Eye Hvel. In Vrilology we refer to the Third Eye as the Bifrost Gland. This is actually two glands, the pituitary and pineal glands. If you close your eyes and concentrate your mind on the spot in your forehead between your eyes, (the Alpha State or Asgard State of Consciousness) you will see an oval shaped object lying on the inside of your eyelids. This is your Third Eye. The Third Eye, or Bifrost Gland, is the means by which you can communicate with beings who exist on planes of reality of higher frequencies.

The color of this Hvel is indigo.

The Third Eye Hvel is governed by the Rune Dagaz, the Rune of enlightenment, but secondarily by Elhaz, the Rune of communication with the Gods, personified by the Valkyries.

The Third Eye Hvel governs issues dealing with the future, the willingness to see into your future; the past, and the willingness to deal with issues of the past that affect your Orlog, or the lack of courage to deal with them. It also deals with your willingness to accept your own abilities to connect with the Gods, to raise your consciousness and accept the truth that you actually have psychic powers.

CROWN HVEL (Asgard): The ninth major Hvel is the Crown Hvel because it is actually on the top of your head. This Hvel is associated with Asgard, and its color is royal purple. The state of this Hvel is essential for all clair-powers and your ability to receive thoughts, information, visions and ideas from the Gods and your Kin-Fetch or collective/racial consciousness.

The Crown Hvel is governed by Othala. This Rune is the Rune of Odin and the Folk collectively.

The Crown Hvel governs thoughts and feelings dealing with the Gods, the Supreme Consciousness, whether we believe in such powers or if we are atheists, religion and spirituality and all dealings with negative experiences from formal religions, and your anger or disillusionment with religion. Our feelings about Divine guidance and our ability to receive direction from higher powers is governed by this Hvel. Many feel threatened by the thought that there is a higher intelligence telling them what to do, and this can affect your Crown Hvel. Our willingness or unwillingness to believe in such higher forces is governed by this Hvel. Trust in the Gods is rooted in the Crown Hvel. If you lack trust in the Gods, or do not believe in higher powers, it is because this Hvel is weak and dirty, spinning slowly.

Kundalini Fire (Charged Vril Energy)

Kundalini is a Sanskrit word meaning either "coiled up" or "coiling like a snake." There are a number of other translations of the term usually emphasizing a more serpentine nature to the word . The concept of Kundalini comes from yogic philosophy of ancient India, which was conquered and settled by Indo-Europeans that referred to themselves as Aryans or Ar-yans. It is from them that we get the name that we give to the original people from which all Indo-Europeans are descended. They retained some of the secret science of Vrilology that was in their possession before their great civilization, located on the shores of the Black Sea, was destroyed in 5600 BCE., and brought it into India, which eventually evolved into the Vedic tradition and lore. In time, this knowledge was transformed by its incorporation with alien ideas belonging to indigenous peoples of southern Asia, and became corrupted. But there is still a great deal to be learned from the Vedic tradition as a source of ancient Indo-European knowledge. We mention Kundalini Fire to show how the ancient knowledge of Vrilology has been transformed by various cultures that can trace their ancestry to the original mother civilization

Kundalini might be regarded by yogis as a sort of deity, hence the occasional capitalization of the term, just as we capitalize Vril, which is the Life Force of the Gods.

According to the yogic tradition, Kundalini (Vril) coils up in the back part of the Root Chakra in three and one-half turns around the sacrum. Yogic phenomenology states that Kundalini

Awakening is associated with the appearance of bio-energetic (Vrilic) phenomena that are said to be experienced somatically by the yogi. Somewhere between the twelfth and fifteenth centuries, Swami Svatmarama wrote the Hatha Yoga Pradipika, which is the source text for the concept of Kundalini. Within Western tradition it is often associated with the practice of contemplative or religious practices that might induce an altered state of consciousness. This is what we mean when we have a religious epiphany that can be induced spontaneously, through some type of yoga, meditation, or in a more destructive way through the use of psychedelic drugs, or through a near-death experience.

This experience is also referred to as "pranic awakening." Prana is interpreted as the vital, life-sustaining force in the body, which of course is Vril. When Vrilic energy is intensified and has an uplifting effect it is referred to as pranotthana. This phenomenon is supposed to originate from an apparent reservoir of subtle bio-energy at the base of the spine, but we will explain that it actually originates well below the base of the spine. The location is at the feet, (above the feet is the "Feet Hvel" and below the feet is the "Sole Hvel") where two Hvels are situated, corresponding to the two original worlds of Musspellheim and Niflheim. It is between these two Hvels that this reservoir of subtle bio-energy is located. It is here that the expansive force of Musspellheim and the contractive form of Niflheim cause Vril energy to build up and become charged with the life-giving qualities. This energy is also interpreted as a vibrational phenomenon that initiates a period or process of vibrational spiritual development.

Two early western interpretations of Kundalini were supplied by C.W. Leadbeater (1847-1934), of the Theosophical Society, and the analytical psychologist Carl Jung (1875-1961). In 1

We won't continue this discussion of Kundalini Fire, but only touched on the subject to demonstrate that knowledge of Vril energy, and how it can be used to transform the individual, has been preserved by Indo-European refugees after the destruction of their ancient Aryan civilization, and has been passed down through the millenniums in other cultures.

The Use of Nauthiz

Nauthiz is a third Rune we need to discuss and use to transform Vril energy currents as they pass through your Hvels. The way Nauthiz is used to modify your Wyrd is through its principle of using the power of resistance to restrict and restrain incoming negative forces, by "fettering" their negative influences, and to eliminate conflict through the power of directed mental force or willpower.

The exercise we will provide you will use Nauthiz to cleanse or bend the energy of each Hvel as Vril flows down the spine to your Sole Hvel. After each Hvel has been cleansed of negativity, you will send Vril back up the spine, passing through each Hvel.

The force of cosmic resistance was born when the universe was manifested. This principle is behind the law: Every action has an equal and opposite reaction. In psychic teaching this law is embodied in the principle of cause and effect. In Vrilology this law is known as Orlog, which means primal layers. And within Orlog there is the force of Wyrd, which is the process where past actions, thoughts and feelings are woven into pathways in your future and present. Remember that a pathway is a path connecting your present with some point in your future. But unlike karma, your future is not set in stone. With the proper knowledge, you can learn to control or affect your future. Thus Wyrd is not simply the end result of what is in your Orlog, but the means to bend your Orlog, and this can be done with the Rune Nauthiz.

When we state that you can cleanse, we do not mean eliminate what is stored in your Orlog, but bend or transform negativity into something positive.

We have covered many topics in the course of these lessons, including how the Norns weave your Wyrd into a web of life from what you have stored in your Orlog, and despite the influence of what past experiences are stored within your Orlog, you still have the power of free will to bend your Wyrd, and thus possess control over your destiny. Most people do not understand this truism, and so they become slaves to their fate.

The Rune that we can use to "bend" our Web of Wyrd is Nauthiz. People are constantly bending their Wyrd by making drastic changes in their lives. They can change their jobs or move to a different city. But most people will find such decisions difficult to make because they do not know how to bend their Web of Wyrd through the use of Runes and especially Nauthiz. The reason why most people find it difficult to change jobs, move, or make other life-changing decisions is they are slaves to their Web of Wyrd, which was woven by what they carry around with them in their Orlog.

The German occultist Guido von List wrote of the Rune Nauthiz: "The need-rune blooms on the nail of the Norn! This is not 'need' (distress) in the modern sense of the word, but rather the 'compulsion of fate'–that the Norns fix according to primal laws. With this, the organic causality of all phenomena is to be understood. Whoever is able to grasp the primal cause of a phenomenon, and whoever gains knowledge of organically lawful evolution and the phenomena arising from it, is also able to judge their consequences just as they are beginning to ferment. Therefore, he commands knowledge of the future and also understands how to settle all strife through 'the constraint of the clearly recognized way of fate.' Therefore: 'Use your fate, do not strive against it!'"

List explains that Nauthiz can be used to bend the forces of Orlog and Wyrd, just as a judo expert uses the weight of his opponent against him–redirecting the force of his opponent to his advantage rather then struggling against it head-on. Thus, Nauthiz should be helpful to you in dealing with negative influences that arise within your life, by removing conflict through the redirection of the negative influences, thus permitting you to achieve your goals.

Whether the obstacles arise from your Orlog, or the Orlog of the situation (could be the accumulation of negativity of the place of employment, the home you live in, your family or the family of your spouse, etc...) you can use Nauthiz like using the stored up energy within the tension of the bow string to redirect the energy to your advantage, by changing the pattern of Wyrd, and thus re-weaving the web. This in essence is what Moses did when he parted the Red Sea. He did not struggle against the currents of the sea, but used the power of need-fire to part the water, and thus removed the obstacle that stood in his way. Northern Lore tells us that the Norns representing the past and present are weaving your Wyrd. Skuld, the Norn representing your future, is tearing up what her two sisters are weaving. This means you have the power to control your destiny if you learn to master the runic energies. You can meditate on Nauthiz and visualize the Norn Skuld, ripping up the weave of the past and the present, and rearranging the threads of your future Wyrd into a pathway more in line with what you desire to manifest in your future.

Endocrine Glands and Sowilo

Certain Hvels are connected to, and affect, various endocrine glands. The glands of the endocrine system are known as the "ductless glands." They affect the physical well being and health of the individual. If the flow of Vril e nergy is disrupted or slowed in any way, this can have an adverse effect on the endocrine glands, and thus affect the health of the individual. These endocrine glands are the master internal controlling mechanism that regulates balance and the relationship between the mind and the body. Since it is the subconscious portion of the mind that controls those body functions that the conscious mind does not deal with, any interruption of the flow of Vril energy through the endocrine glands will cause a disruption of the bodily functions and result in an adverse effect on the body, much in the same way a car will run out of control if the driver falls asleep at the wheel while driving.

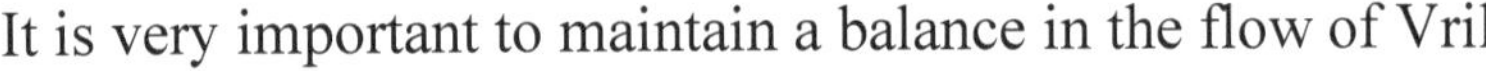

It is very important to maintain a balance in the flow of Vril

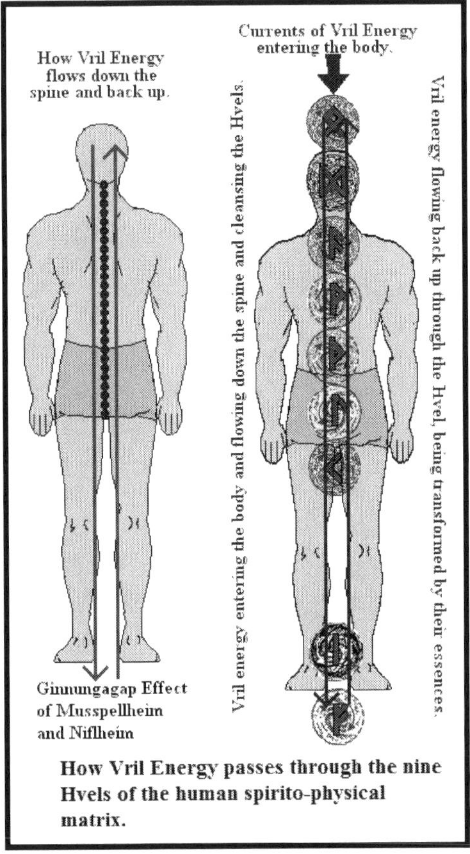

How Vril Energy passes through the nine Hvels of the human spirito-physical matrix.

through these glands. Even the slightest imbalance will generate fluctuations in hormonal secretions. Though they might be extremely small amounts, they are extremely powerful. Once they enter directly into the blood stream, the effect they can create might be subtle, but the effects will be instantaneous, and cause changes in mood, appearance, respiration, digestion, initiative, relaxation, and intelligence.

The use of the runic energies of Sowilo is very effective in cleansing the Hvels. Each Hvel appears like a sun wheel of whirling Vril energy. The sun-like energies of Sowilo can be used to cleanse the passageways in which Vril energy flows, helping to maintain each Hvel functioning at optimum levels of performance. This will assure that energy flowing into each Hvel is increased and balanced so that these "sun wheels" will shine clearly and powerfully, influencing the operation of the endocrine glands. Without the use of Sowilo to energize and cleanse the Hvels, the energy flowing into them will decrease and eventually be blocked by the negative forces of the Orlog, thus causing them to slow their whirling force, and cause the human body to grow sluggish, permitting aging and illness to increase. When the natural balance is restored, the Hvels will grow stronger. This can be done with Sowilo. The upward flow of Vril through the spinal column will then be helped with the runic force of Eihwaz. The end result will be a continuous and increased flow of Vril energy throughout the body, creating and maintaining conditions of natural well being, good health, harmony and wholeness throughout your entire Vrilic energy system.

Exercise to Balance Your Energy Centers or Hvels

1) You should sit in a comfortable position. You do not have to sit on the floor with legs crossed, but you should sit with your back erect and straight. If you are sitting in a chair, make sure it is a straight back chair. You should try to place your feet under the chair so that they are in alignment with your spine. As you sit erect, your spine should be in line with the earth's center.

2) Relax your entire body in the way you have been taught in earlier lessons. Take your time and make sure every muscle in your body is relaxed.

3) Perform your breathing exercises. Feel Vril energy entering your body through your mouth as you breathe in. Feel Vril filling your lungs and hold it for a few seconds. Then exhale slowly.

4) Enter your Asgard State of Consciousness (Alpha State).

5) Once you have achieved your ASC (Alpha), envision a vertical double helix of vibrant Vril energy flowing down along your spinal column. Visualize your spinal column as a huge

Eihwaz Rune, with the top over your head, where the Crown Hvel is located, and the bottom below your feet, where the Sole Hvel is located. Understand that Vril energy is being drawn down from the sun above and then flows down to your feet, where it mixes with the energy of the earth beneath you.

6) Beginning at the top of the Eihwaz, and focus your attention on your Hvels as Vril flows down your spinal column. Starting from the top of your head, visualize your Crown Hvel opening. Watch as pure white light enters your crown Hvel, filling it with a gentle vortex of energy. Visualize the energy forming the Rune Nauthiz within the Hvel cleansing your Hvel of all negativity, releasing any blockages.

7) Vril energy now flows down your spinal column, filling the Third Eye Hvel with Vril energy that whirls and forms a Nauthiz, cleansing it and releasing any blockages. You might have visions of multicolors representing the Rainbow Bridge.

8) The white light moves down to your Throat Hvel, forming Nauthiz and releasing your blockages. Its energies whirl, unleashing the power of Nauthiz to cleanse all negativity within this Hvel. You may feel like chanting or singing certain Runes. Allow the tones to resonate from your throat. Take note of which Runes appear and do not try to chose the Rune. Do this as long as it is comfortable.

9) White light now enters your Heart Hvel, filling it with Vril energy. The same whirling action takes place forming the cleansing power of Nauthiz. You experience a feeling of unconditional love and compassion.

10) The white light enters your Solar Plexus Hvel, filling it with Vril, forming Nauthiz. Gently, your fears, anger, and tensions are released as Nauthiz cleanses this Hvel of negativity.

11) See the white light entering your Spleen Hvel, filling it with whirling Vril energy, forming Nauthiz and cleansing it of all blockages, releasing pain and guilt linked to that Hvel.

12) The white light now enters your Root Hvel, filling it with Vril energy. It whirls about forming Nauthiz, releasing any blockages.

13) The white light now descends down to the Feet Hvel. Once again if fills the Hvel, forming a Nauthiz, cleansing it of any blockages.

14) The white light now enters the lowest of Hvels, the Sole Hvel, located beneath the feet. As it does, it begins to activate the energy of the Sole (Musspellheim) Hvel.

15) Here, Vril energy is harnessed in the Sole Hvel, which is located beneath your feet. This Hvel is Musspellheim, and is ruled by the Rune Fehu. Within this Hvel, Vril energy is caught up and begins swirling about, transformed by the expansive force of the Fire Rune. Visualize the Rune Fehu charging Vril energy and then sending it upward toward the Feet Hvel (Niflheim).

With the correct meditative process we will endeavor to channel the currents of Vril energy entering your body down your spine to the two lowest Hvels located above and below your feet. There, the energy will replicate the creative process that gave rise to the proto-life forms of Ymir and Andhumla, and then send this energy back up the spine, passing through the other seven primary Hvels, causing it to be transformed before disseminating the Vril energy throughout your physical and auric bodies.

16) The heated Vril energy rises to the second Hvel located just above the feet. This Hvel is Niflheim and ruled by the Rune Isa. Vril energy forms fiery sparks that rise from the Sole Hvel, mixing with the icy forces of the Feet Hvel, and combustion occurs. As a generative force, Vril energy is sent back up the spinal cord axis and reaches the Root Hvel (Hel).

17) From the Feet Hvel, Vril energy now rises to the Root or Hel Hvel. Feel it entering and charging the Hvel. This Hvel is ruled by Kenaz, representing generative powers of creation. As it does, visualize Vril forming a Sowilo Rune, radiating bright yellow light like the sun, charging the Hvel, increasing its Kenaz strength.

18) Now visualize Vril energy rising once more in spiraling coils into the Spleen or Svartalfheim Hvel. This Hvel is ruled by Laguz. Feel the Sowilo energy charging and increasing the Laguz energy, strengthening your psychic powers.

19) Vril energy continues to spiral upward, like a whirling Sowilo, filling the Solar Plexus or Jotunheim Hvel. Its radiating power strengthens the Thurisaz power of the Rune that rules this Hvel.

20) Vril now spirals into the Heart Hvel of Midgard. Sowilo charges its energy, increasing the harmonic power of Wunjo that rules this Hvel.

21) Visualize the upward spiraling power of Vril filling the Throat or Ljossalfheim Hvel. The Sun power of Sowilo strengthens the Ansuz energies of this Hvel, increasing your powers to communicate with the Gods.

22) Vril continues to spiral upward, charging the Third Eye of the Vanaheim Hvel with radiating Sowilo shaped Vril energy. The Dagaz Rune of enlightenment is charged and strengthened.

23) Finally, Vril energy flows into the Crown or Asgard Hvel, charging and strengthening the Othala energies of this Hvel with Sowilo energy. The process of cleansing, charging, strengthening and balancing your Hvels is completed.

Through this exercise, Vril energy spiraled up through your spine as if it were a coiled snake. The coiled snake represents the spiraling DNA, opening, activating, bringing you to higher levels of consciousness. (Remember the story of how Odin transformed himself into a snake and passed through a hole to reach the mead of Wisdom?) Allow the energy to flow through your Hvels, concentrating its Sowilo energy to strengthen your individual Hvel energies. See the energy forming a whirling Sowilo within the Hvel wheels as they rotate. Know that your Hvels have been cleansed of blockage and strengthened, increasing their power equally and creating a balance among all the Hvels.

When you are ready, return your consciousness to your physical body. Relax and balancc your energies. You might want to drink some water.

Why Do You Need to Activate and Balance Your Hvels

The human form is part of a multidimensional soul, as we have shown during our exploration of the Soul in earlier lessons, and each aspect of the Soul has its own frequency and vibration linked into multiple aspects of totality of the Soul. Hvels are energy vortexes in our emotional, mental and spiritual bodies. The physical body is a series of separate yet related systems of energy. A Hvel is the interface point between the physical and non-physical form.

Hvels lie along a linear pathway (along the spine) from the Crown Hvel, located at the top of the cranium, to the Sole Hvel located beneath the soles of the feet. These nine Hvels, representing the nine worlds within axis of the Yggdrasill, are symbolic of organized Vrilic energy, functioning as pathways for energy that flows through subtle channels in the spine, and govern the endocrine system throughout the etheric body. As Vril energy passes through and is concentrated within each Hvel, it takes on the life-giving qualities of the Hvels. Each Hvel acts a transformer within the body, coloring the Vril with its own properties. There are seven endocrine glands, each with a vibration and color, and one is assigned to seven of the nine primary Hvels.

Each color of the energy within a Hvel expresses a range of frequencies that fall within specific wavelengths of radiant information. The colors of the visible light system are just above Infrared and below Ultraviolet. The Hvels are specifically designed to act as one level of a tuning antenna. They intercept specific wavelengths of energy containing radiant information, and bring that information down into the density of the body structure to be utilized. Additionally, more refined tuning occurs at the molecular level, as genetic receptors receive information at an even greater level of vibration frequency.

The spin rate of the Hvels is a part of the fine tuning of this system. The higher Hvels spin faster than the lower ones. There is a direct relationship between each individual Hvel center and the specific ranges of energy within the human/creation Matrix. The Hvel is the interface point, the energetic organ linking various aspects of the physical body to its non-physical counterparts...i.e. the Matrix Grid.

It is through this interface that the reality of the human experience becomes apparent. The human being is not the individual and independent being as we perceive. The body is connected to one level of an interlocking series of grids. These grids, having nine sections or sets of vibrations, with nine levels of knowledge in each section, are ranges of experience referred to as Dimensions.

Only the Feet or Niflehim (which send Vril energy into the Root or Hel Hvel), Solar Plexus, Jotunheim and Crown, Asgard Hvels, which correspond to the three wells that feed the tree roots of Yggdrasill, Hvergelmir, Mimir and Urd, are able to access and receive energies from the Higher Self. Any other Hvel can receive these energies only after they have been filtered through one of these three Hvels.

The movement of the feet during your normal waking hours is representative of the generative process of fire mixing with ice creating Ymir. This unorganized, chaotic Vril energy is nourished by Audhumla, which is personified by the earth which your feet walk upon. Vril energy is then sent back up through the seven other Hvels. As it passes through each, it enters and whirls about each Hvel, incorporating the energy-charging nature of each Hvel. As it finally reaches and passes through the Crown or Asgard Hvel, the now perfected mind, the Mannaz Mind, which has been created through balancing the powers of the two halves of the brain, representing Muninn and Huginn, thus creating the Odin consciousness, now sends Vril back down through the spine, passing through the nervous system to every part of the body with its charged powers, to improve and replenish the entire spirito-physical matrix that is the human body/soul.

Through aging, illness, and absorption of negativity in your life, the Hvels begin to collapse into the body and slow their rate of spinning. The ancients knew of this and designed Runic mantras and meditation techniques to maintain the vitality and spin-rate of the Hvels. A Hvel activation (and balance) meditation practice is recommended daily (or at minimum once a week).

Opening and activating your Hvels allows your Vrilic energies to flow up the subtle channels to your Crown Hvel. It is important to first work on opening up your subtle channels through special physical and deep or full breathing exercises that you learned in earlier lessons. Once your channels are open, clearing the Hvels will allow the energies to fully open up and charge your entire system. Even sexual energies can be directed up to the Crown as the Vril energy is activated during sexual arousal.

The way the Hvels transform Vril that flows through our bodies is determined by our Orlog and the residue of feelings, thoughts and actions that fill it, reflecting decisions we made concerning how we chose to respond to conditions throughout our life. We open and close these valves when we decide what to think, and what to feel, and through which perceptual filter we choose to experience the world around us. Our thoughts and feelings thus fill the Orlog, tainting Vril as it flows through our bodies.

The Hvels are not physical. They are aspects of consciousness in the same way that the auras are aspects of consciousness. The Hvels are more dense than the auras, but not as dense as the physical body. They interact with the physical body through two major vehicles, the endocrine system and the nervous system. Hvels are associated with different endocrine glands, and also with a group of nerves called a plexus. Thus, each Hvel can be associated with particular parts of the body, and particular functions within the body, controlled by that plexus or that endocrine gland associated with that Hvel.

The nine Hvels representing the nine worlds of the Yggdrasill are a blueprint or matrix for completing your evolution into a higher form of life. The entire process of charging Vril and using it to recharge every atom within your body with Vril energy, and learning how to guide and manipulate the process, is the secret of Balder Rising. You are using this methodology to awaken the Gods within. It is what we mean when we say — Balder Rising.

All of your senses, all of your perceptions, all of your possible states of awareness, everything that is possible for you to experience, can be divided into categories. Each category can be associated with a particular Hvel. Thus, the Hvels represent not only particular parts of your physical body, but also particular parts of your consciousness.

When you feel tension in your consciousness, you feel it in the Hvel associated with that part of your consciousness experiencing stress, and in the parts of the physical body associated with that Hvel. Where you feel stress depends upon why you feel the stress. The tension in the Hvel is detected by the nerves of the plexus associated with that Hvel, and transmitted to the parts of the body controlled by that plexus. When the tension continues over a period of time, or to a particular level of intensity, the person creates a symptom on the physical level.

The symptom speaks a language that reflects the idea that we each create our own reality, and the metaphoric significance of the symptom becomes apparent when the symptom is described from that point of view. Thus, rather than saying, "I can't see," you should describe it as keeping yourself from seeing something. "I can't walk," means you have been keeping yourself from walking away from a situation in which you are unhappy. And so on.

The symptom served to communicate to you through your body what you have been doing to yourself in your consciousness. When you change something about your way of being, getting the message communicated by the symptom, the symptom has no further reason for being, and it can be released, according to whatever you allow yourself to believe is possible.

We believe everything is possible.

We believe that anything can be healed. It's just a question of how to do it.

Understanding the Hvels allows you to understand the relationship between your consciousness and your body, and to thus see your body as a map of your consciousness. It gives you a better understanding of yourself and those around you.

Hvels are a common concept in several disciplines of alternative medicine and traditional Oriental medicine. A Hvel is a center of energy, which has several functions. In addition to being “representative” of a particular organ or group of organs, a Hvel also controls our being on different levels of consciousness and it links these two representative states.

The concept of Hvel is very important in therapies such as Reiki, meditation, yoga, therapeutic touch, aura, etc. Because of its wider application across a number of disciplines, this is covered as a separate topic.

Chapter Six: How to Use Your Mind to Harness Vril

Know that Vril is a Universal Force

Accept the truth that Vril is a life force that gives form to all things. It is everywhere, in everything, including you. It makes up more than 99 percent of every atom in the universe. It sends a galaxy spinning in the universe, causes a flower to blossom and a volcano to explode, and breathes life into a newborn baby. Like your thoughts, feelings, dreams and imagination, it has no limits. Its dimensions are without limits, it is eternal, and it cannot be destroyed. It is the tool of both the Gods, who use it to maintain order in the universe, and the Giants, who cause chaos to ripple throughout the cosmos. It creates currents of life energy that cause the procession of history to unfold. This force is divine, and it is a divine power within you that you can learn to harness, control and shape to create the future you desire. Trust in your powers to harness Vril, and learn how to use it to change the physical world around you.

Your Thoughts and Feelings Are Instruments You Can Use to Control Vril

You must understand that your thoughts originate with you, and that you can control them and use them to change your life. Realize you can monitor your thoughts, and by doing so you can control your feelings, which generate mental energy to control and shape Vril. Once you understand that your thoughts are the means by which you store and record experiences and how you feel about them, you can begin the process of taking charge of your life and controlling your fate. Your experiences are stored in your Orlog — that part of your soul which is the blueprint by which Vril is shaped, and creates pathways that will lead you into your future. These pathways are what we refer to as Wyrd, or your Web of Wyrd. Thus, your thoughts and feelings are weaving your Web of Wyrd, which means they are creating and shaping your life, and determining your health, your wealth, your love life and your standing within the world. You live the life you imagine, by what you store in your Orlog. Thoughts and feelings manifest the pathways into your future and thus create your physical reality. If you change your thinking, you will change reality.

Know That There is No Limit in What You Can Do

Realize that what you have perceived as possible in the physical world is actually not all; there are unseen forces in the universe. Your thoughts, dreams, and feelings are real, yet you cannot see, weigh and measure them. They have no mass, but they are real. If you believe in only what you can see, hear, feel, taste or smell, you are setting limitations within your life and boundaries in what you are able to accomplish. Vril has existed everywhere since the beginning of time. We lack only the technology to harness its power, but you can do it through the power of your mind. You can decide for yourself whether you will accept this truth, and begin to teach yourself how to harness Vril and use it to change your life, or wait until society learns to harness its power technologically.

Align Yourself with the Gods

The universe is a living force constantly being shaped by the struggle between the Giants, generating chaotic forces in the universe, and the Gods, who are working to counter the Giants and maintain an orderly universe by shaping Vril. You must understand that you have a choice: You can either surrender to the chaotic forces of the Giants, or align yourself with the Gods. If you choose alignment with the Gods, you can use Vrilology to shape Vril in such a way that you will become part of the Gods' design for the universe, and manifest a life of success and joy in everything you do. By aligning with the Gods, you will discover your purpose, and things will come to you effortlessly. The system created and maintained by the Gods is intelligent. Your thoughts and feelings are blueprints constantly being sent out into the universe. If they are positive and affirming joy and happiness, then the Gods will make them a part of their design. But if your thoughts are mostly negative, they will be aligned with the chaotic force of the Giants.

Think of the universe as a great puzzle, in which the Gods and Giants are looking for pieces to put into place. If your thoughts are positive, the Gods will take them and put them into place in the puzzle they are creating, but if they are negative, they will be used by the Giants to create their grand picture of chaos and destruction. You must remember that you possess the power within you to shape those pieces, and the form you give them will determine if they will be used by the Gods or the Giants. Only by aligning with the Gods will you discover your purpose.

The Possible is That Which Has Been Done, the Impossible Has Not Yet Been Done.

Once you accept this truth, you will discover that there is nothing that you cannot achieve. You will begin to change the way you think, and once you do this, you will discover that you will be able to do things that you have always thought were impossible. Know that Vril is always with you, and you can develop the ability to increase its flow into you and use the increased supply of Vril to make things happen that you have always thought were beyond your means.

The energy generated by your thoughts has shaped Vril, creating pathways or Webs of Wyrd, that cause everything that is happening to you right now to happen. It has caused everything that has affected you in the past and everything that will affect you in the future, by the power of your thoughts and feelings. All the wonderful things that make you happy, and all the things you are complaining about have been drawn by the thoughts you send out. You might not want to accept the truth that the terrible things that have been happen to you every day are being caused by you. No one likes to admit they screwed up. It is much easier to simply blame others than to take responsibility for your actions. We jump at the opportunity to take credit for the good things that happen, but no one wants to take responsibility for the bad things that happen to them. This is understandable. Who is going to admit that they wanted to get into a car accident, or lose money in the stock market, or discover their boyfriend or girlfriend is cheating on them, or get themselves fired from their job? But once you have come to terms with this fundamental law of cause and effect, you will be transformed. This is especially true when you realize that you can prevent things from happening to you because you have the power to control them.

One of the most common misconceptions is that "you are the wrong person, in the wrong place and the wrong time." Most people will convince themselves that it was just accidental or coincidental when something happens to them. If you think this way, and continue to do so, your thoughts are going to shape the flow of Vril to create future pathways that will ensure that you will always be the wrong person, in the wrong place, at the wrong time. Let me give you a personal example:

One day I went to the supermarket. I got on the checkout line with a wagon filled with groceries. There were two people ahead of me, and soon there were three people behind me, all with wagons filled with groceries. Suddenly, a cashier opened the next counter and announced she would help the next person, but the last person on my line quickly got in that line, jumping ahead of everyone. My first thought was that it was not fair, and I was going to make a complaint about it, but I immediately caught myself and said over and over, "Cancel!" I canceled the negative thoughts, which quickly defused the growing anger and replaced them with the thought that the line I was still on is moving and there is now only one person ahead of me.

No sooner did I think of this than I heard a crash. Someone passing by the other counter had knocked a large bottle of vinegar to the floor. The broken glass and slippery floor held everything up on the other counter, preventing the shopper who cut the line from leaving. The cleaning attendant arrived immediately, but it took him a good five minutes to clean everything up. By the time I had finished paying for my groceries, and was on my way out of the store, the person who had cut the line on the newly opened counter was still waiting for the attendant to finish cleaning the mess. If I had been the one at that counter, I would still have been waiting. I left thinking, "The Vril was with me!"

So you see, it is up to you to believe you are just the wrong person, in the wrong place, at the wrong time, and that you have no control over the circumstances that affect your life, or to believe that you have control over those things that happen to you in your life. Now, no one has complete control, but you can increase the odds that good things happen to you instead of bad things. Still, whatever you wish to believe will affect the quality of your life experiences. Persistent and focused thoughts will summon whatever you obsess about.

It is even more important to notice how many times during the day your mind returns to something you are obsessing over. The next time you are upset over something, try to be aware of how often in one day you start thinking about it. You will be amazed to discover that when you are not preoccupied with some task, your mind will wander back to the obsessive thought. You might then feel that it is going to take a lot of work monitoring your thoughts all the time. And you will be right, considering that the average person has about sixty thousand thoughts a day. But there is a very simple solution to control your thoughts, and this is by monitoring your feelings instead.

Your Mind is a Thought Magnet

Now that you understand that your mind has frequencies, you must realize that the thoughts you are sending into space will attract similar things like a magnet. Vril is constantly being drawn into you by your mind, to power your body and brain so that you can stay alive. It is the "breath of life" or *Ond*, the gift of life given to us by Odin. As your mind dwells on certain thoughts, those things fill your Orlog, which is shaping Vril coming into you. Your mind will receive Vril that has been shaped by your thoughts and it will create your physical reality, and affecting your body and brain. If you see yourself as a victim, the Vril being drawn into you will manifest situations where you will indeed become a victim. If you see yourself living a life of abundance, Vril will manifest abundance in your life. If you see yourself famous, Vril will manifest situations that will bring you fame. If you see your life as one long struggle to survive in a cruel world, Vril will create roadblocks throughout your life that will prevent you from obtaining those things you want. Your Orlog is creating a present state of mind, shaping Vril that you are drawing in, creating things that will happen to you in your future.

We can sum up simply: Your current, dominant thoughts are creating things that will happen to you in your future. Hence—your dominant thoughts are your future. Your obsessions will manifest themselves in your future. This is not necessarily a bad thing, if you can learn to control the way you think.

Your Feelings Are a Reflection of What You are Thinking

You cannot feel good if you are thinking bad thoughts. Your feelings are the most obvious indication of what you are thinking. If you are always worrying, fearing that bad things will happen to you or obsessing that you are being victimized, you are going to feel miserable. Just as your feelings are good indicators of what you are thinking, you can use your feelings very effectively to help you control and change what you are thinking about. All emotions can be classified as positive emotions that make you feel good, and negative emotions that make you feel bad. You can be happy when suddenly you receive some bad news, and then your feelings change instantly. You get a tightening of the solar plexus as an indication of your feeling bad. Your sudden anger, depression, jealousy, guilt, or depression makes you feel as if you are no longer in control—*a helpless victim of circumstances being shoved around by the powers that be.* The world is cruel and you ask yourself, "Why me?" "Why do these things always happen to me?" You have just changed your thinking process and aligned yourself with the forces that work toward empowering chaos in the universe.

The way you feel is determined by what you are thinking. This is a fundamental law. Your thoughts create the frequency your mind is working with. And when your thoughts are transferred into emotions, they are sending frequencies that shape the flow of Vril into you. The law of cause and effect must work its will, and you begin to manifest your thoughts into events that will play out in your life. When you surrender to bad feelings, you are saying, "This is what I want, so fill my life with circumstances that will reinforce these feelings and continue to make me feel bad!"

Whether you realize it or not, you are constantly thinking and feeling, and this is constantly creating your future. If you are worrying or sad, then you will bring more of that into your life. If you are happy and filled with joy, you will bring those things into your life. Be aware of how you are feeling, because your feelings will indicate what you are thinking about, and will attract more of the same in your future.

Since it is impossible to feel good if you are thinking bad thoughts, you must work to change what you are thinking about. You must accept the fact that you can have whatever you want in life. What do you want most of all? To be happy, right? Then you have to feel good.

You Have Within You the Power to Change the Way You Feel!

Remember that when you are focused on a thought, your mind is working at Alpha, and sending out those frequencies generated by the sustained thoughts, shaping Vril energy flowing into you, creating your feelings and thus manifesting your Wyrd—your future pathway. Look at it this way: your feelings are feedback from the universe, reminding you of the frequency your mind is working in. When you are feeling good, you are being told that you are thinking good thoughts, and when you are feeling bad, you are also being reminded that you are thinking bad thoughts.

So when you are feeling bad, the universe is warning you to change the way you are thinking. "Warning! Warning! Manifestation imminent! Change your frequency now!" This is to let you know that your thoughts are blocking the creation of good things in your future pathway. Your negative frequency is attaching bad things to you, pulling you out of alignment with the Gods. You must change your thoughts before it is too late. Think about something you like, something that will make you happy. You can shift your thinking process into a new frequency by simply saying to yourself over and over, "Cancel!"

If you don't quickly cancel out negative thoughts, you can cause a chain reaction to take place. We have all had those days when everything seems to go wrong. It starts with an unfortunate event, which then sets into motion a series of bad events throughout the day. This is what happens: Something bad happens, which causes you to dwell on it with intense emotion. You can't get it out of your mind, and soon you are sending out intense bad feelings, which shape and mold Vril energy with the same negative intensity. Soon a pathway of negative energy is created that will lead you through a day filled with bad events. So long as you are constantly generating negative frequencies from your thoughts, your feelings are shaping your future track that you will travel. As you experience another bad event, your negative thoughts are multiplied, and your emotional energy increases, shaping Vril, and creating the groundwork for additional bad things to happen. But you can change this chain reaction by simply canceling the negative thoughts. All you have to do is use a simple formula like repeating the word, "cancel," over and over. Then try to think about something else, something pleasant. It might seem simplistic, but once you get your mind off the previous event, you will discover that you have changed the frequency.

This can be done by first entering an Alpha state, and beginning to visualize something pleasant that you want to happen. But you can jump-start this process by filling your vision with an intense, positive emotion. Think of someone or something that makes you happy and brings joy into your life. Feel it! I mean really feel it! Let the vision of this pleasant, joyful event absorb your entire mind. The universe will respond. Your new, positive thoughts will immediately change the nature of the Vril energy flowing into you. Its positive charged energy fields will blaze a new pathway for you, ending the cycle of bad events and turning a potentially bad day into a good day. Your future pathway will new lead to good things.

You can prove this to yourself right now, by taking few seconds of your time to ask yourself: "What is my emotional state right now?" You can sit quietly for a few seconds. Eliminate all distractions. Close your eyes and concentrate on what you are feeling. If you have negative feelings, then think of something pleasant, pushing out all other thoughts, and focus on the positive event you are visualizing. Feel the positive sensation that you are now experiencing, and surrender yourself to it. Smile and even laugh out loud. If you honestly tried this little experiment, you should feel transformed.

You must realize that you have the power within you to create your own universe...that this universe is created by your thoughts and feelings. Therefore, it is important that you develop a personality that is dominated by thoughts of happiness, joy and love. These thoughts will be sent out into a universe filled with currents of Vril energy, shaping them into pathways for you to travel along.

At Least Love Yourself

We all know it is impossible to love everyone and everything. There are plenty of people out there that are impossible to love. There are many things in this world that you cannot love, and should be hated. So please do not think we are asking you to walk around all day with an imbecilic smile. What we are saying is simply not to walk around all day filled with hatred and anger. If your normal personality is filled with negative thoughts and feelings, you will experience those things, those very thoughts and feelings. You cannot harm anyone but yourself with your thoughts.

In the Folk Faith of Balder Rising, we perform a ritual of striking down our enemies. We ask the Gods to protect us against all those who would cause us harm, and send back a hundred times over those negative thoughts that are directed at us. We mentally form a shield of Vril energy around us that deflects and sends back to the sender anything negative directed at us. These negative forces don't have to be from living human beings; there are more powerful forms of negative energy in the vast universe than just that from human beings. A prerequisite for success in this ritual is a state of mind in which you truly love yourself. Once you have truly come to accept who you are, what you are and where you came from, *you will truly love yourself.* This state of mind is what we refer to as the Balder Force. Balder is the God of Love, and thus invincible. Nothing can harm him except blind ignorance, personified by his blind twin brother, Hoder, who is tricked into killing him by Loki, who represents chaos. We need to generate this Balder Force within. This is the essence of the Folk Faith of Balder Rising. This state of loving yourself will generate a powerful shield about you that will deflect any negative thoughts sent your way. It will also help to stop you from sending out negative thoughts and feelings.

See yourself as a Godlike being in harmony with a friendly universe. Know that you are aligned with the Gods. Once you can conceptualize this perception, you will generate just such a universe. You will have transformed your Orlog and used it to create a Wyrd that will be filled with success and happiness.

Chapter Seven: Using Vril to Create the Reality You Desire

The Gods are not judgmental beings. They are too busy struggling to keep chaos at bay so that the galaxies can spin through the universe, stars can form and give off energy, and gravity can hold everything in place. You simply need to decide that from this point in your life, you will align yourself with the Gods. You can do this by merely learning to love who and what you are. Once you learn to love yourself, you can give love to those who are close to you, and you will then naturally live a life of progress, order and easy forward movement through the web of the future. You will have bent your Orlog by cleansing it of negative baggage. This will cause your subconscious to create pathways filled with positive events as you move into the future. Know that your future is not set in stone. In Vrilology, the future is known as "becoming." This means it is ever-unfolding. To assure that it is a bright future, you have only to believe that you have this power and that you can use it. But before you can use it, you need to discover your purpose in life.

Discovering Your Life's Purpose

For you to achieve a life filled with happiness and success, you need to discover one of the most critical fundamental questions you can ask—what truly is your purpose in life? Everyone has one, but the vast majority of us never uncover it, which condemns us to live lives of quiet desperation. Whether we are conscious of it or not, we are constantly searching for that purpose. We are constantly asking, "What is the meaning of life?" The truth is, there is no one universal meaning of life. Each of us has a different purpose, and the secret of a happy and successful life is to discover just what it is for each of us.

In his essay, Spiritual Laws, Ralph Waldo Emerson wrote:

> *Each man (and woman) has his own vocation. The talent is the call. There is one direction in which all space is open to him. He has faculties silently inviting him thither to endless exertion. He is like a ship in a river; he runs against obstruction on every side but one. On that side all obstruction is taken away, and he sweeps serenely over the deepening channel onto an infinite sea.*

I am sure you have all sorts of day dreams about the good life, but is that your purpose? Once you find it, all the good things will come to you automatically, without effort. First, imagine reality as a vast jigsaw puzzle. Secondly, think of yourself as one piece in this vast puzzle. You need to now find the exact place for you to fit into the greater puzzle. Once you discover this, you will fit into it and become part of it. Then everything will feel right and success and happiness will be yours. But how do we discover this purpose?

You can try a simple exercise. First, you need to discover what truly makes you happy. Start by making a list of everything you enjoy doing and makes you happy. Make sure you write it in the present tense, as if you already have what it is that will make you happy. "I am happy because . . ." and then describe it in the smallest detail. Then write down how you can begin to achieve it, but write it in the past tense, as if you have already done it. It doesn't have to be realistic. Don't worry about whether what you wrote will work. Just the practice of seeing yourself doing it, making it come to pass, will begin to shape and mold Vril into pathways that will make it happen. Finally you have to believe that you deserve it. You must be very clear about what you desire; and you must convince yourself that you desire it. And do it with feeling. There are no limits to what you can do or have, but you must know what it is and believe you deserve it. If you wish for money and wealth, then believe that you will receive the necessary money to fulfill your needs. If you visualize too specific and narrow a means to that end, such as that you will win the lottery, you most likely will not win, because deep down you know the odds are too great; but if you see yourself more generally and broadly as receiving enough wealth to make you happy, then money will come to you when you need it to fulfill your needs. In time, the amounts will increase. The formula is an easy three step process of knowing what makes you happy, seeing yourself achieving it, and then believing you deserve it.

Once you discover what it is you want you don't have to keep asking for it. It is like placing an order. You have to place the order once. You know that when you order something on the Internet, or through the mail, it is on its way. You are going to eventually receive it. You don't have to sit around all day wondering when it will arrive — or at least you shouldn't, if you trust the delivery people. You should forget about it. Know that your subconscious is shaping Vril so that what you need will appear in your future pathways — your Wyrd. Once you place the order, you must have complete and unshakable confidence in the delivery service. In fact, it is helpful to believe that it has already arrived and that you already possess it.

You Can Rearrange Your Reality Through Vril

You must learn to think you already have achieved your purpose. If you begin to think that you have not achieved it, or doubt that you will, your thoughts will send out that frequency and shape Vril so that you will not. You can meditate in the Alpha and Theta, imagining that you have already achieved your purpose. By meditating, you are bending your Wyrd. Meditate several times a day if it helps, seeing yourself living your purpose. If you do not have time to meditate, you can simply daydream in the most vivid way possible. When you daydream, you are entering your Alpha state. Do whatever works to convince you that you deserve your purpose and that it is already out there for you. Once this state of mind has been achieved, Vril will begin to rearrange people, events, nations and circumstances for you to achieve your purpose. It will be fit into the plan for divine order in the universe, because your purpose will be based on your love of you, your friends and family, your comrades and neighbors, and your heritage and origins. This is the best way for you to send to the Gods what it is you deed and desire. The Gods will hear your thoughts, and Frigga, Odin's wife, who weaves the webs of Wyrd, will incorporate your needs into the Great Web of the Cosmos.

You really don't need to know how you will achieve your desires. When imagining yourself achieving your desires, have the achievement appear easy. It does not have to be realistic, only effortless. It is just an exercise to help you condition yourself into believing that you will achieve. If you read the history of great men who achieve the seemingly impossible, you will discover that most of them had no idea how it would happen. They just rolled up their sleeves and got to work, knowing that whatever was necessary for them to achieve their purpose would manifest itself at the right time and in the right place. Don't worry about how Vril will bring it about. This is not your concern. The Gods are working tirelessly to maintain order and produce progress. Once you have aligned yourself with them, your desires will manifest themselves through their process. They will receive your thoughts, know your desires, and place them where they will fit into their universe, just as if they were putting together a puzzle and you are just the right piece they were looking for.

You can imagine different ways that it will happen, and the more you exaggerate, the better it will be. They don't have to be realistic. You simply need to know that it will happen. Once you begin to think about whether it will happen in this or some other way, you begin to display doubts, and the currents of Vril energy flowing into you will manifest those doubts and not create pathways to your purpose. As soon as you begin to doubt the validity of your visions, repeat, "Cancel!" over and over. The "how" is not your part in achieving what you desire; that is the duty of the Gods, working to fashion Vril currents into order throughout the universe. If you are convinced you will achieve your purpose, the Gods will work that purpose into place in the order they establish, but if you have doubts, then those doubts will also be worked into the order they fashion.

Think of the Gods building a house for you. They are the builders, but you are the architect sending the Gods your plans. Once they received your plans, they will order the materials, which are the contents of what is housed within your Orlog. They will then begin to construct the house according to your plans and the materials you supplied them with. The quality of materials you send will determine the quality of the house. If you send them low quality materials, you will get a low quality house, but if you send them the top of the line, you will get a high quality house. The choice is yours.

Accept That You Can Do Anything by Harnessing the Power of Vril

Right now, you need to know how wonderful it is going to feel once you have achieved your purpose. Know that the happiness and success will become part of your life once you know your purpose. It is important to feel good, happy and ecstatic. The Gods gave you life. It is a gift from the Gods. Be happy that you are alive. Feel that joy of living right now. Once you do, your mind will be sending out frequencies to shape inflowing Vril to create those pathways filled with more joy of living. Don't just rationally think about it. You must truly feel it! By calling up all your emotional energy, you are manifesting the power to make what you want to come true.

You have to learn to reserve your judgment and suspend your feelings of disbelief. Most people have difficulty believing in what they cannot see. Think about this for a minute. You cannot see a thought, nor can you see emotion, but both exist. You know they are real, yet you cannot touch them or see them. You have to create a Vril Mind Set. Think of yourself as a Vril person. Affirm to yourself out loud that you are a Vril Being — that you are made from the same Life Force that the Gods are made from. Affirm that there is nothing you cannot accomplish. There are no limits to what you can achieve with Vril. Say to yourself, "If I can think of it, I can make it a part of my life." Accept the reality that with Vril, you can do anything you want, especially changing your life for the better. Tell yourself that when you are feeling good, your mind is transforming Vril into pathways that will lead you to what you want in life. You can bend your Wyrd into what you most desire. You are traveling along a pathway created by your good feelings. Therefore, you can only experience those things that will make you feel good. This is the secret of a happy and successful life.

Most people are stuck doing something they hate for a living. Every day of your life, you probably hear people say, "I wish I could change my career." There is an old saying, "If you are doing something you hate, it's work, but if you are doing something you love, it's play." So even if you are stuck in a job or career that you hate, you have got to imagine what will make you truly happy. If you do, and ask for it, and believe that it will come to you, and feel that you desire it with a passion, Vril will form pathways that will lead you to just such a career. Once you have found your purpose, you will no longer be working for a living, *you will be playing for a living.*

It is the same with your desires. If you are constantly crying to yourself about your lot and how you want to change it, it is like swimming against the current. But if you accept the belief that by sending out good feelings about what it is you want, truly want, and know what is your purpose, you will not have try to accomplish it; it will effortlessly come to you. It might take time, and manifest itself when and where you least expect it, but so long as you put it out there and permit it to happen in its own way, *it will happen.*

Learn to Trust Your Instincts

You know that your brain is divided into two halves: the right side is intuitive, while the left side is rational. The problem is, they speak different languages. When you are in the conscious, awake state, Beta, the left side of your brain is speaking to you. But while you are in Alpha, Theta, or even Delta state, the right side of your brain is speaking to you. It is important to be able to enter the Alpha and Theta states whenever you desire, so you can communicate with the right side of your brain. Once you have

Harnessing the power of your desires.

achieved this ability, your instincts and intuitive powers will be able to speak to you loud and clear. When this happens, you must learn to trust them.

When the opportunity arises, you must act. Your instincts will shout it to you, but your left side will tell you to be cautious. Stop and think it over. Ignore the left side of your brain. You must learn to trust your instincts. Your instincts are messages from the Gods telling you what you must do. They are letting you know that they have found a place for you in their greater design, and all you have to do is react. They did all the work, and you have only to act when you are called on to do so. So when you have an intuitive feeling that opportunity is knocking, act. Don't delay. The Vrilic pathways are being blazed for you, and all you have to do is "follow the yellow brick road," so to speak.

You can do this by following a hunch every day. We have hunches every day, but we mostly ignore them. You can practice trusting your instincts by not ignoring them. Each day, try listening to that little voice in your head telling you to do this or that. You will find that they are usually right. This is especially true if you follow everything that you have read in this book so far. If you have a positive outlook, send out positive frequencies, feel good emotions and have a proper attitude, you will have cleansed your Orlog of all negative influences. Your instincts will then lead you down the pathways Vril has laid out for you to achieve your purpose, and you will receive everything that will provide for a happy and successful life.

Know that You are a Vril Being

Though you might seem solid, you are actually made up mostly of Vril. Every cell in your body is made of billions, even trillions of atoms. As we have explained before, the atom is 1 percent neutrons, protons, and electrons, circling what appears to be nothingness. But that nothingness that makes up more than 99 percent of each atom is actually Vril. Therefore, more than 99 percent of you is Vril, while less than 1 percent of you is neutrons, protons and electrons. This is the secret that lies at the center of your existence.

The poet Robert Frost wrote: "We dance round in a ring and suppose, But the secret sits in the middle and knows."

The Chinese refer to this emptiness that fills the center of everything as Tao. They understand that though we appear to be material beings, we are really mostly Vril energy. Without Vril, we do not exist. No Vril, no you.

You are pulsing like a magnet, drawing to you what you are thinking. Unfortunately, your most powerful thoughts tend to be negative and will draw to you the things you do not want. But you can learn to change this, and make sure that those things you really want the most can be drawn to you with this force. You can easily practice how to concentrate on drawing to you only those things you want in your life.

I had no clear idea how I was going to found the Folk Faith of Balder Rising, but I knew that the Gods wanted me to found such a church, so I simply began teaching lessons, and eventually they grew a membership. The members soon wanted to form some kind of permanent entity and the next thing I knew, we had a legally recognized church. "When" and "how" were just questions that I did not ask. I had no sense of time. I knew that it would develop and form itself in due time, because time as we understand it in the West is an illusion.

In the West, we tend to think of time linearly, with a beginning and an end. We look at time as a procession, with each thing happening one right after another. But quantum physics explains that everything is happening at the same time. Once you have become a Vril Being, you will see everything happening in future, present and past simultaneously. Thus, everything that you desire already exists, and the vision of you experiencing your ideal life already exists. You have only to attract it by learning how to condition the two halves of your brain to work together to make it happen. And since time is not an issue, the time it takes for you to manifest what you desire depends totally on your belief in its happening. If you experience a delay in those things you want becoming a reality, the delay is probably due to your inability to manifest them. If you fail to truly believe and feel that you desire what you want and are convinced it can happen, then you have not properly created the frequency with your mind necessary to shape the Vril currents into a magnetic force that will draw those things into your life.

If you think to yourself that what you desire is too big or difficult to create, then your mind will send out those mental blueprints that will cause a delay. What can be manifested through Vril is an effortless task by the Godly forces of the universe. If we think that something will take a long or a short time to manifest itself, then you are setting down on the blueprint a length of time it will take. This is why it is important to mentally see, visualize, what you want to already be a reality. See it in the present tense. If you are overweight and want to be thin, see yourself thin. Feel yourself at the perfect weight. If you want increased abundance, then convince yourself that you already possess this abundance. Time and size are dimensions that exist in your mind, not in the universe. They are created by your mental blueprint and not by the Godly forces shaping the universe.

Remember our discussion of how Odin hanged himself from Yggdrasill so that he could discover the secret of the Runes, which are tools that can be used to harness Vril, giving him the power to shape the universe? Like Odin, we too can learn to harness this force to reshape our reality. In another tale, one of Odin's sons, Heimdall, descends to Earth or Midgard, and teaches those selected by Odin the secret of the Runes. You can join the ranks of the selected Rune Masters through Vrilology and becoming familiar with the Runes, their meaning and powers, and how to master their use as described I this book.

Where I used to work in New York City, there was alternate side parking. I had to be at work at 6 a.m., so getting a parking spot was not always an easy task. I often had to search up to 45 minutes, and most of the time I found a spot three or four blocks away from where I worked. But once I began practicing these techniques, I began finding parking spots right away, and within a block of where I worked. Four out of five days a week, I found parking close to my place of employment or right in front of it. The rest of the time, I had to search for about five to ten minutes and might have to drive two or three blocks away, but people were amazed how easy it was for me to find parking. When my fellow employees asked me what was my secret, I explained to them how Vril worked, and that it could work for them too. No one believed me. And so, I continued to find parking nearby and right away most of the time, while the rest had to search and search.

The secret of Vril is simple. You have to trust and know rather than doubt and fear. You have to accept that the power created by your will can create your reality. The collective process of believing, thinking and feeling that something is happening, is known as will power. Will power is Vril at work. It is your mind, as a Vril Being, sending out frequencies that shape Vril flowing into you and creating pathways that will open your future to great possibilities. Once you realize that everything you see around you, everyone you associate with, everything that happens to you, is the result of your desires, or how your thoughts became energized and created those things within your physical reality, you will understand that you have the power to control your life and destiny, and fill your life with whatever you want, and that there is nothing you cannot achieve. The difference between being a Vril Being and a non-Vril Being is knowing that you have to power within you to create these things.

In our discussion of the multidimensional Soul, we referred to the two halves of the brain as Myne, the right side of the brain, which is the root of memory, the subconscious mind, and our racial memories, and is symbolized by Odin's raven Muninn, and Hugh, the left side of the brain, which controls our rational, analytical and reasoning half of the brain, which is symbolized by Odin's other raven, Huginn. By joining Hugh and Myne, we can forge a bridge over which they can communicate with each other. We too can learn to use our minds in the same way, and thus cause our Third Eye to fully open, thus establishing a communication link between us and the Gods.

This development of a fully integrated brain is fundamental to becoming a fully charged Vril Being. You must surrender yourself to this reality. Surrendering is simply accepting that you are not alone in the universe. You become fully aware that there exists an infinite force working to hold the universe together, known as the Gods. But even more important is the fact that you and the Gods are made of the same Life Force. Once you understand this reality, you will have no problem trusting this force. Secondly, if you know that this force is used by a universal intelligence that we know as the Gods, and that this universal intelligence is shaping Vril to create and maintain order, then by surrendering to Vril, your future will be one of progress and order. All you have to do is know and trust this fact. Once you have accepted that you are 99 percent Vril, you will accept that your thoughts are energized by Vril and you can use your thoughts to shape your future.

Anticipation is a Powerful Force

The reality of your present life was created by your past experiences, which control your thinking process. Once you have cleansed your Orlog by changing how and what you think, you will become a Vril Being and you can begin changing your reality, or bending your Wyrd. This will become a lot easier once you have discovered your purpose. Discovering your purpose gives you direction in life because, like the bird that flies south for the winter, you instinctively know what you want to manifest. This is the secret to changing your life. Anticipate what will happen and it will happen. Instead of simply setting certain goals you would like to accomplish in your life, convince yourself that these things will materialize in your life and they will sooner or later appear — probably sooner than later. Expect them to happen right away — anticipate them.

However, if you exert a great deal of mental energy worrying about something, that something will materialize. If you worry about paying the bills, you will have trouble paying them. If you fear that you will get bills in the mail each day, you will flooded with bills. If you obsess on the fear of going into debt, your mind is conditioning your life to create circumstances which will add to your debt. But if you can change your anticipation, you will change what is being attracted to you. Convince yourself that you can handle all your financial responsibilities, and you will. If you anticipate checks arriving in the mail, your mail will be filled with checks when you need them. If you are confident that you are financially solvent, the pathways you create will lead you into a debt-free future. The reason is simple: your future fills with what you anticipate.

Remember, your past creates your present, and your present creates your future. Most people review their lives and say, "This is who I am." This thinking is a surrender to your past. But if you work at changing your perception of what you are, by rejecting the negativity that has been stored within your Orlog from your past, you will clean house and flush out your Orlog. Think, "That is who I was, but I am not those things anymore." Do not become burdened by the residue of negative things past; if you accept the premise that you are a slave to those thoughts and actions, then you will be.

The simple way to clean house is to replay the disappointments in your life with thoughts about positive action. Eliminate those events that did not go the way you wanted them to by daydreaming that they turned out differently. Recreating those events mentally in a way that turns out positive sends out new frequencies, turning Vril into positive events. We are not telling you to live in a fairytale existence, but simply to find the positive results from events that did not turn out the way you expected. You will no longer be plagued by such negative emotions as depression, disappointment, anger, sadness, worry, fear and hatred, and thus will send new frequencies that will manifest the reverse of those things in your life.

Create your thoughts by visualizing and imagining those things that you want to fill your future, and your thoughts will create that reality. If you wish to obtain those things that have eluded you in the past, act and think as if those things are already part of your life. If you live according to your Vril self, your physical self will conform itself to that vision.

If You are Grateful for What You Have, You Will Get More of the Same

The secret to filling your life with those things you want in the fastest way is to be and feel joyful about it now, in the present.

If you concentrate on the feelings of joy and happiness that you expect, now, in the present, your mind will send those feelings out into the infinite sea of Vril, and your feelings will shape the currents of Vril flowing into you, generating more of the same. By sending out these feelings, pathways will be blazed for you to follow in the future that will be filled with the things that will increase the amount of joy and happiness you are already feeling. Your Wyrd will be created by the law of cause and effect, which gives back to you a hundred times over what you are sending out.

Make a list of those things that you are grateful for in your life, right now. Your mind will concentrate on those wonderful things and attract more of the same to you. Gratitude is a powerful force, and if you are truly grateful for something someone did, or for just being your friend or relative, you can experience this force by letting that person know. Tell that person how lucky you feel that he or she is part of your life. That person cannot help but be moved. You will notice that the person will suddenly see you in a new light and will begin to appreciate you and be grateful that he or she knows you. Like attracts like, this is the rule of cause and effect.

If you are a man and married or have a girlfriend, you already know how moved a woman can be by you letting her know how much you appreciate her, by how grateful you are for just knowing her. Appreciation pulls wonderful things into your life. It is a great trail blazer of a bright and wonderful future. It can knock down barriers and melt away the most resistant obstructions.

Now imagine what it will do for you if every time you wake up, you thank the higher powers for your being alive. Thank Odin, Vili and Ve for giving you life. Simply say, "Thank you for letting me have one more day in this wonderful life." Then begin to run down everything that you are grateful for as you get dressed and wash up. Go over the list you made in your mind. Feel happiness and joy for everything you are grateful for, and you will be manifesting the day to come. Your happiness, joy and gratitude will create the day unfolding before you. It is not as if the Gods hear your thanks and get all mushy-eyed and then reward you. The

Gods are working to create order in the universe. Your positive energy that they receive from your positive affirmations is like mortar that they will use when constructing this ordered universe. They will simply take the positive energy from your affirmations and incorporate it into their work.

If you dwell on all the things you don't want, you are sending out mental frequencies about those things, and remember that the negative affirmations backfire. If your affirmation includes words like "don't want," the "don't" will not register, and it will be turned into some thing you desire. So if you say, "I don't want to get sick today," the Gods will hear, "I...want to get sick today," and you will get sick. But if you affirm every day all the things you are grateful for, you are sending out positive thoughts. Say, "I am grateful for my health and well being," and this positive affirmation will be accepted.

Sending out thoughts of jealousy, envy, resentment, and dissatisfaction cannot help you get what you want, they can only send more of what you don't want. But if you are grateful for what you have, you will get more of what you are grateful for. If you have an old car and need a new one, don't dwell on how terrible the old car is. Be grateful that it has lasted so long, and that the "old fellow" is still able to run. With thoughts like these, you will discover that you will receive those things you need.

Visualize What You Truly Desire

We in the Folk Faith of Balder Rising cannot stress enough the importance of learning to visualize what you want to manifest in the material world. If your mind can see it, it can create it. "One picture is worth a thousand words," is true of Vril. When you can vividly visualize what you want in great detail, you create powerful thoughts and feelings. This causes you to focus intensely on a subject, concentrating energy to empower the frequencies your mind is sending, which creates pathways in your future that will lead you to actualize those visions.

If there is something you want, visualize it first, just as if you were daydreaming about it. Don't just think about—*see it.*

Make sure you visualize it down to the smallest details. Enjoy what it is you are mentally creating, and it is very important that you see yourself already possessing it. Don't see yourself getting it, but already possessing it in the present tense. If you want to buy a house, see yourself not purchasing it, but already owning it. See yourself living in the house of your dreams. Visualize your home as a place of comfort and security. Create separate images of every room in the house. See the furniture, the garden, the front door, the basement—every aspect of the house. If it is a new house, see yourself already living in it. Visualize your home as a loving environment.

When you truly focus on what you desire, you begin to create intense feelings about it. Remember, it is not enough to just think good thoughts, *you must feel them.* Your thoughts create emotions. Make sure you manufacture deep emotions by creating and holding the vision. If you wish for a new house, you must truly feel you deserve it, and then you must truly love living in it. It must feel like your dream house, and the closest thing on Earth to heavenly paradise. Feel this intensely and it will manifest itself. Feelings are the means by which thoughts shape Vril. Your thoughts create images, and your feelings, created by those thoughts, send the frequencies to shape Vril.

Remember our discussion about creating "blueprints" for the Gods? When you align yourself with the Gods, it is important not to think how their divine powers will manifest the end result. That is not your task, but theirs. Don't think about how it will happen, just concentrate on the result. Stay focused on its already existing. Believe that it has already happened. The divine powers will take care of the "how."

Transform Your Thoughts into Holographic Pictures

Let's think about what we said about the universe being like a holographic deck on the Star Trek starship *Enterprise*. It is a very easy task for you to create your own hologram. It is just a visual representation of what you desire and are creating in your mind. When you visualize an image or scene in your mind, you are actually creating your own little universe. You can literally play God by designing it to be just the way you want it to be. This very fact is important, because when you visualize properly, you are doing the same thing that the Gods do. By vividly visualizing something in the most minute detail, your feelings increase in strength, becoming more powerful. The longer you can do so, the stronger will be the mental power. This is why it is so important to keep that hologram alive in your mind. Let us give you an example of how important it is to learn to properly visualize something.

If you have not seen someone for a very long time, and you try to recall what the person looks like, you will discover that you cannot create an image of the person in the smallest detail. You will have difficulty remembering the small details of the way they look. Oh, you will probably be able to describe what the person looks like, but when you try to recall that person's face, you will get a vague image of it, with no details. Unless you have a photograph to remind you exactly what that person looks like, in time, you won't be able to recall the face. So it is important to create a visual image of what it is you desire.

So how do you create a holographic image to help you visualize? You can cut pictures out of magazines, and paste them on a board of what it is you desire. Better, if you are talented at visual art, you can draw exactly what you want. Keep the images as a reminder. Meditate on them if you wish. The better you are able to actually see them, the more powerful will be the feelings you are transmitting to the universe. Don't hold back. If it is a house you desire, collect as many pictures as you can find, or draw them, to describe everything about the house. You can do the same with the front and back yards, the furniture in each room, and the outside of the house, even the area or region of the country you would like to live in and every other detail. You might want to draw a map of the neighborhood, describing the landscape, or even put up a map of the state, county, province or country you wish to move to. Anything that will help you create this "alternative" reality in your mind will generate powerful feelings that will eventually manifest that reality in the material world. Let the Gods know exactly what you want, and they will give it to you. But they have to hear you, *so really feel how wonderful it will be.*

Chapter Eight: How to Use Vril to Obtain Abundance

Without Money, You Can't Get Anything Done.

There usually are two kinds of people when it comes to money. The first are those who believe that money is the root of all evil, and the other believes *greed is good.* There are some religions that encourage their followers to become successful, and some religious actually warn against avarice and usury. The Folk Faith of Balder Rising would like to simply say that after you have completed this lesson, you will learn how to acquire enough wealth to fulfill your needs and desires *without turning into a Mr. Scrooge.* The Folk Faith of Balder Rising believes that its members should lead lives in which they are happy and successful. If that means acquiring huge amounts of wealth, we say, wonderful! We also say that you will not be in danger of losing your soul, as Mr. Scrooge was in Charles Dickens' book, *A Christmas Carol.* In fact, most of you really don't desire to be among the super-rich, though you might occasionally dream about what life would be like if your did. What most people want is to simply have enough money to acquire good things in life, such as a nice home, some leisure time, providing for their family and so forth. This might simply mean that you will need extra money from time to time, maybe as much as doubling your income. Whether you fall into this category, or you are among those who seek vast sums of wealth, you will discover the means to acquire it in this lesson. But you will have to adhere to certain principles.

There is an old saying that everyone has heard and is very misleading. Most people believe power corrupts, and absolute power corrupts absolutely. But the truth is that wealth corrupts and overwhelming wealth corrupts overwhelmingly. Wealth especially corrupts power. But we must not slip into a judgmental process of looking at wealth. Money, after all, is a "necessary evil." In the Folk Faith of Balder Rising, we do not take the view that money is the root of all evil. There is nothing wrong with wanting material things to make your life more comfortable. You will need money to obtain abundance necessary for survival, security, education, and all your personal and family needs. This is the natural law of the society we live in. Unless you want to be a hermit and withdraw from society and bum around, you are going to need money. Money and wealth are indicators of how well you are doing. Money is actually the most material form of energy that can manifest itself in this reality. But the love of money, or perhaps the "lust of money," is the root of all evil. Money is a great corrupting force when one lusts after it and worships it for its own sake. Money is not something to be hoarded, but used, and how you use it is up to you. It can be a force for good or a corrupting agent. How much money and wealth you desire will depend on you. The purpose of this book and the Folk Faith of Balder Rising is to help as many people be happy and successful as possible. As we have explained throughout this book, if you want something, you must generate and send out good thoughts, good feelings. It is the same with abundance and wealth. So if you are motivated by greed, you will not generate wealth, and you might even lose what you already possess.

Focus on Wealth, Not the Lack of It.

The first principle of attracting wealth is that you will never attract it if you concentrate on the lack of it. If your thoughts, feelings and sensations are focused on the fact that something is missing from your life, then you will generate more of its lack. The law of cause and effect will manifest what you are obsessing on. Constant thinking about the lack of money and wealth will generate a life lacking wealth, a life into which it will be impossible to attract more money. If you keep thinking that way, your thoughts will generate many more circumstances in which you will not only not draw more money to you, but will cause yourself to go into, or deeper into, debt. What you obsess on will affect your Wyrd.

Learn to focus on more money flowing into your life, and your future will be filled with opportunities for your wealth to increase. Once you begin to emit signals through the power of your mind, Vril will create pathways in which money will begin to flow to you effortlessly. Your Wyrd will be one filled with the abundance you need and desire. You must begin to think all the time that you have more money than you need to survive. Imagine that you are richer than Bill Gates or the Rockefellers. See yourself hobnobbing with the rich and famous. Daydream about how rich you really are. Really fantasize about how wonderful it is to have more money than you could ever need or want. The important thing to remember is the "is." You must see yourself already prosperous. You must convince yourself that your life is filled with abundance. You will never generate a life filled with abundance and wealth if you believe that you do not deserve it. You cannot just say, "I deserve to be wealthy," but believe that you already are. Know it and your actions will not only reflect it, but generate it without effort.

What Causes Failure and How You Can Create a Successful Life

Before we can begin the work of learning how to harness Vril energy to acquire wealth and success, we need to explore why people fail. Humans are actually designed to stay healthy, acquire everything necessary for success, maintain emotional well being and so forth, and yet, so many people, the vast majority of them, fail to obtain some of these things. Why? Even the most ordinary people should be able to acquire enough of these things necessary for survival. There will always be some who lack the necessary abilities, but if we look about us, we will notice an increasing number of people who fail to fulfill their dreams. The reason lies in the accumulated blockages that we have permitted to dominate the way we think. *The reason most people fail to achieve what they desire is their own obsessions, which manifest within their Wyrd that causes them to fail.* But there is action that can be taken that can eliminate the blockage that will manifest in future pathways, so that we can achieve our natural heritage of abundance.

People unfortunately prefer to obsess on negative things, rather than on positive events in their lives. As a result, our minds are usually working overtime transforming Vril energy currents into the nature of our Wyrd—what lies in wait for us in our future pathways. We must condition ourselves to not obsess on the negative things, but affirm the positive things in our lives. To achieve this, we must first understand what makes us obsess on the negative, and thus causes us to fail. Let's examine some of these reasons.

1) the Fear of Failure: We have a saying: *It is better to try and fail, than to fail because you have never tried.* What this says is simply, most people fail at what they wish to achieve because they are too frightened of failing. This fear will prevent you from ever trying, or cause you to find some excuse to give up. The truth is, most people fail at what they set out to do, but those who eventually succeed do so because they do not let their failures stop them from trying again. Think of Thomas Edison. Do you know how many times he tried to invent the electric light bulb? He tried over 600 times. But each time he failed, he told himself he learned something—how not to make the electric light bulb. He kept on trying until he got it right. Let's look at another case. Babe Ruth of baseball fame. Do you know that the year Babe Ruth hit the most home runs was the same year he also made it into the record book for the most strike outs. He did not fail striking out because he knew that if he did not persist in trying to hit home runs, he would never break the record, even if it meant striking out. So the first thing you most overcome is your fear of failing if you are going to succeed. If your fear of failing takes over, you will never succeed. This is a guarantee, and is what we mean when we say: *It is better to try and fail, than to fail because you have never tried.*

2) Stop Worrying: It is amazing how many people worry about things they have no control over, and even more amazing how they worry about things that have no chance of manifesting themselves in your reality. Studies have shown that out of any 100 things you worry about, 92 of them do not come true. Of the other 8, 4 will turn out to be positive, and thus there was no reason to worry about them, while the other 4 will be negative. So we see that of any 100 things we worry about, 96% of these things we should never have wasted our mental energy worrying about. And that wasted energy was not just wasted, but was fodder for the power of your mind to manifest into a reality waiting for you in your future pathways. The things you worry about are woven into your Wyrd. *So stop worrying!*

3) Low Self-esteem: If you possess a low sense of worthiness, it will manifest itself in low self-esteem, which in turn causes you to doubt yourself. This can affect you on two levels. There is the individual assault on your self-worth, and the collective assault on your self-worth. Let's examine the second cause first.

One of the most treacherous causes for low self-esteem in modern, Western society, especially for individuals of European ancestry, is political correctness. The ideological movement that dominates our culture today blames all of the world's evils on Western, European culture and civilization, as well as on people of European ancestry. If you are of European ancestry, and especially a man, you will be taught that you and your culture and civilization is pure evil. How could anyone who is submitted to such mental torture not suffer from low self-esteem? This cultural and spiritual form of genocide dominates most colleges and universities, and much of our popular culture. The truth is, no one culture is good or evil. Everyone, of every race and ethnic background, should be proud of their heritage, but never to the excessive point of believing they are superior to all others. Be proud of your heritage, yet be aware that it is not perfect. You can break free of the mind-numbing torment of political correctness and increase your sense of self-worth. You can do this by studying the history and culture of Europe, but make sure you avoid most contemporary publications. Instead read older books, or older editions of books, on European History and Western Culture and Civilization.

On the individual level, many people for various reasons, suffer from low self-esteem, caused by their home environment when they were growing up. There are many excellent seminars and exercises, including ones in this book, that will help you to restore your sense of confidence in yourself, as well as your sense of self-worth. Most encourage you to change the way you think, your way of dress, behavior and whom you associate with.

You can transform yourself by seeking to align your self with the Gods. Once you have done this, you *will know* that your life has purpose. Armed with this knowledge, you will begin to transform yourself in ways that you had never thought possible.

4) Guilt: Guilt is a common symptom that we have all experienced, but many suffer an extreme sense of guilt that has destroyed their self-esteem. This is very common within the West. Christians are especially guilt-ridden. From childhood they have been instilled with a sense of guilt based on the Christian theology of *Original Sin*. This insidious concept has screwed up millions of people, and cause them to *hate life*. Guilt is not a natural nor normal state of mind for man. Christianity has caused us to feel guilt over basic human needs, such as sex. The best way to counter this sense of guilt is to, first, forgive your self and try to live a life filled with love—*the love of life!* We should remember that life, the breath of life, is a gift from the Gods. In Odinism there is no concept of sin, original or otherwise.

5) Insecurity: One of the major reasons we do not take the first step in fulfilling our dreams is the sense of insecurity. We fear what others will think of us. Most people possess the desire to belong. They will "go along to get along." This s the herd mentality. We become paralyzed out of fear of what others will think of us, when in reality *you should not care about what other people think about you, because they don't care about you.* You should try and remember that most people will be critical of you because of jealousy. Do not concern yourself with the opinions of others. If you desire something, act boldly and with determination to achieve it.

Wealth Corrupts, and Absolute Wealth Corrupts Absolutely.

This is a truth that we must keep in mind when we seek wealth, prosperity and abundance. Vrilology encourages its members and followers to become financially successful. But to be truly rich, you must not lose your way, your sense of purpose, for if you do, the wealth you acquire will corrupt you and it will become the root of evil in your life. The Rune poems say that we should not hoard wealth and that it should be spread about, but at the same time, that we should not waste it and give it away and become financially destitute. We need to develop a balanced attitude toward money and wealth. If we do not, it can corrupt us in several ways. The most common way is to become obsessive with acquiring wealth and hoarding it. This is the quickest way to lose friends, destroy your marriage and family, and become a very lonely person, who then turns to exaggerated ways to achieve physical gratification in an attempt to fill the void left in life. We have only to look at the many celebrities in show business who start out as decent individuals, and quickly are transformed by their wealth, and the fame that comes with it, into moral degenerates. The danger is from the individual lacking a spirituality that will provide a balance that results in excesses and abuses, but excesses and abuses can be repaired.

The fact is, in the world of invisible forces, wealth and success are the most liquid physical forms of the manifestation of Vril energy in the material world. A shortage of money and success is a reflection of an individual's failure to correctly harness the currents of Vril energy, and to use them to transform that individual's physical environment in Midgard.

Vrilology does not accept the belief that is so prevalent in other esoteric traditions and in many "mainstream" religions: that material existence is evil, or that we must sacrifice material possessions to obtain spiritual purity and higher consciousness. Material success in Midgard can be an indication of either your spiritual evolution or devolution, depending on the way you handle the acquisition of wealth and success. For money is the most obvious form of manifestation of that invisible energy we call Vril, because it is almost as fluid as the Vril currents that we harness and transform into those things we need or desire. All Odinists, whether they practice Vrilology or another form of the Northern

Tradition, should master the science of transforming the Life Force of the Gods into personal success in Midgard. By doing so, they will prove their alignment with the Gods in their great work of maintaining order in the cosmos. By aligning yourself with the Gods, you are drawing the nature of the order they have established into your life, and this is manifested in the success that you achieve in Midgard.

Principles for Acquiring Wealth and Abundance

Most people who read this book will think that now that they understand how to acquire wealth, they have only to buy a lottery ticket and they will win, and become a millionaire overnight. Well, it does not work this way. Deep within your subconscious you have already preprogramed your image of what you are, and in most people it does not include being independently rich. No matter how much you meditate on becoming rich overnight, it will not happen. The principles that we provide for you are really designed for the average person to increase the amount of wealth and abundance in accordance to their needs. You should begin by using the material we provide you to increase your income by 5% to 10%. Subconsciously most of us do not believe we can become rich overnight, nor do we believe we deserve it, but we do believe that we can acquire a small increase in income, and that we deserve it too! Your expectations should be reasonable. Wouldn't it be great if you could increase your income by just 10%? If you continue to apply this principle, in time your income will double. Think of the process of increasing your wealth and abundance as like planting a tree. It will take time for it to grow if you nurture it. But before you know it, you have a full-grown tree. As your income increases, your subconscious mind will come to believe that it is possible for you to become wealthy, and more importantly, it will believe you deserve it. Like planting a tree, it take time. How much time? This depends on the individual

1) Defining Your Purpose in Life: We have touched on this subject before, but we cannot emphasize enough how important it is for you to define your purpose in life. Once you have discovered your purpose, your ability to achieve both material and spiritual abundance will come almost effortlessly. The way you define your purpose is to align your self with the Gods. If you achieve alignment with the Gods, you will be able to tap into their process of replacing Chaos with Order. That order will transform your life, filling it with everything you need to live a happy and successful life.

When you achieve alignment with the Gods, you not only tap into their power to create order, but the Gods can draw on your power to help them in their work. This is the symbiotic relationship that is expressed in the Rune Gebo, the exchanging of gifts, and is what is meant by alignment. This takes us to the next principle.

2) Exchanging Gifts: Have you noticed how some of the richest people engage in philanthropy, giving millions, tens of millions and even hundreds of millions to charities? They understand the principle that if you want to acquire wealth, you must be generous. Many religions expect their members to give regular donations. The reason for this is not greed. There is a power in money when it is given for unselfish reason. Its energy is returned to the giver. This is the principle behind the Rune Gebo. Once you have given, the dynamic force within Gebo brings actual forces to bear, by transforming the Vril currents according to the nature of the act of giving, that will bring you wealth and abundance in exchange for your act of giving. Remember what we never get tired of reminding you? *Like attracts like.*

We once again remind you that shape is one of the principles behind the power of the Runes; notice that the shape of Gebo embodies the principle of exchanging gifts. Each side gives to the other equally. When one side gives unselfishly to the other side, it creates an imbalance in the flow of Vrilic energy that stimulates a compensatory effect of like kind. What you give is given back to you. This is why it is important to give money if that is what you wish to increase in your life. The giving of money causes a momentum that builds with each gift. You are consciously "seeding" your future pathways with that very thing you wish to appear—money. But when you give, give unselfishly. It is best to make a gift and not a loan.

As we said, the rich know the secret to acquiring additional wealth. *"It is better to give than to receive."* The wealthy, who give billions of dollars to charity, do so because they know that if you want to manifest more wealth, *you have got to get it first.* An elderly man on a fixed income who gives five dollars is more enriched than someone worth billions who gives millions. The elderly man on a fixed income is experiencing greater hardship than the Wall Street billionaire. The latter is not making a real sacrifice. He won't even notice it missing among all the billions he has.

When you give a few dollars, or whatever the amount you can afford, to help someone or contribute to the growth and development of something you consider productive and important, you get a good feeling in the pit of your stomach. You know, no matter how large or small your donation is, and it is a real sacrifice, you are performing a noble deed. You start to feel a sense of self-worth. You will also feel grateful for what you have. Say to yourself:

I have more money than I need.

There is an infinite supply of money and abundance and it is on its way to me.

I am receiving more money that I could possibly need.

Every day, I am receiving more money than I need.

Affirmations like this will eventually open pathways into your future for you to make large sums of money.

When you give money freely, and without concern about its loss, you are saying to yourself, "I have plenty of money and don't need all that I have." By being unconcerned about giving up money, you will be attracting money to you. *When you give of yourself with purpose, you will discover money will be flowing into your life in greater amounts.* By giving money away, you are sending frequencies into the Vril-filled universe, and by the law of cause and effect, vast sums of money will begin to flow back to you. Abundance and wealth are the result of your living with a sense of purpose. Money is just like everything else. By living purposefully, you will attract what you want the most. But remember–the desire for more wealth, abundance and money should not be your purpose. It is only when you live your life guided by a purpose that is beyond your selfishness, that you will manifest what you desire. Money and wealth should not be your goals! You should not chase after them! If they are, they will always elude you! The reason is simple. No matter how much wealth and money you acquire, it will never be enough! Your goal must be attainable. It should be the evolution to a higher state of being.

3) Overcoming Limitations: If you concentrate on the lack of wealth, you will never attract wealth. If your thoughts, feelings and sensations are focused on what is missing from your life, then you will generate more of the lack of what you are missing. *Focus on Wealth, Not the Lack of It.* The law of cause and effect will manifest what you are obsessing on in your life. If you are constantly thinking about the lack of money and wealth, then your mind will generate a life in which you lack money and wealth. If you are always reminding yourself that you do not have enough money, then it will be impossible to attract more money. Your thoughts are sending out sensations of how little you have, shaping Vril flowing into you, and blazing pathways that will lead you to more lack of money. If you become preoccupied with the thought of how little money you have, your thoughts will generate many more circumstances in your future in which you will not only not draw more money to you, but will cause you to go deeper into debt.

Learn to focus on more money flowing into your life, and your future will be filled with opportunities where your wealth will increase. Once you begin to emit signals through the power of your mind, Vril will create pathways in which money will begin to flow to you effortlessly. You must learn to think all the time that you have more than enough money than you need to survive. Utilize what we taught you about visualization

4) The Joy of Being Successful: You must learn to see yourself as someone who is naturally successful. If you visualize your purpose in life, and that purpose is filled with abundance, you will discover that you are living a life in harmony with the Godly forces giving order to the universe. *Stop fretting about how much you do not have, and rejoice in all the things you already have and you will fill your thoughts with joy and happiness.* If you are happy with what you have, no matter how great or small, and consider yourself success in having what you do, your mind will send out the frequencies that will mold and shape the Vril currents into pathways in which you will acquire more of what you have. If you are happy with only $100 in your bank account and consider yourself successful in acquiring that $100, your mind will weave a Web of Wyrd that will assure more hundreds of dollars will come to you, and in time you will discover that you have ten times that amount. But if you worry about having ONLY $100, you will never receive more money, because your subconscious will hear only the ONLY, and that's what will be woven into your Web of Wyrd.

You have to create a mind-set in which you are happy about your life. Once you do, prosperity will flow into your life. *Know that Vril will generate wealth in your future.* Remember that the supply of Vril is infinite, and thus the amount of wealth you can generate is also infinite.

Realize that you never have to worry again about such things as money, and prosperity will indeed be a part of your life. You will be creating all the wealth you could possibly want with your thoughts. Trust the universal power of Vril, and know that your vision of yourself as wealthy and prosperous is part of the Gods' design for the universe, and it will come to pass. You might not win the lottery and become a millionaire overnight, but enough wealth will always come your way to assure a happy and secure life. Once you have convinced yourself of this principle, be happy in the knowledge that you can and will generate wealth and abundance.

Know that people who have no money are blocking their access to money though their thoughts. They see themselves without abundance and this creates negative feelings, which in turn, shapes Vril, causing Vril to create pathways leading them to more lack of money

5) Tipping the Balance Toward Abundance: You must see your life filled with abundance. Once you have convinced yourself you are rich, you will be happy. The love and joy that you feel about yourself, and how prosperous you already are, will tip the balance in your favor. Once you spend most of your time rejoicing about having more-than-enough money, instead of the lack-of-money, your future pathways will lead you into a future filled with the former. Know with every fiber of your being that your vision of yourself as rich will be woven into the Gods' grand design for the universe. By finding your purpose, you have aligned yourself with the Gods, and they will weave into their plan for the universe your life of abundance. Know that you don't have to pray or plead or beg on bended knee for what you want. The Gods will give it to you because you have gone into partnership with them in their task of creating and maintaining order in the universe. Once you realize this, give thanks and feel joyful that you have discovered the secret of obtaining happiness and success in your life, and *truly believe it!*

This is the law of cause and effect. The secret to filling your life with the things you want is to *be* and *feel* happy about it now, at this very moment. Concentrate on sending those feelings of joy and happiness out into the infinite sea of Vril that is the universe, and your feelings will shape the currents of Vril flowing into you, generating more of the same. This is the cause that will create the effect, and the effect will be Vril sending all the things that will create more of the same, joy and happiness, into your life. By sending out these feelings, pathways will be blazed for you to follow in the future that will be filled with the things that will increase the amount of joy and happiness you are already feeling. The law of cause and effect is generating back to you a hundred times over what it is you are sending out. And if prosperity is what will give you joy and happiness, then Vril will fill those future pathways with circumstances that will lead you to prosperity.

6) Personal Luck: We will explore the subject of your Personal Luck in a later chapter, but for now know that you can use the methodology provided in this book to transform Vril into *Megin*, which is the Norse term for your supply of "Personal Luck," and maintain an ample supply for your use to manifest what you desire in the material world. Know that you can increase your supply of luck and make it work to transform your life. Your supply of Megin will work to manifest events in your life that will bring to you those things, in this case wealth and abundance, that your mind is concentrating on. Your positive affirmation of being a wealthy person, rich in the good things in life, and possessing a life of abundance, will be transformed into pathways by your supply of Personal Luck in your future.

7) Runes for Increasing Your Wealth: There are many Runes that you can use for drawing wealth and prosperity into your life. Here are some of the most potent Runes you can use:

Fehu: Fehu is the principal Money Rune, representing mobile forces. It is also the primary Luck Rune and can be used to increase your amount of Personal Luck.

Gebo: This is the Rune of the Cosmic Law of Compensation. The crossed arms of equal proportion represent the need for balance. This principle assures equal exchange of energies.

Wunjo: The forces within Wunjo create an energy field where many people can work together harmoniously. You can use Wunjo to help you discover your Personal Purpose, and achieve abundance in every area of your life. It has the power to fulfill your wishes.

Othala: Othala is the converse of Fehu, representing immobile wealth and prosperity through inheritance and property. Use it to bring abundance to your family, organization or any group you are involved in.

Jera: Jera is the Harvest Rune. Its powers represent the energy needed to bring long-term growth and development through the Cosmic Law of Cycles. Its energies assure the right actions of seeding, growth, blooming and eventual harvest.

Berkano: This is the Birthing Rune. Its energies deal with the end of the gestation period of development, and the sudden creation of a new entity, physical or mental. It brings forth the transformed substance into the material world. Its powers govern the process of fertility and birthing equally.

Laguz: Laguz is the Rune of Substance. Substance is the living energy (Vril) out of which everything is made. Use Laguz to harness the Vril currents and shape them into your objective. Laguz represents water. Its powers are similar to the process of filling an empty glass with water. When you use Laguz, you are filling your mental goals with Vril, and thus providing the energies necessary to bring forth into creation that which you desire to manifest.

Nauthiz: This Rune represents the process of manifestation. Necessity and need. Without these two forces you lack the will to begin and carry through with your goals. It is the Rune of resistance and can be used to counter any negative forces within your Orlog that might hinder your success.

Kenaz: The Rune of Creative Fire is the energy needed to bring forth transformation. Its powers give you the technical knowhow to make things happen. If Fehu is the energy that is manifested in the furnace, Kenaz embodies the process of then using the fire within the furnace for creation.

8) Norse Money Charm: You can use the various Runes described to create Bind Runes to draw Luck into your venture or project. You should create a Bind Rune from the Runes that are appropriate to your goal. Let your instincts guide you as to the actual shape of the Bind Rune. You should feel it to be right for you. There is a Norse Money Charm that has been used in the past for harnessing divine response to our needs for substance in manifesting wealth and abundance. We are providing it to you for your use.

The charm's design has outstretched arms that represent the human figure addressing the Gods, similar to the Elhaz. The arms form a cup which can represent a receptive female symbol, as a cup or womb. The intersecting line within the cup is a phallic symbol of fertilization. This charm is especially powerful for acquiring money but can be used for the acquisition of abundance of various forms.

9) Imagine You are Already Rich. To acquire wealth and abundance, you must drive out all disbelief that you can never be wealthy. Create an imaginary life for yourself in which you are rich. See yourself enjoying prosperity and abundance in the here and now. Keep your mind focused on thoughts of how rich you already are. Create an imaginary world for you to visit often, in which you are the wealthiest man in the world. Work on sharpening this image as often as you can in each day. Do not forget that everything in the world is 99 percent Vril, and your thoughts are 100 percent Vril, so your thoughts are more powerful than the material objects around you. Stop imagining yourself a slave to the material around you and see yourself as its master. Know that with the power of your thoughts, you can reshape the material reality you live in. Know that you have a purpose in life, and part of that purpose is to be rich and wealthy. If you can think of yourself as rich, you will create a life in which you are rich. Learn to trust that little voice in your head. It is your intuitive mind speaking to you. Do not be afraid to follow your hunches. They are Vril leading you down the correct pathways into the future you desire. They are glimpses of the reality that the Gods are constantly striving to maintain, and if you can discover their "blueprint for an orderly universe," you will be able to align yourself with the Gods and create a life for yourself that will be one filled with success. The little voices you hear are actually the Gods talking about their work. It is as if you have overheard two successful businessmen talking over their plans to invest their money in a sure-fire venture that will bring them success and rewards. If you make the same investments, you too will prosper. You must make those thoughts that you are entitled to wealth and abundance into the foundation of your vision of yourself. Once you have convinced yourself that this is who you are, wealthy, you will become wealthy.

You must let go of preconceived ideas on how you can obtain abundance. If you have been taught that you have to work hard to obtain abundance and wealth, then your thoughts will bring a great deal of hard work in your life, with very little abundance; your feelings will have created pathways from the flow of Vril to ensure that you will have to struggle for every dime you earn. Instead of thinking that you have to bust your butt for every dollar you make, think over and over how easily money comes to you, and you will send the appropriate frequency that will draw wealth and abundance your way. If you think the only way to acquire wealth and riches is through your job, then you will never achieve abundance, because most jobs will never afford you the opportunity to become wealthy. If you think that wealth is the property of a very select few, and that most people are condemned to a life of toil and struggle, then you will never enjoy a life filled with abundance and wealth. *You have to purge your thinking of such negative and defeatist notions.* Understand that abundance is there in the universe for everyone, and you should not worry about how you will receive it. If you think positive, and fill your thoughts with positive feelings of joy and a love of life, abundance will come to you without you knowing how in advance. Stop worrying about the how. If prosperity is what will give you joy and happiness, then Vril will fill your future pathways with circumstances that will lead to prosperity.

10) Believe that You Can Afford Everything You Desire: If you are constantly trying to figure out how you will get out of debt, you will be attracting more debt. The obsession with avoiding debt or getting out of it is sending powerful feelings that shape Vril, creating pathways that will lead you to more debt. It does not matter whether you are concentrating on getting out of debt or worrying about falling into more debt; you are thinking about debt, and Vril does not respond to the "out of" part. Your strong feelings on debt will draw more of it. If you are really suffering from it, get help with it so you can set up a plan to repay it, and then put it out of your mind. Once you have done this, you can then just think only about prosperity. One way to do this is to play a little game.

The game starts whenever you like by your going window shopping. When you come across something that you really would like to have, not matter how expensive, just say to yourself, "I can afford that." Then visualize how much fun it is have it. You are changing the way you think from "I can't afford that," to "I can afford that." It is the positive affirmation that will help you change your thinking patterns. Do this over and over. Say to yourself, "I can buy that." When you see clothes you would like, say, "I can afford that." When you see that brand new sports car, "I can buy that." Keep doing this and eventually you will develop a more positive attitude toward money. You will begin to feel better about your financial state. You will no longer be worrying about debt all the time, and eventually money will come.

Remember to focus your thoughts and feelings on prosperity, not scarcity. The amount of abundance in the universe is infinite and there is plenty for you. Most people, both rich and poor, have accepted the false impression that there is just so much wealth to go around, and the rich have stolen it. But this is not true. The rich have more wealth because they believe they have a right to it. Wealth and abundance seem to fall into their lap even when they are not trying. It might seem effortless to them. The reason is clear. From childhood, wealthy people are indoctrinated with the notion that wealth is something that will naturally be drawn to them. They take it for granted because it has no real meaning. They never worry about debt, and seem to believe that there is always enough money coming their way no matter happens.

So you see, if you are constantly thinking that you have to work hard for something, then your feelings will create pathways from the flow of Vril to ensure that you *will* have to work hard. Instead of thinking that you have to struggle for every dollar you earn, think over and over how easily money comes to you, and you will send the appropriate frequency that will bring wealth and abundance your way.

Dwarf Powers

Within the Norse cosmology there exist several races of elemental beings, and for our purposes of acquiring wealth and prosperity, we will briefly examine the race of Dwarfs. There are many legends and fairy tales of Dwarfs, who have a great influence over the energy dealing with Substance. In their subterranean realm of Svartalfheim, they mold and shape the material substance into riches. Most legends refer to Dwarfs as misshapen anthropomorphic little people who spend a great deal of time mining for jewels and minerals which they then hammer and meld into great works of art, powerful weapons and fine jewelry. They are beings of material forces.

We suggest you try to meditate on the imagery of the dwarfs, and ask them for their assistance in your quest for material acquisition. There are many fairy tales of Dwarfs weaving straw into gold, or skilled in an artisan craft such as shoe-making. Other tales depict them hoarding treasures. You might find it hard to believe that Dwarfs really exist, but before you dismiss their reality, let us remind you of a survey taken in Iceland in 1975. It turned out that 55% of Icelanders believe in the existence of Dwarfs and Elves. In fact, Iceland has a law that before a road or highway is constructed, the authorities have to first seek the acceptance of the earth spirits (Dwarfs and Elves) and make sure the construction does not interfere or disrupt their own spiritual earthly realm.

Dwarfs are known to be secretive, but in possession of profound wisdom dealing with the acquisition of wealth and abundance. They are known as kobolds, gnomes, brownies, goblins, leprechauns, pook, goodfellow, puck, thumbkin, house-sprites, lares, huldra-folk, nisse, vetta and many other names according to the country where they dwell. Though they are less powerful than the Gods, they possess greater wisdom than humans, especially with all subjects dealing with material possession and craftsmanship. Even the Gods often turn to them for the manufacture of their weapons and wealth, as well as knowledge about the future. We will get into the lore of the Dwarfs in future lessons, but for now we need to understand how they can help you in you quest for material success in Midgard.

Anyone who seeks material success in Midgard should establish a working friendship with the Dwarf-realm. The establishment of Human-Dwarf understanding and love will expand your consciousness regarding the creation of material wealth and abundance in your life. Those of you who wish to obtain for yourselves greater material abundance will be moved to establish a greater understanding of the elemental forces of Earth. To achieve this, you will seek to expand your chosen elemental nature through the power of Love. *In obtaining the knowledge of the Dwarf-forces in your quest for material acquisition, if you are motivated by greed then you will fail, but if you approach the acquisition of abundance and wealth with an understanding of the forces of reciprocity, you must exercise the power of Gebo: the exchanging of gifts. This requires that you develop a perfect balance between the desire to give and gain within your soul.* Just as the Gods give something in exchange for what they receive from the Dwarfs, when you utilize the principle of Gebo, you are extending the force of Love to the elemental forces of Earth, the Dwarfs.

Gods to Call on for Assistance:

There are several Gods you can call on to help you in your quest for wealth and abundance. Here is a list of the most prominent of them.

NERTHUS: She is an early version of the Earth Mother and of the Vanir race of Gods. She is considered Njord's first wife and twin sister.

FREY: His name means "Lord." He is also Vanir; his father is Njord, and mother, Nerthus. His twin sister is Freyja. Frey is a Vanir Sun God and Earth God. His energies will bring you sensual love, fertility, spiritual growth, abundance, wealth, material possession, courage, peace, joy and happiness. He is the Norse equivalent of the Greek Nature God, Pan. He is also is the ruler of the realm of the Light Elves.

NJORD: The king of Vanaheim, he is the God of the seashore. He can bring you great prosperity, especially in trade and commerce, since most commerce was conducted by ships through seaports in ancient times.

FREYJA: She is Frey's twin sister and her name means "Lady." She is most often considered the Goddess of sensual pleasure, love, fertility, beauty, magic and luck, and even war, and she possesses the Brisingama, or Brising Necklace. She had to sleep with four Dwarfs to gain possession of it, and was punished by Odin, which caused her great grief. She wandered Midgard crying tears of gold. Thus she is also a Goddess of material wealth, jewelry, material possessions and abundance. But there is a lesson to be learned from Freyja's experience–sometimes you have to pay the price for abundance if you do not maintain your high standards and virtue.

FRIGGA: Frigga is the Mother Earth Goddess, and wife of Odin. All possessions from the earth, including wealth and abundance, are ruled by her. She is also the Goddess of the Family, so seek her support when conducting business or trade that is family centered. She can give your family prosperity and abundance.

DWARVES: We have already spoken of the Dwarves and their ability to help you gain material wealth and abundance. Seek them out and establish a mutual and loving relationship with them. They are especially helpful with material possessions acquired from within the earth, such as by mining, as well as all manufacturing, inventions and craftsmanship.

Exercises to Create a Mind Set to Acquire Wealth and Abundance:

There is a simple exercise you can do to help you develop a mind set for attracting abundance. The first step is to sit down and write out a list of everything you can think of that makes you happy. You should be able to come up with about 40 to 60 things that you enjoy doing. You can write at the top of the list, "What makes me really, really happy?" You don't have to catalog them in order of what you like to do. For now, just write everything that you enjoy doing.

Next, go back over the list and pick out the top twenty things you like to do best. Then do it again, but pick out the ten top things you like to do from the list of twenty. Finally, pick out the top five things you like to do from the list of ten. You don't have to do it all in one sitting. You can go over and over the list until you are satisfied. You are not trying to list goals and objectives, just things you like to do. They should be things you do well, and really enjoy doing. Things that bring you happiness. The purpose will be to discover your life's purpose. We will have a whole lesson in the future about your Life Purpose. There is a saying, "If you do something you dislike for a living, it's work, but if your do something you love for a living, its play." So you will probably discover that many of the things you enjoy could not be used for your life purpose. That's all right. They might be simply enjoyable hobbies. But there will be a few things that will stand out as a possible Life Purpose. Review these over and over until you decide on one or two that you feel passionate about. But don't fall victim to the negative thought pattern that will cause you to say to yourself, "I really love doing this, but. . . . !!!!!!" No buts, please.

For the next step, we want you to make another list. On top, write, "What I can do to make it happen now?" You are going to have to think about this list of things you can do, so take your time. You might want to incorporate, either for-profit if it is a money-making business, or non-profit if it is not. Or you might want to set up a Web site to begin the process. This does not have to be a business. It could be something you enjoy doing for the sake of doing it. It could be a hobby. It should be something you love doing. If you love to paint, or draw, or write poetry, or short stories, you might want to put them on a Web site for others to read. If you become popular, you can eventually sell your picture or stories. But first step first. You might discover that something you do as a hobby might be professional enough for others to want to pay you to do. But you will never know until you begin doing it.

Another thing you might want to do at first is buy some books on the subject you enjoy. You might have to purchase materials. Write everything down that you have to do to get started. Once you start figuring out what you have to do, you will most likely think of other things to do beforehand. Once you get the juices flowing, they will get you thinking more clearly about how to get started.

Chapter Nine: How Vrilology can help you Obtain a Happy and Loving Relationship

If you wish to manifest a wonderful, loving relationship, you must first define who you are. Remember, the world we live in is created by our thoughts. You manifest your wishes through your thoughts. Our thoughts create the type of person we are, which in turn will determine the nature of our relationship with others. Therefore, follow the simple rule, "Act in accordance with your desires."

Be Sure To Act in Accordance with What You Desire

You have to truly know what you desire in a relationship. What type of person do you want to share your life with. But it is a little more complex than that because you must make sure your actions do not contradict what you desire. For instance, if you are a man and you want to share your life with a loving, caring woman, you must make sure you are not overbearing, selfish and arrogant. Or, if you are a woman, and you want to share your life with a loving man who will be responsive to your needs, you must make sure you are not judgmental, degrading and selfish. It is important to understand that you will receive exactly what you are sending. Make sure your actions, thoughts and feelings mirror what you desire. Begin to live your life in ways as if you have already received what you have asked for. It is through this act of anticipating that your mind generates the reality you wish to create, by acting as if you have already received what you want. Your mind is creating powerful mental frequencies that shape in-flowing Vril.

This method is also true for all your dealings with all acquaintances. Whether the person in question is a family member, a friend, a fellow worker, your partner or your mate, you should at all times act the way you want the other person to act. By acting in ways that you want people to treat you, you will be setting up a field of energy around you that will cause others to adjust to your frequency. Most people will react immediately to your behavior. Think about people you have met. Try to remember their attitude toward you, and especially try to recall how you reacted. You can perform a little exercise by being conscious of each person that you meet through a full twenty-four hour period. Every time you come into contact with someone, take notice of their attitude toward you. Then examine how their attitude makes you feel. Do you immediately feel happy when you come into contact with someone who is happy? If you do, ask yourself why. Try to feel why you immediately respond in the way you do. *Did you feel their happiness?* Do the same for each person you meet. If you meet someone who is angry, do you respond by reacting in anger? Be very sensitive to what you feel when you come into contact with each person.

If you perform this exercise, you will soon discover the transformation you experience when you come into contact with others. Unless you are completely wrapped up in your own emotional storm, which causes you to put up barriers and block out what others feel, your emotional state will be affected whenever you come into contact with the life energy field of each person you meet. Remember our discussion about subatomic particles and how each subatomic particle affects every other subatomic particle it comes into contact with, and continues to do so even when they are millions of light years away from each other? Well, this is what is happening when you come into contact with the life energy field of each person you meet. Your life energy fields, made of Vril, vibrate, and when they come into contact with each other, their frequencies will equalize. The weaker vibration will adjust itself to the stronger. Thus, when one individual is experiencing an intense emotion, it will affect the life energy field of another person experiencing a weaker emotional intensity.

By consciously maintaining a constant emotional state of friendliness and self assurance, you can assure that your mental and emotional state will affect others around you. If you maintain such a continuous frequency of behavior, eventually others will respond to you without realizing how they are acting. Their behavior will adjust to your frequency.

Doing this is not hard. All you have to do is be conscious of the way you want others to treat you, and act accordingly. Be happy, forthright, friendly and open. Your actions will communicate your frame of mind to others. They will see you as friendly, and immediately feel at ease and comfortable around you. They will want to deal with you, and will seek you out because of your friendly behavior. Once you have achieved this frame of mind, you will discover that people will treat you differently, and that they will notice a marked change in you.

Work on Improving Yourself, Not the One You Love

By maintaining a positive attitude toward others, you are creating a field of energy around you in which you can influence others with little or no effort. I am reminded of the movie *Star Wars*, when Obi-Wan and Luke Skywalker ride into town with their two robot companions. They are stopped by two Imperial Storm Troopers looking for two robots. When they ask Obi-Wan, whom the robots belong to, the old Jedi warrior waves his hand and says, "These are not the droids you are looking for." The trooper repeats what he says, "These are not the droids we're looking for." Obi-Wan then says, "You can go about your business." The troops repeat that too. Obi-Wan was exerting a mind-control method on the troopers, causing them to act and think in ways he wanted them to act. In a way, you are doing the same by using your mind to create a field of energy that will affect the way people respond to you. By being friendly, you are sending out mental waves convincing people you come into contact with that you are not a threat, that you can be trusted, and that they should listen to what you have to say.

You will have discovered another aspect of you, as a Vril Being. Remember, 99 percent of you is essentially made up of Vril energy, and this is true of everyone and everything else in the universe. Therefore, if you learn how to control Vril, you can control anyone and anything. All you are doing is manipulating the flow of Vril. You understand that the invisible, Vril part of you is what processes all your actions. In this way you can control and shape your world, and determine the nature of your reality.

Your actions can be translated into very powerful thoughts. If you are constantly displaying a demeanor radiating anger, frustration, hostility, these are the things that you will be confronted with. They will color your energy life field that surrounds you. As people come into contact with it, they will instinctively sense you are unfriendly, and approach you as someone who is hostile and must be confronted. Animals are very adept at sensing this. They can sense fear, anger and hostility, as well as calmness, friendliness, and confidence. They will react to what frequencies you are sending out.

So know that your thoughts are generating what you feel, and your feelings are sending out signals for others to receive and act on. What you generate will be attracted back. Once you set up a field of positive frequencies, the entire universe will react to that. You will be sending to the Gods, who are maintaining the order within the universe, your signals like blueprints for them to incorporate into their grand design. So if you set up your field of love and happiness, the universe will send you more people filled with love and happiness.

If you love and respect yourself, others will treat you the same way. Everyone in your life is a reflection of your thoughts. You are a Vril Being, which means 99 percent of you is Vril energy. The same is true of everyone else. Thus, people whom you are in contact with are not physical beings, but thoughts. How you interact with others is a creation of how you think about others. It is a process created by your thoughts.

How You Feel About Yourself Will Determine How Others Feel About You

You have got to work on improving yourself and your life. Before you can help others, you have to help yourself. I am not talking about becoming a selfish or uncaring person. Many people have dedicated themselves to helping someone, and even begun to sacrifice all their time and energy, because they felt obligated. They feared that if they refused to spend their lives serving those who are in need of help, they were not good people. The thought pattern leading to sacrifice says, "I have to go without because there is not enough for me and the other person." This thought pattern will lead to depression, resentment and bitterness, not only toward yourself, but toward the person you are helping and the world in general.

Many have been taught that to love oneself is wrong, and that to do so is somehow cold, hard and unfeeling. But to love yourself is simply to love your life. And when you truly love who you are, and your life, you display this joy to the world. Others around you are touched by it. This happens in the same way as Obi-Wan changed the thoughts of the storm troopers. Your feelings create a field of energy around you, and anyone who comes into contact with it will be transformed. They will notice your cheerful attitude and they won't be able to resist. This process is based on the simple premise that you must fill yourself with love, joy and happiness, or you won't have anything to give those whom you come into contact with. By doing what makes you happy, you will generate a love of life and others will be moved by what you feel. You will become a beacon in the dark that will attract others seeking those good feelings that you radiate.

Once you change your thinking patterns, and convince yourself that there is abundance for everyone, you will send out thoughts that will change the way others think. You cannot provide for others by sacrificing for them. Sacrifice only creates a condition where you are surrendering everything for another, and that person becomes dependent on you for survival. Instead, you must be there for support, but you must make feeling good a priority, and radiate a sense of joy when assisting others. Don't see it as sacrifice, and don't sacrifice. Radiate confidence and joy, and you will discover that the person who needs help will begin to change their attitude. Gaining confidence, they too will soon discover they can do more and will continue to try to do more for themselves. They might never become totally independent of your help, but they will soon begin to help themselves more and more. This will not only make your task of helping easier, but will help them change their attitude, which in turn will help them master Vril and turn their own life around for the better.

Focus on What You Love About Yourself

There is a simple reason why you have to cultivate a love for yourself. It is simply impossible to love others if you don't first love yourself. When you feel bad about yourself, you draw to yourself those same feelings. People who dislike you will be drawn into your life. But when you feel good about yourself, you will draw into your life all the good things in the universe. You will be creating pathways leading to good health, good relationships, success in your career. Everything that is good is working on good frequencies. So when you feel bad about yourself, you align yourself with the frequencies that will lead down pathways that will bring bad things. As you experience more and more terrible events, you will think to yourself that you are cursed, that you have a miserable life, and that everyone is out to get you. These thoughts and feelings will then fashion the Vril flowing into you to create more pathways that will lead to more of the same. To break the patterns, you have to break the habit of thinking poorly of yourself.

You must never forget that your feelings are born of your thoughts, so if you want to create miracles in your life, you must think of yourself as someone who can manifest them. You must align yourself with the Gods, so that your thoughts will send out positive feelings that will cause them to create pathways that will transform your life into a procession of miracles.

This process will impact the type of people you will meet. The nature of the people with whom we have relationships in our lives will depend on the nature of our view of ourselves. Our relationship with another person is a reflection of our relationship to ourselves. When you love yourself and your own life, you attract others who feel the same. When two individuals can love themselves and their lives, and decide to form a bond with each other, they cannot help but love and enjoy their new life together.

Now you will be asking, "How do I change the way I think about myself?" This is not as hard as you might think. All you have to do is think of one thing that you do love about yourself. No matter how bad you might be feeling about yourself or your life, there has to be at least one thing you like about yourself. Concentrate on this thought and hold it in your mind for as long as you can. If you begin to think about something else, return to this good thought. You will discover that this process will soon draw to you other good thoughts about yourself. Before you realize it, you will have a long list of things about yourself that you like. You will make the remarkable discovery that you are a great human being. Spend time thinking about it and let yourself feel good. Your good feelings will send out frequencies that will shape and form Vril flowing into you. You will begin to attract those good things that you are focused on. Your thoughts will expand and grow, filling your life with more of the same. You must use these good thoughts about yourself to create your relationships.

Focus on What You Love About the Person You Love, Not Their Faults

What you are depends on how you see yourself. Your thoughts originate with you, so you have complete control over your own development and the way you want to be.

This holds true for other people in your life. Stop complaining about them, especially about people close to you: your coworkers, your family, your mate. No one is perfect, and if you continue to dwell on their faults, you will always have those faults to deal with, because they will become a bigger and bigger part of your relationship with them. If you have a negative attitude toward someone, it will resonate every time you are in contact with them, and your feelings will motivate them to resent you. They won't even be conscious of it. Like attracts like. The law of cause and effect causes people to display their negative side if you are expecting them to.

If you are in love with someone, but you are dissatisfied about something regarding their personality or habits, then that will be what you will have to deal with all the time. It will define your relationship. Soon you will be thinking about the faults all the time, and they will grow and consume you. This is especially true when someone behaves in a way that you might not necessarily approve of, though it is not directed against you, nor has it caused you any discomfort. It might just be an issue of your being judgmental. "Oh, God! She is so immature!" "He is so loud!" "She is so self-absorbed!" You can judge the person, even if the person really likes you and enjoys your company, and you might even keep your opinion about their faults to yourself. Eventually, your negative attitude will cause those traits you disapprove of to increase. The person's behavior will take on those traits more often and they will become more intense, all because you are dwelling on them in a negative way.

The best way to counter this development is to make a list of everything that you appreciate about the person. If you are having a romantic relationship with the individual, each day write down one trait you love about the person. Meditate and think about it all day. Do this for ten, twenty or even thirty days. You will soon discover that after you focus on their positive traits, that person will be displaying more and more of these traits toward you. The negative traits will still be there, but you won't be bothered by them, or you might not even notice them any more. They will become invisible to you. You will see only those traits that originally attracted you to the person in the first place.

The worst problem in relationships is that we expect the other person to create happiness in our lives. But most times, they fail to live up to our expectations. The reason for this is simple: The only person who can truly make you happy is you! Everyone else has the opportunity to share in your happiness, but you have to create happiness in your life. You have to create joy and happiness in you and it will shine throughout the universe like a supernova.

The Gebo Principle in Relationships

Gebo is the Rune of exchanging gifts. It energy can be used to cement relationships between individuals. It is a very effective runic tool to establish and build healthy and loving relationships. It is about giving of oneself to another person, who in turn returns the gift of giving. The greatest gift one person can give another person is love–unselfish, all-giving love. This love is an emotional force powered by Vril energy. Since every human in the universe is comprised of Vril, a living dynamic and universal energy which sustains us and responds to our expectations, we have the ability to send this energy to another person, projecting it outward to assist that person in whatever endeavor they are engaged in. By extending our Vril energy to another person, we can support them, especially in their time of emotional need. If we extend love, charged with Vril energy, they will respond in kind. Unfortunately, most of us are unaware of being a Vril being. We are disconnected from the infinite source of this energy. Through our chaotic lifestyles, we have cut ourselves off and so have felt weak, insecure and lacking. We waste our supply of Vril and instead of learning how to increase the flow of Vril into ourselves from the universe around us, we unconsciously and instinctive seek to draw Vril energy from those people around us. It has always been easier to deal with this personal energy deficit by seeking to psychologically steal it from others—an unconscious competition that underlies all human conflict in the world, and especially within the realm of our personal relationships with loved ones, family members, our spouse and friends.

Even in the simple act of holding a conversation with another person, this principle of energy transference occurs. When a person engages another in a conversation, one of two things can happen: that person can come away feeling stronger or weaker. Whether we are conscious of it or not, we tend to say whatever we must in order to prevail in the conversation. This competition is especially true between two individuals who are in a loving relationship. After the initial emotional "high" of the start of a love relationship wears off, one of the two individuals will instinctively try to dominate the relationship. Each of us seeks some way to control, and thus remain on top in, the relationship. And this is also true of the simplest and most fleeting encounters. If we are successful, if our viewpoint prevails, then rather than feel weak, we receive a psychological boost. When we control another human being we receive their energy. We fill up at the other's expense and the filling up is what motivates us. Most people are in a constant hunt for someone else's energy.

By using the energy of Gebo we can learn to exchange the gift of Vril energy between our self and another person. Without the principle of Gebo, you will be taking energy from another person. We must learn to gain energy from the universal source, not other humans. This is one of the most important lessons in this book. In the chapter on health, you learn how you can increase your flow of Vril energy from food, but in order to totally absorb Vril in food, the food must be appreciated, savored. You must learn to appreciate the taste of your food, and this is the reason why we are told by our parents to chew our food thoroughly--so the energy from the food can enter your body. Vril is also absorbed through water and other drinks. Proper breathing is the best way to absorb increased amounts of Vril. After personal energy is increased, you become more sensitive to Vril in all things, and then you learn to unconsciously increase the absorption of Vril.

Remember that Vril is the Life Force of the Gods, and that it is a gift from Odin, who fills us with the first breath of Vril when we are born. This first breath of Vril is referred to as Ond in the Norse myths. It is the divine breath of Odin. When you successfully appreciate this fact, you allow the love that underlies all to enter you. This love is the Balder Force. You are drawing into yourself a love of all things, because all things took an oath never to harm Balder, the Son of Odin. It is this indestructiblc force that fills you, and it is this indestructible force that you exchange with another human when you rely on Gebo to exchange energy. Gebo is thus the exchanging of Vril energy that is colored with a divine love–the divine love that is Balder.

When you get to a level where you feel love, then you can send the energy back just by willing it so with the help of Gebo.

The Magic of Sexual Union

There is one overriding principle that holds true throughout the universe: *Sex is omnipresent and pervasive in the Universe. All manifestations of creation are the results of procreation, and procreation proceeds from the union of the masculine and feminine natures of the Life Force, known as Vril.* This is an immutable law and permeates the symbolic mythology, in not only the Norse, but all Indo-European mythologies. In fact it is at the foundation of all folklore throughout the world.

Mabel Tam wrote in her book, *Sex and the Erotic Lover*:

"Sexual magic is the encounter of two universes: the feminine and the masculine; this union results in love, creation, wisdom and happiness; ecstasy, power and life."

We could not sum up the principle of Sex Magic better.

The Life Force of the Gods, which we refer to as Vril, is impelled with an overriding urge to join masculine with feminine. This compulsion is as unalterable as the rising of the sun in the morning. We can see this primal urge throughout Nature. This law of attraction is prevalent in the world of animals and plants, as well as humans. It even occurs at the atomic level with the joining of the positive and negative polarities, which results in the production of different types of energy. In the reality of electricity and magnetism we can observe the joining of the positive feminine seeking union with the negative male pole. The joining of the positive feminine with the negative masculine results in the creation of a new energy force.

Mystery schools through time have always held to this principle, and this truth has come to be the foundation of modern science. Sex is the all-pervasive, all-present force of procreation. Without sex there is no creation. Creation always results from procreation, and procreation proceeds from sexual activity. Thus, the Great Principle which is at the foundation of all Cosmic activity is the force of attraction between male and female polarities. The motive power behind all creative activities in the Cosmos lies within this most fundamental principle of sexuality. This truth permeates all levels of consciousness, in the realm of physical manifestation as well as on the mental and spiritual levels of existence. The methodology of generation, rooted in the attraction of male and female, is eternal. It is the essence of life, the basis of the order generated and maintained by the Gods in their struggle against the force of chaos personified by the Giants. Anything that is in conflict with this principle is unnatural and a perversion of the natural order of the universe, which is the creation of the Gods, and supported and maintained by the Gods.

We can see this principle played out in the creation tale of the first war waged by the Gods against the Giants. Odin, Vili and Ve are repulsed by the nature of Ymir. Ymir's nature is androgynous. The Gods kill Ymir and create the male-female polarity principle of attraction for procreation by separating Ymir's bisexual nature. The very principle of male and female polarity was the creation of the Gods. They eventually go on to fashion the first human beings, Ash and Embla, from two plants. What is interesting is that the Gods do not first create man and later create woman, as in the Bible. Both are created simultaneously. Thus the confusion of sexuality, such as homosexuality, is the property of the Giants, and exists within the reality of Chaos, while the principle of male and female attraction and sexuality is the essence of the Life Force, or Vril.

Reaching Higher Levels of Consciousness and Spirituality Through Natural Sexual Energy

Our pagan ancestors possessed a far healthier view of sex and the pleasure that one received from sexual activity than people do today. They called on their Gods and Goddesses to fill their lives with fertility, and impregnate all their activities with this life-giving power to give birth to new things. They did not view sexual activity as sinful, and considered the pleasures of sex as their birthright. When people performed sexual activities with each other, they viewed it as an affirmation of their communion with the cosmos. The sexual act was a part of their religious activity and a means to obtain a state of religious ecstasy. To them, life was sex, and sacred sex was sacred life.

All living things are endowed with sexual energies. This sexual force is a life energy. There would be no life, no living organisms without sexual energy. The energies that are exchanged during sex are the male and female principles. One force is impregnating another to create something new, even if it is a deep emotional state of love. In Vrilology, we say that we use tools, the Runes, which represent the male force, to impregnate the female, recessive force, which is currents of Vril energy, and thus give Vril new forms that conform to our desires expressed by the particular Runes used. Can there be any clearer description of the sexual act?

The three monotheist religions have for the most part suppressed human sexuality. This suppression of human sexuality began as far back as Moses and has expanded with the growth of Judaism, continued with Christianity and has taken extreme manifestations in Islam. The life principles that manifest through sex have been turned into a secret doctrine, hidden away within the temples and colleges of mystery schools and other secret religious institutions that exist within and remain hidden from the general membership of the three monotheistic religions. The secrets of sexual magic have become the property of small circles of elite adepts, mostly men, who exploit the life-giving doctrines for their own desire to control and maintain power over the general membership. In many instances, the practice of sexual magic, because of the control by a mostly male ruling elite, has taken on warped and unnatural manifestations. We can see the collateral damage that this practice has inflicted on Christian, Jewish and especially Islamic communities in the form of pedophilia practiced by religious leaders. One can find no end to the recommended deviant sexual practices in the Jewish Talmud. Within Christianity, natural sexual urges have been suppressed and damned as sinful, and the practice of celibacy has warped the natural sexual urges in many Christian priestly orders. In the world of Islam, boys and girls are not permitted to date and the first sexual acts between men and women occur after marriage. Men are encouraged to have sexual intercourse with young boys. Women have to be covered in layers of veils to hide their "Satanic sexuality" so that they do not tempt men from the road of "righteousness." We will simply say that any religious or moralistic teachings that suppress the natural sexual urge will only cause great psychological damage on any society founded on such principles.

Vrilology encourages natural sexual urges, though we must also say that Vrilology distances itself from other esoteric schools that have exploited natural sex magic as a cover for their members' sexual lusts and appetites. We wish to make it clear that such behavior has no place in the Folk Faith of Balder Rising, or in any good, healthy esoteric science. The reason we use the term "natural" sex magic is to reinforce the principle that our teachings can be traced back to the Elder days when *natural meant normal.*

What we are trying to restore to our modern lives is the natural sexuality that our ancient ancestors possessed without having to give it much thought. To them, divine consciousness was not divorced from the physical perspective of the material world. Remember, the Gods dwell within us. Therefore, our physical bodies are temples where the divine dwell. If we seek to raise our consciousness through the growth of our spirituality, then life for us should be one of ecstatic pleasure on the physical level, just as our ancestors lived. *This does not mean we should over-indulge or become decadent, but that the natural pleasures of the flesh, which our biology is fully and naturally designed for, should not be avoided or considered sinful.*

Wilhelm Reich, the Austrian psychoanalyst and natural scientist, explored this ancient wisdom regarding our sexuality. He explained that the Life Force, which we call Vril, but he referred to as *orgone*, flowed freely in vertical energy currents in a similar way to what the Hindus refer to as the Kundalini Fire. Reich explored the relationship of the flow of sexual energy, which is fed by orgone (Vril), to love. This Love Force radiated through the body, outward from the heart, down through the legs and outward through the arms to the hands. When we experience physical love-making with a person of the opposite sex, especially at the sensational peaks, we can feel the sensation of this energy rushing through us at a heightened level, causing us to express our passion through the orgasmic release.

Reich reasoned that humans experience the pleasure of sexual attraction and love-making to ensure the survival of humanity. To deny oneself of such needs results in anxiety, stress and frustration, turning dammed-up orgasmic energy into what he called "body armor." To bottle up or dam the release of our natural sexual urges causes spiritual, mental and physical harm. This pent-up sexual energy needs to be released. Now, we are not suggesting you run out and have sex with the first person you meet, which, in today's day and age, can be dangerous. We are suggesting you seek liberation from harmful concepts that such natural biological functions are in some way "sinful," and should be avoided. You should not feel shame of the physical attraction you might feel to the opposite sex. At the same time, we are not suggesting you jump into bed with every person you might feel attracted to. Remember, there are no good or bad emotions. Love and hate can be good or bad, depending on how you use them. If you fall in love with someone who does not reciprocate your love, or is abusive and exploitive, then love can be a very bad thing.

What we are suggesting is, if you are in a loving relationship with someone of the opposite sex, then you should not feel inhibited to let go sexually. The free expression of your physical love with someone worthy of your love is one of the most wonderful experiences you can truly feel. We should embrace our sexuality as our ancestors did in ancient times, free from psychological, spiritual and religious hang-ups. If you can do this, you will discover for yourself a state of simply being. If you let yourself feel alienated from your bodies, then you will always be burdened with a guilt: that somehow you are disconnected from a greater external force that you are a part of. This sense of alienation will prevent you from successfully completing your spiritual journey of growth and evolution to higher consciousness, to that of a Vril Being.

Learn to Selflessly Love Another Person

If you can achieve this, you will be able to convey a totality in giving pleasure to another. In doing so, you will discover that your lover will reach heights of pleasure that will stimulate their own ability through the Vril energy that you are stimulating within them, and thus this love-giving energy stream will feed back to you, stimulating your own sexual pleasure. It is the unleashing of Vril energy within you that will send you and your lover to heights of ecstatic pleasure, on a higher level of consciousness, where you will experience the existence of the Gods and Goddesses. It is even possible for you to establish a communicative link with the twin deities of love, Frey and Freyja. To reach this state of love is to integrate the energy of Gebo into your soul.

In no other esoteric school, anywhere in the world, is there such a vehicle for the individual to achieve this level of sexual pleasure. Remember what we said about that part of your Soul that we referred to as your Fetch? Your Fetch always takes on the persona of the opposite gender. The reason for this is simple. You Fetch is the means by which you can discover the nature of the opposite sex, and thus, through the establishment of a loving relationship with your Fetch, you will instinctively discover something fundamental about the opposite sex that will help you in your love making. If you and your sex partner both tap into the spiritual dynamics of their Fetch and apply this dynamic in lovemaking, you will attain a transcendental state of mind when you experience orgasm. This will cause you to open up a vast dimension of transcendental awareness of the cosmos that was denied to you before. This awareness of a higher level of existence will enrich your life in every arena of activity, including your lovemaking. This will also accelerate your spiritual evolution into a Godman or Godwoman.

The Sacred Marriage:

Ragnar of the *Denali Institute of Northern Traditions* (runesbyragnar.com) teaches the concept of the Sacred Marriage in relationship to the Norse tradition that is very relevant to Vrilology. He is referring to a state of spiritual elevation in which the male and female elements of our Soul are harmonized, leading us to an evolved state of spiritual balance and obtaining a sense of wholeness. Spiritually, the goal is the formation of a balanced spiritual androgyny that is the formation of what can be described as a total Vril Being, personified by the relationship of Odin, as the teacher of Galdor Science, to Freyja, as the teacher of Seither Science. It is this union of these two disciplines, one male and the other female, that is at the heart of what has been referred to as the Sacred Marriage.

The Sacred Marriage is also the union of the divine with the mortal. It is the establishment, not only of the male and female magical essence, but also the union of the essence of the Gods, or the Creative Life Force, Vril, and us, the Children of the Gods. It is part of your evolution toward becoming a Vril Being.

You should refer to the legend of the Lay of Thrym in the Norse myths. This is the story of how the Giant Thrym steals Thor's hammer. Thor's hammer, Mjollnir, is representative of Thor's powers to defend Asgard against the Giants, and also a symbol of the fertility forces of procreation and evolution. For Thor to remain a symbol of masculine power needed to ward off the forces of Chaos and maintain Order, it is necessary for Thor to become a total Being. Thor needs to regain possession of his Hammer. When the Giant Thrym demands Freyja, the symbol of natural sex Magic, in marriage as payment, Heimdall, the defender of Asgard as well as the progenitor of genetics and the different races of mankind, suggests that Thor dress up as Freyja and go to Thrym's hall to marry Thrym. This tale has many hidden lessons for us to learn, but here, we concern ourselves with the message that even mighty Thor, probably the most masculine of all the Gods, representing the raw male power, must "get in touch" with his feminine side by dressing up as Freyja. Thor's dressing up as Freyja does not have anything to do with homosexuality, but can be interpreted as the need for men to practice and become as skilled in the arts of Seither Science just as much as Galdor, for them to become a fully integrated and evolved Vril Being. The same is true for women, who need to master the arts of Galdor Science, just as much as Seither. Remember, Thor is dressing as Freyja, the Queen of Seither Magic, not as just any woman. This means that men must also study and practice Seither if they are to truly evolve into perfected human beings, creating a balanced order within their spirituality, and thus defeat Chaos, represented by Thrym, who seeks to distort and pervert male-female sexuality by marrying Freyja.

There is a warning in this tale. When Thor dresses up as a woman, Freyja, he is accompanied by Loki. Loki represents Chaos, and is known as a gender-bender in Norse cosmology. His accompanying Thor is a warning of the danger of sexual confusion when one, whether male or female, seeks to obtain the state of the Sacred Marriage. If you are not careful, and confuse Love with Lust, you can easily be led astray into the realm of sexual confusion.

How to Obtain the Sacred Marriage Within Yourself

There is no way you can quickly achieve the state of the Sacred Marriage within yourself. In fact, it is a never-ending, on-going process in which you constantly evolve throughout your life. Even if we obtain a thorough intellectual understanding of the process, it will always remain one of the deepest mysteries of Life. Because it is a part of the process of bonding the consciousness with the subconscious Self, to obtain higher inner levels of consciousness, there really is no ultimate goal, no Holy Grail that you are seeking. But do not let this discourage you. This fact should encourage you because it will frcc you from the concept that you must reach a certain level, and that if you have not reached this level, you have somehow failed. Since there is no end to the process, there is no failure. No matter how adept one becomes, one can always continue to improve oneself in the attainment of this state of the Sacred Marriage.

Now that you understand this fact, let us explain several tools that Vrilology provides you in the quest to attain this state of heightened awareness of the perfected self.

1) First of all, Vrilology acknowledges the power of sex as a tool for spiritual evolution. Unlike Judaism, Christianity, and Islam, which deny the power of sexual forces, and even declare them harmful, Vrilology understands the natural, godly nature of the magical power in the flow of Vrilic energy within the sexual expression of creation, as a tool in the evolution of the being into a Vril Being.

2) Secondly, Vrilology recognizes sex as a natural tool and a gift from the Gods, who created the human species in the form of two genders for the purpose of obtaining both physical and spiritual evolution and development upward. Vrilology realizes that sex is a given aspect that everyone readily and willingly desires to engage; there is no need to motivate one to use it as a means of obtaining spiritual evolution. But we recognize that our modern Judeo-Christian-Islamic morality has warped our willingness to express ourselves sexually, in layers of self-imposed guilt and shame, like Jormundgand, thc World Serpent, that lies under the surface of the world-sea.

In the tale where Thor goes fishing in a boat piloted by a Giant, he struggles with the World Serpent and almost defeats him. But, at the last moment, the Giant becomes fearful of the Jormundgand, and cuts the line, permitting the serpent to escape. This tales explains that we must struggle with the uncontrolled and chaotic forces of our subconscious, and that the Giants are a danger that threatens to unleash this destructive force that can consume us and thus lead us down the road of self-destruction. These desires need only be tamed through an easily inspired growth technique of sexual expression.

3) Thirdly, sex is not only an easily perceived motivator, but its practice can be shared with your partner and lover. Again, we want to remind you that we are not encouraging promiscuous sex. *The practice of natural sex Magic should be performed with a loving and caring partner, someone you truly share a deep*

affection with. It should be with a partner of the opposite sex who you truly care about and cares about you. It is not the initial physical attraction that one experiences with a new partner that qualifies as the tool for achieving spiritual growth. Only after two individuals have established a truly loving and caring relationship sexually, can they begin to use the tool of expressing that deep affection magically.

The purpose of achieving the state of the Sacred Marriage is to manifest an internal transformation that will help you establish a better, loving external relationship with your partner. Thus, the Sacred Marriage is not the establishment of a perfect relationship with your "soul mate," but the manifestation of an internal transformation within yourself, resulting in a spiritual balance between the masculine and feminine spiritual elements within your Soul, which in turn will permit you to establish better relationships with the opposite sex. Achieving the Sacred Marriage internally is not limited to relying on the sexual dynamics of lovemaking, but because this lesson deals with relationships and the male/female polarity, engaging in sex and lovemaking is very relevant and a powerful means to achieve such a state. But we must once again remind you that while assistance from your love partner, and the exchange of energy that accompanies the act of lovemaking, will greatly enrich your lovemaking and relationship, the effect on your lovemaking and the enrichment of your relationship are secondary to the internal union taking place within you. The former are manifestations of the latter.

During these heightened though infrequently achieved peaks of bliss, your level of consciousness will reach heights that you will remember throughout your life. They will be proof that dimensions of higher consciousness do exist beyond our mundane dimension of existence. It is during these peak experiences that you will touch the Divine, the Gods, and their effect on you will provide levels of reflective pleasure that will last a lifetime. Reaching such heights can be achieved through other means, but however you reach them, you will be affected by them in ways that will last throughout your life.

Some Reminders for Establishing a Loving and Caring Relationship

Here are just a few short reminders of how you can work to establish and maintain a caring and loving relationship:

1) Be sure you act in accordance with what you desire.

2) Make sure your actions, thoughts and feelings mirror what you desire.

3) You should at all times act in the way you want the other person to act toward you.

4) Work on improving yourself rather than on improving the one you love.

5) Change the way you feel about yourself, and you will change the way others feel about you.

6) Radiate confidence and joy, and you will discover that the person who needs help will begin to change their attitude and soon will begin to help themselves.

7) Focus on what you love about yourself, because it is impossible to love others if you don't first love yourself.

8) Focus on what you love about the person you love, and not on their faults.

9) Stop complaining about other people, especially about people who are close to you. 10) The only person who can truly make you happy, is you!

Rune Energy to Use for establishing and maintaining a health and loving relationship

There are several very powerful Runes that you can use when dealing with the subjects of sexuality, relationship and male/female polarity. Here is a list of such Runes:

1) Thurisaz: Thor and his hammer, Mjollnir, are associated with Thurisaz. We have touched on this topic already in this lesson, but let us remind you quickly that Thor is one of the most powerful masculine archetypes in the Norse cosmology. He radiates raw male power. His hammer is a phallic symbol of male fertility

energy, and is used as a symbol to consecrate marriages, as well as for the dead and eventual rebirth. Its energies assist in assimilating the polarities of male and female energies into a willful directed pattern of action.

2) Ehwaz: This is the Relationship Rune and symbolized by a person riding a horse. The relationship of rider and horse is one of total trust and dependence. It is also symbolic of a symbiotic relationship between harmonious beings. The trust that exists, especially between the rider and the horse, evolves into loyalty. One can consider Ehwaz as the Rune of Soul Mates. In many Indo-European mythologies there is the story of the twin Gods. In the Norse cosmology the twins are personified by Freyja and Frey, sister and brother, who represent the symbiotic relationship a harmonious pair who personify the forces of strong cooperative love. This Rune can be used to attract the right person for you.

3) Gebo: This is the Rune of Sex Magic. Within its form and energies there lies the secret of exchanged energies, the union of two people, man and woman, to produce a greater power than the two halves. The Volsung Saga illustrates in tale and legend the initiation of Siegfried into the secrets of Galdor by the Valkyrie Brunhilde. Through its powers, one is introduced into the knowledge of the higher worlds within the Yggdrasill through the perfect joining of male and female. This is what we call the Sacred Marriage. This is the greatest gift that can be exchanged and is why Gebo is known as the Rune of gift-giving.

4) Kenaz: As the Rune of controlled fire, Kenaz represents the control of human passion, lust and sexual love for positive purposes. It is the Rune of creativity, joining of two polarities for the goal of creating something new. Two Kenaz Runes joined together, facing away from each other, can form Gebo. As the Rune of crafting, it fashions a new object in the passion of fire. When used in the realm of Sex Magic, it is associated with Freyja, who represents robust sexuality. You can use Kenaz to attract a

lover and increase your sexual potency and virility. Its shape is that of the open womb, receptive of male penetration for impregnation.

5) Ingwaz: This Rune is named after the God, Ing, which is another name for Frey, and is the Rune of male sexuality. It is the potency of the male self-replenishing seed, which is received and held in the womb of the Earth Goddess, eventually to be birthed with a sudden surge of energy in spring. Ingwaz is actually two Kenazs facing each other. It is the Rune of gestation and eventual manifestation.

6) Berkano: This is the Earth Mother Rune that is impregnated by Ingwaz. It is the most powerful female fertility Rune. This Rune represents Frigga, as the Goddess that gives birth after the seed has gestated. It is the Rune of the life-giving energy.

7) Uruz: As the Rune of Health, you can use its energies to restore sexual potency. It contains the primal energies of creation. This energy is indestructible, raw and primitive; it represents the primal urge for sexual intercourse and reproduction. Though it is usually considered a male sexual force, it can be used by both men and women to cause sexual desire to manifest with overwhelming force in oneself or one's mate.

Chapter Ten: Increasing Your Supply of Personal Luck

The Northern Idea of Luck

You now have an understanding of how Vril energy flows into you in currents, and how, through the power of your mind, you can fashion it into whatever you desire. There are many ways to do this, but for now, we want to explain how you can transform Vril into what we refer to as your *Personal Luck* or *Megin.*

Megin is the Norse term for your Personal Luck. Everyone is born with a certain amount of luck. With each individual, the amount is different, just as some people are bigger than others. Some are smarter than others. Some are better artists than others. And so, some people are luckier than others. But unlike with other esoteric traditions, through Vrilology we teach you how you can increase your luck.

Just what is Personal Luck? The first quality of Personal Luck is that it is a mobile force. Personal Luck can be recognized, measured and shaped according to your individual will. The universal force that fuels it is Vril. There is a Norse myth where Odin, Hoenir and Lodurr create the first man and woman. Each God provides them with a special and unique gift. Odin's gift to them is *Ond*, or Vital Breath. This Vital Breath is the flow of Vril energy currents that sparked life within them. Vril flows throughout your body and soul. It is that part of your soul, called the Hamingja, where Vril is transformed into your Personal Luck, also known as Megin.

Megin is Vril transformed into a personal force known as Luck. This power source is a form of energy that is distinct from any physical power or strength. The amount of Megin, or Luck, you possess determines the amount of success and good fortune you will experience in your lifetime. It can be used to heal, to improve and maintain your physical health and well being, to make things happen, to increase the power of your will, and to provide success in whatever you wish to do. It can even give you the power to control your destiny. It resembles charisma, but it is far more powerful than simple charm, popularity, or ability to persuade. The foundation to all this is the process of transforming Vril into Megin.

Let us give you an example of how I used this power when I needed it. Where I worked, there was alternate side parking. I usually found a spot right away, every morning, because I used this principle of increasing my luck. One day, I forgot that I had planned to leave work early, and parked on a street where the alternate side parking rule was enforced from 11:30 am to 1 pm. Well, when I left work at noon I discovered that people had double parked their cars, which resulted in blocking my car. I tried to find the owner of the cars blocking my car, but failed. A couple of local men told me to take my car up on the sidewalk and get out that way, but there was a sign pole on the other side of my car and try as hard as I did, I could not maneuver my car past the pole. Both men offered to try and failed. I was now getting mad, but before I completely lost my temper, I remembered the principle of drawing on my supply of Personal Luck. I quickly changed my mental attitude by laughing at the situation and making jokes of my predicament. Remember—like attracts like! The other two men also joined in making jokes about the situation. Just then, another man came walking down the block. He stopped and asked me what the problem was? I explained the situation, and after examining the situation, he said he could get the car out, and asked me if I wanted him to try. I said of course. Well! He had be to some kind of Houdini, because in a few seconds, he was able to get the car out. He maneuvered the car past the pole and onto the sidewalk. I thanked him., and he told me that was real lucky, because he was on his way to the subway and he never walked down this block before. I asked him what made him come this way. He said he didn't know, but that he just had a feeling that he should go this way today.

By changing my attitude, I changed the pattern of Vril energy and it brought just the person I needed to get me out of the predicament I was in. We need to review something about the nature of that part of the soul, known as the Hamingja, before we can show you how to harness Vril and transform it into Megin.

Your Hamingja

Personal Luck is something that all European pagan/heathen traditions believed not only existed, but was possible to harness, and that it was possible to increase the amount one possessed. The Romans even had a Goddess to personify Luck by the name of *Fortuna*, who they believed chose mortals to be her favorites—Fortune's Favorites—who seemed to lead charmed lives. Caesar was believed to have been one of Fortune's favorites, and lived a charmed life, achieving success in everything he did, until his luck finally ran out. Too bad he did not know how to recharge his Luck.

The Hamingja is that part of your multidimensional Soul that harnesses Vril energy and transforms it into Luck, or Megin. You can refer back to the chapter on the Soul to refresh your understanding of the Hamingja in relationship to your multi-dimensional Soul. Luck is stored within the Hamingja, which gives your entire auric, or life-energy, field greater potency and much more flexibility for the workings of the human will. The Hamingja serves to concentrates one's personal Megin much as Scottish bagpipes act to store air for future melodies. The Hamingja is a kind of reservoir for the storage of your Megin energies, which become your Luck.

By studying Vrilology, we know:

1) We can strengthen the walls of the Hamingja by using the Rune, Elhaz, and thus store greater supplies of Luck or Megin.

2) To increase your supply of Luck by using the fives Runes representing the five elements: Fehu (fire), Uruz (earth), Laguz (water) Ansuz (air) and Isa (ice), to transform Vril into a very specialized form of life energy that is Megin.

3) One can learn to send or discharge your Luck to help others by using the Rune Fehu, the Sending Rune.

Methods to Increase Your Personal Supply of Luck

Making a relatively simplistic assumption, we can say that the amount of Luck in your life is equivalent to your Hamingja's ability to draw in Vril energy and convert it to Megin, and its capacity as a reservoir to store this psychic energy reserve.

It is usual for most people to experience their best Luck during their early years. During your youth, the Hamingja is still fresh and full of Megin. This original source of Luck is what is passed down to you from your share of the energy treasury of your family's ancestral stream. This is the reason why things appear to happen naturally and effortlessly for most people when they are young. If you gave it serious thought, you would notice the numerous experiences or "lucky" synchronicities that happened to you when you were young.

As you grow older, your body changes, and you take on greater responsibilities. This causes the level of the energy you need to function to increase, causing you to draw on greater amounts of Megin energy stored in your Hamingja, causing the level of your reservoir of Luck that you can draw on to decrease. As you move through life passages, and the "skeletons" accumulate in your Orlog, the capacity of your Hamingja to produce Megin decreases. This accumulation of negative Orlog (thoughts, feelings and acts) will cause the flow of Vril into you to slow. The amounts of Vril necessary to support your bodily functions will increase, drawing on more and more Vril, faster than your Hamingja's ability to convert Vril into Megin, thus causing health problems and old age. Vril energy necessary to create Megin will be diverted from your Hamingja. This process will quickly deplete the reserves of Luck in your Hamingja. If your Hamingja is not refilled with fresh Megin energies, your Luck will progressively decrease and eventually dry up.

If you develop health problems, your supply of Megin will be used first to counter these bodily diseases and other health emergencies. This unintended depletion of your reservoir of Megin energies will ensure that your relative level of Luck remains low and eventually decreases to the point when it will be spent altogether. You will instinctively draw on your supply of Megin stored in your Hamingja in the event of an emergency. Unfortunately, people are unaware of the nature of their Hamingja, and thus fail to restore their level of Megin. This supply is normally kept at an adequate level to meet daily needs, but not sufficient to give you what you knew as "good luck" in the past, and is definitely not adequate to protect you from threatening situations now and in the future, unless you actively work at restoring it, as well as learning how to increase the Hamingja's ability to generate and hold greater amounts of Megin.

We want to point something out here. In most occult lore, it is taught that an individual human is limited to a fixed allocation of Megin energy, or Luck, in a lifetime. Vrilology does not hold to such an assumption. We know that if an individual does not learn how to preserve his Megin and refill his Hamingja after discharging Megin, he certainly would appear to "run out of luck." But this does not have to happen.

How to Increase Your Luck

There are several things you can do to maintain a healthy supply of Megin and prevent the loss of Luck. Here are a few suggestions:

First: Stop Excess Drainage: Avoid extreme displays of negative emotion (anger, jealousy, bitterness), which will cause unnatural drainage of your Hamingja, as well as unbridled exuberance that fills the atmosphere around you with energy supplied from your Hamingja. If you are politically active and attend demonstrations or protests, this activity will drain your Hamingja, and you should be sure to recharge it afterward. If you attend such entertainment activities as sports events, or attend a rock concert, your energy will be drained from you. Great orators cause audiences to unleash great vortexes of unbridled enthusiasm, which they then harness and shape to change the course of events in the world. Rock stars who can elicit great convulsions of emotional discharges from their audiences are performing similar feats, harnessing the discharge of Vril energy for their personal wealth and fame, or to support their favorite causes. If you have ever attended such events, you might remember feeling "drained" afterward The reason for this is you *were* drained of your supply of Megin. In all cases, you would want to recharge any discharge of energy that normally would escape from such excessive emotional expressions.

You should take note that great amounts of the Vril energy flow out of your eyes and consciously monitor this process in the normal course of the day. You are constantly scattering great amounts of energy by giving attention to trivial focus points during the day, all day long. We're sure you are familiar with the term that *your eyes are windows to your soul.* What you might not realize is how significant this saying is in terms of human energy flow. If you don't learn how to consciously draw the shades on your eyes, you will continue to needlessly discharge energy from your reservoir of storage. You will learn more about the significance of your eyes and how to use them to control the exchange of Vril later on in this book.

You will want to remove yourself from the vicinity of *psychic vampires*, who love to drain you of your Vril energy, in the same way as a vampire sucks your blood. These are people who constantly go on and on about how terrible things are, how horrible their lives are, about how miserable life is in general and how the world is coming to an end, or conspiracies, the existence of enemies and threats everywhere, and how we are all poor, helpless victims like sheep waiting to be sent to the slaughter house. After listening to such monologues of doom and gloom, you usually feel drained, but the person who talks about such horrible eventualities is recharged and excited, and so filled with *your* life force they can hardly stand still.

Second: You Need to Increase Your Storehouse of Energy on a Regular Basis. You will learn how to do this in the exercise that we provide in this chapter. It is not hard and is very effective. By chanting and meditating on the described Runes you can strengthen your Hamingja and increase its reserve of energy. We will go into this method in more detail in a moment.

If you don't have time to perform the exercise every day, do it once a week. In the meantime, there are several ways you can draw on extra reserves of Vril energy to convert to Megin by touching plants and trees on their new growth. You should consciously send the life force to your Hamingja from the plants and thank the plants for their help. The life energy of the plants will be absorbed into your Hamingja.

You should also do deep breathing exercises, which will gather more of the Vital Breath or Ond from the atmosphere of Earth into your Hamingja. Deep breathing, when done properly, will increase the flow of Vril currents into you.

Pet owners will tell you that there is an exchange of healthy energy between themselves and their pets, and medicine has now discovered the effectiveness of owning a pet in the healing process and maintaining good health.

Get in the habits of regular physical exercise and proper eating to maintain good health and vitality. This will help you to lessen the loss of Vril energy during your daily routine.

Avoid the use of recreational, mood-altering drugs or excessive alcohol consumption. Both will deplete your reserves of Luck.

You do not want to constantly expend precious Megin in restoring yourself to health after a disease or sickness, so keep yourself in good physical and mental health.

Third: You Should Constantly Visualize the Build-up of Energy. As you visualize the Runes you use to increase and maintain your Luck, acting in their prescribed manner, visualize the energy flowing into your Hamingja. Visualize your Hamingja as a vaguely defined concentration of energy like a camel's hump on your back, between your shoulder blades. As the camel drinks great amounts of water, its hump will actually grow. You should imagine the same thing happening to your Hamingja. Notice how it is differentiated within your larger auric field by its level of concentration, and imagine it growing larger and more intense as you work to increase its powers to produce and store greater amounts of Megin.

As you mentally redirect the energies generated by your runic meditations into your Hamingja:

1) Visualize your Hamingja as a center of concentrated energy. Then see it expand to accommodate this new influx of Megin, just like the camel's hump expanding as it fills with water.

2) Clearly see your life energy field that surrounds you become more defined with increased density at the edges, making it an impermeable container, preventing possible leakage from within, or intrusions from outside.

3) Visualize some kind of release valve within your auric field. This device will permit you to send amounts of the energy stored within to loved ones, or for other specific magical workings.

The Hamingja is one of the most effective tools you will possess for solving life's daily problems, most of which are caused by a lack of Megin energy to influence life events.

Remember the pathways into your future that we referred to as Wyrd? Well, this method will help you to refashion and design the Vrilic energy currents into whatever it is you desire, by adding power to your will to make things happen that are advantageous for you in life. We will explore the subject in greater detail in the next lesson. You will also be able to send this energy to help others close to you. This is very important in creating and maintaining a healthy and loving relationship.

Of course it takes serious mental preparation, and a great amount of mental concentration, along with a rudimentary knowledge of the practical techniques of energy transformation that we provide in this book, to refill the Hamingja. Unfortunately, most people never maintain a higher level of commitment to something that is not material, and usually grow lax, and eventually, due to laziness, abandon a sure fire method of increasing their psychic potential. Even if the knowledge of the Hamingja were commonly known, most people would still lack the motivation, stamina and discipline to develop the skill to make it work.

Hopefully you will no longer be one of these people. If you are willing to spend the time and energy necessary to unravel the deeper mysteries in Life, the workings of the unseen energy dimensions revealed to you in this book, you will no longer be just one more poor soul trying to struggle through life, for you will have discovered the techniques that the successful people have discovered, or instinctively know, to provide them with that “extra edge” that brings them success in everything they do.

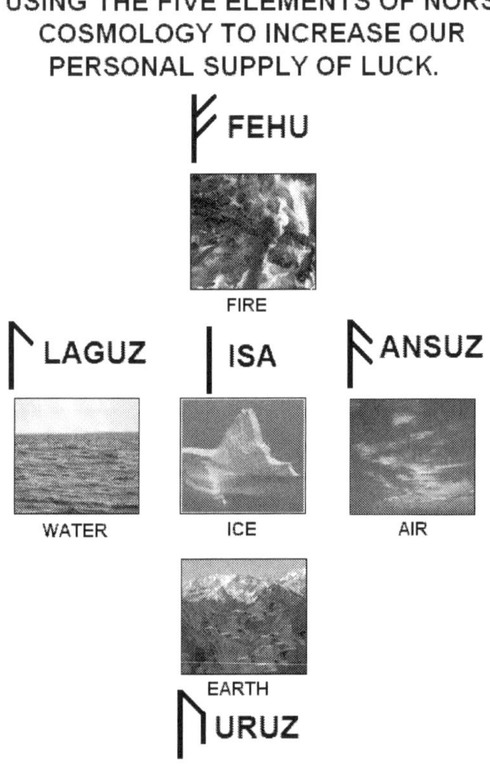

By harnessing the five elemental powers of Norse cosmology, we can transform Vril currents that enter our spirito-physical bodies into Megin, which is our personal supply of Luck, by chanting the corresponding Runes.

Exercise to Increase Your Luck and Strengthen Your Hamingja

The Runes you use to help you maintain your supply of Luck are Fehu, Elhaz and Sowilo. Fehu, the Rune of Luck, is known to increase the production of Megin within your Hamingja as it transforms Vril energy currents that enter your body. The Rune Elhaz, the Guardian Rune and *the Rune of Balder Rising*, will act to strengthen the walls of your Hamingja, giving it a greater capacity to hold new energies. Sowilo, the Sun Rune and *the Rune of Balder Risen*, is another Rune you can use to maintain a healthy supply of Luck. You can meditate and chant these Runes whenever you wish to increase your production of Megin. But if you want to seriously increase your ability to transform Vril into Megin, you should perform the exercise described below at least once a week. It will increase your Hamingja's ability to produce Megin (personal luck) substantially.

There are five elements, instead of four, in the Norse cosmology. They are, **earth, fire, water, earth** and **ice**. By chanting the Runes associated with these five elements, you can increase the capacity of your Hamingja to hold produce and hold increased volumes of Vril energy. The Runes you will be chanting are: **Fehu** (fire), **Uruz** (earth), **Laguz** (water) **Ansuz** (air) and **Isa** (ice). You will then chant the Rune **Elhaz**, used to strengthen your Hamingja so that it can hold additional amounts of Megin. You will chant each Rune nine times.

Let's begin the exercise:

1) Sit in a comfortable chair with your feet flat on the floor, or, if you prefer, in the Lotus position, and close your eyes.

2) Hold your head well balanced, not slumped.

3) Concentrate on your skull and feel the muscles in it relax—totally relax. Let all tension drain from it. Now do the same with your face. Then your neck, your shoulders, your arms, your hands. Then do the same with your chest, your waist, your hips, your upper legs, your lower legs, and finally your feet. Make sure you are completely relaxed.

4) Enter your Alpha mental state Do this by slightly raising your eyes under your closed eyelids. Hold them there, but make sure you are not straining to do so.

5) Begin to count backwards from ten to one. If you need more time to enter into a deep state of consciousness, count backwards from twenty or thirty–you decide how much time you

will need. Maintain one second intervals between each number, so don't rush the countdown.

6) Hold your mind in a state of rest. You are now going to take several deep full breaths. Breathe in, and draw the air into your Solar Plexus.

7) Hold your breath to the count of nine. Then slowly exhale. Repeat this breathing method nine times.

8) Visualize the first Rune, Fehu, before you. See the Rune before you, as if you are looking at it being projected on a movie screen. Hold the image for few seconds. Remember that this is the Rune of fire.

9) Begin to chant *Fehu, the Fire Rune*, in a long, drawn-out fashion nine times. As you do, feel the energy of the sun flowing down into you from above, charging you and filling your very being. Do it nine times.

Next chant the Rune *Uruz, the Earth Rune*, in a long, drawn-out fashion nine times. As you chant, feel the Vrilic energy of the earth beneath you rising through your legs and mixing with the Vrilic energy already pulsating within you.

Next chant the *Rune Ansuz, the Air Rune*, in a long, drawn-out fashion nine times. As you chant, feel the Vrilic energy of the air flowing into you through your nostrils and mouth, whirling down into you and mixing with the Vrilic energy already pulsating within you.

Next chant the Rune *Laguz, the Water Rune*, in a long, drawn-out fashion nine times. As you chant, feel the Vrilic energy of the air flowing about you as if you were in a gentle whirlpool. Feel the energy of water entering your pores and mixing with the Vrilic energy already pulsating within you.

Next chant the Rune Isa, the Ice Rune, in a long, drawn-out fashion nine times. As you chant, feel the Vrilic energy of the ice solidifying, growing stronger, and expanding like the glaciers moving across the earth, mixing with the Vrilic energy already pulsating within you.

Finally, chant the Rune Elhaz, the Rune of the Hamingja, transforming the Vrilic energy within you, strengthening the walls of your Hamingja. Imagine the Hamingja as a huge balloon expanding as it is transforming Vril into Megin. Feel the walls of the Hamingja growing stronger as it expands.

10) Remain still with your eyes closed, and imagine yourself charged with this energy, knowing that it there for you to use.

11) You will count from one to five and then open your eyes.

How to Send Your Luck

If you use these exercises you will have a life energy field filled with Megin, charged with Luck. At any time you can send your Luck to another person. If you are in close contact with someone you can mentally send Megin by using the Fehu Rune, which is both the Rune of Luck and the Sending Rune. Some traditions simply refer to this as sending part of your "life energy" to another person. If you wish to enter your meditative state as we just described, you can. Once you enter your meditative state, visualize the person you wish to send your Megin to and then visualize Fehu. Fehu has two upward lifting arms. Visualize Megin rising out of these arms and toward the person who is your target. See the currents of energy flying toward the person and entering them, filling their life energy field. You can do this as often as you want, but make sure you recharge your own supply of Megin.

We want to introduce you to a Norse magical runic formula guaranteed to work. You can use this formula with any Rune, or combination of Runes, depending on what it is you seek to accomplish. We will use it for increasing your Luck, holding it and sending it. There are several Norse-runic formulas you should know. They are *Lathu, Gibu, Auja* and *Alu.*

Lathu means *I summon.*
Alu embodies *I manifest magical inspiration.*
Auja means *Luck.*
Gibu is connected to the Rune Gebo and means *I give.*

Thus, when you chant *Lathu Alu*, you are saying, *I summon or invite magical inspiration.*

When you chant *Gibu Alu*, you are saying, *I send or give magical inspiration.*

Now, if you add a Rune after the incantation and include Auja for Luck, such as *Lathu Alu Fehu-Auja*, you are summoning the magical inspiration of Luck. Fehu is Luck Rune, so by combining it with Auja for Luck, you are increasing the Megin being summoned.

You can do the same for sending Luck. If you change a Runic formula from Lathu to Gibu, such as *Gibu Alu Fehu-Auja*, you are sending the magical inspiration of Luck. Gibu sends runic energy, and Fehu is both the Luck Rune and Sending Rune.

OK, how do we use this formula?

1) Perform the steps to get into a relaxed state and enter your Alpha State of Mind, or Asgard State of Consciousness, by raising your eyes under your closed eyelids and count backwards from 20 to 1.

2) Take a deep breath and suck air into your solar plexus. Hold it for 9 seconds. Then, as you release it, chant the Rune Fehu. Keep an image of it in your mind as you slowly release your breath and chant the name of the Runic chant ***Lathu Alu Fehu Auja***. Do it 9 times.

3) If you wish to then send the Luck, you do the same, but say ***Gibu Alu Fehu Auja*** and visualize a current of energy flowing from you to the person you wish to receive your Luck.

You can chant the Runic formula mentally or loudly, depending on where you are when you are performing this chant. If you do it mentally, just let your breath escape as you concentrate on the image of the Rune in your mind.

Chapter Eleven: How to Use Vril to Generate Good Health

Vrilology does not encourage you to use the techniques that it offers in the arena of healing as a substitute for traditional medicine, but rather to assist in the healing process. The power of the mind to harness the Life Force, Vril, and use it to assist in healing should be helpful to you in your recovery. And though it is possible to perform "miracles," this does not mean that miracles will happen by avoiding traditional medicine, nor can miracles be guaranteed. No doctor will make a promise that you will recover from any illness, for no one can predict what will happen in the realm of healing and medicine. One's failure to recover can be due to the power of the mind to counteract medical treatment, just as it can assist in the healing and recovery process.

What we are is the result of what we think about ourselves. We are the creation of our thoughts. Medical science is beginning to understand just how powerful a hold our minds have over our physical state, health and well-being. Before we go any further, you should perform a little exercise. First, remove your clothes and stand in front of a full-length mirror. Then truly examine your body. Third, shut your eyes and imagine in every detail what kind of body you would like to possess. You must visualize your physical body in a state of perfect physical health. Once you have created this "new you," examine it in every detail. Fourth, open your eyes and look into the mirror. See your new body before you. Examine your new body just as you imagined it, and then ask yourself, "What is stopping me from actually having that body?" Finally, ask yourself if you believe you can manifest this new vision of yourself. If you do, you can.

Remember, your body is made up of atoms and atoms are more than 99 percent Vril energy. Through your thoughts and feelings, Vril can be molded into whatever your mind can imagine. Everything about the physical vehicle that you see as your body is a manifestation of your mind. The growth of your body from infancy to adulthood is the result of your DNA harnessing and shaping Vril energy flowing into you. Your DNA is a blueprint stamping its code onto Vril to create your physical form as it grows. Once you reach a certain point in your aging, the currents of Vril flowing into you slow down, and your body can no longer receive enough to maintain itself. This causes deterioration that we associate with aging. But you can be trained from youth to use your mind to control the formation of your body, by giving form and shape to Vril flowing into you as you grow up. You can also increase the amount of Vril flowing into you as you grow older, which slows down the aging process and helps you to live a great deal longer than the normal life span. Medical science theorizes that our bodies have the potential to live up to *two hundred years*. If this is so, can't we learn how? We can!

Use Vril to Create Your Physical Health

1. By now you recognize that Vril does exist, even though you cannot experience Vril with your five senses, and you understand that you are a Vril Being. Accept that there is an invisible, all-powerful force of life that fills the universe and makes up more than 99 percent of every atom. Once you have assimilated this belief system into your thinking process, you will discover that you can flow through life like a leaf floating on a current of water.

You should perform the little mirror exercise we described every morning when you get out of bed, and right before you go to sleep at night. Instead of an unattractive, unfit, and unhealthy body, see a superior Vril Being with good health and a youthful demeanor standing before you. If you see yourself as unfit, Vril energy radiating within you will reinforce this perception and act accordingly to make your body conform to this unhealthy view. But if you see yourself as healthy and youthful, your belief will cause Vril to work toward manifesting this self in the physical world.

2. By creating positive thoughts about your body you will harness Vril and cause it to transform your reality to match your

thoughts. Your mind creates about 60,000 every day, which in turn generate your feelings.

You have within you the potential to control your body. Your will is the architect that designs your body, and though this will is invisible, and cannot be weighed or measured, it still exists. Your will is your mind harnessing Vril. Learn to use it to create the reality you want for yourself. Use it to make the impossible come true. Accept the truth: *Your thoughts are created by you, and you can use them to transform your physical world.*

3. The power of your mind to use Vril has no boundaries. There are no limitations to what you can accomplish with your mind. Trust the truth that there is no limit to what your mind can do to transform the physical world. This is true especially of your health. You can replace illness with health. Once you accept that you can control the state of your well-being, you will be able to act on this truth. Your powers of conception will begin to work toward keeping you healthy. When sickness does appear, your mind will have the power to help cure you. Every cell in your body is dying and replacing itself, and this process is powered by Vril. Know too that your mind can fashion and shape the currents of Vril, work to prevent the depletion of Vril—whose depletion causes your body to deteriorate with age and permit illness to invade your microcosm—and even increase its flow to ensure continuous good health and physical well being. You possess the means to replace your cells with new and better cells, and through this power you can change your poor behavior, bad eating habits, and all unhealthy conditions, and make the miraculous happen within your physical being.

4. Change your perception of what is possible by saying, *The possible is that which has been done, and the impossible is that which has not yet been done.* You have got to change your idea of what is possible and what is impossible. Throughout history, if something had not yet been achieved, like man flying, it was considered impossible. Imagine if you asked someone who lived five hundred years ago if it was possible to go to the Moon. They would have locked you up. But we do fly and travel to the

Moon. With this understanding that nothing is impossible, you will be able to move mountains. But if you believe that your illness is incurable, then it will be. If you believe that your life is one great struggle against the process of aging and illness, then it will be filled with sickness and rapid, premature aging. Know and accept that you have the power to use Vril to transform yourself, and design your physical life as you want it to be.

5. We rely on our five senses to perceive the physical world around us. The sensations that we receive are then sent to our conscious, rational mind, in the left side of the brain. But the right side of the brain speaks a different language from the left side, like two different computer systems, MacIntosh and IBM. We have got to come up with a program that will permit the two sides of our brain to talk to each other. We have to learn to move beyond reliance on our five senses.

Everything in the universe cannot be explained logically, especially the process of your own thoughts and feelings. Try to explain the emotions of love or hate. You can't. There is no logical explanation for our feelings, but they do exist, and they are extremely powerful forces that govern our lives. You have got to understand that the universe is grand and there are realms that exist beyond our five senses, just like the sounds a dog can hear that we cannot, or the infrared color spectrum that insects can see and we cannot.

When Someone is Convinced He Is Being Cured--He Will Be Cured

You have the power to cure yourself within your own mind. Don't take my word for it. Let's think about the placebo for just a moment. Placebos have been used to test the effectiveness of people's ability to heal themselves. Tests have been conducted where individuals are given what they are told is a medication that will cure their illness. Unknown to them, only half the test group is given the medication, and the others are given sugar pills–placebos. The remarkable thing is that there is always a certain percentage of people who take the sugar pills, thinking it is the medication that can cure them, and are cured. The reason they are cured is simple: they believe they are taking the cure and so their minds expect their bodies to heal, and they do.

Once again, we are not recommending you abandon traditional medicine. What we *are* saying is that your mind has the power to work with the cure suggested by the health provider. If you have a life-threatening illness, and you are told you should take the cure, do so, but use your mind to work with the treatment to make it more effective. What you must do is to maintain a positive attitude when undergoing treatment of any kind. In a way, the medical treatment will help your mind to work wonders in healing your body. But you have to work to maintain the proper attitude which says that the universe is filled with limitless abundance that includes good health. When you surrender to depression due to illness, your mind is working against any cure administered to you by the health care establishment. But if you maintain the proper attitude you will draw on the Vril and shape it into the good health that you desire.

You Can Have the Body You Want

Let's go back to that full-length mirror. Once again, take a good look at the body you have. Are you satisfied? Do you see the perfect body you want? Most people will say no. Even the most physically fit will find fault with something about how they look. The truth is, if you are short, you will not grow another foot of height, no matter how hard you try, because it is not in your DNA. It is possible, over several generations, to use this process to help certain genes within your DNA to come to the fore in each successive generation until your descendants get a superior body. This is a form of genetic engineering. But right now, we must concentrate on the here-and-now. How do you improve the body you were given?

Let's take an example that most people today can identify with—weight. Most people in today's society suffer from some kind of weight problem. This is especially true in the United States where obesity is becoming epidemic due to bad eating habits. As a result, even our children are suffering from obesity. But this does not have to be.

If you are constantly dwelling on the need to lose weight, you will always need to lose weight. The focus on the need causes Vril to manifest itself in giving you the need to lose weight. It will prevent your body from easily losing weight and keeping it off. So you gained weight because you already felt yourself gaining weight. People always gain and lose a few pounds in the course of daily, weekly and monthly activities. But as soon as you gain a few pounds, you begin to worry about getting fat. This causes the mind to create powerful feelings by which you are now always worrying about gaining weight. And what happens when your emotions are working full time on a growing obsession? They are shaping the life-giving Vril flowing into you to cause you to gain weight. You cannot lose weight or keep it off if you are thinking fat thoughts.

We are given many excuses for gaining weight. We are told we have a slow metabolism, or a thyroid problem, or it is hereditary or we have bad eating habits. All these reasons can be valid if we believe them. We are finding something other than ourselves to blame for weight gain. Food, genes, and metabolism are not responsible for your being overweight. Your thoughts are responsible for your weight problem. They will continue to be the cause of your being overweight. Just accept that your thoughts are the primary cause for everything that happens to you, and you will be able to eliminate such problems as being overweight.

As you look into the mirror, visualize what you think is your perfect weight. Create a vivid picture of yourself at the weight you desire. If you find old pictures of yourself when you were at your desired weight, place them around your home so you can look at them often. Once this image of yourself replaces the present overweight image, you will begin to think of yourself always at this desired weight. Cut out pictures of people from magazines with similar perfect-weight figures. Surround yourself with images of people with their perfect-weight bodies. Avoid people who are overweight, and keep your mind focused on your goal. Your mind will begin to "think thin thoughts" and those thoughts will begin to shape Vril into molding your body into that desired weight.

You must come to believe that there is a perfect weight for you and you already weigh that much. Act as if you are already at that weight. Think to yourself every day that you can feel the pounds dropping off. Feel yourself getting thinner. Write it on paper and display it where you can see it. You might even want to buy the clothes for this desired weight so they will be in your closet to remind you every day that the desired weight is waiting for you. This desired weight is the natural weight for you. Convince yourself that you have only to act, think and believe and your body will adjust itself to this natural weight.

Avoid doing anything that will remind you of your weight problem. If you see yourself hopelessly overweight, you will always remain overweight—and hopeless. Your negative image of yourself will manifest a negative body. Think about how wonderful it is to be at your natural weight, and how good you feel because of this natural weight. You can even imagine your excess weight as layers of clothing that you are wearing, and you have only to remove each layer, one at a time. Once you have removed all the layers of clothing, your natural weight body will be revealed. So begin shedding your excess clothing right now.

Concentrate on Perfect Health

Create an image of yourself already in perfect health. Imagine yourself as Superman. You possess a super body, with super health. You are stronger than the average man, able to leap buildings at a single bound, and faster than a speeding bullet. Know that nothing can hurt you except kryptonite, and your kryptonite is your negative thoughts. If you want to remain Superman, with his super body and health, you need to avoid kryptonite.

Now think of yourself as Dorian Gray, possessing eternal youth. You do not age, but the painting of yourself does. Imagine you too have a painting of yourself and every time you begin to think of bad health or an imperfect body, you are thinking of that painting and not you. When thinking negative thoughts, and holding a negative image of yourself in your mind, you are molding the incoming, life-giving Vril, into currents of energy that will create pathways to a future where your negative thoughts and images become a reality.

Don't just believe, but *Know* you have, within your mind, the power to think yourself into perfect health. *Know* that this power *will* slow down the aging process, and you *will* live a longer and healthier life. Do whatever it takes to convince yourself that a better and healthier body is here, waiting for you. If you fear going bald, or your hair turning gray, then do what it takes to reverse this image of yourself. If you are turning gray, then see yourself with your natural hair color. If it takes a little hair coloring to convince you that your hair is not turning gray with age, then apply a little to your hair so that you can maintain an image of yourself with your natural hair color. After a while you will discover that the graying process has been reduced, or at the least slowed down. This is true of balding. If your hair is beginning to thin, then act in every way as if your hair is still full-bodied. If you want to use one of the present-day formulas for thinning hair, then do so, especially if it will help you to convince yourself that your hair is not thinning.

Laughter is the Best Medicine

I'm sure you have heard this saying before. Nowadays, Hospitals even employ clowns and comedians to entertain their patients. Hospitals even bring in pets for patients to hold and pet. Lovable animals help cheer up the sick. Why are hospitals doing this? *Because modern medicine has discovered that people who are ill will begin to heal themselves more readily when they are cheerful and happy.* This is why many people begin to get better once they leave the hospital and return home. The familiar surroundings, filled with their loving family, often help them begin the healing process. And the best way we can begin to help the mind heal itself is by maintaining a cheerful disposition by laughing.

You know that when you laugh, you feel great. It is impossible to be sad when you are laughing. If you are ill, don't dwell on it. The worst thing is to sit around all day worrying about your illness. Your negative thoughts will be reinforcing Vril flowing into you to work on making you sicker. Keep your mind busy with things you love doing. Talk to people who make you happy. Watch movies and television shows that are funny. If you are stuck in bed, watch videos of comedy movies or your favorite comedy television shows, all day long. Watch and do anything that will help you to laugh.

Dwelling on Illness, Will Attract More of the Same

The last thing you want to do is talk about your illness all day long. Most people like to talk about "what ails them." If you are always talking about your illness, you are focusing your mental powers on it, and the life-giving Vril will create more of what it is you are concentrating on. Turn your thinking around, and see yourself getting better, living a life of perfect health. Do what the doctor tells you, but don't obsess over the illness. That's what the doctor is there for. You are paying him to make sure you get better. You concentrate on being healed.

And don't talk to others about your illness. If anyone asks you how you are feeling, tell them you are feeling better every day. If you talk about how bad you feel, you will continue to feel bad and this condition will get worse. If someone asks you, "How are you feeling?" just remind yourself that you are feeling wonderful. You can make a joke about your illness. Say something like, if I continue to feel this way, I might go for a long hard run around the block later, and then laugh about it.

Have you ever noticed how most doctors don't get sick? Doctors, especially general practitioners, are in contact with sick people all day long, and yet they never get sick, or they seldom get sick. The reason is simple. They are thinking about and focusing on helping patients get better. They are not thinking about how ill their patients are, but how can they help them recover and feel better. These thoughts create a shield around the doctors that keeps them invulnerable from all the germs and bacteria they come into contact with every day. The best doctors have a good bedside manner. They remain cheerful and constantly remind their patients how well they are doing, and that they will soon recover. They know that most of their patients trust them and a simple positive affirmation from them will help with the healing process.

You are Only as Old as You Feel

This is another old saying, commonly quoted. There is also a great deal of truth behind these words. If you feel yourself aging, you will continue to age more rapidly. As you grow older, you can slow down the aging process by simply thinking yourself young. I know from personal experience. I am more than a half century old, and yet, I still think of myself as twenty. I still have the same interests I did at twenty. I have not discarded what I believed, enjoyed and found fun and interesting when I was twenty. I still do what I did at twenty, though not as much of it. And most people tell me I look about ten years younger than I really am. This is because I work at maintaining a youthful disposition.

For instance, I never take the elevator to go up or down just a few floors. I try to walk quickly, and maintain a youthful stride. I refuse to act like I am growing old. If I can, I would prefer to walk to the store, rather than take the car. I exercise and try to be as physically active as I can. My mind refuses to see me growing old, and my body listens to my mind. I can still do everything I did at twenty, just maybe not as much of it. But why should I accept limitations just because I have lived longer? Even if you live to be two hundred years old, you will slow down, but you have the power within yourself to slow the "slowing" process. There is truth in that old saying. You really are only as old as you feel. And feeling is all in your mind.

There are plenty of examples of this, and if you think about it, I sure you can come up with two or three individuals over sixty, or even seventy, who still do everything they did at twenty or thirty. I know someone who is one hundred years old. She is still active, and everyone who knows her has always been amazed about how youthful and active she still is. For decades people would say, "She still walks to the store," or, "She is as sharp and fit as she always was." When she is asked how she stays in such good shape at such an advanced age, she simply says, "I never think about how old I really am. I just go and do whatever it is I want to do, and never ask if I can do it."

Begin to Heal Yourself Now

Stress kills! Everyone knows too much stress in your life will kill you. Stress can physically age you, turning your hair white and causing you to lose weight, and cause an overall decline in your health. It can cause your heart to fail, increase your blood pressure, and many other medical problems. Your mind can destroy your body, but it also has the power to heal it and keep it healthy. Unhappy thoughts lead to an unhealthy body, while happy thoughts lead to a healthy body. Your emotions are constantly changing your body for better or worse. Physicians will tell you that by just smiling, you can improve your mental and physical well being, alleviate stress and even slow development of age wrinkles in your face. But you cannot smile if you are suffering under the bombardment of unhappy thoughts.

It is a shame that too many people have to work at being happy. But the truth is, there are too many unhappy people in the world. And for the most part it is the little things that make us unhappy. Every time you feel unhappy, sad, depressed, or angry or are overcome with any negative emotion, think about something or someone who makes you happy. You have got to want to be happy. Ask yourself why you would want to be unhappy. The thing is, we are overcome with negative emotions, and before we can control them, they overtake us. Something happens and you react. We all do, and so do I. But I consciously drive such feelings out as soon as they appear. I begin to think about something that will bring a smile to my face, or someone I love and cherish. I think about how fortunate I am, and then the thing that made me unhappy does not seem that important anymore, and I wonder why I even got upset in the first place.

Principles Necessary to Use Vril for Healing

There are several principles you must understand when you use Vrilology for healing:

1) Within you is an inherent ability to use the flow of Vril to control your physiological process beyond what traditional medicine claims is possible.

2) The ability to harness Vril, and use it to heal yourself and others, involves the coordination of your body, mind, and the spirit.

3) When you obsess on something, you are drawing more of it into your life. Your mind sends out vibrations from your thoughts and emotions, which shape the currents of Vril flowing into you, creating pathways into your future, filled with what you obsess about.

4) Adverse thoughts and emotions manifest adverse psycho-physiological effects, while positive thoughts and emotions manifest positive psycho-physiological effects.

5) The power that resides within your mind is far greater than you imagine. Within it is the power to affect your body processes, including the power to heal, rejuvenate and prolong your life.

6) By changing the way you think, you can use your mind to make you well, or sick. It is possible to use Vrilology to unlock the power of your mind and channel the Vril currents flowing into you, to make yourself radiantly healthy, improve and maintain a vigorous immune system, and slow down and even reverse the aging process, so that you can look younger and live a longer, healthier life. You can also increase your energy levels, improve your mental processes, improve your cognitive abilities, and improve your memory.

7) Vrilology can help you to lose weight.

8) Vrilology can help you to fall asleep, and remember your dreams.

9) Vrilology can help you not to doze off when you are drowsy.

10) Vrilology can help to eliminate headaches.

11) Vrilology can help you to wake up at a given time without the use of an alarm clock.

12) Vrilology can be used to help you overcome addictions.

13) You can use Vrilology to use your dreams to help you find a solution to a problem.

14) It can help you to study for a test or remember complicated material.

15) You can learn to coordinate both halves of your brain so that they can work more fully together.

These are just a few things that you can learn to accomplish through Vrilology, but to do so, *you must learn to use the full potential of your mind.*

Here is a little riddle that can help to explain what we mean. Say you are standing on the shore of a lake. There is an island in the center of the lake with everything you desire in life, but there is no bridge to the island. There is also no boat for you to use to get to the island. The shore of the lake is bare, so there are no trees for you to make a raft. How do your get to the island? The answer is, you swim. But what if you do not know how to swim? The answer is, *you learn!* So you must learn how to use your powers to make things happen. This is done through meditation, visualization, the proper method of breathing, and applying the use of Runes as a tool to help you to harness and control the Vril currents flowing into you.

The Danger from Stress and Anxiety

If we want a healthy mind and body, it is best to maintain a balanced disposition *free from stress and anxiety* as much as possible. *This is why Vrilology is based on love, joy and happiness, and why Wunjo is so important to us and our health.* Good health is a prerequisite for happiness, and happiness is necessary if we are to maintain good health. The negative emotions, if not controlled and properly used, will drain the Life

Force from us, deplete our supply of Vril, cutting off its vital life-giving energies to certain parts of our bodies and eventually leading to poor health. Any doctor will tell you that too much stress and anxiety, which is the result of wrong thought-patterns, will cause physical damage to our bodies. Wrong thoughts lead to wrong behavior, which can also damage our health.

If your health is not everything that you wish it was, then you should examine the method of your thinking. You have to keep in mind that every one of your thoughts produces an impression in your mind. These impressions are like seeds that you are implanting into the soil of your subconscious. There, they will form tendencies. These tendencies, will in turn, attract similar thoughts, and before you know it, you have grown a whole crop which must be harvested. This harvest will dominate your thoughts and feelings. If they contain disease germs, the harvest will be sickness, decay, weakness and failure. *You have got to understand that you must constantly ask yourself what it is you are growing—just what it is you are planting in your subconscious.*

This is why it is so important to learn to focus our mind and control our thoughts, emotions and urges so that we can set our actions toward a precise objective, resulting in the harmonious relationship and cooperation of body and mind. This harmonization of our desires by the will of the mind will manifest in peace of mind and good health.

Directing the Flow of Vril in Your Body

You must learn to direct Vril toward those areas of your body where you want to increase the flow of its power. Be very clear in your mind about where you want Vril to flow, and how you want it to affect you. For instance, if you have a cholesterol problem and you want Vril to flow through your vascular system to lower your bad cholesterol, you should *will* the process. *Within your mind visualize currents of Vril energy coursing through your vascular system, breaking down the bad cholesterol.* Imagine that you can actually feel the cholesterol disintegrating and your blood flowing freely. This does not mean that you should cease using any prescribed drugs. Don't be foolish. In fact, if you are taking medication, visualize the medication working more efficiently and without side effects. *Vril should be used help your traditional medical treatments to work more efficiently.* If we were to dedicate our lives to training ourselves in the use of Vril, and pass this knowledge down to our children, perhaps in a few generations we could advance to the point where we have the power to cause mutations within our bodies by the shared power of the collective will. At the moment, our Bifrost Glands are so atrophic from lack of use by our race over thousands of years, we cannot expect to reverse this condition overnight. It is possible that some miraculous manifestations might occur, but we are not yet collectively masters of Vril to the point of abandoning traditional medicine or science.

Using Runes to Heal with Vril

The use of the Vril should be done in conjunction with the Runes. Always remember that the Runes are a marvelous tool, given to us by the Gods as a means by which we can harness our shared Life Force (Vril). This is especially true when dealing with healing. We can use different Runes for what ails us. When meditating and chanting to draw on the Vril, we should employ the Runes to draw on and shape the healing power of the Vril. Here is a list of what Runes should be used for different medical problems:

Fehu—Chest and respiratory problems.

Uruz—Problems with muscles and tendons and anything to do with body strength and muscular tissue.

Thurisaz—Heart.

Ansuz—The mouth, teeth, throat, tongue. Stuttering and all speech impediments.

Raidho—Legs, feet, knees and gluteal muscles.

Kenaz—Cysts, ulcers, abscesses, boils, cuts, lacerations and all injuries associated with fevers and infections.

Gebo—Poisons and toxins.

Wunjo—Problems associated with breath, breathing and the respiratory system.

Hagalz—Lacerations, grazes, scraps, cuts and wounds.

Nauthiz—All problems associated with the arms, elbows, hands and fingers.

Isa—Loss of feeling and sensation, numbness, paralysis and other problems dealing with the nervous system.

Jera—Problems dealing with the bowels and digestion.

Eihwaz—All problems dealing with the eyes and vision.

Perthro—Anything associated with reproduction, child birth and the sexual organs.

Elhaz—Problems dealing with the head, brain, headaches, anxiety, stress, or mental and psychological disorders.

Sowilo—Burns and all problems dealing with the skin.

Tiwaz—Rheumatism, arthritis and all problems dealing with the joints and hands.

Berkano—Fertility problems.

Ehwaz—All back and spinal problems.

Mannaz—Sprains, dislocated joints, pulled tendons, cramps, especially associated with wrists, ankles and feet.

LAaguz—Kidneys.

Ingwaz—Problems dealing with male genitalia and reproduction.

Dagaz—Mental illnesses, distress, phobias, nervous problems and anxiety.

Othalaz—DNA, genetic problems and inherited illnesses, and anything dealing with inherited traits.

The best way to use the Runes is to first choose the individual Runes associated with your problems, and then chant those Runes that have specific healing qualities. Runes dealing with protection and the Life Force include Uruz (vital force), Thurisaz (protection), Kenaz (controlled energy), Wunjo (harmony of forces), Elhaz (life and protection), Sowilo (life and rebirth), and Laguz (life energy). *Uruz, Elhaz and Sowilo are three very important Runes in the healing process and should be used whenever you seek to use the Vril in healing.*

Uruz, Sowilo and Elhaz–the Three Primary Healing Runes

Uruz is the first among Runes you can use to heal and restore good health. Its rune-energy is the most vital of runic forces when dealing with self-healing, restoring the original pattern of the physical form with recuperative Megin energies, and its power is to restore vitality. Uruz represents the great nurturing force of the cosmic bovine that gave life to the Gods. It nourished Ymir. Its ancient symbol is the now-extinct aurochs, a mighty ox that once roamed the forests of Europe. The aurochs stood taller than a man and had a horn spread of twelve feet. It represents forces of protection, strength, tenacity, courage, protection of home ground and a fierce sense of independence.

The energy that is shaped by the runic forces of Uruz is associated with growth and overcoming obstacles. It is the runic symbolism of the *will to power*, the *will to live*. It runic energies are raw, primitive power, and you can use it to fill yourself with strength, persistence, durability and the ability to survive any ordeal.

Uruz is the primary healing Rune within the Elder Futhark. Its powers to heal come from its power of archetypal patterning. *It draws on Megin (Vril energy transformed into your Personal Luck), and uses it to restore the initial pattern found in the individual's etheric or subtle body, which is known as the Hamr.* Vril energy that flows into each of us is shaped into patterns that fit nicely into the perfected blueprint vibration of the physical body enjoying perfect physical health. Proof of this Hamr shape is revealed to us when an amputee claims that he can still *feel* the phantom limb after the physical limb has been removed. When the physical body shifts in its vibrational resonance so that it no longer conforms to this blueprint, which is the original Hamr energy shape, it becomes prey to all sorts of disease, illness and other ailments that can cause harm to your physical well being and good health.

Just as the physical body can shift away from its original invisible energy pattern, so too it can be restored to its Hamr pattern when sufficient Megin is diverted and shaped into a healing force through the use of several Runes, foremost of them Uruz.

Uruz is especially useful in harnessing telluric Vril energy rising from the Earth streams into your being. Earth energies are a very potent force for healing, and Uruz is especially useful in harnessing and shaping these energy currents. We were born of Mother Earth and her nurturing powers are very effective in self-healing. Uruz draws these telluric Vril currents up through your body and then returns them to the Earth.

The second most effective Rune you can use in the healing process is Sowilo. *It is the Rune of the Sun and Cosmic Energies.* It is very effective is enhancing your powers of self-healing with high levels of positive Vrilic energy. It can be used to increase the powers of your hvel for greater psychic optimum health.

Sowilo, as the Rune of the Sun, representing the falling rays of the sun's energy toward earth, is a counter force to the runic energy of Hagalaz, which is the Rune of hail or falling ice. Just as Fehu is the polar opposite of Isa in the cosmic relationship of Ginnungingap to Musspellheim (Fehu) and Niflheim (Isa), so is Sowilo, as the falling rays of the Sun, the opposing force of Hagalaz, falling hail, in the physical and mental world.

In Norse cosmology, *Balder is the Shining God, the Sun God, the Bright One*. He survives Ragnarok, and his resurrection heralds in the new, golden age that is Gimli. Thus he is the principal deity associated with Sowilo. He represents the regenerative powers of Vril, the Life Force, which flow through the human body, charging fire in your metabolism. The energy of Sowilo gives heat to the body, *making us warm-blooded.* This is why blood is warm. It is charged with pure, undiluted fire, giving energy and vitality to all your worldly endeavors, as well as your good health.

The flow of Vril energy is drawn down from the Sun overhead, and instills great energy into your healing work. This form of Vril energy, drawn from the Sun, can be used to manifest great transformations in the health of the physical body. The cosmic energy drawn from the Sun through the use of Sowilo can increase the potency of Uruz's healing potential. Think of a solar battery storing solar energy and then using this energy to aid in heating your home. The principle behind the use of Sowilo in healing is similar.

The third of the Healing Runes is Elhaz. Elhaz is the *Rune of the Valkyrie*, and is used to strengthen your Hamingja. It can be used to strengthen the walls of the Hamingja and thus increase its capacity to hold larger amounts of Megin. *Elhaz is the Life Rune*. It is the Rune that assures the resurrection or rebirth of Balder. *As Sowilo is the Rune of Balder Risen, so Elhaz is the Rune of Balder Rising*. It is this regenerative power that will help with the process of improving your health and well being.

Elhaz is associated with two Goddesses. The first is Freyja, as the leader of the Valkyries. She brings the dead to Asgard, where she divides them with Odin. This is the process of being reborn into a higher form of consciousness. The second Goddess in Idun. She is the Goddess of Eternal Youth. She feeds the Gods and Goddess every day with Golden Apples, which symbolize the Vrilic power of youthfulness and vitality. The golden apples are symbols of the Sun and its golden rays with the power to heal.

The Valkyries are sometimes depicted as swans, or Swan Maidens. The swan has always been associated with eternal youth, regeneration and rebirth.

Elhaz also is the primary Protection Rune. Its powers can be used to provide protection from harm, including illnesses and sickness. When drawing on Elhaz's powers, one is enveloped with so much Vril energy that he or she becomes scared of evolving into a Vril Being. When drawing on the shaping powers of Elhaz, you are causing the Divine powers within you to rise, thus causing you to evolve into a state of well being and good health that brings you closer to the Gods.

Exercise to Teach You to Help Your Doctor to Heal You

Do not fool yourself that you should not seek medical assistance or think that using Vril is a substitute for medical science, *because it is not!* In fact, *you should use Vril in conjunction with medical science.* If you have a serious problem and your doctor is assisting you with medication or treatment of some kind, you can and should use Vril to assist in empowering the treatment—*to help your body to react positively to the medical treatment.*

When you are being treated for an ailment, you can assist the medical aid offered by traditional medicine with a simple exercise. You should by now be able to perform this exercise with ease. *This exercise should be performed three times a day.*

1) Sit in a comfortable position with your eyes closed and roll them slight upward toward your eyebrow under your closed eyelids so you can enter your alpha state. If you are doing this in bed, prop yourself up with several pillows to help prevent you from falling asleep.

2) Slowly count backward from 20 to 1, waiting one second between each number. But before you begin counting, mentally see the Rune, Raidho, which is *the Rune of the road to right results.*

3) Perform your relaxation exercise, concentrating on different parts of your body, beginning with your scalp, and work your way down to your toes. As you do, relax them. Take your time. You should be totally relaxed by the time you reach your toes. Feel yourself entering a deeper state of meditation.

4) Once you are completely relaxed, begin to visualize yourself as youthful, radiant, healthy, attractive, vibrant and filled with energy. See yourself in a state of perfect health.

5) Ask yourself mentally, "Why do I have this health problem?" Then let your mind wander freely. Just let it go blank and wait.

6) Visualize the Rune of Ansuz, *the Rune of communication and knowledge.* Ask the Gods for the knowledge to help you cure yourself. Know that they will provide this knowledge eventually. Know that when the time is right, you will know what course of action you will need to take to be cured. You can call on the Goddess, Eira, *the Goddess of medicine and healing.* You can ask Eira to help your doctor. Ask her to give him the knowledge necessary to heal you.

7) Visualize a screen before you. This screen represents the past. Visual an image on the screen of yourself ill. Imagine yourself suffering from whatever it is that is wrong with you. Now slide the screen to your left and see a second screen, which represents the present. See yourself being cured. It can be any image. You can be cured from the touch of the Goddess Eira, or your doctor. Just visualize yourself in the process of being cured. Now slide this screen to your left and see a third screen, which represents the future. On this screen, see yourself cured. You are once more perfectly healthy. Let's say you are suffering from a stomach ulcer. You should then choose the appropriate Rune for ulcers. This would be Kenaz. Visualize Kenaz, and feel its powers disintegrating your ulcers. *Feel its powers healing you!*

8) Say to yourself, "I will always maintain perfect health in body and mind." Visualize Uruz, *the Rune of Healing. Feel Uruz's powers working in conjunction with Kenaz, healing you!*

9) See yourself cured. You are in perfect health once more. Hold this thought of yourself in perfect health. Visualize it in every detail. See yourself happy, vigorous and healthy. Hold this image for about five minutes. As you do this, visualize the Rune, Sowilo, *the second Rune of Healing, and the Rune of the Sun.*

10) Begin to count from 1 to 5. As you do, see yourself filling with the energy of the sun. Concentrate on Sowilo, the healing powers of the sun. Count one, two, three. When you reach three, stop and say, "When I open my eyes on the count of 5, I will feel fine, in perfect health, feeling better and better every day of my life." Continue counting...four, five...and then open your eyes and affirm mentally, "I am wide awake, feeling wonderful and in perfect health. I am feeling better and better each day of my life." You can visualize Elhaz, *the Rune of resurrection and rebirth.*

This is one simple method to help with the healing process by changing the way you think.

Using Vril in General Self-treatment

You can administer a form of general self-treatment by lying down in a comfortable position and relaxing your entire body. Then, *concentrate on the Solar Plexus.* Use your will *to direct the flow of Vril up to your brain and then down through your nervous system.* Feel it flowing downward to the left and right foot. Concentrate on this until you feel a tingling sensation in your feet, or a general feeling of awareness. You should then move up the body, doing the same thing with the lower legs, the upper legs, the reproductive region of the body, the abdomen, and then the solar plexus, the lungs, chest and throat. Then proceed to do the same with your shoulders, upper arms, lower arms, hands and finally with your fingers. At this point, you should proceed to do the same as you did with your feet, directing Vril to your head. Wait until you feel the same sensation that you felt in your feet. After this has been accomplished, concentrate on directing Vril to your spinal column, downward from the brain through the spinal cord and outward through the connecting nerves. Next, concentrate on the sacral plexus at the lower part of the spine. Concentrate on this region until you feel a thorough tingling sensation. By now, you should be charged with Vril. Continue to lie comfortably. Visualize your entire body radiating with the power of Vril. Rest quietly for a few minutes, slowly letting your mind relax, permitting all your thoughts to escape from your mind. You should rise refreshed and energized. This method can be varied, so you might want to experiment, depending on what parts of your body need recharging.

Nourishment

The first thing we would like to say is that there are no dietary requirements nor restrictions on what you can eat or drink. Vrilology does not desire to control anyone, nor seek to forbid or demand that its followers and practitioners submit to constraints of eating and drinking certain foods and drinks. Unlike certain religions, there is no taboo on what you can eat or drink. But Vrilology *does encourage* good habits of eating and drinking. The reason for this will be made clear in this lesson. We do suggest one refrain from ingesting toxic materials, drugs, depressives and mind-bending substances for recreation. The reason is simple:

Besides the negative effects they can have on your physical well being, such things will cause you to lose control of your mind and senses and thus manifest a state of chaotic thinking, which can be very harmful, especially when practicing Vrilology or any esoteric discipline.

Vrilology encourages good eating and drinking habits. Moderation and balance! This is the best rule to follow when eating or drinking. The reason for this becomes clear once you understand how you can acquire Vril from the substance you eat and drink.

Types of Food and Vril

We all know that our bodies require certain daily amount of vitamins, proteins, nutrients, calories, fats and other elements found in foods, but medical science fails to recognize the need for Vril for the maintenance of good health. Our bodies speak to us through cravings. It is the way our bodies tell us that we are deficient in certain elements necessary for our well being. Most animals still have this infallible instinct that tells them what they need for their physical well being, and we also once possessed a well developed ability to ***instinctually know*** what our bodies were lacking. But because of our modern, sanitized, sterilized and artificial living environments in megametropolises, our natural instinct to select the proper various types of food best adapted for our needs has atrophied. The majority of us live under artificial conditions that have not only warped our natural instincts, but contributed to the development of an unnatural habit of ingesting foods that are unhealthful at best, and even dangerous to our well being in many cases. We do not have the space to explore proper diet and good nutrition, for these subjects can be acquired easily from various sources including your library or the Internet, we will try to explore the relationship of food and drink as contributory factors to our good health in relationship to their Vril-containing properties.

Food that we humans need for good health can be divided into three general classes:

1) protein or nitrogenous foods—meats, nuts, peas, beans, etc.—which are tissue-builders of the system;

2) carbohydrates—sugars, starches, gums, breads, etc.—which are both tissue builders and heat-producers; and

3) fats—animal fats, vegetable oils, butter, etc.—which serve principally as heat-producers.

The various types of food possess different amounts of Vril. Foods rich in proteins contain large supplies of Vril that are easily assimilated into our body chemistry. Carbohydrates are especially rich in large amounts of Vril that can be absorbed into the human body. While fats contain much needed heat-producing material needed for our bodies to function and maintain good health, they contain small amounts of Vril available for us to absorb. While different authorities disagree as to the exact amounts of each category necessary for good healthy, *it is agreed that a well balanced diet is necessary for good health.*

Dietary Requirements and Race

Those of you who were born before 1980, and might remember government reports encouraging a well-balanced diet that consists of bread, butter, beefsteak, potatoes, eggs, milk, green vegetables and so forth, would have noticed in recent years changes in this program. Recent reports discourage the ingestion of red meats, milk and other products. The reason for this change in *what constitutes a healthy diet* is due to *the changing racial makeup* of our population. The previous diet recommended was geared to a population in the United States that was about 90 percent European in ancestry. But today, the European percentage of the United States population has declined to about 60 percent. The rest are made up of peoples from Africa, Latin America, Asia and the Middle East, who require a different dietary requirement for good health. Most non-European descended populations find milk to be not only unhealthful, but downright dangerous due to their intolerance to lactose, while most people of European ancestry are lactose tolerant and find it a wonderful source of nourishment and vitamin D. Thus, we must take into consideration the difference in dietary requirements of different races.

Despite the political correctness that race does not exist except as a social construct, *race does exist in physical reality!*

Vrilology is a European folk religion, and best suited for people of European ancestry, though we do not discourage individuals of other, non-European ancestries from studying Vrilology, and hope everyone of all racial backgrounds can benefit from what we teach. We only mention this point about race and nutrition for the good of everyone. Whether you are of European ancestry or non-European ancestry, we want to warn you about the different dietary requirements of different races so that everyone can adjust our program to their individual biological needs and requirements based on their racial background.

The Pleasure of Taste

Remember your mother telling you, when you were a child, *to chew your food thoroughly?* Well, mother knew the importance of the proper mastication of food, without knowing why. There are physiological reasons for chewing your food thoroughly. By saturating your food with saliva, there is less waste when the food passes through your stomach and intestines. By giving your stomach an easy time of performing the task it was designed to do, we are able to employ the energy and blood necessary for servicing the brain. The ancient occultists never suffered brain lethargy from over-eating.

The ancients knew that the proper mastication of food is the best way to acquire the greatest nourishment from your food. They did not possess knowledge of modern chemistry, but they knew that one of the most effective ways to absorb Vril from your food is through the nerve-endings of your tongue and mouth. Once food passed down into the digestive system, most of Vril within foods was lost if the food was not chewed thoroughly, so it was important to masticate it before swallowing. They felt that so long as some taste remained in the food, there was still a supply of Vril that was not being absorbed. Only after all taste was removed from your food by thoroughly chewing it, was all available Vril extracted from your food. Thus, they ate slowly, taking their time to chew each mouthful carefully so as to extract every last bit of Vril and absorb it through the nerve-endings in the mouth and tongue. They also claimed that by doing so, they obtained a pleasure from eating that even the biggest glutton could never experience or conceive. You possess the sense of taste as a means to encourage you to extract the greatest pleasure from your foods, by chewing it thoroughly before swallowing.

Once you learn to adjust your eating habits, you will discover an increase in energy, health and vitality. This is from the greater amounts of naturally extracting a greater supply of natural Vril energy from your food.

Eating to Live Rather than Living to Eat

You should live by the rule: *Eat to live, don't live to eat.* It simply means to avoid excess and you will experience the true normal pleasure and satisfaction in all of Nature's functions. In Vrilology there is no sin, and we reject the idea of the "seven deadly sins," as described by Christianity. One of these sins is gluttony. We do discourage gluttony, not because it is a sin of character, but because it is unnatural. Thus, unlike Christianity, and other religions, which often encourage fasting, Vrilology rejects both gluttony and fasting because both are unnatural and contribute to the body falling into an unnatural state which is also unhealthy. Gluttony will cause lethargy, and fasting will only weaken your body's ability to fight off illness. In both cases, your body's ability to absorb the necessary supply of Vril, to continue functioning properly and assuring good health and long life, is interrupted. *Balance!* This is the key to good health, both physically and spiritually.

The Importance of Water as a Source of Vril Energy

The ancients understood that great amounts of Vril could be extracted from water. This is why water is not only so important to maintain life, *but is the source of life.* Life cannot exist without some supply of water. *Water is the source of all life. The currents of Vril energy are often compared to currents of water, and the universal supply of Vril is referred to as a sea of Vril.* Therefore, it is important to understand the proper way to drink water. The ancient elders drank water in small sips. If you were ever in the Military, you will remember being instructed to take small sips of water and holding them in your mouth for a few seconds before swallowing when you suffer from dehydration, and never take large gulps. Of course, what you were being instructed to do, even if the military did not understand the nature of Vril, was to permit your mouth and tongue to absorb the greatest amounts of Vril from the water before swallowing. Our ancestors believed that the body could not extract Vril from water as effectively once it was swallowed, and then the water served only the physiological functions of irrigating the body and carrying away refuse material.

The process of extracting the greatest supply of Vril from water through sipping also provides the greatest pleasure in quenching thirst. This is shown to be true by the popularity of the use of straws by people today. There is a different taste to whatever it is you are drinking when you drink it through a straw. It would indicate that we acquire greater satisfaction or gratification when sipping a liquid through a straw. It would seem that the essence of the cooling liquid is absorbed more effectively in this way and provides greater refreshment. This is also true of hot drinks, which are naturally sipped because they are too hot to drink in gulps. This is why we get great satisfaction from drinking our hot cup of coffee, tea or hot cocoa.

Laguz: How the Water Rune can Provides for Mental Health and Well Being

Laguz is the Rune of Water, or Primal Waters. By studying the runic nature of Laguz, we can learn something of how water is such a powerful conveyer of Vril energy. *Water is representative of the subconscious.* This is vital in generating vitality and vigor not only for your physical body but also in maintaining and ensuring its good mental health and well being.

Water is the symbol of the subconscious. As in any body of water, there is much happening below the surface that you cannot see. *Thus, Laguz, as the Rune of Water, symbolizes the invisible Life Force or Vril.* Water represents the subconscious mind and your emotions in dream therapy. To get wet, or find yourself in a body of water, while you are dreaming usually means you have entered your subconscious mind. There are dangers lurking beneath the calm surface of any body of water. This is why the sea of the unconscious mind can be a terribly turbulent and uncontrollable realm to enter by the uninitiated. If you have a lot of emotional baggage, you can discover terrible monsters lurking in your subconscious, waiting to pounce on you as soon as you enter. I am reminded of the movie, *The Forbidden Planet*, staring Walter Pigeon, who plays a scientist who discovers alien technology that enhances the power of his mind. The result is the manifestation of a terrible monster in the physical world, from his subconscious or "Id", that he cannot control, and he begins to hunt down and destroy anyone who might stand in his way or oppose him. You should be warned that these monsters are real, and your mind has to confront them, but the good news is that these subconscious beasts can be controlled for good through mastery of runic skills. This danger is reflected the way Vrilic energy flows through Laguz. It rises up its shaft and down the arm, similar to Uruz, but when it is released, the direction it then takes can be unpredictable. This is the nature of water. Unless you are very careful in planning how to control the flow of water, you can easily lose control of it. There is great power in water, especially in running water. It is much more difficult to control than one might imagine. This is also very true of our emotions. Emotional forces are not the property of the left side of the brain, the rational mind, but of the right side of the brain, and rooted in our subconscious.

We can visualize the two halves of the brain as the ocean and the sky above it. The right side is the sea, with all its hidden properties existing below the surface. The left side of the mind is the sky overhead. The interesting thing to note in this analogy is that water is constantly being vaporized and rising up into the air, just as the hidden properties of the right side of the brain (the subconscious) are constantly invading the left side of the brain and interfering with the logical, rational thinking process that is taking place there. It is possible to help to balance the flow of Vrilic energy between the two halves of the brain by using the following Runes:

Laguz, as the Rune of Water (the subconscious mind).
Ansuz, as the Rune of Air (the conscious mind).
Dagaz, as the Rune used to bridge the two halves of the brain.
Raidho, the Rune of right paths.

Raidho can be very useful whenever you wish to direct something into a controlled and proper movement.

Laguz represents the many rivers that flow out of the Well of Hvergilmir located in Niflheim, fed by the melting ice along its frontiers. These rivers are the source of Vril currents of energy that fill the universe. Northern creation myths use a symbol of yeast like rime to portray the invisible currents of Vril energy that are the foundation of the material universe. As we have described before, this living energy, Vril, is the Life Force of the universe. It is the essence of every atom, comprising over 99 percent of the atom. Since everything in the universe is made up of atoms, everything is made up of Vril, including our thoughts. It is in this way that our thoughts, through their variation of vibrations, ideas and thoughts can be transformed into reality, taking physical manifestation. One who is an adept in Vrilology can project his thoughts into patterns formed by his mind's ability to change the vibratory frequencies of Vril currents, energized by his emotions (water) and desire (fire) that will eventually materialize in the physical universe. *We can see the polarity of the universal principle of male/female fertilization that is at the root of all Nature.* In this case, the shaped thought patterns are the male principle fertilize the female Vrilic energy currents to give form to the physical world.

Because the mind is such a powerful instrument in shaping Vril energy currents, we must never forget the relationship between our conscious and subconscious minds. Look at water and how it manifests itself in the physical world. Water can manifest itself though underground wells or rivers. The earth is riddled with underground streams of water that occasionally rise to the surface in the form of springs, and often turn into powerful rivers that can greatly transform the physical nature of the surface of the planet. This is similar to the way our subconscious minds can affect the conscious mind.

Laguz can be used to help you to delve deep into the unconscious realms of your subconscious mind, as well as that of the collective unconscious. You can use Laguz to help develop your clairvoyant abilities or Second Sight. This will enable you to be sensitive to shifts in the subconscious currents of Vril energy around you and within you. You can develop your Second Sight and be aware of events before they are actualized in the physical environment.

Because Laguz is associated with water, which is the element of the unconscious, hidden forces of Life, and emotions, it is considered a feminine Rune. Though it is also considered a Rune of Twins, associated with Njord, the God of the Sea or Seacoast, and his twin sister/wife, Nerthus, Laguz is often associated with the powers of what has been referred to as *woman's intuition.*

Chapter Twelve: You are a Vril Being

If you clasp hands, you will feel yourself as a solid, living being. But we are actually 99.999... percent Vril energy. The remainder is subatomic particles. It is the power of Vril that holds the particles together within your atoms, and keeps your atoms from flying off in every direction. It is Vril that makes you appear solid, even though it is a form of energy.

Having read this far, you should be ready to move beyond skepticism and accept the truth that you are a Vril Being. Once you become aware of your Vril self, you will know there is an unseen, invisible world that you can experience. And once you have experienced this unseen dimension, and understand it and how it works, you will know that you can use your mind to tap into its laws to work miracles in the visible universe. Once you have achieved this evolutionary growth and development, you will know that you have evolved into a superior human being—you have become a Vril Being.

The Reality of Vril is Everywhere

You have only to look around to know that the wondrous universe is impossible to fathom without accepting that there is a higher force beyond the material. The universe that we can see with our five senses is far too complex and wondrous to have been created without the intervention of a divine intelligence. The more you examine the universe, the more you have to accept that. How did the whole thing get started? Scientists will talk about the Big Bang, but how did this happen? What was before it? What caused it? Scientists know that some kind of invisible force holds the entire universe and reality together. They have become aware of the trans-dimensional nature of the universe, but they still can't explain consciousness and what happens to it after death. These things exist within the invisible realm of the Gods–the realm powered by Vril.

Everything in the universe is Vril! Understand that Vril is everywhere and in everything. It is pulsating, vibrating and flowing fields of spiritual energy.

We truly live in fortunate times in regard to the tradition that we are teaching. New discoveries in scientific fields in general and quantum physics in particular have contributed a scientific foundation to what ancient mystics and philosophers have known through the millennia—a greater understanding of Vril, helping many realize that Vril is not based on any mystic "belief," but has a scientific foundation.

Each of us is transmitting frequencies that affect what happens in the universe. We also know that all energy vibrates at different frequencies. Being mostly Vril, we also vibrate at different frequencies. Which frequency we vibrate at is determined by whatever it is we are thinking or feeling at any given moment. This is determined by the conscious state your mind is working in at any given time—alpha, beta, theta, or delta. Everything in the universe, including everything you want and desire, is also made of Vril energy and is vibrating. Everything is Vril, and everything is vibrating.

When you think—which is all the time, even when you sleep—you are sending frequencies into the currents of Vril energy flowing into you. This causes Vril to vibrate at the same frequencies. You are thus causing Vril to build pathways into a future that will include what you want. As you focus on what you want, you are causing Vril currents to change the vibration of atoms of whatever you desire, so that they will be attracted to those pathways. You are causing it to move into those pathways through the vibrations you are sending out. You, a human being, have a brain superior to that of animals, and thus your mind is a much more powerful instrument in attracting what you desire to manifest in your future. Your superior brain permits you to more effectively focus on what you want. An animal's brain can do this, but less effectively, because their minds are governed by their instinctual needs.

You should remember that how the future pathways manifest in your life is determined by how you think and feel. Like attracts like, so if your thoughts are positive and motivated by joy, happiness and harmony, then whatever you want will appear in your life and bring more of the same. But if you are consumed by anger, hatred, and other negative thoughts and feelings, then the things that are attracted to you will do so in a way that will bring more negativity to your life. Charles Haanel (1866-1949) wrote in his excellent book, The Master Key System: "To be conscious of this power [that in the Folk Faith of Balder Rising is called Vril] is to become a 'live wire.' The Universe is the live wire. It carries power sufficient to meet every situation in the life of every individual. When the individual mind touches the universal Mind, it receives all its power."

What is a Vril Being?

Most people think of themselves as a physical being possessing a soul or spirit. This spiritual entity is usually thought of as identical to your physical body and existing within it. When you die, it leaves the physical body and floats off somewhere, depending on your religious beliefs. The truth of the matter is, your physical body exists within your soul or spiritual entity. Every atom within you is made of Vril. Vril makes up not only your physical form but is also the essence of your morphic energy field that extends beyond your physical form.

Let's understand something about Vril. It is a form of energy, but on a different plane of existence. Vril, like all energy, can never be created or destroyed. It has always existed and always will exist. It can be changed and transformed, and does change form. Now remember that Vril is a "Life Force." It is the same Life Force that makes up the divine powers, the Gods. The Gods of our ancestors' religions are just like energy. They are immortal, but they too are not permanent; they change form and evolve.

What makes one a Vril Being? The Gods created us with Vril. By thinking us into existence, by instilling us with their consciousness, they gave us form; to give us life, they filled us with Vril currents that we refer to as Ond, the breath of life. We are all Vril energy creatures, made of the same substance that the Gods are made from, but the difference between a Vril creature and a Vril Being is the latter has discovered the techniques to control Vril and use it to transform his universe, including himself. *This makes the Vril Being semi-divine because when he has achieved this state of being, the state of Balder Risen, he is now aligned with the Gods!*

The Control of Vril Energy Within the Spirito-physical Body to transform yourself

By now you have come to the realization that we are all beings composed of energy–Vril energy. *The purpose goal of the Folk Faith of Balder Rising and Vrilology is to transform Vril into a harmonic frequency so that we will become aligned with the Gods.* Vril is constantly entering your body and is being channeled throughout your body to power your entire being, both spiritual and physical. You soul is powered by the Vril currents. These currents are disseminated throughout you to replenish Vril energy in every atom of your body. Your mind, both subconsciously and consciously, is working to channel these currents of Vril energy in many different ways. How your mind channels Vril will depend on what is stored within your Orlog. Your Orlog is part of your soul and acts like a filter which Vril passes through and thus takes on the quality and nature of whatever is stored there. We have explored how you can cleanse your Orlog of negativity that might be stored there. By understanding the nature of Hvels and their role in shaping Vril energy, you will be able to purify and change the nature of Vril currents by balancing the energy-shaping natures of your Hvels.

What Are Hvels?

We have discussed how your thoughts, emotions and actions act collectively as a filtering agent of Vril energy, changing its nature and controlling its flow throughout your body and soul.

The matters you think about, especially when you obsess over them, will control your emotional state, which in turn charges your Vril energy, causing it to take on their nature. *In others words, the things you obsess on the most will affect your Hvel energy centers.*

The word *Hvel* is Norse for wheel or whirling center or vortex. Hvels are centers of Vril energy within the human body where Vril is concentrated, which have correspondence to the organization of psychic powers of the mind that are powered by currents of Vril that flow through your body. At junctions where two or more rivers join, the flows of water interact and their force of movement will cause whirlpools or vortexes, containing powerful currents that can cause ships, boats and people to either sink or crash. The same is true of the flow of Vril energy throughout your body. As Vril courses throughout your body, there is a large number of small points where the nervous system branches off in different directions. At these points Vril coalesces into tiny whorls, like pools of water that become whirlpools. In India they are referred to "Chakras" (Sanskrit for "wheel") and there are claims that there are hundreds of such points of whirlpool energy throughout your body. The Chinese use them in their science of acupuncture. We refer to these Chakras as Hvels, which are whirling centers of Vril energy. We have already examined the Hvels in Chapter Five, but let's look at them once more.

We will concentrate on the most important Hvels, which are associated with the worlds of the Yggdrasill. The Asians refer to only seven major Hvels or Chakras. In Vrilology we consider there to be nine main Hvels, aligned along the axis of your body with your spine. Seven are located deep within the center of your physical body. The eighth is above the feet and the ninth is below the feet, which location is also part of your multi-dimensional extended Soul.

The Nine Principal Hvels

Vril energy enters the bio-energy system of the human body through many avenues, but primarily through the head, being attracted to the power of the mind. The mind is represented as the "crown center" or the Asgard Hvel. It is then sent down the spinal cord by way of the sympathetic nervous system trunk channels that travel through the ganglia. *As it travels down the spinal cord it is like the unorganized Vrilic energy that filled the universe at the beginning of time, that gave rise to the Ginnungagap.* It passes down to the feet where it congregates in two Hvels: one located below the feet which corresponds to Muspellhim, and one just above the feet, corresponding to Niflheim. Within these Hvels the Vrilic energy takes on the qualities of fire (expansive force) and ice (contractive form). It is here, where the two feet usually perform motion in the form of walking, that the forces mix and re-create the combustion of life in the formation of Ymir. Sparks rise from the Sole Hvel and mix with the Feet Hvel, causing a reaction similar to the Big Bang. Creation takes place. *Thus, between the Feet Hvel (Niflheim) and the Sole Hvel (Musspellheim Hvel) we see the Ymir Factor take place.* The Vrilic current that now flows upward, back up the spinal cord (Yggdraill or Eihwaz Rune), is chaotic, like Ymir, but it will pass through the other seven Hvels corresponding to the other seven worlds of the Yggdrasill. As it does, it will be transformed, just as Ymir was transformed by Odin, Vili and Ve.

As Vril passes upward and moves through each of the other Hvels, it is transformed in different and specialized ways. *It is this process of Vril moving upward, passing through each Hvel or world, that mirrors the slaughter of Ymir by Odin, Vili and Ve, and how they took his parts, refashioning them in an orderly way, transforming formless and chaotic energy into a systematically organized cosmos.* Here are the Hvels, their associations with the nine worlds, and primary and secondary associations with Runes:

1) Crown Hvel – Asgard – Othala (Dagaz)
2) Brow or Third Eye Hvel – Vanaheim – Dagaz (Elhaz, Mannaz, Othala)
3) Throat Hvel – Ljossalfheim – Ansuz
4) Heart Hvel – Midgard – Wunjo (Perthro, Sowilo)
5) Solar Plexus Hvel – Svartalfheim – Thuriaz (Jera, Uruz)

6) Spleen Hvel – Jotunheim – Laguz
7) Root Hvel – Hel – Kenaz (Fehu)
8) Feet Hvel – Niflheim – Isa (Hagalaz)
9) Sole Hvel – Muspellheim – Fehu

In addition, two Runes are important in relationship to the Hvels generally: Sowilo and Eihwaz. *Sowilo represents the Vril currents coursing through the body, while Eihwaz represents the spinal column or cosmic axis (Yggdrasill).* What is interesting is the shape of these two Runes. If you examine them you will discover that Eihwaz is an elongated version of Sowilo, but tipped on its side.

At the Root Hvel, which represents Hel, the realm where the ego is asleep and unaware of its true esoteric heritage, Vrilic energy causes the inner Self, the awakening Ego-self human being, to regain consciousness of itself and its true heritage, and then rise from the Netherworld much as Balder rises from the Netherworld and heralds in the Gold Age of Gimli.

Once Vril energy reaches your Mind, after passing through all the Hvels, it is then sent back down your spinal cord along the nervous system to every part of your body, feeding Vril energy to every atom within your body and soul.

The Hvels in the lower regions of your body whirl at slower rates than those located in the higher areas of your body. They spin clockwise as viewed from above. If you were looking directly at a person, you could imagine them spinning on their side, like a ceiling fan suspended from a ceiling. In the illustrations that we present, we show the Hvel spinning as if they were fans standing up so that you can better grasp the various natures of the Hvels.

Within the seven upper Hvels, energy spins faster in those Hvels located in the upper parts of the body and slower in the lower regions. The Feet and Sole Hvels have a different nature that we will explain shortly. The hues of the energy also appear to be of different colors that are reflected in your life energy field that is also known as your aura. The changes in the color of your aura reflect how Vril is affected when it passes through your Hvels. The state of each Hvel will affect Vril in different ways. Obsessions create imbalances because when you obsess over things, the Hvels dealing with them will become *under*-active. This will affect the flow of Vril throughout your body, thus preventing some parts of your body from receiving the much-needed Vrilic energy, and this permits decay, causing illness and aging. Having an over-sized or over-active Hvel is not a problem, it is only when there is extreme imbalance among the Hvels that they get out of hand.

We won't into detail once again, but you might want to review each Hvel its purpose by re-reading that section of Chapter Five.

Kundalini Fire (Charged Vril Energy)

Kundalini is a Sanskrit word meaning either "coiled up" or "coiling like a snake," though there are numerous translations emphasizing a more serpentine nature to the word, such as “serpent power.” The concept of Kundalini originates with the yogic philosophy of ancient India, which was conquered and settled by Indo-Europeans who are referred to as Aryans or Ar-yans. It is from them that we get the name that we give to the original people from which all Indo-Europeans are descended. They retained much of the secret science of Vrilology from the lost Ur-civilization, located on the shores of the Black Sea, which was destroyed in 5600 B.C.E., and brought it into India. As refugees from that great cataclysm, the knowledge they brought with them to India was incomplete, and eventually evolved into the Vedic tradition and lore. In time, this knowledge and lore were transformed from its incorporation with alien ideas belonging to indigenous peoples of southern Asia, and became corrupted. But there is still a great deal to be learned from the Vedic tradition as a source of ancient Indo-European knowledge.

Kundalini might be regarded by yogis as a sort of deity, hence the occasional capitalization of the term, just as we capitalize Vril, which is the Life Force of the Gods.

According to the yogic tradition, Kundalini (charged Vril energy) coils up in the back part of the Root Chakra in *three and one-half turns* around the sacrum. Yogic phenomenology states that *Kundalini Awakening* is associated with the appearance of bio-energetic (Vrilic) phenomena that are said to be experienced somatically by the yogi. Somewhere between the Twelfth and Fifteenth Centuries Swami Svatmarama wrote the *Hatha Yoga Pradipika,* which is the source of the text for the concept of Kundalini. Within Western tradition it is often associated with the practice of contemplative or religious practices that might induce an altered state of consciousness. This is what we mean when we have a religious epiphany that can be induced spontaneously, through some type of yoga, meditation, or in a more destructive way through the use of psychedelic drugs, or through a near-death experience.

This experience is also referred to as "pranic awakening." Kundalini is "charged Prana energy," or charged Vril energy. Prana is interpreted as the vital, life-sustaining force in the body, which of course is Vril. When Vrilic energy is intensified and has an uplifting effect, it is referred to as pranotthana. *This phenomenon is supposed to originate from an apparent reservoir of subtle bio-energy at the base of the spine, but we will explain that it actually originates well below the base of the spine.* The location is at the feet—below the Feet Hvel and above the Sole Hvel, the Hvels corresponding to the two original worlds of Musspellheim and Niflheim. It is between these two Hvels that this reservoir of subtle bio-energy is located. *It is here that the expansive force of Musspellheim and the contractive form of Niflheim cause Vril energy to build up and become charged with the life-giving qualities.* This energy is also interpreted as *a vibrational phenomenon that that initiates a period, or a process, of vibrational spiritual development.*

Two early western interpretations of Kundalini were supplied by C.W. Leadbeater (1847-1934) of the Theosophical Society, and the analytical psychologist Carl Jung (1875-1961). In 1932, Jung held a seminar on Kundalini yoga, presented to the

Psychological Club in Zurich. His lecture on the subject is today considered a milestone in the psychological understanding of Eastern thought by the West, as symbolic transformations of inner peace. Jung presented Kundalini yoga as a model for the developmental phases of higher consciousness. He was interested in it because the Indian tradition is descended from Indo-European esotericism. He interpreted its symbols in terms of the process of individuation (Princeton University Press Book description of C. G. Jung - "The Psychology of Kundalini Yoga", 1999).

We won't continue this discussion of Kundalini Fire, but only touched on the subject to demonstrate that knowledge of Vril energy, and how it can be used to transform the individual, has been preserved by Indo-European refugees after the destruction of their ancient Aryan civilization, and has been passed down through the millenniums in other cultures.

The Use of Nauthiz

Nauthiz is a third Rune we need to discuss and use to transform Vril energy currents as they pass through your Hvels. The way Nauthiz is used to modify your Wyrd is through its principle of using the power of resistance to restrict and restrain incoming negative forces, by "fettering" their negative influences, and to eliminate conflict through the power of directed mental force or willpower.

The exercise we will provide you will use Nauthiz to cleanse or bend the energy of each Hvel as Vril flows down the spine to your Sole Hvel. After each Hvel has been cleansed of negativity, you will send Vril back up the spine, passing through each Hvel.

The force of cosmic resistance was born when the universe was manifested. This principle is behind the law: *Every action has an equal and opposite reaction.* In psychic teaching this law is embodied in the principle of cause and effect. In Vrilology this law is known as Orlog, which means *primal layers.* And within Orlog there is the force of Wyrd, which is the process where past actions, thoughts and feelings are woven into pathways in your future and present. Remember that a pathway is a path connecting your present with some point in your future. But unlike karma, your future is not set in stone. With the proper knowledge you can learn to control or affect your future. Thus Wyrd is not simply the end result of what is in your Orlog, but the means to bend your Orlog, and this can be done with the Rune Nauthiz.

When we state that you can cleanse, we do not mean eliminate what is stored in your Orlog, but bend or transform negativity into something positive. The Rune that we can use to "bend" our Web of Wyrd is Nauthiz. People are constantly bending their Wyrd by making drastic changes in their lives. They can change their jobs or move to a different city. But most people will find such decisions difficult to make because they do not know how to bend their Web of Wyrd through the use of Runes and especially Nauthiz. *The reason why most people find it difficult to change jobs, move, or make other life-changing decisions is they are slaves to their Web of Wyrd, which was woven by what they carry around with them in their Orlog.*

The German occultist Guido von List wrote of the Rune Nauthiz: "The need-rune blooms on the nail of the Norn! This is not 'need' (distress) in the modern sense of the word, but rather the 'compulsion of fate'–that the Norns fix according to primal laws. With this, the organic causality of all phenomena is to be understood. Whoever is able to grasp the primal cause of a phenomenon, and whoever gains knowledge of organically lawful evolution and the phenomena arising from it, is also able to judge their consequences just as they are beginning to ferment. Therefore, he commands knowledge of the future and also understands how to settle all strife through 'the constraint of the clearly recognized way of fate.' Therefore: 'Use your fate, do not strive against it!'"

List explained that Nauthiz can be used to bend the forces of Orlog and Wyrd, just as a judo expert uses the weight of his opponent against him–redirecting the force of his opponent to his advantage rather then struggling against it head-on. Thus, Nauthiz should be helpful to you in dealing with negative influences that arise within your life by removing conflict, through the redirection of the negative influences and thus permitting you to achieve your goals.

Whether obstacles arise from your Orlog, or the Orlog of the situation (could be the accumulation of negativity in a place of employment, the home you live in, your family or the family of your spouse, etc...), *you can use Nathuiz like using the stored energy within the tension of the bow string to redirect the energy to your advantage, by changing the pattern of Wyrd, and thus re-weaving the web.* This in essence is what Moses did when he parted the Red Sea. He did not struggle against the currents of the sea, but used the power of need-fire to part the water, and thus removed the obstacle that stood in his way. Northern Lore tells us that the Norns representing the past and present are weaving your Wyrd. Skuld, the Norn representing your future, is tearing up what her two sisters are weaving. This means you have the power to control your destiny if you learn to master the runic energies. You can meditate on Nauthiz and visualize the Norn Skuld, ripping up the weave of the past and the present and rearranging the threads of your future Wyrd into a pathway more in line with what your desire to manifest in your future.

Endocrine Glands and Sowilo

Certain Hvels are connected to, and affect, various endocrine glands. The endocrine system is one of ductless glands. They affect the physical well being and health of the individual. *If the flow of Vril energy is disrupted or slowed in any way, this can have an adverse effect on the endocrine glands, and thus affect the health of the individual.* These endocrine glands are the master internal controlling mechanism that regulates and balances the relationship between the mind and the body. Since it is the mind, especially the subconscious portion, that controls those body functions that the conscious mind does not deal with, any interruption of the flow of Vril energy through the endocrine glands will cause a disruption of the bodily functions and result in an adverse effect on the body, much in the same way a car will run out of control if the driver falls asleep at the wheel while driving.

It is very important to maintain a balance in the flow of Vril through these glands. Even the slightest imbalance will generate fluctuations in hormonal secretions. Though they might be extremely small amounts, they are extremely powerful. Once they enter directly into the blood stream, the effects they can create might be subtle, but will be instantaneous, and cause changes in mood, appearance, respiration, digestion, initiative, relaxation, and thinking.

The use of the runic energies of Sowilo is very effective in cleansing the Hvels. Each Hvel appears like a sun wheel of whirling Vril energy. The sun-like energies of Sowilo can be used to cleanse the passageways in which Vril energy flows, helping to maintain each Hvel functioning at optimum levels of performance. This will assure that energy flowing into each Hvel is increased and balanced so that these "sun wheels" will shine clearly and powerfully, influencing the operation of the endocrine glands. Without the use of Sowilo to energize and cleanse the Hvels, the energy flowing into them will decrease and eventually be blocked by the negative forces of the Orlog, thus causing them to slow their whirling, and causing the human body to grow sluggish, permitting aging and illness to increase. When the natural balance is restored, the Hvels will grow stronger. This can be done with Sowilo. The upward flow of Vril through the spinal column will then be helped with the runic force of Eihwaz. The end result will be an continuous and increased flow of Vril energy throughout the body, creating and maintaining conditions of natural well being, good health, harmony and wholeness throughout your entire Vrilic energy system.

Exercise

1) Sit in a comfortable pose. You do not have to sit on the floor with legs crossed, but you should sit with your back erect and straight. If you are sitting in a chair, make sure it is a straight back chair. You should try to place your feet under the chair so that

they are in alignment with your spine. As you sit erect, your spine should be in line with the earth's center.

2) Relax your entire body in the way you have been taught in earlier lessons. Take your time and make sure every muscle in your body is relaxed.

3) Perform your breathing exercises. Feel Vril energy entering your body through your mouth as you breathe in. Feel Vril filling your lungs and hold it for a few seconds. Then exhale slowly.

4) Enter your Asgard, or Alpha, State of Consciousness (ASC).

5) Envision a vertical double helix of vibrant Vril energy flowing down along your spinal column. Visualize your spinal column as a huge Eihwaz Rune, with the top over your head, where the Crown Hvel is located, and the bottom below your feet, where the Sole Hvel is located. Understand that Vril energy is being drawn down from the sun above and then flows down to your feet where it mixes with the energy of the earth beneath you.

6) Begin at the top of the Eihwaz, and focus your attention on your Hvels as Vril flows down your spinal column. Starting from the top of your head, visualize your Crown Hvel opening. Watch as pure white light enters your crown Hvel, filling it with a gentle vortex of energy. Visualize the energy forming the Rune Nauthiz within the Hvel, cleansing your Hvel of all negativity, releasing any blockages.

7) Vril energy now flows down your spinal column, filling the Third Eye Hvel with Vril energy that whirls and forms a Nauthiz, cleansing it and releasing any blockages. You might have visions of multiple colors representing the rainbow bridge.

8) The white light moves down to your Throat Hvel, forming Nauthiz and releasing your blockages. Its energies whirl, unleashing the power of Nauthiz to cleanse all negativity within this Hvel. You may feel like chanting or singing certain Runes. Allow the tones to resonate from your throat. Take note of which Runes appear, and do not try to choose the Runes. Do this as long as it is comfortable.

9) White light now enters your Heart Hvel, filling it with Vril energy. The same whirling action takes place forming the cleansing power of Nauthiz. You experience a feeling of unconditional love and compassion.

10) The white light enters your Solar Plexus Hvel, filling it with Vril, forming Nauthiz. Gently, your fears, anger, and tensions are released as Nauthiz cleanses this Hvel of negativity.

11) See the white light entering your Spleen Hvel, filling it with whirling Vril energy, forming Nauthiz and cleansing it of all blockages, releasing pain and guilt linked to that Hvel.

12) The white light now enters your Root Hvel, filling it with Vril energy. It whirls about, forming Nauthiz, releasing any blockages.

13) The white light now descends down to the Feet Hvel. Once again it fills the Hvel, forming a Nauthiz, cleansing it of any blockages.

14) The white light now enters the lowest of Hvels, the Sole Hvel, located beneath the feet. As it does, it begins to activate the energy of the Sole (Musspellheim) Hvel.

15) Here, Vril energy is harnessed in the Sole Hvel, which is located beneath your feet. This Hvel is Musspellheim, and is ruled by the Rune Fehu. Within this Hvel, Vril energy is caught up and begins swirling about, transformed by the expansive force of the Fire Rune. Visualize the Rune Fehu charging Vril energy and then sending it upward toward the Feet Hvel (Niflheim).

With the correct meditative process we will endeavor to channel the currents of Vril energy entering your body down your spine to the two lowest Hvels located above and below your feet. There, the energy will replicate the creative process that gave rise to the proto-life forms of Ymir and Andhumla, and then send this energy back up the spine, passing through the other seven primary Hvels, causing it to be transformed before disseminating the Vril energy throughout your physical and auric bodies.

16) The heated Vril energy rises to the second Hvel located just above the feet. This Hvel is Niflheim and ruled by the Rune Isa. Vril energy forms fiery sparks that rise from the Sole Hvel,

mixing with the icy forces of the Feet Hvel, and combustion occurs. As a generative force, Vril energy is sent back up the spinal cord axis and reaches the Root Hvel (Hel).

17) From the Feet Hvel, Vril energy now rises to the Root or Hel Hvel. Feel it entering and charging the Hvel. This Hvel is ruled by Kenaz, representing generative powers of creation. As it does, visualize Vril forming a Sowilo Rune, radiating bright yellow light like the sun, charging the Hvel, increasing its Kenaz strength.

18) Now visualize Vril energy rising once more in spiraling coils into the Spleen or Svartalfheim Hvel. This Hvel is ruled by Laguz. Feel the Sowilo energy charging and increasing the Laguz energy, strengthening your psychic powers.

19) Vril energy continues to spiral upward, like a whirling Sowilo, filling the Solar Plexus or Jotunheim Hvel. Its radiating power strengthens the Thurisaz power of the Rune that rules this Hvel.

20) Vril now spirals into the Heart Hvel of Midgard. Sowilo charges its energy, increasing the harmonic power of Wunjo that rules this Hvel.

21) Visualize the upward spiraling power of Vril filling the Throat or Ljossalfheim Hvel. The Sun power of Sowilo strengthens the Ansuz energies of this Hvel, increasing your powers to communicate with the Gods.

22) Vril continues to spiral upward, charging the Third Eye of the Vanaheim Hvel with radiating Sowilo shaped Vril energy. The Dagaz Rune of enlightenment is charged and strengthened.

23) Finally, Vril energy flows into the Crown or Asgard Hvel, charging and strengthening the Othala energies of this Hvel with Sowilo energy. The process of cleansing, charging, strengthening and balancing your Hvels is completed.

Through this exercise, Vril energy spiraled up through your spine as if it were a coiled snake. The coiled snake represents the spiraling DNA, opening, activating, bringing you to higher levels of consciousness. (Remember the story of how Odin transformed himself into a snake and passed through a hole to reach the mead of Wisdom?) Allow the energy to flow through your Hvels, concentrating its Sowilo energy to strengthen your individual Hvel energies. See the energy forming a whirling Sowilo within the Hvel wheels as they rotate. Know that your Hvels have been cleansed of blockage and strengthened, increasing their power equally and creating a balance among all the Hvels.

When your are ready, return your consciousness to your physical body. Relax and balance your energies. You might want to drink some water.

Why Do You Need to Activate and Balance Your Hvels?

The human form is part of a multidimensional soul, as we have shown during our exploration of the Soul in an earlier chapter, and each aspect of the Soul has its own frequency and vibration linked into multiple aspects of totality of the Soul. Hvels are energy vortexes in our emotional, mental and spiritual bodies. The physical body is a series of separate, yet related systems of energy. This system is referred to in the ancient lore of the Indo-Europeans and referred to by the Norse as Hvels. In the Indo-European Indian or Vedic tradition, Hvels are called Chakras. A Hvel is the interface point between the physical and non-physical form. Hvels lie along a linear pathway (along the spine) from the Crown Hvel, located at the top of the cranium, to the Sole Hvel located beneath the soles of the feet.

These nine Hvels, representing the nine worlds within axis of the Yggdrasill, are symbolic of organized Vrilic energy, functioning as pathways for energy that flows through subtle channels in the spine and govern the endocrine system throughout the etheric body. As Vril energy passes through and is concentrated within each Hvel, it takes on the life-giving qualities of the Hvels. Each Hvel acts a transformer within the body. The purpose is to bring into the system a higher frequency of vibration, from the subtle portions of the Matrix Grid, into the thicker frequencies for purification and healing of negative energies. There are seven endocrine glands, each with a vibration and color, each assigned to one of the primary Hvels.

Each color of the energy within a Hvel expresses a range of frequencies that fall within specific wavelengths of radiant information. The colors of the visible light system are just above Infrared and below Ultraviolet. The Hvels are specifically designed to act as one level of a tuning antenna. They intercept specific wavelengths of energy containing radiant information, and bring that information down into the density of the body structure to be utilized. Additionally, more refined tuning occurs at the molecular level, as genetic receptors receive information at an even greater level of vibratory frequency.

The spin rate of the Hvels is a part of the fine tuning of this system. The higher Hvels spin faster than the lower ones of the top seven. There is a direct relationship between each individual Hvel center and the specific ranges of energy within the human/creation Matrix. The Hvel is the interface point, the energetic organ linking various aspects of the physical body to its non-physical counterparts...i.e. the Matrix Grid.

It is through this interface that the reality of the human experience becomes apparent. The human being is not the individual and independent being we perceive. The body is connected to one level of an interlocking series of grids. These grids, having nine sections or sets of vibrations, with nine levels of knowledge in each section, are ranges of experience referred to as Dimensions.

Only the Feet or Niflehim (which sends Vril energy into the Root or Hel Hvel), Solar Plexus,(Jotunheim), and Crown (Asgard) Hvels, which correspond to the three wells Hvergelmir, Mimir and Urd that feed the tree roots of Yggdrasill, are able to access and receive energies from the Higher Self. Any other Hvel can receive these energies only after they have been filtered through one of these three Hvels.

The movement of the feet during your normal waking hours is representative of the generative process of fire mixing with ice creating Ymir. This unorganized, chaotic Vril energy is nourished by Audhumla, which is personified by the earth which your feet walk on. Vril energy is then sent back up through the seven other Hvels. As it passes through each, it enters and whirls about each Hvel, incorporating the energy-charging nature of each Hvel. *As it finally reaches and passes through the Crown or Asgard Hvel, the now perfected mind, the Mannaz Mind, which has been created through balancing the powers of the two halves of the brain, representing Muninn and Huginn, thus creating the Odin consciousness, now sends Vril back down through the spine, passing through the nervous system to every part of the body with its charged powers to improve and replenish the entire spirito-physical matrix that is the human body-soul.*

Through aging, illness, and absorption of negativity in your life, the Hvels begin to collapse into the body and slow their rate of spinning. The ancients knew of this and designed Runic mantras and meditation techniques to maintain the vitality and spin-rate of the Hvels. A Hvel activation (and balance) meditation practice is recommended daily, or at minimum once a week.

Opening and activating your Hvels allows your Vrilic energies to flow up the subtle channels to your Crown Hvel. It is important to first work on opening up your subtle channels through special physical and deep or full breathing exercises that you learned in earlier lessons. Once your channels are open, clearing the Hvels will allow the energies to fully open up and charge your entire system. Even sexual energies can be directed up to the Crown as the Vril energy is activated during sexual arousal.

The way the Hvels transform Vril that flows through our bodies is determined by our Orlog and the residual feelings, thoughts and actions that fill it, reflecting decisions we made concerning how we choose to respond to conditions throughout our life. We open and close these valves when we decide what to think, and what to feel, and through which perceptual filter we choose to experience the world around us. Our thoughts and feelings thus fill the Orlog, tainting Vril as it flows through our bodies.

The Hvels are not physical. They are aspects of consciousness in the same way that the auras are aspects of consciousness. The Hvels are more dense than the auras, but not as dense as the physical body. They interact with the physical body through two major vehicles, the endocrine system and the nervous system. Hvels are associated with different endocrine glands, and also with a group of nerves called a plexus. Thus, each Hvel can be associated with particular parts of the body and particular functions within the body controlled by that plexus or that endocrine gland associated with that Hvel.

The nine Hvels representing the nine worlds of the Yggdrasill is a blueprint or matrix for completing your evolution into a higher form of life. *The entire process of charging Vril and using it to recharge every atom within your body with Vril energy, and learning how to guide and manipulate the process, is the secret of Balder Rising. You are using this methodology to awaken the Gods within. It is what we mean by Balder Rising.*

All of your senses, all of your perceptions, all of your possible states of awareness, everything that is possible for you to experience, can be divided into categories. Each category can be associated with a particular Hvel. Thus, the Hvels represent not only particular parts of your physical body, but also particular parts of your consciousness.

When you feel tension in your consciousness, you feel it in the Hvel associated with that part of your consciousness experiencing stress, and in the parts of the physical body associated with that Hvel. Where you feel stress depends upon why you feel the stress. The tension in the Hvel is detected by the nerves of the plexus associated with that Hvel, and transmitted to the parts of the body controlled by that plexus. When the tension continues over a period of time, or to a particular level of intensity, the person creates a symptom on the physical level.

The symptom speaks a language that reflects the idea that we each create our own reality, and the metaphoric significance of the symptom becomes apparent when the symptom is described from that point of view. Thus, rather than saying, "I can't see," you should describe it as keeping yourself from seeing something. "I can't walk," means you have been keeping yourself from walking away from a situation in which you are unhappy. And so on.

The symptom served to communicate to you through your body what you have been doing to yourself in your consciousness. When you change something about your way of being, getting the message communicated by the symptom, the symptom has no further reason for being, and it can be released, according to whatever you allow yourself to believe is possible.

We believe everything is possible.

We believe that anything can be healed. It's just a question of how to do it.

Understanding the Hvels allows you to understand the relationship between your consciousness and your body, and to thus see your body as a map of your consciousness. It gives you a better understanding of yourself and those around you.

Hvels are a common concept in several disciplines of alternative medicine and traditional Oriental medicine. A Hvel is a center of energy, which has several functions. In addition to being "representative" of a particular organ or group of organs, a Hvel also controls our being on different levels of consciousness and it links these two representative states.

The concept of Hvel is very important in therapies such as Reiki, meditation, yoga, therapeutic touch, aura, etc. Because of its wider application across a number of disciplines, this is covered as a separate topic.

Chapter Thirteen: the Formation of a Vril Being

We are sure you have heard it said many times that we use only a small part of our brains. This is very true. The difference between the powers of your mind that the average person uses, and the power that lays dormant is enormous. The purpose of Vrilology is to help you to increase the potential of these dormant powers, you can live life to its fullest in Midgard. The surest way to achieve this end is to evolve into a Vril Being

By now you should be aware that you are actually something of a storage battery. You have the capacity to draw in greater amounts of Vrilic energy and store it within your Hamingja and transform it into whatever you need, including improving yourself physically, mentally, psychically and spiritually. In this chapter you will begin to discover ways to discharge this energy, and use it to transform yourself both internally and externally, which includes making changes to your personality and character.

Characteristics of a Vril Being

Your personality is formed by your Wyrd, which in turn is the result of what has been stored up within your Orlog. Much of what is in it is the result of your own experiences, but some of it is inherited from your ancestors. Remember you are essentially made up of Vril energy, which is the Life Force of the Gods. Thus, the real you is Divine. But it is imprisoned within the layers of your Wyrd, formed from what is stored within your Orlog. You need to free the Divine within you so that it can grow and evolve into Vril Being. But what is a Vril Being?

We need to explore just what are the characteristics of a Vril Being. Some individuals have a greater natural ability to utilize their Vrilic potential, and thus display some, if not many, of the characteristics of a Vril Being, without being conscious of what they are doing. A Vril Being can be either a man or a woman, so if we use the male gender in talking about a Vril Being, please understand it is only to simplify the grammar and not to infer that only men can become a Vril Being.

A Vril Being is one who appears to possess a magnetic personality. He generates energy that can be considered charisma even when he is in a state of rest. In fact, this state of rest is the natural state of being for a Vril Being. It is characteristic of his ability to be in charge of himself and the world around him at all times. Unlike your personality, which acts like a suit of armor that might protect you, but also imprisons you and hides you from the world around you, your Vril personality is more like an invisible force shield, in that your Higher, Inner Self is visible to the world around it, for all to see, or more correctly stated–*for all to feel.*

No matter what the situation he finds himself in, the Vril Being will always appear calm and in charge and never fidgety and nervous. This conveys the presence of a great reserve of inner strength that cannot exactly be defined by those who come into contact with him, but will always be noticed and felt. The reason is simply that it is a reservoir of a limitless power.

Your eyes are a powerful device to transmit Vril energy, and this is every effective when used to influence others. The eyes of a Vril Being have the power to reach within another and hold him within his grip. When focusing his eyes in this way, his eyes are not looking into the eyes of the other person, but are fixed on the point between their eyes known as the Third Eye or Bifrost Gland. By fixing his gaze at this point, he can cancel out the other person's mental powers in the same way you might shut down a generator by turning off the power switch. His glance goes right through the other person with an intense, boring gaze that overwhelms the victim, who is seldom aware of what is happening to him, and thus is seduced instead of conquered. When the victim speaks, the Vril Being will never make eye contact, keeping his gaze fixed on the point between the eyes, but when the Vril Being speaks, he will concentrate on either the right or left eye, depending on the effect he is wishing to send. His look is masterful and yet kindly and his intention to control is never obvious. The reason for this is simple. *Unlike a psychic vampire that seeks to drain you of your energy, the Vril Being is sending you energy, causing you to be charged up, and then seeking to merge your empowered energy field with his. This creates a symbiotic relationship between the two beings rather than one of parasite and host that a psychic vampire establishes with his victim.*

The Vril Being interaction with others is always polite and he is always willing to listen, but despite his politeness, his indomitable will is always present beneath the surface. *He will instinctively sense that he is a man that must be obeyed because he knows exactly what he wants and is in no hurry, because he is confident that he will get it.* The Vril Being understands the Law of Cause and Effect, and thus is so sure of his ability to make whatever he desires happen, this confidence in his own ability acts like a light that draws the moth to it.

We can see the *male force* impregnating the *female form* in the way the Vril Being interacts with the normal human being. The human being will feel the strength of will that the Vril Being possesses, and the normal human being must submit to the power of the Vril Being's conscious strength.

As you grow as a Vril Being, you will outgrow the need to display evidence of your power, yet you will know that, as one who has mastered the mechanism of Vrilology, you have a right to everything you desire, including influence, popularity, fame, success and wealth. People who come into contact with a Vril Being will want to do so again and again. Others will willingly tell him what he wants to know. They will want to please him. His mind has the power to sway others. He understands the Law of Cause and Effect. He knows how to use his power effectively and can elicit whatever he wants from those he comes into contact with. He does not perform this by forcing his will on others, but rather by implanting the seed of what he desires from others within them. He does not deplete their Life Force, but sends his own, and thus establishes an energy bond between himself and those around him.

Those who do not possess a Vril personality might also seek fame, fortune and success, and might possess a forceful personality, but as they try to influence others by forcing them to change their opinions, instead irritate them. Such a person magnifies what others are already feeling, especially if others are afflicted with negativity. If others are peevish, he intensifies their irritation; if they are depressed, he deepens their gloom, if they are happy, he will depress them, sucking the joy out of them. The reason for this is that he is always trying to suck the life out of others for his own enhancement. Without realizing it, he is drawing the Life Force from others to lighten his own gloom. Others come away from their contact with him depressed, irritated or angry because he acts as a weight on others, imparting something of his own grievances to them so that he can lighten his own load.

This type of non-Vril being never stops complaining, and babbles on and on about the ills of the world, about how terrible his life is and how dark and depressing life is in general. He is the creature of impulse who is always warning of the approaching doom. He seems to draw great strength from imputing doom and gloom in others, trying to enslave them within his own discontent. How unlike he is to *the Vril Being who possesses an attitude of mind which governs his circumstances, and therefore is in command of the world around him.* The Vril Being is aware of the state of the world, but unlike the non-Vril individual who is always airing his grievances, always complaining, inviting failure, seeking confrontation, and wasting energy, the Vril Being does not air his grievances publicly, nor does he seek sympathy or flattery. He recognizes the force in every desire, and makes that force his own by giving hope and confidence to those he comes into contact with. He instills hope, joy and a new-found strength in others, and then draws that strength to him, creating a collective bond for all to share. *He makes himself the divining rod for the collective good of the many.*

The Runic Principles Behind the Vrilic Personality

Let us examine quickly the Runic principles behind what we have just discussed. First, the Vril Being is confident, self-assured and calm. There is a strength within him that does not escape. This is the Runic principle of Isa at work. The strength that he possesses is powerful and yet healing. It eliminates stress, anxiety, worry and other negative forces. Here we see Uruz at work. The strength of Uruz can be overpowering, and yet it is the Healing Rune. This strength, while under control and self-contained, also shines forth for others to experience when they come into contact with the Vril Being. He is like a distant star. You can see him from a distance, but only when you come into close contact with him can you experience the warmth and light that he radiates. Here is the principle of Sowilo. He radiates a force, but it remains his own, under his control. This is the duality of Sowilo and Isa, and together they produce the principle of Fire and Ice, the formula for creation. Thus, his power is generative and not destructive. It creates, uplifts and enlightens and does not destroy, dragging one down into doom and gloom. He can and often does send this power to others who come into contact with him, bringing success, joy and harmony into the lives of others. Here we see the principle of the Runes Fehu and Wunjo. *Because of this Runic formula, the Vril Being both leads and teaches, and so he is not just a teacher, nor just a warrior, he is a warrior-priest.*

Extracting Vril Energy from Your Desires

You know by now that your desires are powered by Vrilic energy currents, and that they contain enormous power, for they can affect your development as a human being, as well as creating the nature of your Wyrd. *Desires are emotionally charged mental commands acting to harness Vril and shaping it into whatever is the nature of the desire.* This process is governed by the laws of attraction and repulsion. Remember—*like attracts like!* But a fully evolved Vril Being is not a slave to his desires, but knows how to extract the energy of his desires, store that energy within his Hamingja, and then shape it into whatever purpose he needs it for. We have said before that your desires, which are emotions, are not to be negated, but controlled, so that you can tap into their power. Normal human beings are unable to control their desires effectively, and thus people waste an available source of unlimited energy. This wastefulness weakens your power to attract specifically what you want, and instead draws into your future pathways those things that you actually do not want to shape your Wyrd. Therefore, if you cannot learn to master your desires, you will be wastefully discharging valuable Vril, which a Vril Being would instead store to use for what he truly wants to manifest in his Wyrd.

You must understand that your desires are not something to be feared or considered stumbling blocks, but an available source of power, to be drawn on and used to hasten your evolution into a Vril Being. There are both positive and negative desires. Impatience, anger, jealousy, dissipation, indulgence and vanity are some examples of the later. But of all the desires, vanity has the most draining effect of all on us, because it is seldom recognized, especially in the most obscure manifestations, taking such insidious forms that one hardly realizes he is trying to gratify his vanity. But by using Runes, especially Isa, you will learn to insulate yourself against the weakening effects of uncontrolled discharge of the Vrilic energy that feeds the desire.

The Power in Secrecy

It is important that you cultivate the art of keeping a secret. It is only natural to want to broadcast good news to as many people as possible. But by doing so, you are feeding your vanity. The Vril Being is different from the general population; you can begin to develop your ability to contain the energy that lies within your desires by practicing the art of *keeping a secret*. Regarding your opinions and attributes, keep in the dark those with whom you come into contact. Every day, see how often you can refrain from telling an acquaintance some news that you have just received. You will discover how difficult it is to "bite your tongue," or "hold your tongue," because of the desire to tell someone, especially people close to you, the news that you have learned. But by refraining from telling, you will be storing the energy that feeds your desire to broadcast, within you. Like money in the bank that draws interest, this stored up energy will beget a force that will draw more force to it. The amounts of Vril energy that you will be able to hold in reserve within your Hamingja, for you to use for your important enterprises, will increase in accordance with the number of secrets you can learn to keep to yourself.

Your ability to control your urges will somehow create a condition which will increase the force and strength stemming from your desires tenfold. Think of how a dam stores up water and uses it to create energy to be utilized for great efforts. You will be doing the same, storing up your power and using it under controlled conditions for what you wish to manifest.

By developing the ability to keep a secret *you will soon develop an air of mystery about you.* There is a saying that a deep river is silent. The world yields authority to those whom it cannot understand. The Vril Being is a mystery to those he comes into contact with, for he appears unfathomable. So you must learn to appear steadfast and refrain from bizarre behavior. Eccentricity can be fatal for the Vril Being. There is truth in the saying that it is best never to let *your enemies* know what you are thinking, but this is also true of *the public in general.*

When someone comes to you with some information, display appropriate concern, but do not express surprise; receive the news kindly and calmly and without comment,. The person who is informing you will be astonished that what has so deeply affected him has made so little impression on you. By showing interest without reaction, you are conveying the sense that even the most astonishing news does not upset you because you possess an inner strength that comes from deep mental discipline and balance. He will be not only astonished, but curious, and respect the stability that is evident in your self-control and contemplation. You can easily maintain your self-control by the use of Isa. Whenever you feel the urge to react, think of this Rune and hold its shape, and thus its energy, in your mind.

Familiarity breathes contempt! There is a great deal of truth in this saying. By not revealing everything you know, you will cultivate a sense of mystery and awe within those whom you come into contact with. With the vast majority of people you meet, remain steadfast in your thoughts and actions, and never voluntarily surrender your opinion on most subjects. When asked your advice, give short replies that are direct and to the point. In conversation, draw out the other person. When in a group, speak last after everyone else has exhausted their opinions. You voice will then seem like the wind that sweeps away the fall leaves. As long as you are able to maintain a mystery about you, you will appear as a power beyond the ability of most people. You will appear, and rightly so, as a being who moves outside the normal flow of time and space, as if you occupy a dimension of reality that is just beyond the reach of the average individual. Others will react in many ways, including apprehension, curiosity, suspicion, wonder, mystification and confusion, but whatever the reaction, others will find you a force beyond their control and will respect and even fear you as such. By preserving this air of mystery you become an attraction to friends, and enemies will stay clear of you.

Conserve Your Need to Seek Approval from Others

There will be times when you will feel the need to act clever and impress others. This is a desire for approbation—one of nature's most subtle forces that feeds our vanity. But it is a force that drives us against our will and sober thought, and causes us to shoot our round prematurely. We have said that in conversation, whether with an individual or in a group, always refrain from speaking up first. Sit back and listen to what is being said. Let others exhaust themselves in debate and argument. Permit the passions to fly while you remain calm and detached. Take up a position out of the way, in the back or off to the side, as if you are not part of the group. Only after everyone has revealed their thoughts and exhausted themselves in expressing themselves and defending their point of view, should you speak up. And then do so in a matter that appears not to take issue with what has already been said, but state your point of view as fact and not to be disputed. The others will have to turn and bend to listen to what you say while you remain in command, sitting or standing comfortably.

When holding a conversation with an individual, let the other person talk his head off, and then when you feel it is time to respond, begin by first asking questions. Question the other person's point of view, causing him to think about what he said as he defends his opinion. Only afterwards should you state your opinion and then be direct and to the point.

Keep your desire to express your opinion for the purpose of approbation under control. Don't state your point of view to impress others, but to make a point. Keep under control your desire to impress, and it will become a force of attraction. By repressing the need to constantly react to argument, you will build up the force of your attraction, and soon develop a growing sense of self-respect and unconscious dignity—a feeling of power that you will feel growing within your very nerves. You will then notice the change in the way others treat you. People will want to talk to you and seek you out for your opinion.

Learn to Use Your Eyes

Remember how we described how you can concentrate your gaze on another person to either block their influence over you or to convey either an emotional or a logical response? We discussed how you can use this method to block the influence of psychic vampires, and prevent them from sucking your Life Force from you. We will review this methodology once more.

First let us examine what we refer to as the central gaze. When you wish to gain the upper hand over someone who is trying to dominate or influence you, you should concentrate your gaze, both eyes, on the point between their eyes, at the bridge of their nose. Most people, when looking at another person, without realizing it, concentrate their gaze on the person's right eye. The reason for this is that the right eye, which is connected the left side of the brain, is the receiver of logical information. Therefore when someone is talking to you, and is trying to influence you, they will naturally concentrate their gaze on your right eye. You can block their influence by concentrating your gaze between their eyes. *Make sure when you are doing this you do not glare or scowl.* You do not want him to know you are trying to block his influence. Remain calm and even friendly. You will discover that he will soon begin to shift his eyes uneasily, finding it difficult to hold you

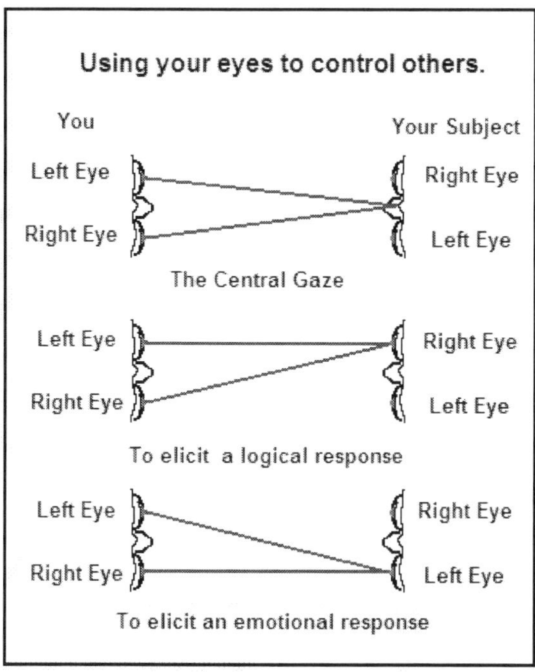

gaze. When you are talking to him, continue to gaze between his eyes. When he speaks, listen respectfully, but concentrate on this point at the bridge of his nose. *You must remain calm and friendly.*

When you wish to influence someone through logic, or through a rational argument, concentrate your gaze on their right eye, for this eye is connected to their left brain, the seat of logical thought.

When you wish to elicit an emotional reaction, concentrate your gaze on their left eye, which is connected to their right brain, the seat of emotions and the subconscious mind.

How to Use the Negative Forces in Your Orlog to Your Advantage

You must understand the significance of what is inside your Orlog, and how to negate or bend the negativity that is stored there by using the Runes Perthro and Nauthiz. Every desire, emotion and thought that you have experienced, both negative and positive, as well as inherited, is stored within your Orlog and effects your Wyrd. These forces determine your personality and character. For the ordinary person, they forge a suit of armor that also acts like a prison in which we are confined, controlling us and our actions, and thus creating future pathways filled with everything we do not want. But by developing your character you can control this process, by remembering that every desire, emotion or thought is a mental force fed by Vril energy. By controlling your desires, especially the negative ones, you can harness their energy and use it for your own purpose. Thus, you become the master of the energy that powers your desires, denying the power of your desires to enslave you. You are not repressing your desires, but learning to use their energy effectively. You can accomplish this by using several Runes.

First, use Perthro, the Rune of your Orlog. Meditate on Perthro and see it as an open trunk filled with all your desires. Now think about which desires have the greatest hold over you, and that you therefore need to control. It does not matter if they are negative or positive. You want to identify those desires that radiate with the most powerful currents of Vrilic energy.

Next, meditate on Nauthiz, the Rune that can create a counter force to control the desires you have chosen. You can visualize this in any way you want. Let us give you an example. See Perthro as an enclosure filled with wild horses. Then visualize Nauthiz as a cowboy with a lasso rounding up each horse until they are all under control.

Once all your horses are under control, concentrate on taming them by meditating on Isa, the Rune of constriction of unwanted forces, to bring them under control. You are now concentrating on controlling your will power, bringing your desires under control, not to eliminate them, for you cannot eliminate what is in your Orlog, but to control the energy behind each desire and channel the collective power of this energy, so you can shape and direct it as you wish.

You now want to meditate on Ingwaz, the Rune of gestation and sudden release. With this Rune you can store the energy of your desires and use its power to transform this energy into something else. Then, when it has been transformed, you can then release it into what it is you need to manifest.

This exercise is effective for mastering those desires you know you need to control. You can perform this exercise at any time, to help you to master the forces within your Orlog. But what happens when you are suddenly struck by one of these desires?

Previously when you felt a certain desire overcoming you, you would be upset and wish it did not affect you, but now you will welcome the opportunity to harness the energy behind it. Concentrate on the desire and slowly inhale with the full breathing method, filling your lungs to their capacity, drawing the Vril deep within the solar plexus. The inhaling should take about nine seconds. As you inhale, think to yourself that you are consciously appropriating the full force of this desire. While doing this, concentrate on Isa, the Rune of constriction.

The next step is to hold your breath for a full nine seconds as you concentrate on Hagalaz, the Rune of devolution and evolution. This Rune will banish the harmful effects and transform the energy into patterns perfect for your purpose. As you do this, think to yourself how you have transformed this force into a source of energy that is at your command.

Finally, exhale for nine seconds. As you do, think of the Rune Elhaz, and say to yourself mentally that this energy is being transformed into a powerful weapon for you to use when you have need of its power.

Like everything, practice makes perfect. It will take time for you to perfect this method, but you will notice an instant reaction by people you use this method on, even if it is not a radical change. You will discover a new sense of self-respect and confidence. In fact, there will be a noticeable physical transformation after each conscious retention of the force of desire that will manifest itself in the sensation of power and fullness.

Try this out on someone with whom you have not had a close relationship or friendship, to see if you can capture his or her attention. It should be someone who is friendly but has not taken a noticeable interest in you, someone whom you always seem to exhaust yourself trying to get closer to, but who left you drained from each encounter. It could be a neighbor you meet every day, or better, someone at your workplace you are sure to run into daily. *You can begin by not doing anything.* Practice the law of conservation of forces by not talking about things that would flatter your ego to talk about. Think about when you have tried to impress, only to feel drained, foolish and non-magnetic. Instead, bottle up your desires. Conserve the desires of the flesh as well as of the mind. Capture the force behind your desires. Bottle up the currents of Vril energy and transform them into Megin, your Personal Luck.

The energy you are storing and transforming into Megin will attract its opposite from other people, even without your conscious effort. Others will notice a change about you in your manner, because your actions will unconsciously change. Good things will drift in your direction, but do not be disappointed if the big things you want do not manifest themselves immediately.

As you continue to store up your Megin, it will radiate in your auric field. Others will not visibly see it, but they will react to it because your personality will have begun to change. Subtle changes will gradually begin to take place. Your eyes will grow brighter, your skin clearer, your posture will become more erect and your face will take on the expression of confidence and radiate a joy for life. You will see the world in a new light, one in which you are no longer the unfortunate object of subtle forces acting against you, but a conscious force yourself. You will become a star in the darkened sky of humanity, shining brightly.

When you encounter the person who has not taken an interest in you so far, do not try to start up a conversation with him, but smile slightly, and knowingly make contact by applying the method of directing your gaze between his eyes. Do this every time you meet the person. You will notice a marked change in his behavior, as if he is seeing you for the first time. He might eventually even stop you and start up a conversation. If he does, continue to use the central gaze directed at the point between his eyes.

Exercise to Develop the Masterful Gaze

We have so far emphasized the importance of not glaring or scowling when concentrating your gaze on the other person whiling holding your glance attentively. You might want to practice the next exercise. It will help you to hold your gaze on a fixed point without being obvious about what you are doing. First of all, remember that you should not use the method all the time, but only selectively, when you *need* to be impressive. There is such a thing as being oppressively impressive, and this should be avoided. Use your newfound powers with skill and pleasantness. Wear an interested expression when you wish to please. Avoid perpetual smiles, which will appear undignified. This is why you should practice this exercise, *so that you can find just the right expression that will fit your face when using this method.* You want to cultivate the impression of *good-humored power*. Nothing is more attractive than this combination.

Now for the actual exercise. You will need a good size mirror, a comfortable chair and a pencil or some washable marker. That's pretty much all you need, besides fifteen minutes a day. The mirror should be big enough to reflect your entire face at a distance of two or three feet. Place the mirror on a table or a wall and sit in your chair facing it. Place a mark with your pencil or washable marker on your forehead over the bridge of your nose, right between your eyes. Sit and stare at the dot in your reflection.

Find the right expression that expresses interest and friendliness without being undignified. Then hold your gaze unfalteringly upon the spot between your eyes, trying to remain perfectly motionless. Try as much as possible to avoid blinking. This will be difficult at first, but in time you will be able to hold your gaze without blinking for longer and longer periods of time. A little trick to help you avoid blinking is to slightly raise your lids every time you feel like blinking. The relief to the nerves is nearly the same as blinking. Do not be discouraged if you find it hard to refrain from blinking, it takes a little practice. Try to do this exercise for up to fifteen minutes, but there is no need to do it longer than this time.

The best time to perform this exercise is in the morning or after you have taken a nap. Your body is fresh and relaxed. You can also perform this exercise after you meditated or performed your relaxing exercise in which your entire body has entered and held a total relaxed position for about 30 minutes. You can start out by performing the exercise for five minutes and then lengthening it for one minute each day until you reach fifteen minutes. You will soon notice that you have developed a steadfast and forceful gaze, and when you do look into the eyes of other people, their eyes will shift uneasily while you calmly apply your central gaze into the center of their forehead. If you faithfully apply this exercise, you will have developed a masterful gaze.

Projecting Your Willpower by Using Laguz

You can use the Rune Laguz, which is the Rune representing Vril, as well as the unconscious mind, psychic powers and especially the ability to mold Vrilic energy currents into the right pattern. *The shape of Laguz is one of taking the flow of Vril and changing its direction under the control of your will.*

First, you can perform simple exercises to develop your concentration by drawing both a circle and a square at the same time. Take two pencils and hold one in each hand. At the same time, draw a square with one hand and a circle with the other. They do not have to be perfect. The purpose of this exercise is to perform two tasks at the same time. You can also do other variations of this method. A good one is to pat your head with your right hand and simultaneously rub your belly with the left hand. The variations on this method are limitless. Such exercises will help you to strengthen your ability to concentrate. But first, let us remind you of something very important about concentration.

The most effective way to concentrate is not to clench your teeth, harden your muscles, scowl fiercely and goes at your task in a brutal fashion. Doing so is a waste of energy. Remember, we do not wish to fight against the currents, but control the currents and make them flow in the direction we wish to send them. When directing your will's power toward an objective, remain calm, relaxed, intelligent and joyful. In this way, you will not be setting up Vrilic barriers, but opening yourself to the flow of Vril currents. You mind has limitless power. By permitting the currents of Vril to flow freely through you, your developed will-power will fashion and direct their flow into whatever goal you wish them to flow into. In this way, you will very quickly be able to direct your will toward an objective without a great deal of preparation. You will only have to visualize Laguz and your mind will send your will's power toward the intended goal.

A good example of how this works may be seen when you are driving on the highway. If you see a car on the road being driven in a erratic fashion, you can project Laguz onto the car and then send the Runes Raidho and Wunjo toward the driver so that he will drive in the right fashion, in harmony with the rest of the cars on the road. When driving, you will not be able to perform your relaxation or meditation. You will want to quickly and effectively send your mental command through the use of your concentrated will-power. Laguz is a very effective way of doing this. When trying to mentally control a person you are face-to-face with, just project Laguz onto that person's head, especially the forehead if you are facing the subject, and send your mental command.

The Third Eye or Bifrost Gland

Many esoteric traditions, both ancient and modern, speak of the Third Eye as a conduit of psychic abilities. It is usually thought to exist at the point between your eyes on your forehead. Today, we have determined that it is physically located in the central interior of the brain, consisting of both the pituitary gland and the pineal gland, which collectively we refer to as your *Bifrost Gland,* referring to the Rainbow Bridge that joins Midgard with Asgard. If you examine it closely, a sort of bridge is formed from the pituitary gland, located behind the root of your nose to the pineal gland, located just behind and above it, near the center of the head within your brain.

Using Your Eyes to Project Your Willpower

A dynamic current of Vril energy creates an interaction between these two glands, creating a bridge of energy when the Bifrost Gland is stimulated. It might feel like a warm spot at the center of the forehead. As you develop your psychic abilities, the vibrations of both the pineal and pituitary glands fuse, forming this bridge, just as the Bifrost Bridge connects Midgard and Asgard, permitting communication and transportation between these two realms. This enables you to tap into information that can be retrieved from the astral plane of consciousness known as Mimir's Well in Norse cosmology.

The pineal gland is known as the Crown hvel (chakra), which is the point at which cosmic knowledge and energies from Asgard enter the human mind. The pituitary is known as the Third Eye hvel (chakra) which receives the knowledge and energies, and recalibrates their frequencies so that they can be perceived by human consciousness as intuitive cognition. This bridge of Vrilic energy creates a pathway when stimulated, and is represented in Norse cosmology as the Rainbow Bridge or Bifrost. It is this *energy charged bridge that is the source of our communication with the Gods and other realms of the Yggdrasill.*

Through the study and practice of the lessons offered in the Yggdrasill Training Program, by developing potency of your Bifrost Gland, you become more sensitive to the finer emanations of various levels of consciousness, both higher levels and lower levels. This will eventually permit you to see the mediating images of the Elder Norse tradition, as well other images that exist within the many dimensions of the multiverse, which are normally invisible to ordinary physical sight.

Your Bifrost Gland is a means through which you can experience your clairvoyance, clairsentience and clairaudience or collectively, your "clair" powers, as well as second sight, prophecy and hyper-cognition. When your clair powers manifest themselves, *you will experience images, sounds or physical sensations of taste, smell and touch even though you are not within the physical range of such sensations.*

All humans possess natural instinctual abilities that we can refer to as human intuition. These sensations bypass the thinking processes of the brain, resulting in a non-thought that provides an awareness that is beyond the five physical senses. Human intuition is *the process whereby, the mind is able to tap into the universal well of knowledge (Mimir's Well) and draw on new information to formulate a new thought or idea.* This is unlike the more common process of the mind tapping into your subconscious, which is a storehouse of information that you might not remember, but were once familiar with, transforming the data into new un-thought-of patterns of manifestation.

The Denali Institute defines human intuition as *"an awareness of information that one did not know before through education or past experiences, and did not logically think out or reason through. It happens spontaneously, willed or unwilled, and comes from the supra-conscious mind unclouded by the subconscious belief system.*

Opening Your Third Eye with Mannaz

Mannaz is a very effective Rune you can use to open your Bifrost Gland. If we examine Mannaz, we discover several hidden runic shapes within its form. The upper portion of Mannaz is the Rune Dagaz. *Dagaz is the Rune of Illumination and Enlightenment.* Its shape corresponds to the two halves of the brain, or the right and left hemispheres, and the Third Eye manifesting at the junction in the center. If we split the Rune in half, we discover two Wunjo Runes, facing each other, as if they are kissing or embracing. Thus, we not only have the union of the right and left hemispheres of the brain, but the joining or balancing of the male and female components of the evolved human soul. *Thus, Mannaz is the Rune dealing with the powers of the consciously elevated mind, evolved to its fullest potential. This happens when you conduct your Bifrost Gland to begin the process of reforging the broken links between Midgard and Asgard.*

In the first century, the Roman historian Tacitus wrote in his *Germania*, about the early Germanic tribes of his time. He described a certain God and his son. Let us quote from *Germania*:

"In their ancient songs, their only form of recorded history, the Germans celebrate the earth-born god, Tuisito. They assign to him a son, Mannus, the author of their race, and to Mannus three sons, their founders, after whom the people nearest the Ocean are named Ingaevones, those of the center Herminones, and the remainder Istaevones. The remote past involves guesswork, and so

some authorities record more sons of the god and more national names . . ."

In *Germania*, Tacitus establishes a link between two Gods and mankind. The God Tuisito, an Earth God, gives birth to a son, Mannus, who is responsible for the creation of the three classes of man. This tale is later repeated in the Elder Edda poem *Rigsthula* (Song of Rig). It is obvious by the names that Mannus is associated with the Rune Mannaz. Tuisito is another name for Frey, and in this lore, Frey's son is Mannus, or Rig. In the preface to *Rigthula*, there is contained a reference that Rig is actually Heimdall, an Aesir God, who is also referred to in the Song of Sybil as the progenitor of the races of mankind, so the associations become blurred. In the first paragraph of the Hauksbok version, the Seeress begins, "*Hear me all you hallowed beings, both high and low of Heimdall's children.* I

In Norse Lore, Frey has a twin sister, Freyja. They are referred to as the Lord and the Lady, and reputed to have had sex with one another. This tale of brother and sister having sex with each other is repeated often within the Vanir race of Gods, and Frey and Freyja are considered the offspring of the marriage of another brother and sister, Njord and Nerthus. *The meaning of this is the esoteric union of the divine male and the divine female, united in the creation of the perfected human type personified as a Vril Being.* It is this union of the male (force) and female (form) that is significant within the Vanir, who are Earth and Sea Gods and Goddesses that deal with reproduction, generation and evolution. One has to ask then, who are the parents of Heimdall if he is associated with Mannus, who is Vanir, while Heimdall is considered Aesir.

Heimdall's mother is considered the "Nine Waves of the Sea." Are the nine waves the daughters of Aegir and Rand? Perhaps not, for though they are considered part of the pantheon of Gods, they have Giant origins. Instead, let us consider that the nine waves are really nine lives and thus associated with the cat, which in folklore has nine lives. And since Freyja is the Goddess associated with cats, we can assume with some validity that the nine waves are really a reference to Freyja and that she is Heimdall's mother, while Odin is Heimdall's father. Thus Heimdall can be considered both Vanir and Aesir at once. This would also provide the link between Heimdall and Frey, who is the male counter-part to the Vril Being archetype that Frey and Freyja would represent.

We can see similarities between the Runes Mannaz and Ehwaz. Mannaz incorporates the shape of Ehwaz, the twin dynamics of male and female, with the awakening of Dagaz, or daylight and illumination within higher consciousness, plus the twin shapes of Wunjo, joy in harmony, as well as the twin shapes Laguz, the Rune of higher consciousness.

Heimdall is referred to by several names, including the "White God" and the "Shining One." *His role represents a special one in which he imparts a certain spiritual purity of higher consciousness that is imparted to us through our DNA or genetic link with the Gods.* We can see from this tale that *all mankind is descended from the Gods*, but not all have the same relationship with the Gods. *In this way, we know that different races must seek linkage with the Gods in different ways*, through different traditions, thus interpreting the Gods differently, seeing them in different manifestations. *And since the Divine and mortal share a bond in which they exchange the Vrilic energies, there is a transformation among the Gods through their relations with the different races of mankind, thus evolving different races of Gods.* Could it be that the story of Rig not only tells us of the division of mankind into different races, but also the reverse flow of the Vrilic energy, which creates a division among the divine, *and thus gives birth to the many different pantheons of Gods that are worshiped through the world?* Can this be an explanation of why the Gods possess different and alien forms in other alien dimensions?

We recommend you use Mannaz to meditate ro help create a spiritual harmony among the many transpersonal constructs found within your Vrilic energy field, so that they be incorporated into a synchronicity that will lead you toward the evolved state of a Vril Being. When you feel a spiritual disconnect, or imbalance in your physical or Midgard existence, you should meditate on Mannaz. Mannaz will help to restore a harmony of the many forces within your Inner World through synchronicity.

Activating Mannaz within your life will unleash the great potentials within your Higher Self that will lead to the opening of your Bifrost Gland.

Second Sight or Spae-craft

There are many names for second sight, but basically, it is the ability to see into the future. One who possesses second sight can perceive things before they happen. It is referred to as precognition in the field of parapsychology. It has been referred to as sooth-saying, spae-craft or fore-seeing. It is a clairvoyant ability possessed by both men and women, that the Folk Faith of Balder Rising considers one aspect of Seither.

Through most of pagan Europe, women with such abilities were considered oracles, and the most famous was the Oracle of Delphi in ancient Greece. In ancient Rome, it was believed that certain women were especially adept in forecasting the future, and were known as Sibyls. Among the Norse, women were thought to be especially gifted with psychic powers, and male leaders often sought them out for advice and counsel.

Men with such powers were often pagan priests of the temples. The Celtic druids were famous for possessing such powers, and Merlin is the most famous magician in folklore possessing second sight. They were depicted as wearing a hooded robe and carrying a staff. The hooded robe was a means of isolating the soothsayers from the physical world, permitting them to receive information from the astral realms. The robes were usually black, gray or blue in color, though the druids are reputed to wear white.

Laguz, which is represented by a lake, is considered the Rune of Psychic powers and especially second sight. The lake is representative of the primal waters of the subconscious realms of higher, astral dimensions, from which one can tap into the universal fountain of infinite knowledge. *Laguz* is important when you work to develop a disciplined mind with the purpose of unleashing these psychic powers within you. The Old English Rune Poem says, "when the horse of the sea needs not his bridle." This means anyone who seeks to develop his psychic abilities, delving into the subconscious waters or currents of Vrilic energy should possess a sufficiently developed self-control to master the energies, just as a rider should be skilled enough to control the horse that he rides. The most skillful rider is one who feels himself one with his steed, and so the most skillful master of the energies of Laguz is one who is fully integrated with his powers and possesses a confidence in his abilities to use them.

Telepathy and Esp

When two individuals synchronize their psychic abilities, they may develop a form of communication we refer to as telepathy or ESP. When this happens, one person is a sender and the other a receiver. Telepathic communication can happen between two or more living individuals, or between the living and the deceased. It can manifest itself in visions, thoughts, voices, hypnotic states or trances, emotional sensations, illnesses, psychic messages or automatic writing, and this phenomenon is sometimes referred to as a *telepathic impress*. A natural form of telepathy is common in women who have children. A mother will often feel that her child is in danger or has need of her help.

ESP, or Extra Sensory Perception, was a term coined by J. B. Rhine of Duke University in the 1940s. For our purposes, we use the terms telepathy and ESP to refer to the skill of psychic communication, or the sending and receiving of telepathic communication or messages. Two Runes that we use for this skill are *Fehu, the Sending Rune, and Ansuz, the Receiving Rune*.

The first thing you might notice about these two Runes is their similarity in shape. It is not an accident that they are so similar, both resembling the letter "F," but the antennae are pointing up in Fehu, as if sending forth or upward, while in Ansuz the antennae are pointing down or inward.

FEHU is the Sending Rune. It is used to send messages, images or energies. Fehu is the Rune of mobile power, fire or energy, and expansive forces of Musspellheim. It is related to the expansion of the ability of your Hamingja to generate Luck or Megin and utilize its power to make things happen, thus sending forth its energies into the objective reality surrounding you. It can be used to increase the power levels of your auric fields. You can use its energies to draw on its power to send messages or Vrilic energies. You have learned in previous lessons how to use Fehu to send your Luck, but you can also use it to send messages to influence people and events. Psychic communication between two people and other acts of ESP or telepathy can be achieved by drawing on the sending power of Fehu.

ANSUZ is the Rune of Communication and the Receiving Rune. You can use it to receive communication in the form of Hypercognition, by which you can receive messages or information from the universal source of infinite knowledge, or Mimir's Well. This is why this Rune is associated with Odin as a shaman, for he gave an eye to drink from the well, whose waters represent infinite knowledge or the currents of Vrilic energy that fills the universe. You can use Ansuz to communicate with others physically through speech or through transpersonal forms of communication. Its energies can enhance your clairvoyant or "clair" powers. The Runic energies of Ansuz can be used to raise your vibratory level through the force of ecstatic inspiration, transforming your abilities to receive telepathic impulses. This process of raising your vibratory levels will also increase your ability to send. By using Ansuz, you can develop the powers to manifest spontaneous telepathy in another receptive person or people. Orators will use Ansuz by itself to generate vibratory waves of ecstatic energy to excite large groups of people. But when you wish to send a message aimed at a particular individual or target, under the controlled authority of the power of your will, you should use Fehu.

Chapter Fourteen: Learn to Increase the Body's Supply of Vril Energy

The Gods Dwell Within Us

There are 50 million cells within the human body. Each cell is made up of molecules and our molecules are made up of atoms. It is estimated that there are 7 billion billion billion atoms in the human body. About two thirds of these are hydrogen atoms. Hydrogen atoms make up about 90 percent of all atoms in the universe. To understand the proportions of an atom, let's say the proton within the hydrogen atom is the size of a tennis ball. The electron orbiting it is another ball whirling about it at a distance of 200 miles. But what is amazing is that the electron is not always there because it is flashing in and out of our universe. It is this orbiting action of the electron around the proton that captures and harnesses Vril energy and gives it a frequency unique to the type of atom it is.

The hydrogen atom is truly a wonderful object because it has a single electron orbiting a nucleus of one proton. Magnetic Resonance Imaging, known as MRI, can measure the way different concentrations of positively charged hydrogen protons vibrate within the human body after being subjected to a powerful rotating magnetic field. Whenever we look at the electron it flashes conveniently into view. In its true state it is a blur-like wave or string, but whenever we look at it, it changes its reality into a ball-like object that we refer to as a particle, or sub-atomic particle. The reason for this transformation is that when we look at the electron, it is actually aware of our observation, and makes itself easier for us to observe because of its sensitivity to our thoughts. But what is most interesting is that we are made up of these transforming atoms and whenever we look at ourselves, they are forming themselves into solid objects. This begs the question: *Are we really entities of energy that are being transformed into solid objects when the atoms become aware that our consciousness is observing them?* Is there consciousness within the atoms?

Remember, atoms are more than 99 percent made up of Vril energy, which is the Life Force of the Gods. Thus the atoms are the Gods, or the realm within which the Gods dwell—Asgard!

The electrons within our atoms come from somewhere else. They are actually wavy lines or strings, vibrating sound frequencies, that come from larger wavy lines or strings, known as superstrings. No one knows where superstrings come from, but we can hypothesize that strings (or waves) are to humans what superstrings are to the Gods.

If we examine our inner space, we discover that it is very much like outer space. It appears to be made up of vast amounts of nothingness, but that's not exactly correct, for the nothingness is actually made up of Vril energy, both within the inner space of our bodies and the vast distances of outer space. We know that energy and matter makes up less than 5 percent of the universe and that the rest of the universe is made up of what science refers to as dark energy (Fehu--the fire of Musspellheim) and dark matter (Isa–the Ice of Niflheim), which are opposing properties of Vril.

But let's get back to the atom. Atoms actually "talk" to each other. How they perform this feat is still a mystery, but it has come to be described as "entanglement" by the scientific community. Just what is entanglement?

When we observe an electron, it settles into a rotation around the atomic nucleus, spinning in one direction which appears to be random. Entanglement occurs when a twin atom's electron simultaneously spins in the opposite direction. Thus, if one spins clockwise, the twin spins counterclockwise. What we must be clear is that one atom does not *cause* the twin atom to spin in the opposition direction, because that would imply a time delay. *Entanglement happens instantaneously, in unison outside our known dimension of time.*

This phenomenon has been tested in the same laboratory over and over, but what really amazed scientists has been the same result happening when tested over longer and longer distances. This has led them to conclude that entanglement is a phenomenon that exists not only outside our known understanding of time, but also independently of distance, so the result of entanglement is referred to as a non-local event. Entangled electrons exist anywhere in the universe, even when separated by millions of light years, and yet the entanglement is not weakened by distance. *It is as if distance does not exist.*

The sub-atomic world of electron behavior gives credence to the belief that psychic abilities function on this level of reality, which is the realm of quantum physics. This is the realm of higher consciousness in which the Gods dwell.

Rupert Sheldrake, a British evolutionary biologist, has come up with an interesting theory that explores the existence of *morphic fields*. These are invisible energy fields of information that all living creatures possess. They are made up of Vril energy and are part of the extended Soul. Sheldrake believes they exist in a dimension apart from the physical realities of the known universe, and thus they possess quantum qualities. These fields interact with each other among different individual members of the same species and are the reason why flocks of birds fly in coordinated formation or why fish swimming in schools turn spontaneously without any of the hundreds of individual members colliding into each other.

Sheldrake theorizes that these living fields exist in the past, present and future simultaneously and govern both human and animal behavior, forming a living matrix upon which the physical bodies are formed. Thus, this would fit the description Vrilology gives of the physical body existing as one of many parts of the Soul.

In the world of medicine, there is the image of the caduceus that is commonly used as an emblem used to denote the medical profession. The caduceus is a rod with the twin serpents entwined on the rod, climbing towards spreading winds, that signifies the Greek god Hermes (Mercury to the Romans and Odin to the Norse). The caduceus can be found on many medical logos and even used to denote communication and travel. It has been used for many centuries by many diverse people, including the Sumerians over four thousand years ago to represent the emblem of their god, Enki, the Lord of the Sacred Eye (Odin), and by the Greeks as a symbol of healing. It has been used by alchemists, such as Sir Isaac Newton, as a symbol representing the power of transformation.

The intertwining serpents also look every much like the coils of electricity that one notices in the Tesla coil that Nicola Tesla invented and claimed could harness infinite amounts of electricity and send it over vast distances. The coiling serpents also represent the twin coils of energy representing Hvels. Our spiritual, mental and physical well being depends on the unfettered movement of Vril energy through the body, and its passage through the nine Hvels, representing the nine worlds of the Yggdrasill. The image of Vril energy, coiling down and up once more along the cosmic axis of the Yggdrasill that the human spinal cord represents, is seen in the caduceus, coiling about each Hvel and then reaching the uppermost realm of Asgard, which is depicted as the open wings, denoting the attainment of highest consciousness, and thus oneness with the Gods.

The twin serpents wrapping around the Hvels control the flow of Vril energy entering and exiting each Hvel, as rooted in the universal principle of Male-Force and Female-Form. The twin coiling streams of energy is the female form wrapping itself about the male force of the rod or staff. It is interesting that in the Norse cosmology, the first man and woman are described as being created by the Gods from living trees (representing the Life Force or Vril energy) and are named Ask and Embla. Ask is thought to be the ash tree and Embla is the elm tree. But some believe Embla is actually a vine that grows by wrapping itself about the trunk of a tree. This would fit nicely with the symbolism of the caduceus and the relationship between the universal principle of Male-Force and Female-Form.

Our health depends on Vril flowing continuously and uninterrupted through the Hvels and then passing throughout the body. This can be achieved by maintaining a balance of energy in each Hvel, which helps to cleanse one's Orlog, and thus creating harmony throughout the body. We need to understand the flow of this energy through the body and how it affects every cell, gene and atom.

If you examine the shape or model of the DNA, you will discover the similarity between it and the caduceus. Interesting enough on its own, the DNA strand also resembles a series of Dagaz runes aligned side-by-side. It can also resemble a variation of the Ingwaz rune.

Ingwaz represents Frey, the God of fertility and thus DNA, while Dagaz represents enlightenment. Once again, the combination of these two Runes represents the principle that *the Gods dwell within us.* The double helix of caduceus represents the flow of Vril energy into us, moving down the spinal column (Yggdrasill) and then undergoing transformation at the junction where the bottom two Hvels (Niflheim and Musspellheim) are located. It then flows back upward along the spinal column, undergoing additional transformation as it passes through each of the other seven Hvels, representing the other seven worlds of the Yggdrasill, and then is disseminated throughout the spirito-physical matrix of the Soul. We can see that DNA, which possesses a form similar to the variation form of Ingwaz and Dagaz, is behaving like billions of tiny superconductors, or collectively as one great superconductor.

What is a superconductor? *"A superconductor is a substance that conducts electrical energy incredibly fast because there is little or no resistance."* For instance, if you freeze mercury at 269 degrees below zero C, it loses all its electrical resistance and becomes a superconductor. Other elements, such as tin, aluminum, titanium, zinc and tungsten, also become superconductors at extremely low temperatures. Scientce began to look for a superconductor that functions when warmer so that it could be incorporated into computers, making them extremely fast.

Scientific American magazine ran an article in 1995 describing how a strand of DNA became ten thousand times more conductive in the presence of the superconductor ruthenium. Additional experiments demonstrated that a combination of DNA and carbon coated rhenium, another superconductor, achieved this state at room temperature. Thus, when DNA is extracted from a living being, dried and added to a superconducting compound, it appears to enhance the compound's superconductivity at temperatures nature prefers. Thus, we can speculate that when DNA is nestled cosily in its friendly environment within the nucleus of a cell, it behaves as a superconductor, acting as a balancer of opposing magnetic forces, allowing another dimension of energy (Vril-the Life Force of the Gods) to enter into its midst.

Vrilology teaches that Odin spoke three Runes into Balder's ear as he laid dead on his funeral pyre. These Runes are Dagaz, Nauthiz and Ansuz, and they are the runic formula for Balder's resurrection, and with this resurrection the rebirth of the Gods. Dagaz is enlightenment that one achieves with Vrilology, Nauthiz, the need to reestablish the connection or bond between the Gods and their children, and Ansuz, the state of spiritual ecstasy one achieves with the ability to communicate with the Gods. The secret of achieving this state of higher evolutionary consciousness in rooted within our DNA, a realm where the Gods dwell. If we accept the notion that our DNA is an advanced form of superconductor, generating Vril energy throughout the spirito-physical body or Soul, then we can understand the principle behind the runic formula that Odin spoke to Balder.

DNA–Where the Gods Dwell

If we examine closely the structure of DNA, we discover that only 10 percent of our DNA is directly involved in setting the genetic structure of our bodies. Scientists have puzzled over the function and purpose of the other 90 percent and have labeled it "junk DNA." Many hoped that this mystery would be solved once we had completed the Human Gnome Project, and while this pioneering research has revealed much about the nature of our genetic heritage and nature, we are still in the dark as to the purpose of "junk DNA." But we are slowly beginning to see beyond the mere chemistry of the DNA and its mathematical coding, into a world of quantum dimensions, a realm where the Gods dwell.

For a long time, scientists in Russia have examined DNA with a more holistic vision. They have examined its nature from outside the box, so to say, by exploring its electrical and vibrational qualities instead of just its chemical nature. With the understanding that light is necessary for life, their research has revealed that DNA molecules respond to photons of light. Their research has led them to claim DNA molecules actually receive, harmonize, store and transmit light. This is done mostly in the same shade of blue as the sky.

Interesting about the nature of light is that its particles or quanta can also be considered to be waves, but stranger still is the issue of color. A red rose is not red because its surface is red. When light shines on a red rose, the red color of the spectrum is reflected. It is this reflected red light that we see when we look at a red rose. The rest of the color spectrum is absorbed. With white objects, all colors are reflected, and thus white objects tend to be cooler because they are reflecting more of the light. Black objects, on the other hand, absorb all colors and thus are hotter because they absorb all the energy of the light.

Light has healing qualities that can have a positive effect on the body because it is energy that enhances the healing process. Russian research has shown that our DNA, which acts as a receiver and transmitter, is involved in this process. They have included the assistance of linguists in their research. They discovered that the so-called "junk DNA" is constructed in precisely the same way that our languages are with syntax and grammar. We can speculate from their research that human language has its origin in the life encoded within our very DNA, and has been transmitted into our consciousness. Could this be the result of the Gods providing us with consciousness? Empowering us with the ability to communicate with them and each other?

If we take the three Runes representing DNA—Dagaz, Nauthiz and Ansuz—we discover that the first of these Runes, Dagaz, represents light and the God Heimdall. Heimdall is known as the "White God," and white is the totality of the light spectrum. Heimdall also is the guardian of Bifrost, the Rainbow Bridge. The rainbow is what we have when we break white light up into the various colors of the spectrum. Another nature of light is heat, and the Rainbow Bridge is often referred to as the fiery bridge. This is the second Rune, Nauthiz, the Rune of Need-Fire. The third Rune is Ansuz, the rune of communication, which is sound and the transmission of thought and consciousness. We can understand that Dagaz, light or enlightenment, is transmitted through communication, Ansuz, and between them is the need to do so, which is Nauthiz. Thus, with us, within our DNA, is the need and means to communicate with the Gods.

We know now that our DNA resonates not just with light, but also with sound. Remember—*everything vibrates!* This is how we can chant the Runes and use their frequencies to transform the world around us, as well as transform ourselves. *Since our DNA resonates with both light and sound, it is possible to actually change our DNA through the vibrational qualities of the Runes.* Thus, we can discover the soothing or harmful effects of all forms of music, as well as the spoken word. Here we have the nature of the Rune Ansuz revealed to us.

Experiments were conducted in Japan exposing water crystals to different types of music. Dr. Masaru Emoto noticed that the shape of the water crystal changed when exposed to various types of music. This was true even when they were exposed to different words. Words would be written on a piece of paper and suspended on the water. Loving and kind words and certain types of music, such as classical music, produced beautiful crystalline shapes. This was true even when the same word was written is various languages. Angry and hateful words, and music such as gangster rap or hard rock, produced bizarre images. Even the intention of the way the words were used caused different effects. It was as if the water "knew" the emotional intent of words and sounds that were employed. This principle is behind the practice of chanting and prayer.

Before going on with our exploration of DNA as a conductor, we need to take a look at the standard electrical coil that we find in our electric kettle. It has a conducting cable through which passes an electrical current. This produces an electromagnetic field, which in turn heats the water. This is known as the "standard coil." But if we double the coil, by wrapping the coil in tight circles around a ring, the North and South electromagnetic fields cancel each other out. We can see this in the "bifilar coil." But if we configure the coils into a figure-eight shape known as the "Möbius coil," all the magnetic fields cancel each other out, leaving a magnetic vacuum. The same effect is produced by the "toroid coil."This is a space beyond magnetism, like the space created between the mag-lev train and the rail it rides over. *This is "entangled space" where connecting electrons of opposing spin open to another dimension where energy exists outside our concepts of space and time, known by science as "free energy," "zero-point energy," and "scalar energy," but Vrilology refers to it as Vril.*

You might ask, "What has this to do with the DNA?" Well, the double helical DNA is constructed of many tiny but extremely powerful Möbius coils laid end to end. We now know that Vril energy is being transmitted by every molecule of DNA, within every one of our 50 trillion cells continuously, to receptors all around the body. You can imagine it working similar to an old-fashioned slide projector, which projects tiny transparent images onto a large screen. But unlike the slide projector, DNA is projecting Vril energy, which is other-dimensional energy, instantly and holographically, not onto a flat screen, but throughout the entire matrix of our three-dimensional body. A good analogy to how the DNA molecule holds within its fields the data of the entire body is the hologram, where the smallest part holds all the information of the whole. The microscopic double helix of the DNA therefore leaves its imprint within the matrix of the whole body.

Some scientists believe that there are differences between the 3-dimensional hologram and the DNA model, which acts as a projector for a 4-dimensional reality, as time itself is processed by this molecule. This takes us into speculation on the relationship of

DNA's shape to the Möbius coil, which is a figure-eight and possesses the shape of Dagaz.

Thus, in both the Möbius coil and Dagaz, we have the figure "8." In is interesting that the Norse year is divided into eight parts. Thus, if we draw a circle and divide it into eight parts, which is the symbol for the Norse year, we actually have a circle with nine points. The ninth point is located in the center where all the other eight points meet. These nine points represent, once again, the nine worlds of the Yggdrasill. The ninth point, located in the center, is Midgard, which is at the center of the cosmological diagram that the Yggdrasill represents. It is here that the natures and influences of all the other eight realms converge and manifest themselves collectively. Thus, this is the center of reality, the place where consciousness can be transformed.

We inhabitants of Midgard might not necessarily recognize our realm as a place where we can achieve higher consciousness, because it exists in a dimension that is "other worldly." At first sight, when we observed the year divided into eight parts, we did not recognize the center as the ninth point. Nor did we understand its significance because its nature exists in a dimension that is beyond our three-dimensional sense of reality.

The illustrations of the nine points of the eight part division of the year and its significance in extra dimensional reality can help us to better understand the extra dimensional nature of the Dagaz Rune. If we take the DNA helix, which is made of two strands coiling about each other like the Möbius coil, and view it head-on, we can see that it looks like the eight-part yearly circle. Running down the center of the helix would be the ninth point, which would form an axis around which the double helix would twirl. Thus this would form the Yggdrasill. It is this vortex nature that Victor Schauberger, the Austrian engineer who tried to harness Vril energy mechanically, used as the principle in his experiments, creating a convecting double vortex that created an implosion, and thus releasing infinite amounts of "free Vril energy."

We can see that our DNA, in addition to coordinating the construction of the physical structure of our bodies, using runic principles, dynamically constructs a map of the multi-dimensional spirito-physical Soul, which the physical body is a part of, in the form of a holographic matrix. This ensures that the building blocks know where to piece themselves together, both within the physical realm of Midgard and within the extra-physical realms of the other eight worlds of the Yggdrasill, which is depicted in the shape of the whirling double helix of the DNA. *It is remarkable how our most ancient ancestors grasped the significance of the double-helix of the DNA, and the fundamental truth of our physical and spiritual growth and relationship with the Gods, long before Watson and Crick won their Nobel Prize for their discovery of the nature of the DNA.*

This double-helix structure involves trillions of information fields that are projected by our DNA, interacting with each other on a scale that is beyond our wildest imagination, which send ripples of morphic fields of Vril (Life Energy) reverberating, not only throughout our physical body, like ripples on the surface of a lake (our bodies are made up mostly of water), but also throughout the Vril-powered energy field or Soul that extends beyond the physical body. This creates a boundary between the microcosm within our selves and the macrocosm of the universe. So as our understanding of our DNA deepens, we can begin to perceive it as a vital link between our earth-bound (Midgard) mortal/physical body and the more ethereal realms (the other eight worlds of the Yggdrasill) of our immortal, timeless Soul, and the Gods who dwell within our DNA. It is no coincidence that the Möbius coil, as well as Dagaz, has a shape similar to our double-helix DNA and is the classical sign of infinity.

If we were to turn the double-helix DNA on its side, and look through it, we see the toroid coil, and within a toroid coil, magnetic fields are cancelled out. *The center, where the magnetic fields are cancelled out, becomes an opening or window to another dimension—Asgard—where the Gods dwell.* If we could shrink ourselves down and enter this realm, we would experience perfect alignment with the Gods. This would be a dimension of perfect peace, where all around us we would witness a fierce electrical storm raging. This perfected state is the order that the Gods establish and work to maintain. The electrical storm whirling about it is the forces of chaos that is represented by the Giants, who seek to storm Asgard, but are unable. *It is this realm of perfect alignment with the Gods that we seek to establish in Midgard.*

Thus, to become a Vril Being is to evolve into an entity governed by peace and contentment, impervious to the world of pain and suffering whirling about you.

Achieving this state is what we mean by—BALDER RISING!

Morphpgenic Fields and Vril

Rupert Sheldrake proposes that there is a field of energy within and around a morphogenic unit which organizes its characteristic structure and pattern of activity. This energy field is made of Vril. Essential to Sheldrake's model is the hypothesis of "morphogenic resonance." This is a feedback mechanism between the field and the corresponding forms of "morphogenic units." The greater the degree of similarity, the greater the resonance, leading to habituation or persistence of particular forms. So, the existence of a morphogenic field makes the existence of a new similar form easier. According to this concept, the morphogenic field underlies the formation and behavior of "holons" and morphogenic units, and can be set up by the repetition of similar acts and/or thoughts. The hypothesis says that a particular form belonging to a certain group which has already established its (collective) morphogenic field, will tune into that morphogenic field. The particular form will read the collective information through the process of morphogenic resonance, using it to guide its own development. This development of the particular form will then provide, again through morphogenic resonance, a feedback to the morphogenic field of that group, thus strengthening it with its own experience, resulting in new information's being added (i.e. stored in the database). Sheldrake regards the morphogenic fields as a universal database for both organic (living) and abstract (mental) forms.

In lay terms, the theory proposes that any form looks always alike because it "remembers" its form through repetition and that any new forms having similar characteristics will "use" the pattern of similar forms already existing as guide for its appearance.

That a mode of transmission of shared informational patterns and archetypes might exist did gain some tacit acceptance, when it was proposed as the theory of collective unconscious by renowned psychiatrist Carl Jung. According to Sheldrake, the theory of morphogenic fields might provide an explanation for Jung's concept as well. Also, he agrees that the concept of Akashic Records (term from Vedas representing the "library" of all the experiences and memories of human minds or souls through their physical lifetime) can be related to morphogenic fields, since one's past (an Akashic Record) is a mental form consisting of thoughts as simpler mental forms (all processed by the same brain), and a group of similar or related mental forms also have their associated (collective) morphogenic field. (Sheldrake's view on memory-traces is that they are non-local, and not located in the brain.

What creates these morphogenic fields? Perhaps the consciousness that creates its own reality creates its own morphogenic field, and the collective consciousness of a particular species or race of beings generates its own group energy fields that are maintained as a group awareness. Within this morphogenic energy field, new data banks are constantly being downloaded with new information or learning, which helps to fashion the nature of the morphogenic fields. Eventually, a critical mass is reached from the new data that results in a transformation within the DNA of the group that generates the collective morphogenic fields. The entire race or species that represents the group will simultaneously become aware of the new patterns created by the new information or behaviors. This feedback is what is known as morphogenic resonance.

An experiment was conducted using a species of white rat. It was bred over many generations to learn the swimming skills needed to swim a maze immersed in water. It was discovered that after many generations, the descendants of the original rats were born with an innate knowledge of how to swim the maze, even if they had never seen the maze. All the rat descendants were able to swim the maze as well as, or better than, the trained rats of the previous generations. In time, all members of this species of white rat seem to be born with this innate ability without having to be taught.

The DNA is the tuner from which the morphogenic resonance of each species or race receives instructions. Vril energy is constantly flowing into the organism, replenishing the supply of energy that powers the atoms. From the frequency of the vibrating atoms Vril energy powers every cell within the organism, including DNA. The overflow of Vril energy creates a morphogenic field around the organism. The mind is taking Vril and painting it with the thoughts and feelings that it experiences, and transforming the morphogenic field. Since the DNA of all members of a given species and race is almost identical, or at least much closer to the frequency of the morphogenic fields of all members of its own genetic group than to the morphogenic fields of those organisms belonging to a different genetic group, the collective morphogenic fields of a genetic group can easily exchange and share the data that is shaping the nature of the morphogenic fields of all individuals belonging to the same genetic group. Here we have the scientific basis for the Kin-Fetch.

Morphogenic fields are associated with the properties of life. Each cell, tissue, organ and structure within the body has its own individual field, which determines the qualities and characteristics expressed by the individual organs. By this principle, your DNA is merely the hardware, but the energy field, made from Vril, determines the characteristics that you inherit from your parents. From the collective field of your family, race and species, you download the biological traits that determine what you are. Your morphogenic field is linked to the morphogenic field of your parents, relatives, families and other individuals who are genetically related to you. The closer the relationship, the greater the connection between your morphogenic field and theirs.

Thus you inherit those characteristics of mind and body through the morphogenic field. Morphogenic fields are, after all, made of Vril energy.

Every form of life, from the tiniest cell to the great blue whale, has a morphogenic field. Sheldrake writes that, *"The whole point about morphogenic fields is that nature as we know it is mutable and adaptable. Anything which influenced or imposed a pattern upon chance could bring about a causative influence in nature not violating any of the laws of physics."* Richard Barlett, in his book *Matrix Energetics*, describes an experiment involving chicks. "In it, day-old chicks were put in the same room with a robot that had a picture of a mother hen on it. The robot had been programmed to move randomly; however, when the baby chicks looked at it, the randomness was disrupted. When observed by the baby chicks, the robot's patterns of movement deviated toward the chicks to a statistically significant degree."

Sheldrake sees morphogenic fields as the underlying force behind the psychology of crowds. Organized rituals, both social and spiritual, will manifest a certain spiritual mental outlook that will come to dominate and influence the entire society, affecting the way everyone within the community, especially if they are closely related genetically, causes them to act, feel and think pretty much the same way. The Catholic Church survived two thousand years, even when faced with spiritual challenges from within and outside the spiritual body, because of the continuous ritual acts performed everywhere within the Church, in a uniform way. It is only in the last fifty years that the Catholic Church has seen a breakdown of the uniformity of its rituals due to the ever expanding diversity, culturally and racially, within the ranks of its members. The Catholic morphogenic field is dividing into many different morphogenic fields that do not communicate with each other. The cause is Vatican Two, which has abandoned the two-thousand-year traditions and rituals that were the glue that held the Catholic Church together. Rituals must be performed with the correct movements, gestures, words and music throughout the world. This morphogenic resonance creates the correct conditions for morphogenic resonance to reinforce the spiritual unity among those who perform the ritual, even if they are spread out across the face of the earth. This would be true even if there were human settlements on different planets in other solar systems separated by hundreds of light-years.

This can be explained through an understanding of quantum physics, which has shown that effects in the quantum realm are non-local in character, because information is transmitted or entangled at the proton level of reality, making it available to other protons everywhere in the universe, and possibly in the multiverse. This is the foundation for the phenomena of telepathy. Thus, we now can understand that all information, thus, all knowledge in the universe, is available to everyone through the power of our minds. This is what we mean by Mimir's Well. It is the well of knowledge. Odin drank from it. He gave up one eye, which was placed in the well. This is metaphor for his ability to tap into the quantum ocean of infinite knowledge. Richard Bartlett writes: "My point is that when you free up your thinking from its normal linear patterns, you can begin to access and integrate new information directly from Zero Point Energy Field: what some physicists have referred to as the Mind of God." In Vrilology, we refer to it as *the Eye of Odin.*

We must understand that the longer a technique has existed and been practiced, and the more people who practice this technique, the greater will be its power to change reality. Let's use the methodology that Vrilology employs, the Runes. The Runes are gifts from the Gods. They possess a natural power to harness Vril energy, and each Rune as its own character, which shapes Vril in unique and individual ways. This power of the Runes that is invested in the runic symbols, and their ability to harness and channel Vril by Rune Masters, is similar to the principle behind morphogenic fields, which are created by Vril energy. The truth is, *morphogenic fields are not just active in organic entities or biological species, but in systems of thought and belief.* Everyone who uses Runes will have full access to the specific morphogenic field associated with the use of Runes, and will be able to call *right now* on the vast ocean of knowledge that existed in the past, exists in the present and will exist in the future. Remember there is no time, no present, past or future in quantum reality. There is only now! The same is true for Norse cosmology. Odin knows the future as well as the past, and this explains the confusion of time that exist within the myths. Many have commented on the confused nature of the chronology of the myths.

The experiences, knowledge and traditions dealing with the use of Runes by anyone and everyone who has ever mastered their use and discovered and understood their mysteries is available to those today who are practitioners of Runes. *By creating a bond with the Runes, by absorbing their essence within us, they resonate so completely within us, within every atom within us, that we must employ them because their nature becomes our nature.* This creates a link between those who master the Runes, absorbing their resonance within our morphogenic field, and thus, changing the resonance of our morphogenic field so that it is in harmony with that of the Runes. This causes us to be linked with the power grid of runic energy, and this is when real Runic Magic manifests itself in miraculous ways because you have created a link with the infinite source of data concerning the Runes that exist *within the infinite Quantum Ocean of information known as Mimir's Well.*

Body Energy Work

Now that you have a greater understanding of how Vril energy functions in passing through your spirito-physical self by creating morphogenic fields and regenerating your atoms, you can work toward expanding your ability to increase and control the flow of Vril energy throughout your body. Learning how to do this is essential. Some of the techniques that you will work are:

1) Deep Physical Relaxation
2) Breathing
3) Shadow Memory Recall
4) Energy Body Stimulation
5) Quieting the Mind

6) Primary Energy Center Stimulation
7) The Hel State of Consciousness
8) Energy Body Loosening

You have already developed the ability to enter a deep relaxation where you become so comfortable that your mind and body will almost disassociate, which will take you to that "fuzzy" edge between sleeping and waking, which combines the Alpha (which we refer to as the Asgard State of Consciousness–ASC) and Theta (which is referred to as the Gladsheim State of Consciousness–GSC). This ability to enter a deep physical state of relaxation is the foundation upon which the rest of the work rests. Now we will begin to explore how to enter the Hel State of Consciousness, the Delta mind, which we experience when we enter deep sleep. This is why we refer to it as "deep trance." This is the condition where you remain in a self-aware, lucid state while working in a deep physical relaxed state or Delta mental state, similar to lucid dreaming.

Learning to control your breathing is something that you have by now become proficient at. Deep, full or reverse breathing helps to increase the intake of Vril into your body. It promotes relaxation, helps to clear the mind and increases the flow of Vril energy.

We have examined the way the nine primary Hvels transform Vril energy that flows into your body and then passes through your energy matrix that underlies spiritual, biological, emotional, and mental processes associated with the complexities of living. The ability to stimulate, raise and manipulate your personal supply of Vril energy is invaluable in your evolution into a Vril Being.

Once you have mastered the techniques to deliberately manipulate the flow of Vril energy, permitting you to store, build up, activate, use, shape and project Vril energy, causing manifestations within yourself and the world around you, you will have begun your transformation into a Vril Being. Once you have developed this state of being, you can join the ranks of the

Einherjar (those who work with Odin) and *Sessrumnir* (those who work with Freyja), or both, and exist in alignment with the Gods, assisting them in maintaining order and harmony in the universe.

Body Awareness

Learning awareness of your physical body is the first step in becoming aware of your energy body. By "energy body," we are referring to the matrix of Vril energy that is flowing throughout your physical body through your nervous system, thus creating a network or matrix of energy that duplicates your physical body. Through the nervous system through which Vril energy flows throughout your spirito-physical form, thus regenerating every cell in you, you can stimulate Vril by physically stimulating your physical form. This can be done by the most simple method of scratching and rubbing different parts of your body.

Exercise One:

The first step is to scratch your skin at different points of your body to cause a light tingling sensation that helps you become aware of the energy coursing through you.

1) Begin by scratching your knee, either right or left, with the nail on your index finger. Do this long enough to cause a tingling sensation. Close your eyes and focus on this point and forget about the rest of your body. Center all your attention on your knee. Continue to do this for about thirty seconds.

2) Do the same for the other knee.

3) Begin to explore other parts of your body. Do the same to your big toes, your thumbs, elbows, your thighs, your nose. Perform this procedure anywhere on your body as often as you like. The more you do it, the better you will be able to sense Vril energy within you.

4) Using the nail on your finger tip, trace a line from your big toe up your leg, over your kneecap, and along the inside of your thigh to the crotch. Do this several times on both legs. As you do this, feel the tingling sensation on your skin as you run your finger nail over it.

5) Perform this same procedure on your arms. Beginning with your thumb, run your finger nail along the insides of your arm (the skin there is more sensitive) over the insides of your elbow to the top of your shoulder.

Once you have performed these exercises, you should be able to replicate the same sensation along your skin with your mind, without touching your skin with your finger nail.

Exercise Two:

The next step is to familiarize your self with the energy within your hands.

1) With the fingertips of your right hand, gently rub the top of your left hand. Begin with your thumb. Run your fingers up and down your thumb, from the fingernail to the top of your hand, where it meets your wrist. Do this nine times. Close your eyes and concentrate on the tingling sensation on your skin as your rub your fingers over your thumb and hand.

2) Do this nine times to the index finger, rubbing it the tips of your fingers along the top of that finger, over your hand to where it meets your wrist.

3) Perform this same brushing action on each of the other fingers.

4) Perform the same procedure on your right hand with the fingertips of your left hand.

5) With the fingertips of your right hand, return to your left hand and gently run them in a circle over the top of your left hand, between your knuckles and wrist, with your eyes closed. As you do this, feel the tingling sensation. Concentrate on that sensation. Then do the same with your right hand.

6) With the palm of your right hand, gently brush the top of your left hand, up and down, from your fingertips to your wrist. Do this with your eyes closed and concentrate on the tingling sensation within your skin. Repeat the same procedure on your right hand with the palm of your left hand.

7) Hold both hands before you (you can rest them on your knees or the arm of your chair) and *feel* Vril energy pulsating

within both hands, as if energy is sweeping along your hands, from your fingertips to your wrists and back to your fingertips. Do this with your eyes closed and feel the pulsations bouncing up and down your hands, as if someone were brushing out the insides of your hands.

Exercise Three:

Perform the same procedure by your hands on your feet as you just did on your hands. Use the opposite knee to rest the foot on that you're stimulating.

Exercise Four:

Now we will concentrate on the soles of the feet, where your Musspellheim Hvel is, while the top of your feet is the location of the Niflheim Hvel. So your feet, as a source of Vril energy stimulation, are very important.

1) Brush all of your toes one of foot simultaneously. Then perform this exercise on the other foot.

2) Scratch or rub the sole of your foot. Be gentle, as the sole is very sensitive to tickling. Begin with one foot and slowly move your fingertips in a circular motion about nine times. Then, begin to brush your fingertips along the entire sole of your foot, from your toes to the heel. Then switch feet and do the same to the other foot. If you wish to spend more time on the soles of your feet, please do so. It is important to feel the surge of energy.

3) Use the entire hand, fingers and palm, to brush the entire sole of each foot from the toes to the heel.

This entire exercise up to this point should have taken three or four minutes. If you wish to take longer, please do so.

4) Place your feet on the floor and feel the surge of energy pulsating in both feet at the same time, moving back and forth between toes and heels. Close your eyes and concentrate your mind on the sensation of pulsating energy.

Exercise Five:

Once your feet have been properly stimulated, you will begin working on the stimulation of energy in your legs and thighs.

1) Begin with either leg. With your fingertips placed on your toes, rub, scratch or stroke the whole length of your leg, by moving your fingertips up the top of the foot to your ankle, over your shin to your knee and then, continue to move up the front of your thigh to your hip. Then, retrace the path down your leg, back to your toes. Perform this stroking action about nine times.

2) Repeat this stroking motion on the underside of your leg, beginning with the ankle and moving up until you reached the back of your buttock.

3) Repeat the two stroking techniques on the other leg. Avoid touching the genitals, as stimulation of this area can cause erotic sensations that might cause distractions.

4) Next, repeat the entire stroking of the top and underside of your legs, but this time, perform the stroking stimulation of both legs at the same time. You can close your eyes, but whether or not you keep them open, concentrate on the tingling sensation of Vril energy coursing up and down your legs.

5) Sit with your legs stretched out before you or even lay down, but make sure you do not fall asleep. Begin at your toes and with your mind, feel Vril energy coursing up your leg to your hips and then feel it coursing back down to your toes. Repeat this over and over. Feel the energy coursing through both legs at the same time. Begin slowly and eventually increase the speed of Vril energy coursing up and down your legs, from your toes to your hips and back down to your toes, without touching your legs. Continue this “bouncing” action for about five minutes.

The Development of Your Body’s Energy

These exercises should be practiced over a long period of time. *Take your time.* Do not rush the process. You should have a sense of your ability to stimulate and command Vril energy. When you begin the exercises on how to manipulate Vril energy, you should have a strong sensation of the flow of Vril. You will feel a surging, bubbling and rushing sensation that will cause your skin to tingle. It will be as if water is rushing through your body. This is one reason why the Rune for Vril energy is Laguz, which means "lake" and represents "water." Over time, these sensations will decrease, causing many to think they are doing something wrong. *Actually, it is the reverse. The greater your ability to control and manipulate your personal supply of Vril, the more likely the sensations will decrease.* The strong energy sensations you experience early in your lessons are the results of resistance within your energy body to the increasing flow of Vril. But as the energy body adjusts to the increase in flow, the sensations will decrease because the pathways in which energy flows will have expanded.

Some of the sensations you might experience will be:

1) a tingling or vibration sensation in the soles and toes of your feet

2) a sensation of water rushing through your legs and arms

3) tingling within your bones, arms, hands, feet and legs

4) tingling up and down your spine

5) spasms and cramps in your muscles

6) the sensation that ants are crawling all over you, similar to the sensation one gets when part of one's body "falls asleep"

7) prickling sensations

8) hot and cold sensations, especially in the palms of your hands and the soles of your feet.

Once you have learned to command the flow of Vril, your body will adjust and the tingling sensations and other physical reactions will decrease and disappears altogether. This is similar to what an athlete experiences as he exercises. His body will ache as his muscles develop, but eventually he will be able to perform with increased physical endurance and little or no physical pain.

The Fundamental Energy Body

Each of us has a fundamental energy body that is connected to the physical body. In fact, the two are intricate components of your multidimensional Soul. The physical body is dependent on the continuous flow of Vril energy to maintain its physical well being, as each atom requires Vril energy to maintain its atomic integrity. The amount of Vril energy available for this maintenance function will decrease in most people because of negative thoughts, actions and feelings that they obsess about. *This negativity diverts huge amounts of Vril energy from replenishment of your body. This causes aging and illness.*

On the flip side, the exercises that we have taught you, such as increasing your personal luck, also will divert increased amounts of Vril energy from replenishing your body. This is why it is important to learn how to increase the inward flow of Vril energy and become a master of its use and manipulation.

Learning to increase the flow of Vril will assure the necessary flow of Vril energy, so that your fundamental energy body can continue to properly perform its functions, which include maintaining the proper balance of biological functions and mental dexterity, assuring the maintenance of your Hvels' ability to cleanse and channel Vril energy, and providing the necessary amounts of Vril energy for your mind to assure supply for your spirito-physical body.

The Expansion of Your Energy Body

When performing the exercises provided to you in this book, you are learning to increase the storing of Vril for the manufacture of your personal luck, for faring forth, for remote viewing, to increase your protection, or as necessary for the well being of your spirito-physical body. When you are young, you naturally absorb huge amounts of Vril energy, and your requirements are not as great, even though your physical activities might be more strenuous than when you are older. But as you age, your obsessions increase, your mind becomes more preoccupied with thoughts, feelings and actions that are negative, which might become so routine that it will be hard to break the pattern, and this results in the waste of greater amounts of Vril. So you will need greater amounts of Vril energy to prevent yourself from aging and becoming ill. Now, if you begin to practice the techniques we teach in Vrilology, you will need even greater amounts of Vril energy, but Vrilology also teaches you how to increase your flow of Vril, which actually increases your ability to do more with less. This is why you need to learn how to naturally increase your ability to expand the flow of Vril energy coming into you.

Once you have incorporated what you are learning in this book, your subconscious mind will adjust itself and your flow of Vril energy will increase without your even being aware of it. *This is part of what we mean when you have achieved a state of Balder Risen. You have achieved alignment with the Gods, and you are like a leaf that rides the currents of a river, moving along the currents of Vril energy effortlessly.*

Let's continue with our exercises.

Exercise Six:

We will return to your hands and proceed to apply the same method to your arms.

1) Brush one hand's entire palm and the palm side of the fingers. Begin with one hand and slowly move your fingertips in a circular motion about ten times. Then, begin to brush your fingertips along the entire palm, from the tips of your fingers to your wrist. Then switch hands and do the same to the other hand. If you wish to spend more time on the hands, please do so. It is important to feel the surge of energy.

2) Place your hands on either your knees or the arms of the chair, palms facing up, if you are sitting, or next to your sides if you are lying down, and feel the surge of energy pulsating in both hands at the same time, moving back and forth between your fingertips and wrists. Close your eyes and concentrate your mind on the sensation of pulsating energy.

3) Place the fingertips of your right hand on the underside of the fingers of your left hand, and rub, scratch or stroke the whole length of your arm, by moving your fingertips over the palm of your left hand, across the wrist, up the inside of your arm, passing the inside of your elbow up to your shoulder. Then,

retrace the path down your arm and back to your fingertips. Perform this stroking action about nine times.

4) Repeat this stroking motion, on the top of your arm, beginning with the top of the fingers, over the top of your hand and moving up until you reach the top of your shoulder, right to the base of your neck.

5) Repeat the two stroking techniques on the other leg.

6) Place both hands on your knees or the arms of your chair, or at your sides, and imagine the surge of energy moving up and down both arms at once. Concentrate on the tingling sensation of Vril energy coursing up and down your arms.

Exercise Seven:

We will now target your spine, the upper body region and finally the entire body.

1) Sit comfortably in your chair with your hands on the arms of the chair or your knees. Keep your eyes closed so you can concentrate on what you are doing. Begin at the base of your spine, concentrating your mind at the tailbone, and move your awareness up the full length of your spine to the top of your head. Feel Vril energy slowly rising through your spine to the crown of your head.

2) Slowly feel the energy moving back down your spine to your tailbone. Repeat this over and over. Begin slowly and eventually increase the speed of Vril energy coursing up and down your legs, from your tailbone to the top of your head and back down your tailbone. Continue this "bouncing" action for about five minutes. *Make sure you breathe normally while doing this. The spine energy bounce tends to interfere with the natural breathing pattern. This can cause shallow breathing and intermittent breath-holding.*

3) You should lie down for this exercise, as you will want to keep your body straight. You might wish to keep your arms raised over your head and your legs together. Once you are in this position, begin at the soles of your feet, and mentally trace your awareness up your legs, through your body, your torso, head, and

arms and finish at your fingertips. If you are unable to raise your arms over your head, you can rest them at your sides, but your awareness will rise no further than the crown of your head. Then trace your awareness back down to the soles of your feet once more.

4) Repeat this by bouncing your awareness up through your entire body and down again, and as you do, *feel* the flow of Vril energy rising through your entire body and then retreating back down it once more. Repeat this bounce over and over, and slowly increase the speed by which it passes through your body. Do this for about five minutes.

Harnessing and Storing Vril

As a result of these exercises, you should be able to effectively stimulate your energy body. The exercises were designed to help loosen up the flow of Vril energy, remove blockages and strengthen the network of pathways through which Vril energy flows. The newly discovered sensation of Vril flowing through your body can be a fantastic spiritual awakening. If you have not already come to the realization that you are not just a physical machine but an energy entity, you certainly will come to accept this reality by the time you have completed this training program.

The first set of exercises was designed to loosen up your body so that Vril can more easily flow through you. Now we must learn how to harness this energy and store it so that you can use it for whatever purposes you will need it for. Using Vril for the manufacture of personal luck, protection or success can be costly, so you will need to increase its flow so that your body, both physically and spiritually, will have a sufficient supply of Vril to power its normal activities. It might seem as if we have put the cart before the horse in demonstrating how to use Vril for such purposes before we demonstrated how to increase its flow and store it, but we needed to demonstrate how Vril can change your life for the better before we introduced you to the advanced techniques that will take a great deal of dedication and determination on your part.

We cannot stress enough how important it is to master the art of increasing the flow of Vril for such activities. You cannot do too much energy raising. You should put aside a couple of hours each week for this purpose.

We Are Energy Beings

By now you should be familiar with the knowledge that we are energy beings, and that our physical form is just a reflection of this energy body. Though we might appear to be solid flesh and blood, underneath our fleshy exterior we are composed of the most highly structured matrix of Vril energy. This matrix includes your Hamingja, your many Hvels, the primary ones and the hundreds, even thousands of smaller Hvels, your entire multi-dimensional Soul, regions where Vril energy can be stored and parts of your body that can be used to exchange Vril energy with other people. These are the palms of your hands, soles of your feet, eyes, lips, mouth, tongue and genitals.

Each of these energy circuits have various purposes and are all interconnecting, supporting each other's requirements, and are all integrated parts of the energy matrix's synchronicity. Each of us absorbs a small amount of Vril energy for our normal daily functions. This flow of Vril energy decreases as we age because of the negativity we accumulate through negative thoughts, feelings, actions and especially our obsessions. We absorb Vril in various ways: eating, drinking, and breathing, from our environment and from people we are in contact with. As we grow and mature, and our Orlog becomes filled with the negativity we stored there, our requirement of Vril increases, but this increased negativity will actually cause the amounts of Vril flowing into us to decrease. This process assures aging and illness and eventually death. Think of it this way. Imagine each negativity to be a lead bar you acquire and must carry with you at all times. As you accumulate more and more lead bars, the effort to carry them around with you increases. It will take more and more energy on your part to support their weight. It is the same with Vril. The more negativity you carry around with you in your Orlog, the larger amounts of Vril energy you will need. Eventually, it will not be enough and it will affect your Wyrd—your future pathways in life.

Asgard, Midgard and Hel

There are three major energy storage regions within you. The first is the subnavel region that corresponds to Hel. It is ruled by the Rune Kenaz, controlled fire. This region acts like a furnace, causing energy to increase in intensity and sends it towards a given purpose of creation. The second region is near the heart and corresponds to Midgard. It is ruled by the Rune Wunjo, and represents harmony. Thus, the fire sent by Kenaz is made harmonious with whatever tasks you set for it. The energy of Kenaz is thus used in a constructive way for manifestation. The third region is between the Third Eye and the Crown and is represented by Asgard. The Rune is Othala. This represents the highest manifestation spiritually, representing Odin himself. Thus, the Asgard region represents spirit, the Midgard region represents Vril itself, the Life Force, and Hel represents the sexual energy of creation or generation. Like this training program, in which the first level is Hel, where the sleeping self is awakened for the first time to its true heritage, so too is this region very important in raising energy that is stored in your body. Thus, of the three regions, only Hel should be filled with energy storage action, which we will describe in the exercises to follow. It is from here that "charged" or "shaped" energy flows upward, along the axis which represents the Yggdrasill, to the higher storage regions of Midgard and Asgard. This we have your awakening taking place in Hel, representing the subconscious, manifesting itself first in the conscious, or Midgard, which thus takes you to a higher manifestation of consciousness in Asgard.

Clearing Your Mind

We are now going to discuss how to develop your ability to tame your mind. This is the ability to silence internal mental dialogue and keep your mind clear of vocalized thought. There is a voice in your head that is constantly talking, making observations, reminding you of things, constantly restating the obvious to you over and over. This chatterbox is the biggest obstacle to developing your mental and psychic powers. It is sometimes referred to as *involuntary subvocalization.* It is the major cause for obsessive thought. If you cannot control this internal dialogue, you will never be able to prevent yourself from obsessing on the negative, which is the greatest obstacle to developing your powers of internal projection where the expanded energy body is generated, which is the first step toward wakening-induced faring forth. It is vital that *you first master the internal dialogue and relax and focus your thoughts for a sustained period of time*.

Let's us first state that by learning to clear your mind, or taming your thoughts, *we are not referring to shutting down all thought.* Your mind will still be aware of mental imagery, body awareness, actions, visualization and so forth, but your mind will cease its chatter. You can observe an object and be aware of it and its characteristics, even examine it, but your mind will not discuss it. There will be no internal dialogue. *You will learn to think and act without words.* Thus, a tamed mind simply means no word-based chatter. The internal dialogue or involuntary subvocalization will be replaced by a relaxed state of mental silence, not unlike when you silently try to listen to a far-away or faint noise. *You actually do this all the time, every day, without realizing it. Your internal dialogue is shut off whenever you are watching television, a movie, listening to music or daydreaming. This also occurring just before you fall asleep, when you enter your Alpha or Asgard State of Consciousness, which you should by now be an expert at inducing.*

It can be a little disconcerting at first, and might even seem somewhat lonely, because we are so conditioned to listening to the little voice in our heads chattering away over and over. Holding this relaxed mental state will take practice and concentration, but in time it will come much more naturally to you, and you will eventually become used to it and look forward to it.

The ability to tame your internal mental dialogue can be used for all sorts of positive purposes, including the reduction of worrying. The greatest cause of stress comes from our inability to quiet our mind. Our inner voice will constantly discuss problems we face every day, and discuss it over and over until we become obsessive about them. This is the greatest problem we face as regards storing negativity in our Orlog. Our internal dialogue acts like a recording machine, typing into the files of our Orlog all the things that we should not be obsessing over. Once you have developed the ability to quiet your mind, you will be able to use this talent to reduce stress, eliminate obsession and create a clear-thinking mind for you to use to help you perform those tasks that you really should master for your own improvement and evolution, but spiritually in your physical reality.

A disciplined mind that has developed the ability to silence its own internal dialogue is not only stronger but has greater powers of self-awareness and focus than other minds that are incapable of doing the same.

Taming the Mind

Early attempts to master mental quietness probably caused tension headaches, especially when practicing entering your Alpha and Theta states, but by now you should be able to enter this state effortlessly. You probably noticed that the brain has quickly accommodated your needs as you practice. Let us give some suggestions to help you further develop your ability to tame your mental chatter.

You can easily do this by focusing your mind on any physical or mental task. This will easily clear your mind and develop the ability to focus. Physical activity is especially effective in learning to shut down the mental chatter. Even the simple exercise of walking can be very effective. Take a long walk and as you do, turn off the inner speaker. Simply observe everything you see, as you walk. Use your senses of smell, sight and hearing to observe and examine. *Do not mentally comment on what you perceive.* Simply notice it all without talking about it to yourself in your mind. You should also avoid daydreaming as you walk, concentrating your mind on the things you pass and observe.

Other ways to practice are to listen to music and concentrate your mind on the sound without commenting about it to yourself. You might do the same while watching television. It you are physically exercising, concentrate on the physical efforts of your body without making comments. Just take in the physical exertions of your body. If at any time your mind wanders, simply refocus your attention back on the task at hand.

Another method we have taught you to enter a meditative state is to count backwards. This can be very effective in shutting off the mental chatter. By counting backwards, you are progressively causing your mind to retreat backwards toward a desired goal, as opposed to counting forward. Numbers are also very effective in shutting off the verbal chatter. You can also use Rune chanting to the same effect. Runes are not words in the traditional sense. Though they have esoteric meaning behind them, they can be very useful in learning to concentrate your mental powers. Eliminate the mental dialogue by visualizing the form or shape of each Rune in your mind and holding the image without speaking. The best Rune for this exercise is Isa, which is the Rune of Concentration and used to quiet your mind.

Chapter Fifteen: Your Vril Personality and the Balder Force

Personal Magnetism or Super-charged Megin

Vril can be used to create a strange and miraculous force known as personal magnetism, which enables the Vril Being to attract, influence, dominate or control others. Throughout history great individuals have appeared to possess this strange, mysterious power, which enabled them to attract or influence others, both as individuals and on a grand scale. In some cases, such individuals received instruction from occult teachers, while others stumbled across the existence of this power within themselves. Many of them, in their writings or sayings, have testified to their knowledge and use of this most wonderful power. Its best definition might be *a powerful, unique force to influence others that is little understood, but whose existence is readily felt. The individual who possesses it, in the form of mental force or a super-charged personality, influences or exerts control by attracting, controlling, dominating, or influencing other persons.* But this would imply that only certain individuals possess personal magnetism and that the remainder of humanity is devoid of it. This, in our opinion, is a mistake. The truth is, each and every individual is in possession of a certain degree of personal magnetism, and each person may increase and strengthen that power by knowledge and practice. What this personal magnetism is, is your personal supply of Luck, or Megin, which is super-charged Vril.

You should review the section of this book that discusses how to transform Vril into Megin or Personal Luck.

Everyone possesses some degree of personal magnetism, perhaps even to a considerable degree, which manifests itself as a field of Vrilic energy, called an aura. . Even the most repellent persons are really manifesting a high degree of personal magnetism, but in a negative form which drives people from them in the same manner that others attract people to them, just as magnets can repel as well as attract. This energy field affects the minds of other persons coming within its influence.

This personal energy field varies greatly in degree of strength, extent and general character, among different individuals. The average person has but a weak personal energy field, which extends but a short distance on all sides of him, while the strong characters are surrounded by a widely expanded personal energy field of great power, especially when they are aroused by any strong emotion, feeling or desire. The personal energy field of those strong individuals usually extends great distances from the person, and is fairly saturated with strong dynamic magnetism, which impresses itself strongly upon those coming within their field of influence.

We radiate what we feel, what we think and especially what we obsess on, affecting those around through the personal energy or Vril field that surrounds us. This is true of people possessing a weak energy field. If your personal energy field is colored by good-cheer, brightness, and happiness, it will cause persons with whom you come in contact to be affected by these attributes. But if you radiate feelings of gloom, pessimism and discouragement, these sensations will adversely affects persons coming near you. What we want you to understand is that every person, even those possessing the weakest and most negative power, may develop his or her personal magnetism.

We have explored the nature of the multidimensional aspect of the Soul and especially the Orlog and how it acts as a filter, through which Vril passes, taking on the characteristics of what is stored within it. *By carefully practicing what Vrilology teaches regarding how to transform your Self, any person possessing sufficient will, perseverance and determination can learn to clean out his Orlog and bend what is stored within it to his will. He can then will himself to develop from a puny state of magnetism into a conduit of giant magnetic powers. But this requires determination, constant practice until a certain stage is reached, and an indomitable will.*

Mental and Physical Aspect of Personal Magnetism

Your success in cultivating a Vril Personality will depend upon creating a balance of your physical and mental conditioning. Mental magnetism flows from your mental state—how you think, feel and react to the world around you—while physical magnetism flows from the way you carry yourself—your appearance, the expression on your face, the way you walk or hold yourself. Some persons have more mental magnetism, while others have more physical magnetism, but the individual who really manifests the highest degree of personal magnetism is the one who is developed along both poles of activity, both phases of magnetism – physical as well as mental. This type of person possesses a Vril personality.

Your mind creates thought waves and then projects them, beyond the limits of the brain, into your Vrilic aura or life energy field, and even beyond the range of your own personal energy-field when necessary. When accompanied by the physical magnetism generated by the other pole of magnetic activity, this mental magnetism strongly affects other persons coming within the field of action of these thought waves.

For these thought waves to manifest themselves sufficiently to produce marked results, they need a good supply of physical magnetism. You need to use your mental powers not only to affect others around you, but also to transform yourself. This will result in your acting, talking and behaviing in such a way that others will find themselves physically drawn to you. Their emotional state will take on your emotional state, which will be transmitted by your physical behavior. This physical appearance will be one of joy and harmony with the world around that will manifest itself as an air of self-confidence and friendliness.

As stated in learner lessons, the mental state of the Vril Being must be one of Wunjo–harmonious joy. The knowledge that you possess the power within you to harness Vril and use it to transform your reality into one of your choosing, should produce a state of mind of cheerfulness, hopefulness, and supreme confidence that will vibrate in your life field, causing the life fields of all those who come into contact with you to resonate with yours. THE IS

THE BALDER FORCE! Once you have achieved this state of being, you have already achieved the first step in affecting the reality around you without any conscious effort on your part.

Likewise, if your mental state is one of gloom, depression and lack of self-confidence, the vibrations caused by you of a gloomy, depressed character will impress its resonance on all individuals coming in contact with you, and your gloomy mental states will manifest itself by creating a gloomy existence within the objective realm of Midgard.

Why are some individuals sought out by others while other individuals are avoided? The reason is the reaction others have when they enter into the extended life-energy field that individuals produce. If your life-energy field is charged with the runic energies of Wunjo, they will cause others to react positively to your Balder Force, creating an air of harmony and joy in any interaction between yourself and others. People who come into contact with you will feel a harmonious joy and cheerfulness that will cause their attitude to change and make them amenable to your suggestions. In the same way, if your life-energy field is one of gloom and doom, others will be repelled by contact with you. *You might refer to this latter type of persona as the Hoder Force, one of darkness, depression and gloom that one is engulfed in when one exists in a state of blind ignorance.* You might be able to disguise your thoughts from others and even wear a mask of false facial expression, but the mental vibrations of your personal atmosphere *will give you away.*

Most individuals fall into a third category of people who leave little or no impression on others they come into contact with. The reason is that their mental states are so varied, inconstant and fleeting that they neutralize each other, and fail to impart a definite shade of thought-color to their life-energy field that they project. Remember that we are all creators of energy–Vrilic energy–that is constantly vibrating. The frequencies of our vibrations will be affected by the stronger vibrations of those whom we come into contact with.

You need not despair if you are constantly preoccupied by undesirable thoughts and emotions that affect your personal energy field, for these sensations are the result of what you are carrying around with you in your Orlog, and we have explained how you can bend or cleanse your Orlog of these undesirable influences. Once you have mastered this technique, you will be able to entirely change the character of your mental state, and thus transform your personal atmosphere from the very worst to the very best.

The Nerve Force

The physical properties of personal magnetism depend on two coordinated manifestations of what might be referred to as the "nerve force": (1) the transmission by way of the nervous system of a plenteous supply of what has been described by some as a "nerve force"; and (2) the conscious projection, by the will, of that supply of nerve force into the personal atmosphere, and even to a greater distance under special conditions. What is meant by "nerve force" is simply Vril energy converted into super-charged willpower, which controls all physical movements. It is sometimes referred to as "nerve force" because Vril energy is channeled through the human body by way of the nervous system, down to the most delicate nerve filament. Vril does not flow through the nervous system like blood through arteries and veins, but like an electric impulse flows along the nervous system. Not all Vril that is transmitted through the body does so by the nervous system, but currents intended to assure the unconscious or instinctual functions of the body, such as breathing, or heart pumping, or hair growing, and the replication of cells as they die, are powered by Vril through the nervous system.

Certain parts of the brain are great reservoirs of this Vrilic nerve force, as are also the groupings of nerve-matter called a plexus, prominent among which are the solar plexus and the sacral plexus.

As you already know, Vril is constantly flowing into you from the infinite source that fills not only our universe, but the multiverses. The atmosphere is charged with Vril, which is taken up and absorbed by the nervous system, and stored away in its great reservoirs, from whence, in turn, it flows over the nerves when required, by the physical or mental needs of the individual.

The body absorbs this universal source of life force through breathing. The "breath of life" is Odin's gift and known as Ond. The process of breathing, in its higher and lower forms, not only extracts oxygen or other elements from the air, but also extracts Vril at the same time. Once this is understood, we can understand why living things perish as soon as their process of breathing be interfered with. The understanding of this secret of nature throws a much-needed light upon the important part played by breathing, in the life of all creatures.

The harvest of Vril energy to maintain a healthy and vigorous life can decline over time. But in some individuals, the amount of energy does not decrease but increases. This can be an involuntary phenomenon, or one produced by the individual's discovery of how to harness and increase the flow of Vril consciously. We have all heard of and probably met certain persons flowing with vigorous amounts of Vril, radiating this energy within their life-energy fields, perceptibly to those shaking hands with them, or even just coming into their vicinity. These individuals radiate health and vigor, exerting a positive healing and invigorating effect on those with whom they come in contact. We are invigorated when we meet them because they absorb amounts of Vril greater than their needs require, they are release the surplus Vril into the atmosphere around them toward all who come into contact with them, thus causing others to react positively to their very presence. This is what we mean by the Balder Force. *This is the essence of the difference between a Vril being and an average human being.*

In a similar manner, some individuals who lack sufficient Vril go around unconsciously absorbing Vril from others, and, in extreme cases, becoming vampires sucking the Vril from those around them. Who of you have not met this type of person, and have not noted how depressed and weakened one is after having been in the company of such a person for some time? The average person does not need any further proof in this case, beyond that afforded by his or her own experience. These individuals are blind to what is happening. They are examples of the Hoder Force.

You might ask why all persons are not equally endowed with this energy since it is readily available. The answer is that the life habits of individuals differ, and just as one is physically strong and robust, and another weak and delicate, so is one individual strong in Vril, and another weak in it. This can also be the result of what has been inherited from one's ancestral stream and stored in one's Orlog. Moreover, a change in the life habits of the person will inevitably result in a change in the amount of Vril absorbed and retained by him or her.

Try to remember occasions when you came into contact with someone whom you could describe as having a strong personality. It could've been anyone in any walk of life—a religious leader, a lawyer, a politician, an orator, a businessman—anyone whose success depends upon interacting with other persons. You were probably conscious of a strength and power being radiated by that person, a power you probably felt was not mental or intellectual strength alone. It seemed, instead, to be a force that moved you physically. So strong is this power in the case of some of the world's great characters that they seem to personify will power – mighty centers of vitalized energy, affecting all with whom they come in contact.

There are many men and women who possess great intellectual powers, but are not "magnetic" as the term is generally used. They do not radiate or throw off force, and the element of physical magnetism is almost entirely absent. They seem to be centers of great intellectual energy – but nothing more. Their intellect is well developed, but they seem to lack that "something" which impresses persons.

The "magnetic" person is almost always in possession of an indefinable something, which we call "strength" and energy. He may not be a stout, large person – he may even be a scrawny, lank individual, of slight frame and small stature – but even in the last case he will be "wiry", like a coiled wire spring full of latent energy. The magnetic person is never the weak, flabby, jellyfish type. Even on their deathbeds, magnetic persons, weakened by disease, radiate this magnetic power of attraction. No matter what their outer appearance, they seem to be in possession of a something within them which stores and radiates strength and power.

Let us clarify what we are describing. We are not claiming that this physical nerve force (Vril channeled through the nervous system) alone constitutes personal magnetism or the Balder Force. There are many men and women who possess and radiate this physical nerve force who are not personally magnetic in the full sense of the term. The combination of mental and physical magnetism is needed to produce the full phenomenon of personal magnetism.

Vril Powered Thought Waves

Another important factor of personal magnetism concerns the part it plays in the phenomena of telepathy, hypnotism, mental influence, and similar phenomena in which the mind of one person acts upon the mind of another. It works by "vitalizing" the thought waves with currents of Vril energy, which is then projected outward toward those whom the magnetic personality contacts. This power can be felt in the person's eyes, through his fixed stare, or by the sound of his voice, or sometimes just by being in his presence.

This power to move you is especially true in those orators, whether spiritual, political or scholarly speakers, who have the power to convince you of the righteousness of what they say, not so much by the logic of their argument, but by the force of their conviction which is felt, rather than understood. You will grasp this concept better if you recall someone who delivered a speech or lecture about some topic, and did so with brilliant logic, marked intellectual ability, and filled with good, sound thoughts, yet whose delivery seemed dead, dull, colorless and lifeless. To you it lacked the life, vigor, and the force of the delivery of another speaker who might have possessed the same intellectual gifts as the previous speaker, or even less intellectual power; you were moved more by the force of his delivery than the intellectual logic of his thoughts, because his speech radiated life and strength, and consequently, magnetic power. The reason for this is that the former lacked vitalizing force, while the other possessed this in abundance. Think this over carefully, until you "get it" – for this gift to generate Vril-powered thought waves, and project them outward, is one of the great secrets of personal magnetism and the foundation of a Vril personality.

Once you have developed the ability to charge yourself with increased currents of Vril, and consciously or unconsciously acquired the art of combining it with thought waves, your speech or thoughts will be charged with dynamic force, reaching and affecting those with whom they come in contact. Like a high-power rifle, Vril drives the thought wave like a bullet to this mark, hitting the bull's eye with a tremendous impact, and making a powerful impression on the mind of the other person or persons. There are persons whose words seem fairly alive—so vital is their action upon the minds of others—because these persons have powerful Vril personalities or physical magnetism used in connection with their mental currents. They flash out this combined force toward their audiences of many persons, and the latter are fairly lifted off their feet by the power.

Mastering Fear and Anger as a Way to Control the Distribution of Vril

Let us review some simple principles that we have already explored regarding the nature of Vril:

(1) You do not generate Vril. Vril is absorbed through breathing and ingestion of nourishment, food and water. This absorption of Vril is known as Ond, and is the Gift of Odin.

(2) Your body absorbs certain amounts of Vril necessary to survive, but through incorrect living habits, thoughts and feelings, the amount of Vril your body can absorb will decrease, preventing your cells from receiving the necessary Vril to assure good health, causing illness and aging, resulting in premature death.

(3) Through proper living habits and exercises, especially by using the Runes in meditation and chanting, you can increase the amount of Vril that you can absorb.

(4) Using the Runes as a tool within the methodology of Vrilology, you can harness the power of Vril to manifest phenomena of your choosing, transform yourself into a Vril Being, increasing your ability control your destiny.

(5) You need to understand what is meant by the Balder Force, or the possession of Supreme Confidence. Balder knew he was invincible and thus feared nothing. *This is the first principle of the warrior. Self-confidence and fearlessness–the confidence that one can handle any situation that might manifest itself.* To achieve this state of Balder Force, one must master one's fear and anger.

Let us consider the subject for a moment. When you are frightened or angry, you breathe with a different rhythm than when you are calm and peaceful. Each emotion, up and down the scale, has its own appropriate rhythm of breath, which invariably manifests at the same time. Different physical conditions also manifest in correlated breath-rhythms.

If you study the way of the warrior, you will notice in most warrior-societies, the image of the warrior is one of self-control, an individual who speaks little and is a pillar of calm and confidence. We can see this in the Japanese Samurai, the master of oriental martial arts, the American Indian warrior, the Spartan phalanx and Roman legion, as well as the discipline in the soldier of the modern-day army. They are all taught to master their sensations of fear and anger.

You will find that a few moments of anger-breath or fear-breath will result in your experiencing a sensation of anger or fear. Likewise, you will find that the deliberate assumption, on your part, of the breath-rhythm of peace, calm and self-control will be sufficient to induce that particular state of feeling in you.

In this connection, let us remind you that when you are endeavoring to control your temper, and maintain your pose under extreme provocation, you will find that you instinctively strive to control your breath-rhythm, which shows a marked tendency to fly off into a state of rapid panting and gasping. Remember the advice to "count to ten whenever you feel yourself getting angry?" So long as you can maintain your steady controlled rhythm of breath, you will maintain your poise and self-control.

Let us then agree that there is a breath-rhythm which nature uses to restore Vril to the depleted system, after a great demand upon it in the direction of either a strong mental, emotional, or a severe physical strain; and that a deliberate assumption or "acting out" of this particular breath-rhythm will result in your being able to quickly absorb a greatly increased supply of Vril for the purpose of use in personal magnetism.

The Fehu-Isa Stretching Exercise

We will now present a simple exercise to help increase of the flow of Vril through your nervous system, and consciously use it to vitalize your mental powers. This exercise will help Vril to flow more easily through your body and support the previous methods you learned in earlier lessons, designed to increase the absorption and flow of Vril through meditation and chanting. You will be surprised at the increased ease that you have developed by mastering this exercise.

The combination of this Fehu-Isa exercise will not only increase the frequency and strength of the vibratory rate of your life-energy field; others too will notice the difference. You in turn will notice that other persons will be conscious of something in your handshake and touch that surprises them. They will not understand exactly what affects them, but they will be conscious of some strange feeling pervading them. The best plan will be for you to keep your secret to yourself, and to avoid any impression of being out of the ordinary. You wish to create confidence, not fear, and the strange and mysterious causes fear rather than confidence. *So keep your own secrets, and always present a cheerfulness and confidence in all your mannerisms with other persons. This will help others to readily accept your new-found powers, and they will even be drawn to you as if you were a source of light in their otherwise dark and dreary lives.*

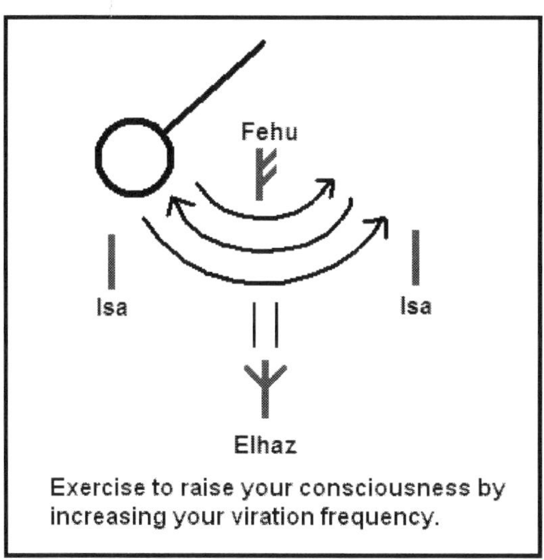

Exercise to raise your consciousness by increasing your viration frequency.

The Rune Fehu has the property of expansion of force, causing energy to expand, while Isa is the Rune that possesses the power to hold together and contract that same force. Together they form a pulsation principle of expansion and contraction, which is at the foundation of the action of stretching one's muscles. This runic force is at the heart of nature's own favorite way of distributing to all parts of the body Vril to be absorbed into the system. It is nature's way of sending vitalizing and invigorating Vril currents to the places where Vril is needed.

This "stretching" is something far more than a manifestation of laziness, weariness, or fatigue. It is an instinctive action resulting from nature's recognition of the need of a fresh supply of Vril. Do not mistake and confuse causes and effects in this matter.

The Fehu-Isa complete stretching exercise is a twofold motion: an extension of the limbs, followed by a tensing or contraction of muscles that draw back in the extended limbs or parts of the body.

Both of these motions are actually forms of "tensing" or contracting the muscles. The extension movements result from the tension or contracting of the opposite set of muscles. The principal muscles of the body are arranged in opposing sets, one being used to push out, and the other to draw in, the limb or portion of the body. When in the process of stretching you first extend and then draw in the limbs, you really are tensing the opposing sets, in order.

Nature's purpose in tensing the opposing muscles seems to be that of "squeezing out" something from the muscles. And that is exactly what it is – a squeezing out of something. Of what? Of the old, stale, weakened Vril energy that produces physical magnetism. Why? To what end? To the end that the supply of fresh, vital, strong currents of Vril energy may rush in to take the place thereof. Here we have the principles of creation in the duality forces of fire and ice, which are represented in the runic forces of Fehu, expansive fire, and Isa, contractive pull of ice.

The nerves themselves and the muscles are kept vitalized and invigorated by the same form of energy, coming from the same source. Moreover, the fresh supply of Vril pouring into the muscles and cells, from the great reservoirs of the Vril stored in your Hamingja, leave the latter more or less depleted, and cause them to call for a fresh adequate supply from the universal source. In short, the stretching process sets into operation the whole machinery of the distribution of the system's supply of Vril, and results in the whole nervous mechanism's being given a new impetus.

The Fehui-Isa principle is the secret of the adept's method of distributing a fresh supply of Vril through the nervous system to all parts of the system, at will, thus rendering himself a veritable dynamo of physical magnetism. The ordinary stretching is simply an elementary form of Vril distribution. This Fehu-Isa principle of stretching is behind the form of calisthenics generally known as "the tensing exercises." In that system you may find the seed of an even more efficient system. The tensing system of calisthenics is taught for the purpose of exercising the muscles, but it has been found to not only develop the muscles, but benefit the entire biological system. This is the result of the Fehu-Isa exercises greatly invigorating the entire system, by distributing Vril throughout the human body.

When performing the stretching exercises, we should move calmly and slowly, almost "lazily", in tensing the muscles, in turn extending and then drawing in, instead of moving vigorously. Movement should be in slow-motion, for in this way there in no depletion of your supply of Vril, but rather, a constant taking in and distribution of Vril from the centers to the parts, and consequently a marked increase in vigor, vitality and vim. The difference can be understood perfectly only when one practices these exercises for oneself. You will note the practitioners of Tai-chi performing such exercises in the same fashion.

Let's begin the exercise:

1) Absorption of Vril is necessary to begin this exercise. So step one is to lie down in a comfortable position, and completely relax your body. Now begin your full or reverse breathing exercise to ensure a ready supply, and free and full distribution, of Vril. Before Vril can be distributed it must first be absorbed, and the breathing exercises are designed to increase the flow of Vril being absorbed by the body.

2) Then perform a short energy generating exercise to cause Vril to freely flow throughout your nervous system. By now in your training, you should be very sensitive to the increased inflow of the Vril during the breath-rhythm exercise, and you will feel the tingling sensations as it courses throughout your body.

Remember, never overdo the exercises, or force yourself to perform them when you do not feel like it. Avoid anything approaching artificiality in the matter.

3) Once you have charged your body with increased Vril energy, still lying on your back, extend your arms upward over your head, to their full extent – stretch them out easily but thoroughly as far as they will go. As you stretch, slowly chant Fehu. Then slowly chant Isa as you slowly pull your arms in. Repeat several times.

4) Stretch the arms out sideways from the body chanting Fehu – and then in as you chant Isa. Do this several times.

5) Stretch the legs in the same way, chanting Fehu, and then chant Isa as you draw them back in. Do this several times.

6) Stretch the neck several times, chanting Fehu, and then contract it chanting Isa.

7) Stretch the hands and fingers, by moving the hands backward and forward from the wrist, clenching and unclenching the fists: opening and closing the fingers. Chant Fehu as you stretch and Isa as you contract.

8) Stretch the feet and toes, in the same general manner as in the case of the hands and fingers, chanting Fehu and Isa.

9) Turn over and lie on your stomach, with your face down on the pillow or floor, and repeat the above exercise in this position. This will bring into play a number of muscles not employed in the former position. Always chant Fehu when you stretch and Isa as you contract.

10) Rise to your feet and stand with your legs spread out, the feet several feet apart, with arms extended upward and outward. This will bring your body into the general shape of the letter "X." Then rise to your toes and stretch upward as if you were trying to touch the ceiling. Chant Fehu as you do, then contract as you chant Isa. Repeat several times.

Upon completion of this exercise you will discover a sensation of rest and renewed strength. It is important to chant Fehu and Isa as you stretch and contract, bring their runic forces into play in the great creative and life-generating process that these two Runes possess in their synthesis. Their runic energy will assist you when you are tensing your muscles, in the act of stretching and then contracting the limbs, helping the process of "squeezing out" the old, worn out, depleted supply of Vril, and absorbing in its place a fresh supply of vigor, vitality and vim from the great reservoirs of the nervous system and Hamingja.

The Sowilo Principle of the Vril Personality

The Vril personality can be summed up with the Rune Sowilo. Sowilo has a dual nature. It is the Sun Rune and personifies Balder, the Son of Odin. Balder is the source of what we refer to as the Balder Force, which is the sense of supreme confidence that one must maintain to ensure the generation and radiance of the Vril personality. Once you are assured of the power that the Vril personality generates, your sense of invincibility grows, because you understand that with a thorough expertise of the use of the Runes, you have the ability to harness Vril and use it to transform the world around you to conform to your desires, which includes causing others to submit to your will.

This sense of invincibility is the confidence that nothing can hurt you. Balder possessed this supreme confidence because his mother, Frigga, convinced everything in the universe to take an oath not to harm her son. The one exception is mistletoe. The implications of this exception have been touched on earlier and will be discussed again later. For now, you need to understand that this sense of supreme confidence, or Balder Force, is represented in the nature of Sowilo as the Rune symbolic of the Sun, as a shield. This sun shield is actually a double Sowilo connected in the center, which forms the swastika. Despite the negative association of the swastika with the Nazis, it is traditionally considered a good luck symbol throughout western history, and still is associated with good luck in the non-Western world, especially among the Hindu and Buddhist cultures. The swastika as a sun shield is a power symbol of protection and acts like a force field in science fiction dramas.

Sowilo as a symbol of the Sun, associated with Balder, is only one aspect of the Rune's nature. The Rune's shape is actually that of a lightning bolt and thus is also associated with Odin's other son, Thor. Thor possesses a hammer, Mjollnir, which he throws as a weapon that destroys anything it strikes. It is often referred to as a thunderbolt, and Thor is the God of Thunder, or Storm God. Unlike Balder, who possesses supreme confidence, and thus is unconcerned about threats, and shines like the sun, radiating supreme confidence, Thor is the personification of the thunderstorm. When he loses his cool, his fury and rage is uncontained. He is the aggressive force that is projected outward.

So you have in Sowilo the nature of the Sun personified by Balder, radiating great energy that makes you untouchable, as well as the power to project outward, sending the power of Vril toward a target as Thor does.

The projection of this Balder Force, which we can describe as the Mjollnir Force, is done by training your mind to use its will to send its Vril-charged thought waves by consciously projecting this physical force just as Thor does when he throws his hammer.

Sowilo equals Thor plus Balder

We want to emphasize that your Vril personality, charged with Vril energy, can consciously project this vital energy in the same way. The projection of this physical magnetism into your personal life energy field or aura, which is actually a personalized field of Vril energy that has been transformed by what is stored within your Orlog, thus taking on a characteristic unique to you, will affect others who come into contact with you. They will get an instant impression of you from the nature of your personal energy field. This is what is meant by your physical magnetism. *It is considered a "physical" phenomenon because people who come into contact with it will feel its effects.*

There really is no great secret formula to master the art of projecting one's physical magnetism by the power of the will. It is actually a very simple procedure, consisting of three steps. The first is acquiring a belief in, or realization of, one's powers to so project the force. The second is the actual willing or commanding the force to be projected. Different methodologies may be used to acquire this skill; therefore the third process is discovering which tradition is best suited for you, based on your own, individual genetic heritage.

Various methodologies reflect the different cultures around the world, which have grown out of the diverse cultures of mankind, and are rooted in the diverse genetic compositions of the many races of humanity. What one must discover is that certain traditions, on how to master this skill, will work better for individuals due to their genetic makeup due to their genetic heritage. *There is no one universal method that will work exceptionally well for everyone. Vrilology is a methodology, rooted in Western tradition, and works exceptionally well for individuals who are of European or Caucasian heritage.*

Belief is a very important aspect of mastering this skill. The will never acts in a direction which the mind believes impossible. It is almost impossible to use this technique to acquire wealth by willing yourself to will the lottery, because deep down in your subconscious, your mind refuses to believe that the odds are in your favor; but you can accept the fact that you can receive reasonable sums of money when you have need of them, and thus, you will receive the correct amounts of wealth as you your needs require. The disbelief acts as a brake on the will – do you see the point? Belief does not necessarily render accomplishment certain, but it removes the barriers of disbelief, the latter preventing any accomplishment by the will. There are many things that we would be able to do if we could only believe that we could do them – but disbelief acts as a brake and a barrier to the efforts of the will. Realization of one's power will often gain half the battle of accomplishment for him.

Exercise: Increase Your Vibrates to Evolve Your Consciousness to a Higher Level of Reality

Here is an exercise to help you increase your level of consciousness. This exercise will cause your level of consciousness to increase so that you can enter the higher states of consciousness, and thus, help yourself evolve into a Vril Being.

Step 1: Enter your Asgard State of Consciousness (Alpha state), which by now should come easily and quickly through the proper way of relaxation, breathing and focusing.

Step 2: Visualize the Rune Isa. Concentrate on Isa. Let its qualities of stillness and ice resonate within your mind. Meditate on Isa for several minutes until your mind is completely still. Feel the power of ice causing contraction to the point where all movement ceases and there is only motionlessness. Now chant Isa nine times, in the long, drawn out method. Feel the power of icy contraction resonating within you every time you chant Isa.

Step 3: Visualize the Rune, Fehu. Let its qualities of movement and fire resonate in your mind. Fehu is the Rune of sending. You can use its power to cause movement. Feel its energy flying away from you, expanding. Now chant Fehu nine times, in the long, drawn out method. Feel the power of fiery expansion resonating within you every time you chant Fehu.

Now you have visualized and absorbed the natures of Isa and Fehu.

Step 4: Begin chanting, not in the long, drawn out method, but by simply reciting the names of the two Runes over and over. It should sound like this: *Isa, Fehu, Isa, Fehu, Isa, Fehu, Isa, Fehu, Isa. . .* As you chant Isa, imagine a pendulum in position to your left. When you chant Fehu, see it swing to your right. Then imagine it stopping as you chant Isa again. Then as you chant Fehu once more, see it swing back to the left. Continue to do this, chanting *Isa, Fehu, Isa, Fehu, Isa*, as the pendulum swings back and forth. As you continue to chant, increase the tempo every few minutes so that you will eventually go faster and faster.

As the pendulum swings back and forth, faster and faster, feel the life-creating energy building up within you from the amalgamation of the icy nature of Isa and the fiery nature of Fehu. Just as it happened at the beginning of time, when the ice of Niflheim and the fire of Musspellheim, amalgamated and caused the formation of life in the form of Ymir, creating the first consciousness, so too feel the powers of Isa and Fehu, merging and causing the evolutionary process building up within you, causing your consciousness to evolve to a state of higher consciousness.

Step 5: As your consciousness evolves, begin to visualize the Rune, Elhaz, and feel its power of evolution rising within you. Imagine Balder rising from the Netherworld to herald in the Golden Age of Gimli within you, and know that you are evolving into a higher state of being—*into a Vril Being.*

An Experiment With the Time and Space

You should perform a simple exercise that should provide you with proof that your mind has the potential to control time and space.

By now you should be able to place your mind into a deep state of Theta. What you are going to do in this exercise is place yourself in such a state while watching the second hand of a clock or watch. You are going to discover that the second hand has stopped. It really is a startling experience and one that you can easily do. But to perform this exercise, you really need to command control over your mind. So, if you have mastered the methods we have given you in previous lessons, you should be able to perform this exercise with no problem.

Step 1. Place a clock or watch with a second hand on a table in front of you. No digital time pieces. It must have a second hand that you can watch move about the face of the clock. Make sure you can easily see the hand. Then, sit in a chair and lean with both elbows on the table if you wish. Make sure you are in a relaxed position.

Step 2. Use your exercise for relaxation. You can close your eyes when you are doing this, if it helps, but you will open your eyes once you have reached complete relaxation and look at the second hand moving around the face of the clock or watch. Concentrate on the way the hand moves about the face of the time piece. Notice its rhythm as it moves. Don't force yourself to do this. It should all be done quite effortlessly.

We now come to the crucial part of the exercise.

Step 3. Remain in your position and close your eyes. Think of a favorite place where you love to be. It can be a real location or an imaginary place, but some place where you will feel at peace and enjoy yourself performing your favorite activity. Here, you need to recall your lessons on visualization. We want you to visualize yourself at your favorite place, performing whatever it is that will bring you great joy and contentment. Don't just imagine it—*visualize it!* If you are at the beach, then feel the sun on your face. Smell the salt air. Feel the sand between your toes. Touch the water. Hear people enjoying themselves, or the sound of seagulls calling to each other. You have to *really feel as if you are there*. Don't just think you are there—be there! Use all your senses. The results will be more effective if you choose a relaxing activity that a hectic one. Lie on the beach, rather then playing a game.

Step 4. When you feel that you have surrendered to the visualization, slowly open your eyes just a bit. *Don't focus on the watch or clock.* Instead, just let your gaze fall on the time piece, as if you are a disinterested observer of the entire affair. If you have followed the instructions correctly, you might notice that the second hand sticks in a few places, slow down, or even stops for a while. If you are very successful, your might even able to stop the second hand for quite a while. For most people, this is a shocking experience. The natural reaction is: "This is impossible!" The moment one feels shocked, the second hand will resume its normal speed. You can perform this experiment over and over, and when you get to the point where you are no longer shocked by the second hand standing still, you will be able to watch with half-open eyes the face of the time piece, while remaining in a meditative state, and keep the second hand from moving for as long as you wish.

Now, you might ask: "What in the name of Asgard, Midgard and Hel is going on?" We believe that while you remained at the table, watching the time piece, your mind went off to the beach, and left the "hardware" unattended. What we mean by the "hardware" is your sensory organs and your brain. While they were processing and producing information, your mind or consciousness, which makes sense of the information, went to the beach. This is an example of remote viewing or out-of-body travel. From the moment the watch stopped to the moment it resumed movement, you were out of your body. Really! In cases where the second hand only slowed down, the observer was split. He was partially on the beach and at the table. But if the second hand stopped completely, it is the same as a camera that was recording a moving image, and then stopped recording, while holding the last bit of data it was recording until it resumed once more. You sometimes notice this happening on digital television. You will be watching a show and then suddenly, the picture freezes for a few seconds. When it resumes, it has skipped forward in time to where the video would be if it had not frozen.

If you have not been successful in your first attempts to freeze the hand of the clock, you might want to experiment with the Rune, Isa. Isa is the Rune of contraction, inertia, and stillness. So when you have entered your favorite place, and reached a state of stillness and peace, you might want to meditate on Isa before opening your eyes. Isa will help you to still your mind.

This little exercise is an example of the potential power that resides within you. Know it! Feel it! And believe it because you have demonstrated it for yourself, and not because someone has convinced you to believe it. This is the essence of Vrilology. It is a religion based on knowledge, and not on faith alone.

Chapter Sixteen: As a Vril Being, You Have the Ability to Transform the World Around You

Our minds have the power to manifest those things we spend a great deal of time daydreaming about. Then why don't these things materialize for most people? The reason is simple–most people spend a great deal more energy thinking about the things *they don't want*. In fact, we dedicate a great deal of energy to the effort of not wanting things. But remember what we said in earlier chapters? The divine forces of the universe do not hear "don't," "not," "no," and other negatives. When you say, "I don't want to be sick," the divine forces hear, "I want to be sick." When you say, "I don't want to be fat," the divine forces hear, "I want to be fat."

You Create More of What You Fight Against

In the world we live in, we spend far too much time fighting against those things we would like to eliminate from our lives and society in general. The time, effort, mental energy and feelings we dedicate toward eliminating something only reinforce those "somethings" in our lives and society. Fighting against something only creates more of it. We create what we focus on. If you are dominated by anger, hatred and bitterness, those emotions will create more of what you are trying to destroy. Your obsessions direct a great deal of emotional energy toward shaping Vril into those things we seek to destroy. The divine powers of the universe do not hear the word "don't." Thus we are creating what we don't want. Karl Jung said, "What you resist persists." When you are concentrating on something, you are creating more of it. Your thoughts about it are drawing more of the same to you.

If you are preoccupied with trying to make the world a better place, but feel totally helpless because all your efforts, time and determination have achieved nothing, and all you have for it is failure, then you have to ask, "Have I been fighting for something, or against something?" If you are honest, you will realize the reason you have failed to make the world around you better is that you have been motivated by the desire to oppose something you consider wrong. Many people think they are for something, but if you ask them what it is they are for, they will begin by telling you what they are against. They will tell you they want to eliminate crime, eliminate drugs, eliminate immorality. Eliminate! Eliminate! Eliminate! But they will never tell you what it is they are fighting *for!* The reason is they don't know what they are fighting for.

You cannot win by only being against things. If you fight against something, you are in effect contributing all your thoughts and feelings to drawing more of it into your life, and you bring more of it into the world around you. Opposing something says, "I don't want this thing because it is bad for me and society in general." But Vril does not hear this. What it does hear is, "I want this thing because it is bad for me and society." "I want to eliminate crime," is heard as, "I want crime." So you continue to draw what you oppose into the world, your negative feelings transforming Vril into exactly what you are trying to fight.

If you have ever been involved in politics, you will then understand that if you want to win, you must have a positive message. The must successful political leaders in history are those who offered their followers a vision of what they want to create. It does not matter if you think that vision good or bad, or if they are sincere about establishing it. What is important is that the leader or leaders of a movement will convince thousands and even millions of people to focus on the creation of that vision. The Twentieth Century had many examples of this method.

When Franklin D. Roosevelt ran for president in 1932, did not travel around the country complaining about how terrible things were during the depression. He traveled from state to state telling listeners how he could turn things around, and how, if they joined with him, they could work together to restore the good times, and make the United States a better place for everyone. *Happy Days Are Here Again* was his campaign song, not *Nobody*

Knows the Troubles I've Seen. That actually was the theme of the Republicans, and their candidate, President Hoover, who lost to Roosevelt.

At the same time, in Germany, we saw the rise of Hitler. However the politically correct regard Hitler today, what he actually campaigned on was how all Germans should unite, put aside their political differences, and work to create a new and better "folk community." He told his listeners pretty much the same thing Roosevelt told his listeners: "Happy days are here again, if only you will vote for me." Millions of Germans believed him and focused on his message of hope. Very little of what he said during his campaign was negative. He seldom mentioned those things he hated, and told the German people that they were superior and could achieve anything, if only they united and worked together. This is pretty much what FDR said at the same time in the United States. And this message is still true. If you want to change the world, you have to concentrate on a positive message, with a positive vision.

By Focusing on Negative Events, You Create More of It

You cannot change the course of events by opposing the changes taking place. You can only fight one idea with another. Everything that happens in the world started with a simple idea. A single thought can move mountains, and the same is true for the course of history. Great changes take place in history because people *believe in something.* It takes only one thought to begin the process. As more and more people turn their thoughts and their feelings toward the realization of that idea, their thoughts give life to the original idea, causing it to grow bigger and bigger, until finally it becomes a wave that sweeps over and transforms society and the world. It becomes reality because we focus our minds on it. But if we turned our minds away from it, it would no longer cause us to act and react. It eventually evaporates and exists only in the pages of dusty history books.

The lesson is simple: *If you want something to happen, or even to stop something from happening, don't focus on stopping what you oppose, but rather think about what you want to happen.* If you support a cause, the cause should support the formation of an ideal. You must dedicate your mind, thoughts, and feelings to the establishment of a positive, forward-moving, and exciting ideal, and not turn your attention toward stopping the establishment of an idea or policy. When you turn your thoughts to eliminating something, you are actually concentrating on that something and contributing toward its establishment, increasing its strength and reinforcing its growth.

There is nothing wrong with understanding what you oppose, because it makes clear in your mind what you desire. But it does not make very good sense to concentrate all your mental and physical energy in opposition to something. You must work toward the establishment of something. You should spend your time and energy on explaining, describing and advocating the idea you seek to propagate. The more you talk about something, the more Vril is being fashioned to materialize it within the reality around you. If you talk in opposition to something, Vril does not hear the negative. So if you are focusing on what you don't want, Vril hears only the subject and gives more energy to making it a reality. Whether you are for or against something, by your focusing on it, that something will become stronger.

If you want to change the world, you must not focus on negative things. Focusing on the negative only brings more of it. Your obsession only strengthens what you seek to eliminate. To be against something is to hate something. Hatred has never been a motivating force for people to give their lives for something. People are willing to surrender themselves, including their lives, for something they love. Before you can make something a reality, you must make people love what you are trying to establish.

Dedicate Your Time and Energy to Creating What You Want

Understand that you are not powerless to make your thought a reality, even if it is something that will manifest itself on the world stage. You have the power to turn each of your thoughts into a building block of a new reality. But you must focus on what you want to happen, not on what you don't want to happen. Concentrate your thoughts and emotional energy on what you want to materialize in the physical realm. You must understand that you have the power within you, within your mind, to make things happen by emitting feelings of love and support toward what you love and want to create.

As you focus on the things you believe to be good and helpful, Vril will fashion itself to make those thoughts a reality. Others will agree with you and begin to think as you, reinforcing the power of Vril to transform your ideals into reality. Feelings of love will bring more of what you love into the world; feelings of hatred will only bring more of what you hate into the world.

Use Kenaz as the Rune to control energy and craft it into an object. It is the Rune of Transformation. You can also use Raidho with Kenaz. Raidho is the Rune of Divine order. Use it to channel what you craft into the right results. Also use Wunjo for the fulfillment of wishes and the realization of true will. Wunjo will create a harmony between you and the world around you so that your desires can be fulfilled. Finally, use Ingwaz to incubate your creation until it finally is released into the real world of Midgard as part of your reality.

Sigil Magic

So what exactly is a sigil? In a nutshell, one tried-and-tested way you can create a sigil is by writing a sentence expressing your deepest desire then turning into a symbolic picture. Then you can fill this picture with energy and forget about it – and wait to see if your goal comes true.

In magical terms, a sigil is a tool – it's a shape you design that tricks your mind into creating a specific effect into your life. Creating sigils to work magic was made popular by mystical artist Austin Osman Spare, in his "The Book Of Pleasure." He said:

"Sigils are… a means of symbolising desire and giving it a form that prevents thought on that particular desire… and allows it free passage to the sub-consciousness."

So what does that actually mean?

The biggest problem with creating magic is your conscious mind, dammit! It's your psychic censor and it keeps telling you what you should think, even if you don't agree with it. The theory goes that if you believe there's no way you can magic a laptop into your life, then of course your magic won't work. Remember, your conscious mind is very powerful at telling you there's simply no logical way you can draw a magical picture that will somehow get you a laptop three weeks later. You have to trick it to let it know who's boss

Making a sigil gets you PAST your conscious mind. The good news is that your subconscious is way more powerful than your everyday common-or-garden consciousness is your subconscious. It will ALWAYS be more powerful, because your conscious mind only works when you tell it to. Your subconscious mind, on the other hand, works ALL THE TIME. If you can tell your subconscious to do something, it will chug away at the problem without you even 'thinking' about it, 100% of the time, and your magic will be far more likely to work.

The theory goes like this: the conscious mind is not directly capable of performing magic (in fact, it inhibits magic), so the subconscious mind must have the magical intent implanted in it somehow it so that it can 'unconsciously' manipulate the magic-steeped world around us to bring about the result.

The method for creating a sigil is simple, creative and generally a lot of fun. It can be done alone, or with a small group of like-minded friends.

Unlike complicated magical rituals, you will need

1) Something to write with. Any normal pen or pencil will work.

2) Blank paper, at least three or four sheets.

3) A comfortable, distraction-free place to work.

4) About 30 minutes, including prep time.

To make our sigil, we're going to do, basically, five things:

1) Write down our desire as a statement of intent

2) Turn it into a picture (a sigil)

3) Simplify that picture and make it look more magical

4) Charge the picture up with magical energy

5) Ground ourselves, forget about the sigil and go and do something else – confident that the sigil is now in our unconscious which is going to do all the magical work for us. Remember, our subconscious understands images and symbols better than anything else, so it's best to send it a symbolic form of our wishes.
Let's make your first sigil:

How to Make a Magical Sigil
1. Create a Statement of Intent. First, write down your desire very clearly, like this:IT IS MY WILL TO BE OFFERED RED FRUIT

Scan the letters and cross out any repeating ones, as follows:

IT xS MY Wxxx xO BE xFxxRxD xxx xxUxx

Which leaves us with the following letters remaining:

ITSMYWOBEFRDU

There. Now you've done the first stage – creating your statement of intent, and simplifying it.

Magical notes: What lies behind creating a statement of intent?

What you've just done is taken a conscious desire and broken it down into something your conscious brain doesn't recognise any more: a meaningless string of letters. The more energy you put into turning your sentence into something unrecognisable, the more you leave your annoying conscious mind behind and hammer the message into your powerful subconscious.

The creation of the Statement of Intent is really important. Austin Osman Spare preceeded all of his magical statements with the prefix "THIS MY WISH…" followed by the description of what he desired. Maybe you don't have to, but it does make the exercise feel more formal and special. You could also use THIS MY INTENT, or THIS MY WILL – whatever works for you.

Also, the statement of intent must be expessed only in positive, not negative terms. The subconscious has the annoying habit of perceiving everything positively. For example, if you want to pass an exam, do not express it as “I will not fail my exam” — the deep mind ignores the “not” and hears this as “I will fail my exam”! Instead, express it as something like “I will pass my exam with flying colours”.

Also, sigil magic is simple and powerful. A good way to begin is to choose some simple, unimportant result — one to which you aren’t personally attached, so your conscious mind doesn’t care what the results are. Like:

IT IS MY WILL TO BE OFFERED RED FRUIT

Such a wish is entirely unimportant, but not something that one runs into every day, so it’s a good test. See how long it takes for the wish to manifest. The practical side of such exercises is that success increases one’s confidence that MAGIC WORKS, which in turn makes success more likely for more important objectives.
There is no way to prove if sigil magic works (or not) except by trying it yourself. Never believe the hype. Create your own. Moving on…

2. TURN YOUR STATEMENT OF INTENT INTO A MAGICAL SIGIL

So far, you’ve got your simplified Statement of Intent: ITSMYWOBEFRDU

You’re now ready to go on to the next stage and turn this string of letters into a picture – your magical sigil.

On your piece of paper, make a basic, rough sketch linking the various letter shapes together, combining some of them as you go along (for example, an “M” is a “W” upside down, “I” is contained in “T”, “F” is part of “E”, “D” sits snugly in “O”, etc.):

Next the image is simplified and refined.

The magical sigil above contains all the letters in “it is my will to be offered red fruit”.

It’s been given extra embellishments to look spooky and distract the mind.

Most homemade sigils look a little spooky or alien – like UFO writing or witchy wall-scratchings. There are no rules as to how

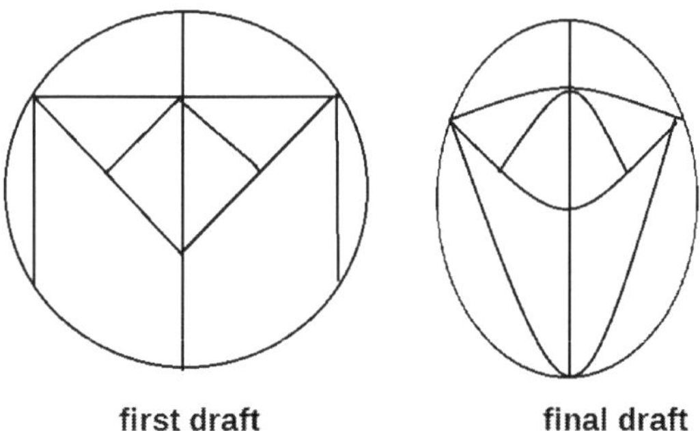

your sigil should look as long as it works for you.

Magical notes: What lies behind turning a statement of intent into a graphical sigil?

Your goal is to make a shape that your mind can easily visualize. You also want it to look artistically impressive and somehow special – like a magical logo. Again, this is for ease of visualisation later. However, what you're aiming for is a design that can be easily recalled by short term-memory, but not by long-term memory – you'll want to forget about the sigil. So too much simplicity is not a good thing. Easy enough to visualise in the ritual, easy enough to forget later on – that's the key to a good sigil.

3. CHARGING THE SIGIL

Charging the sigil means infusing it with your energy. You have to get yourself to a point where you are full of energy but not really thinking anything, and then pour this energy into your sigil. There are several good ways to charge your sigil:

a) Meditation

The simplest form of meditation is to hold the image of the sigil in front of your eyes and stare intently at it at the peak of gnosis and, to use Spare's description, 'drink it into the mind'. It's really effective if you draw the image on a wall mirror (with a medium that can be washed off) and stare at it. In effect you will also be staring into your own eyes by making sure the image you drew on the mirror is over your eyes. Try to get into a state of "not-thinking" but at the same time obsessively concentrating on the image of the sigil to the exclusion of everything else. Not the meaning of the sigil, but simply the graphic image itself as pure abstract, unconnected to any meaning – a picture and nothing more.

b) Masturbation

We're not joking. Masturbate while visualising the sigil in your mind's eye. With the masturbation method you're likelyto get yourself to a point when you're full of energy and no thought, ie. orgasm. Hurrah! At the point of orgasm, visualise the sigil becoming big and bright and then exploding/disintegrating into nothingness. That's it! Sigil charged!

c) Wild dancing

If you don't like masturbating but do like dancing, pour yourself into wild wanton dancing – leap everywhere, go wild, spin round and round, get out of breath – it doesn't even have to be to music. You just have to get to a point where you feel full of adrenalin and power and tingly and aren't really thinking anything. Then visualise the sigil in your mind's, eye, see it becoming big and bright and then let it explode/disintegrate into nothingness. And stop dancing.

d) Laughter

Stare at the sigil and laugh. Working yourself up into a real stomach-aching laughter.

e) Holding your breath.

Once again stare at the sigil and hold your breath. Place you hands over your mouth and nose so you will be completely cut off from any air. Hold your breath while staring long and hard at the sigil while your mind is a blank. Do it until you can't hold your breath any more and you begin to feel light-headed. The take a breath right before you feel you are going to pass out.

4. GROUND YOURSELF

Destroy the sigil (for example, burn the bit of paper that it's on). Now do something completely different. Do the washing up. Go for a bike ride. Do something completely grounded in reality. The sigil is over, done with. You don't care any more. Your subconscious might care (the bit that's still doing the magic) but you and your conscious mind are now totally uninterested.

5. FORGET ABOUT IT

Finally, it's important to separate yourself from the magical ritual you've just done. Don't do any meditation, other magical operations, or talk about the working with anyone. At least, not the first time you do a sigil – you need to find out what works for you. The idea is to shut the doors to the subconscious. It also keeps it from easily floating back into the conscious mind until the short term memory dumps it, which according to psychologists takes about three hours.

So just sit back, get on with life, and in a few days or weeks, you'll probably pass your exam, or be given a delicious piece of fruit.

Congratulations! You just made a sigil!

You Can Accept the Unlimited Supply of Vril to Create Whatever it is You Want

The universe is your plaything. Sounds egoistic? So what? You have the power to make the Vril-filled universe give you everything you desire. The universe is more than willing to oblige. Know that you can use Vril to make what you desire a reality. You have only to align yourself with the positive forces that are the Gods, creating and maintaining order in the universe, and your thoughts will be transformed into blueprints that the Gods will incorporate into their design to maintain that order. The Gods offer all things to everyone through the law of cause and effect, but for you to make this happen, you have to understand the nature of the universe, the role the Gods play in maintaining its order, and how Vril is the means by which that order is manifest.

You have the power to experience only what you want. There is no reason for you to be a slave to events you think are beyond your control. Vril fills an infinite universe, and thus there is an infinite supply of Vril. Once you accept this, you know that the abundance you seek is infinite. There are no limits to what you can achieve if you know how to use Vril to transform your dreams into reality. Everyone has the ability to tap into this endless source of power. The powers that rule the world have known this for thousands of years, and have been working at this process behind closed doors.

A group known as Lucian's Trust has members across the world meet at a certain time on a certain day and meditate on the changes they want to manifest. They are not alone. Every power in the world works at this process. The Freemasons, the Catholic Church, the Muslims, the Buddhists, the political left, Satanists—everyone who understands how to use Vril uses it to work at making their vision of the world a reality. We've already seen in Chapter One how the Bohemian Grove members pool their mental powers to harness Vril and turn it into the reality that will guide the course of history and create the reality that they desire. This is not a bunch of nuts. They are who rule the world. They run the houses of worship you worship at. They control television and radio, produce the movies you watch, write the news you read, and teach your children in the schools and universities. They are the politicians you elect and trust with the power to run this country. They are the military leaders who run our armed forces and fight our wars. They are the most successful people in the United States, and the most successful people throughout the world are doing the same.

There is an old saying, "If you want to be successful, do what successful people do."

To align yourself with the Divine Powers of the Gods, use the Rune Elhaz. This is the Valkyrie Rune. The Valkyries are agents of communication between you and the Gods. The shape of the Rune is one which we take up when we wish to communicate with the Gods. It is the Rune of linking Midgard with Asgard. Also use Eihwaz, the Rune of communication between the various realms of the Yggdrasill. Finally you should use Gebo, the Rune of Exchanged Gifts or union, in this case between you and the Gods.

Your Defined and Held Mental Attitude of Yourself and the Outer World

The process of transforming the physical world you live and play out your life within is the result of two coordinated manifestations of mental power, the first of which was "the holding of ideas within your mind until your life energy field is charged with the vibrations of the particular mental states." This can be done by using the correct Rune or combination of Runes. Let us now consider what are these "certain mental states" which are to be held.

In the first place, these "mental states" are not so much any set of particular thoughts, *but rather are stated mental attitudes of oneself in relation to your outer world.* Your firmly held and defined mental attitude will impress itself upon everything in the objective world you come into contact with, and the Runes you use will help the process. Even your physical appearance and persona will conform to this state of mind; your voice, the way you walk and your general appearance all grow to reflect this inner state of mind you possess. Moreover, your mental atmosphere becomes so charged with certain vibrations, that those who come in contact with you will actually feel your mental attitude reflected in your personal life-energy field and adjust themselves to it.

Your life energy field will be charged with this mental attitude you hold of yourself, defining your persona and affecting everyone and everything you come into contact with, and it will be composed of the variety of beliefs, feelings, thoughts and actions that you have stored within your Orlog. In most individuals, what is stored in their Orlog will prevent their mental attitude from manifesting a forceful character. This is why it is so important to use Nauthiz to bend your Wyrd, and use other Runes to refashion it into what you desire.

But in the case of the strong individuals, it will be found that there is always a strong fixed mental attitude – a strong desire which colors all thoughts; a powerful ambition which gives tone to all the rest; or a firm resolve which fires the entire mental character. This strong vibration is carried out into the personal life-energy field, where its influence is felt, and men react thereto.

Simply stated, mental attitudes can be divided into four classes–positive and negative and alpha and beta.

Let us examine just what we mean by positives and negatives, alpha and beta attitudes by listing some of their attributes.

Positive: courage, masterfulness, dynamic thought, self-esteem, comradeship, openness, generosity, helpfulness.

Negative: arrogance, criticism, doubting, jealousy, vanity, fickleness, vindictiveness and sarcasm.

Alpha: activity, initiative, assertiveness, continuity, forcefulness, taking charge, being outgoing.

Beta: self-distrust, fear, slavishness, waiting for orders, sluggishness, static thought, withdrawal, unreliability.

This list might be extended much further, but I think that you will have caught the idea by this time. Run over the list of the strong positive qualities of the strong men of your acquaintance and endeavor to reproduce them in you. Run over the list of weak, negative qualities of the weak persons you know – and endeavor to "cut them out" of your mental attitudes.

Mental attitude resembles yeast, in the sense that if you insert a single bit of the ferment in your mind, it will begin to grow, until it finally fills your entire mind. It tends to reproduce itself and color all your other thoughts. This is true of both desirable and undesirable mental ideas, but – and remember this well – here is a most hopeful and encouraging fact: a positive idea will tend to kill a negative one, and the alpha mental state will outshine the beta mental state; so you see Nature is fighting on your side. The best way to kill and destroy negative mental ideas and the beta attitudes is to plant a good crop of positive and alpha in their places, and then encourage the fight; all the negative and beta will go under surely. It is like pouring fresh water into a basin of dirty water – in time the water will become clear; or, again, like flooding a room with sunshine – the darkness will be destroyed.

The second manifestation of mental power is: "The conscious projection of the mental current from the brain centers, by the action of the will of the individual."

There are actually two forms of this second manifestation of conscious projection:(1) the projection into the personal atmosphere with the intended purpose of influencing everyone who comes into contact with you; and (2) the specific projection of a direct current into the mind of another individual, for the purpose of direct influence upon such person.

Most people color their individual life energy field by the character of their mental states without being aware of what is taking place. The intensity of their force depends upon the degree of mental activity of the person. The person of inactive thought, ideas or feeling will lack almost all intensity, while the person of the active mind will display a marked degree of intensity compared to the former group. These two categories of individuals makes up most of humanity.

There also is a small class of individuals who consciously work to develop one's life-energy field. This strong interest really combines the two elements of feeling and attention, respectively. Feeling is a strong mental element, and attention is a direct application of the will. While they might not fully understand the nature of the Orlog, these persons have awareness that their obsessions, which colors their energy field, will affect anyone who comes into contact with them. They also possess some understanding of how to project their thoughts and feelings into the minds of others. It follows that such persons must strongly project their mental states into their personal atmosphere, although unconscious of the same, and without a deliberate employment of the will for this purpose.

The strongest and most powerful effect is produced by those individuals who understand the process, and who consciously and deliberately project their thought into their personal atmosphere, where it joins and is vitalized by their physical magnetism, so that its full effect is manifested upon those who may come within its field of influence. In this category we place the Vril Being.

Successfully projecting thought-color and power into your life-energy field is identical to success at projecting your will into the mind of other individuals by harnessing the power of Vril. To succeed you must: (1) believe in your power to so project; and (2) actually project your will. The use of the will in the matter of projection consists of the actual willing or commanding of the thing itself. Remember what Yoda said to Luke Skywalker? "Don't try, do!" The mental currents are very obedient to the will, and in fact depend almost entirely upon the will for power to move and act. And do not forget this, for it is important: *The will is moved largely by desire. If you doubt your ability, your doubt will cancel your desire.*

If you strongly desire that your personal atmosphere be colored by your thought currents, and at the same time picture the thought currents flowing out and filling your life energy field, you will have little left to do in the direction of the conscious use of the will. *Remember that your thought currents are actually currents of Vril energy colored by your thoughts, which are in turn colored by what is stored in your Orlog. What is stored in your Orlog is empowered and charged with Vril energy and thus become powerful desires that can and will dominate your thought process. This is why it is so important to learn the methodology of bending or cleansing the things stored there so they do not control your thoughts.*

Super-Charged Megin Currents

In previous chapters we examined how you can transform Vril energy into Megin, your personal supply of Luck. We also explored how Vril energy enters your body, moving along the axis of your spinal cord to the two lower Hvels, Niflheim and Musspellheim, and then moves back up, passing through the other seven Hvels, incorporating the different quality-transforming natures of each Hvel until it reaches your brain. From your brain, it once again moves down your spinal cord, this time channeling itself through your nervous system into every corner of your spirito-physical body. You also learned how to raise your energy levels, to charge your body with Vril energy, causing it to rush up and down your body, its conductor.

What we need to remember is that Vril will be filtered through your Orlog, that part of your Soul where all your feelings, thoughts and actions, as well as what you have inherited from your ancestral stream, are stored. This is fundamentally important if you wish to understand how your individual life energy field is colored. We have explained how you can cleanse your Orlog by using Nauthiz, and thus bend your Wyrd. This is accomplished by controlling what your mind obsesses on, which will affect your projection of personal magnetism, which is super-charged Megin.

The individual's supply of super-charged Megin is formed by a combination of his physical and mental force, which tends to run in currents, and is transmitted in waves. The life energy field or aura of the person is, in fact, composed of many waves of Megin, circling around the confines of his aura, a constant wave-like motion being maintained, and a rapid rate of vibration always being manifested.

It is these waves of Megin which, when coming in contact with the mind of other persons, set up a corresponding rate of vibration there, and thus produce a mental state in them, corresponding to that of the mind of the person sending forth the Megin.

You should keep your life-energy field well charged at all times, by performing the exercise for transforming Vril into Megin, and then projecting your supply of Megin into your life-energy field at least several times during the week. No special number of times is absolutely necessary. You can perform the exercise once a day or several times a week. You might also use the shortened version of the exercise, using only the Runes Fehu, Uruz and Elhaz, to quickly recharge your supply of Megin when you feel depleted. You should use your own judgment in this matter. You will soon learn to feel when your aura is weak, and when it is strong. These things come to one by practice and actual experience. You will soon learn what it is to "feel" the condition of your Hamingja, just as you now feel heat or humidity.

Whenever a situation arises where you are about to come into contact with others whom you wish to influence, or who may want to influence you, you should charge yourself well with Megin. If you have the time, perform the long version of transforming Vril into Megin. This will assure that you have a large supply of Megin for you to project into your personal life energy field, which will thus charge your aura making it strong and positive, instead of weak and negative. The principal thing in battle is to be fully prepared for any emergency, and this rule is applicable to the case of the uses of Megin as a form of personal magnetism in your dealing with other persons.

The currents of Megin not only constantly flow about, within the confines of your life-energy field, but also often push outward toward other persons who attract your attention. In such cases, the aura seems to stretch out toward the other persons, and even to envelop them in its folds. You should understand that this is an involuntary action of the Megin, and not a conscious or deliberate projection of the currents of Megin from your mind to the other mind. There is an almost automatic action of the Megin charged life-energy field in the way just stated, when another person arouses your interest or attention.

This phenomenon is a non-deliberate action of the will, or an automatic action. The will is called into operation the moment the attention is attracted. In fact, the attention is a positive act of the will, and, consequently, the will sets into motion the Megin currents in the direction of the object of attention. This phenomenon automatically occurs whenever you converse with another person, or address a public assembly. You attention is concentrated on others, and your mind subconsciously begins projecting in their direction a series of currents of super-charged Megin, the vibrations of which must affect them unless their own vibrations are of a more positive nature. Most individuals possessing a great personal force, because they either consciously or unconsciously possess the ability to generate and project their Megin, can make their field of personal magnetism felt by all who come into contact with them. But most of these individuals make little use of a technique known as the "direct flash."

The Direct Flash Technique

The direct flash projects a mental command backed up by a ample supply of Megin for the purpose of extracting a positive response from others. *It involves holding a command within your mind, accompanied by a mental picture of a desired action you wish another person, or persons, to perform. Once you have formed in your mind this image of what you want to manifest, you charge it with a supply of Megin and this discharge a deliberate flash by the power of your will.* You are consciously projecting a discharged flash, like a spark of personal electricity, into the aura of another individual, or of particular persons, or into the atmosphere of a crowd of people.

The key to the "direct flash" consists of the deliberate action of the will in projecting or "flashing" into the mind of another person a certain direct statement or command, backed up by a powerful current of Megin. Here a few exercises you can employ in developing your powers.

Exercise One:

Stand before your mirror and gaze positively and firmly at your own image, just as you would gaze toward another person. In fact, you must imagine that you are really gazing at another person. Then, send that imaginary person – pictured by your reflected image – the message: "I am stronger than you!"

By now you should be familiar with the principle of employing the power of your will so that you are not merely thinking or saying the words of the command, but actually willing the command, just as you would will the raising of your hand. You should have cultivated this power of willing, and truly believe you have the power to use your will to make things happen. When you go to sleep at night, you know that the sun will come up in the morning. You do not have to want it to or hope it will. You simply know it will, and then you go to sleep, giving it no more thought because *it will happen!* This faith in what is reality is what you must cultivate in your ability to make things happen by the power of your will. Once you know something will happen, you no longer have to give it so much thought.

In sending the message, "I am stronger than you," you must accompany the effort of the will (by which you send forth the thought-command) with a strong mental conviction that you are stronger than him, and also with the belief that he will be impressed by this fact and will accept your statement, just as surely as the sun will rise in the morning. You must get yourself into the mental attitude of demanding that he accept your statement, not that you merely request him to do so. In this form of influencing there is no such thing as "requesting" – it is all a matter of "insistent command" – do not forget this. Once again we refer to Yoda—"Do! Do not try! Do or do not!"

When you command, you take the first place for yourself, and push the other person into the second. In practicing before your mirror, remember this, and endeavor to raise yourself into the first position. You will know when you have done this, by the peculiar feeling of superior magnetic strength that you will experience.

Once you have mastered this principle, you are in a position to practice the next stage of the exercise before the mirror. You might be anxious to try your power on other persons, but before you proceed, make sure you have thoroughly mastered the mechanism of direct flash before the mirror, and only then will you will be ready to begin practicing on real people.

Exercise Two:

Surely you have been employing many of the techniques you have learned in this training program on other people by now, so practicing this exercise on real persons should not be new to you. You will want to employ the runic energies of Laguz for psychically influencing others, and Fehu for its sending power.

This next exercise is very simple. We want you to cause a person who is walking ahead of you, on the street, to turn around as if he had heard some one call out to him by name.

As you walk for some little distance behind theanother person, whether on the street or in a park or other public place, concentrate your fixed attention on the person, gazing at the lower back part of his head. Visualize the Rune Laguz there and then, employing the runic energy of Fehu, sending him first a strong flash of Megin force, this being followed by the "direct flash" command, "Hey you! Turn around," just as if you were actually calling out aloud to him. You may even whisper the words so softly that no one else can hear them; this may help you to put force into the command at first, but you will soon outgrow the need of the same. At the time you send the flash command, you must actually WILL that the person to turn around in your direction. Put all the magnetic force within you into this effort.

Sometimes the other person will turn his head almost at once, and look inquiringly behind him in your direction. But in most cases, he will be apt to first grow uneasy and restless, and begin by glancing from side to side, as if looking for someone. Eventually, he will almost (but not quite) turn his head around. He will finally glance backward somewhat furtively and suspiciously. No two persons act precisely alike in this respect, and furthermore, the same person will act differently under different conditions. There are certain times at which the conditions seem to be more favorable than at others, for various reasons, as you will discover for yourself.

You will find that the best results will be obtained while the other person is proceeding idly along, without his attention being directed particularly in any direction.

The mind is more open to outside influences when its attention is not fixed on a particular task. This is the result of an

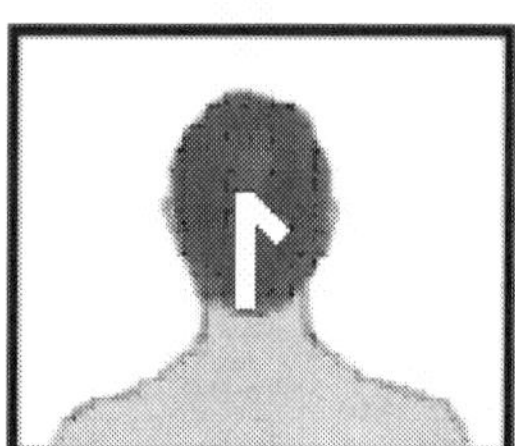

Visualizing Laguz on the back of subject's head.

established rule of psychology, and will be found to be operative in all cases, as for instance, if you call a person when he is preoccupied with a deep thought, he will probably not hear you call him, though under other conditions he would turn readily. This exercise should work well when people are walking because when you walk, your mind has actually slipped into the Alpha state, and thus, it is functioning on a higher level of consciousness, which makes it more readily susceptible to the psychic influence of the runic energy of Laguz.

Exercise Three:

You can perform this exercise in any crowded location, such as a movie theater, church, or any place people are sitting in rows. You begin by fixing your mental gaze at the lower back of the head of some person sitting in front of you. Once again employ the Runes Laguz and Fehu, and then send him the "direct flash" command: "Hey, you! Turn around and look at me!" Use all the Megin force within you, putting the force of your will behind the command.

You will notice the same peculiar result as in the preceding exercise--the fidgeting in the seat, the uneasiness and restlessness, the final quick turn of the head in your direction, followed by the confused expression of countenance. In both of these cases, you should maintain a calm, uninterested gaze ahead, apparently not noticing the person. It is not well to have persons get the idea that you are experimenting upon them, any time. There is no power so potent as the silent, reserved power. So keep your own counsel, and do not scatter and weaken your force by talking about it to others - far less by boasting about it.

The Direct Command

Once you have acquired the technique of the "direct flash," you should be able to manifest what is known as "the direct command" without much additional instruction.

By "the direct command" you will flash a direct command or demand into the mind of another person, backed up by the concentrated runic forces. The "direct command" is really a high form of the "direct flash," and is the method whereby the latter may be used to the highest degree of effectiveness.

In the "direct command" you flash your command to the mind of the other person, mentally, of course, but in exactly the same way that you would make an actual command by spoken words. You form the words of the command in your mind, carrying with it as strong a mental picture as you can create, backed up by the runic forces of:

Laguz (molding Vrilic substance into psychic patterns),

Kenaz (harnessing and controlling the Vrilic forces),

Raidho (channeling the power along the correct path),

Thurisaz (the projection of focused power to break resistance),

Fehu (sending directed expansive force), and

Ansuz (release of mental fetters thru ecstatic force.)

You then mentally flash the command to the other person with as much magnetic force as you can muster.

Test of Wills

The method taught here to develop your personal magnetism is governed by the universal fact that there are various

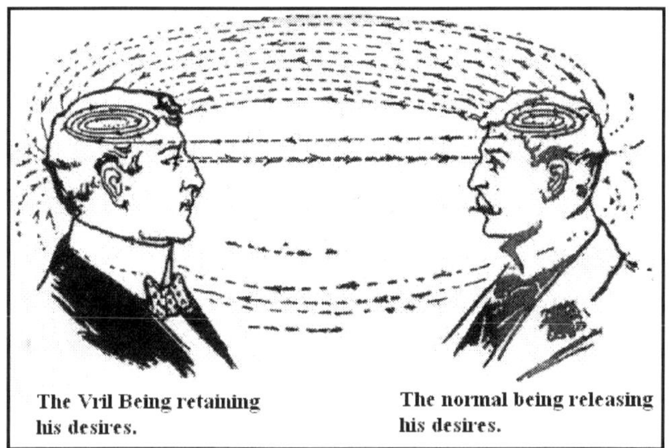
The Vril Being retaining his desires. The normal being releasing his desires.

degrees of power, and that, all else being equal, the stronger power will prevail over the weaker. It is true that the individual, by a superior knowledge of the science of defense and offense, may often triumph over a superior degree of strength in the other person. This fact is as true of personal magnetism as it is of physical strength. The skilled Vril Being may overcome his stronger adversary, just as the skilled boxer may overcome a stronger man, or a skilled fencer may disarm and defeat a much stronger opponent.

Many traditions speak of the "test of will," or the power to command others. Yet what is this will power, which influences others? What is it that makes us accept, and adopt too, the advice of one person, while precisely the same advice from another has been rejected? Is it the weight or force of will, which insensibly influences us, the force of will behind the advice? That is what it is! The person who thus forces his or her advice upon us has no more power to enforce it than others; but all the same we do as requested. We accept from one what we reject from another. The reason is that one person has a greater command to harness Vril and transform it into Megin, that special something that empowers his charm, personality, charisma or personal magnetism, which eliminates barriers in the psyche of others, causing their mental resistance to melt away just as surely as the warming rays of the spring-time sun melt the icy snow of winter.

This is of exceptional importance. The Vril Being does not force others to bend to his will. He extends his super-charged Megin outward, into the life energy fields of those who come into contact with him. They in turn are seduced by the force of his super-charged Megin and willingly follow his lead because "it feels right!" Others want to accommodate themselves to the Vril Being, for they feel energized in his or her presence.

Note the individual who possesses knowledge or natural talent to harness Vril in greater quantity than others, and to transform it into Megin to empower his will with personal magnetism. There may be abler men, cleverer men; but it is this one who can, by this subtle power, make other men obey him, not through coercion but through seduction. This type of persuasion is achieved by extending your energy field outward, giving energy to others, which cause them to feel a "high" from the super-charged energy that they are receiving. This has the opposite effect of someone that forces others to bend to his or her will. They are taking energy from them, weakening their ability to resist and thus causing them to feel defeated. Their submission is only temporary, until they find the power to resist.

Corporeal Magnetism

There is another way of influencing others through the use of Megin-powered personal magnetism. It is the subject of what may be called "corporeal" magnetism. By "corporeal' is meant, "pertaining to the body." We use the term "corporeal magnetism" to indicate and designate the conveyance of Megin by means of physical contact, as, for instance, by the touch of the hands, lips, tongue, feet and genitalia.

Corporeal magnetism is the projection of Vril-charged Megin to another person over the channels of the nervous system of both persons, instead of through the ether as in the case of ordinary projection.

Through corporeal magnetism, not only are the healing treatments given by the use of the hands. Vril passes over the nervous system of the healer, making the leap between the finger-tips and the body of the other person. Thru this process, something more than just the healing energy is passed from one person to another.

In "corporeal magnetism" a "mental force" is passed from one person to another. This transmission of energy from one individual to another is felt physically. A simple example is the handshake. The handshake often conveys the strongest kind of personal magnetism. In the touch of the hand is often found the strongest kind of emotional vibrations. This is the power behind the sensation of "touching." As we already mentioned, this power of touching, in which corporeal magnetism is transmitted from person to person, is most effective through the physical contact of hands, feet, lips, tongues and sexual organs.

In the kiss, especially if the tongues are used, there is often to be found the most active form of emotional vibrations, as almost everyone knows. The transmission of corporeal magnetism is most effective through sexual contact, where all these physical means of transmission of this form of energy are employed. In short, by bodily contact there may often be conveyed the most wonderful or dangerous forms of sexual magnetism.

Powerful sexual emotions are often aroused by a kiss, or touch of the cheek, or even the holding of hands. The holding of hands, the thoughtless kiss, pressure of the cheek, the physical embrace, or close physical contact, all afford and furnish a "direct line" for the passage of this sexually charged Vril energy through corporeal channels. It is possible, by close physical contact, to convey your emotional vibration to a member of the opposite sex, and use this power to seduce the person who is the object of your sexual desire by arousing reciprocal vibrations. In ritual sexual magic between two willing partners, who share deep emotional bonds of mutual love, the individuals involved will reach heights of magical bliss during orgasm that some claim, and we agree, permit the practitioners to reach a level of consciousness that is the equivalent to that in which the Gods of the Vanir and Aesir exist.

You have also probably noticed that many individuals whose business it is to influence you in any direction, such as politicians, preachers, promoters, salesmen, etc., have a habit of placing their hands upon your shoulders, during the conversation – or laying their hand lightly on your arm while speaking to you – in some cases, giving you a final pat on the back as they urge you to "sign right here, and close the deal." Have you realized that this is a form of corporal magnetism, and that it is often very effective?

The Balder Force

The ultimate goal of evolving into a Vril Being is to manifest the Balder Force within you. As a Vril Being, you radiate this Balder Force, rendering you virtually, though not entirely, invincible, for even though Balder was untouchable, even he could be killed, and was killed, through the use of mistletoe, the one thing in all the universe that did not take the oath never to harm him. We need to explore the meaning of this myth to understand the Balder Force and the nature of Vril Beings.

Balder is the Son of Odin and Frigga. He tells his mother he has a dream that he will die, and Frigga then causes everything in the universe to take an oath never to harm her son, but overlooks mistletoe. In celebration of Balder's invincibility, each morning the Gods gather on the fields of Asgard and take turns throwing their weapons at Balder. But because of his invincibility, none of the weapons can harm him. Everyone rejoices because so long as Balder lives, Ragnarok, the end of the universe and the death of the Gods, will never take place.

But not everyone rejoices. There is one who hates Balder. He is Loki, the great "corrupter" from within. Loki is a Fire Giant who convinces Odin to take him into Asgard and live among the Gods. He even becomes blood-brother to Odin. But as times goes on his influence in Asgard is that of corrupting their divinity.

Loki convinces Balder's twin brother, Hoder, to take part in the games. Hoder has refrained from doing so because he is blind and has no weapon to throw at Balder. Loki fashions a dart from mistletoe and gives it to Hoder. He leads him to the field and helps him aim the dart at Balder, and throws it. But instead of harmlessly falling to the ground, the dart strikes Balder, killing him. Loki has fashioned a poison dart. Mistletoe is a powerful herb from which one can make either a love potion or poison.

This story is significant. Balder is Odin's instrument of his rebirth, and the rebirth of the Gods after Ragnarok. *It is through Balder's death that he survives Ragnarok, because he is in Hel, the Netherworld, when it takes place. Balder represents the purity and light of the Gods. He is the embodiment of the secret that is Vrilology, which is the process by which we can awaken the Gods that dwell within us, filling us with their power and essence, transforming us into Vril Beings. It is this establishment of the Balder Force within us that is the creation of the Golden Age of Gimli. Gimli is not some mythical paradise, but a state of being within us.*

Hoder, Balder's twin brother, is blind. He represents the darkness of ignorance. It is this state of being that we are born into, and live our lives, ignorant of our true heritage as the Children of the Gods. While in this state of ignorance, we can be tricked by Loki, the agent of Chaos, into living chaotic lives.

Mistletoe represents a poisoned form of love, which is perverted and thus will lead us away from living a life of pure love. Balder represents the true, pure LOVE FORCE. It is this Love Force that makes us invincible. It is a state of being in which we hate no one, including ourselves. We know of our divinity and this makes us invincible. Once you KNOW you are invincible, because of your knowledge of how to harness and control Vril, you live in a state of bliss. Once you have achieved this state, which is referred to as both the BALDER FORCE and BALDER RISEN, you become the pillar or axis of a new realm in Midgard which is Gimli.

The runic formula for this state of being is Elhaz, Sowilo and Tiwaz.

Elhaz is the Rune of Balder Rising, the rebirth of Balder within you. It is the Life Rune and it represents you as a student, studying Vrilology. It is the Valkyrie, who is your instrument for communication with the Gods, embodying the power of protection. It is the means by which you become a divine instrument, and causes an awakening of your Higher Self within.

Sowilo is the Rune of Success, embodying the power of both the Sun (Balder) and Lightning (Thor). Its heat (supreme knowledge of Vrilology) melts the inertia and static existence in a state of ignorance (Isa or ice). It is a surge of action, of potential elemental force and divine thunderbolt. Its powers of the sun form a protecting shield around you, making you invincible, while its lightning force gives you the power to destroy all who try to harm you.

Sowilo is a powerful protection and offensive Rune. It is shaped like a lightning bolt, which represents the aggressive force personified by Thor, who throws his hammer, Mjollnir, which is in turn symbolic of the thunderbolt. Sowilo also represents the Sun, and Balder is the Sun God. As the Sun, Sowilo is protection and the defensive force, representing the invincibility possessed by Balder. When you whirl Sowilo, it takes on the appearance of two Sowilo Runes forming a whirling Swastika. We can create a powerful Runic symbol of the Swastika representing the shield, and a lightning bolt Sowilo projecting out from the center, where the two Sowilo Runes are joined. This symbol is a form of Helm of Awe, which is also a powerful protection symbol.

Tiwaz is the Rune of Social Order. It is the Rune of Victory. Its power fills you with a sense of self-sacrifice, leadership, authority, valor in battle, and social harmony, and is personified by the God Tyr, who sacrificed his right hand so the Gods could fetter Fenrir, representing Chaos.

Elhaz is Rune # 15, whose digits add up to 6 (1+5=6). Sowilo is Rune # 16, which adds up to 7 (1+6=7), and Tiwaz is Rune # 17, which adds up to 8 (1+7=8). If we then compute 6+7+8, we get 21, whose digits sum to 3 (2+1=3). Three is the divine number of Odin, Vili and Ve, who slaughtered Ymir, representing uncontrolled Vril or Chaos, and created Order from his parts. Thus we have within the three Runes of Elhaz, Sowilo and Tiwaz the Order-giving power of Odin, Vili and Ve, and the means to triumph over Chaos.

Projecting the Power of Self-defense as a Vril Being

As a Vril Being you will gradually develop a power within yourself that will give you an advantage over most people whom you come in contact with. Still, there are always the very strong individuals to be reckoned with, and this is why you need to learn how to disperse and dissipate the personal magnetism of such persons. The defensive methodology that we provide you is far simpler than you would think at first, but you must understand that if you are to master the technique, you must first learn how to project effectively.

The secret is this: In defending oneself against projection by another in any or all of its forms, you have but to project toward the other person a strong denial of his power to influence, affect, or master you. That is the whole thing in a nutshell. Of course, you must understand that you need to master how to energize yourself, raise your levels of Vril energy, form a symbiotic relationship with Gods who will assist your evolution, and master the principles of Vrilology that are laid out in this book.

But, for now, we want to remind you of the very important fact that in this denial you do not really destroy or lessen the power of the other person. You only neutralize his magnetism so far as it affects yourself, or those whom you wish to protect. In other words, instead of destroying his weapons, you merely turn them aside, and cause them to glance off, leaving you unharmed. This is what we mean by the Balder Force.

By regularly reinforcing your personal energy field with large quantities of Megin, produced by the increased flow of Vril into your spirito-physical body, you will render yourself immune not only from the direct flash, and direct demand or command, of others, no matter how strong they may be; but also from the general contagion of the mental atmosphere or auras of others. By proper concentrated effort along these lines, you may render yourself absolutely immune from the force of the personal magnetism of others, if you so desire. Or if you prefer, you may shut out only certain individuals from your field, and allow the beneficial magnetism of others to enter it. In truth, you are your own master, if you but exert your power.

There is of course the other plan of fighting aggressive magnetism with aggressive magnetism – this is the real magnetic duel in its plain form, and may be used when desired. But if you merely wish to repel the aggression of others, you have but to use the defensive plan of the denial, as I have just told you.

In forming the mental statement which accompanies all forms of the use of mental magnetism, as you have seen, you merely express (mentally) in a few, strong positive words, the idea you wish to reach the other person's mind. Well, so it is in the case of magnetic self-defense. You simply mentally state in a few strong words that you deny the power of the other person. You will find, as you experiment, that in the very words "I deny," there is a mighty dynamic power of defense. It is the mental idea behind these words which, figuratively, wipes out of existence the other person's magnetism, at least so far as you, yourself, are concerned. It is the great shield of defense. Let the full meaning of the word “deny” enter into your mind – you will find it contains a new meaning and strength, when considered in this connection.

This defensive process merely enables you to throw off, and render yourself immune from, the aggressive intent of others, and does not enable you to master them or to compel them to do your bidding. In order to accomplish the latter, you must beat down the guard of the other person; protect yourself at the same time; and then carry the day by a direct Vrilic assault upon him. You can do these things if your opponent fights you with the weapons of aggressive magnetism only, but if he denies your power, he is immune, and you cannot affect him; just as if you deny his power, you are immune – in case both deny, then the battle is drawn, and neither win. The denial is not a weapon of aggressiveness – it is merely the shield of defense. Remember this! Of course, if you use both shield and sword, you will have a double advantage, providing he does not also use the shield. For if you can repel his magnetism, and at the same time use your own – then he is at your mercy. But if he knows enough to also use his shield – then the battle will be drawn, and neither will win a decided victory. Do you catch the idea? Think it over until it is plain to you.

When you repel the magnetism of one of the persons who have been using it without knowing the nature of his power (and there are many who so use it – the majority of them, in fact) you will be amused to see how "broken up" such a person becomes. He will become bewildered at his failure to influence and affect you, and will often become embarrassed and, in some cases, actually entangled in the currents of his own magnetism. It may even happen (it often does, really) that such a person will become so confused by his apparent loss of power, that he will lose his assurance and consequently his ability to attack. In such cases, he becomes an easy subject for a magnetic rush or broadside on your own part, which will quickly drive him into a disastrous retreat. Of course, if he has a scientific knowledge of the subject, he will not be so taken off guard, but, recognizing your knowledge and power, he will pass it off with a smile, and relinquish the attack.

Dagaz and the Shield of Invisibility

Before we move on to the next lesson we want to discuss one more aspect of Invincibility–*invisibility!*

When one possesses the Balder Force, one is rendered invincible, which means you no longer are a target for life's little and big problems. You can move through life free from most difficulties. When you are confronted with a problem situation, you can easily deal with it and move on. This Force includes the ability to render things, including yourself, invisible. This is accomplished by utilizing the runic energies of Dagaz. According to The Denali Institute of Northern Traditions (runesbyragnar.com), you can simply visualize Dagaz over any object you possess and no one will notice it.

Remember the old saying? "If no one sees or hears a tree fall in the forest, it did not happen." The principle behind this saying is that if no one sees you, you are not present, even though you are physically present. The reason for this is that visibility is based on consciousness or attention of human consciousness to any object or person appearing in the energy environment. This can be done through the use of runic energy dynamics of Dagaz, which is the Rune of Day, or "Daylight."

Everything vibrates! And that which does not vibrate has no perceptible reality. Though objects in the objective reality appear solid, the truth is everything is made up of energy. Everything is made up of atoms, and atoms are 99 percent energy–Vril energy. An atom is a collection of subatomic particles–protons, electrons and neutrons. The space between them is filled with pulsating, oscillating electromagnetic fields that are either in a state of motion or at an instant of rest. Remember our lesson on achieving higher consciousness? We explained the pendulum principle of Itzhak Bentov. In his book, *Stalking the Wild Pendulum*, he explained that when the pendulum reaches its point of rest, it becomes nonmaterial for an instant blink of time, while at the same time it reaches almost infinite velocity. This blink is the dynamics of Isa, the Rune of contraction and inertia, while the movement is the dynamic of Fehu. The pendulum swings with the movement of Fehu, halts for an instant that is the dynamic of Isa, and then swings back again. Here we have fire and ice at work. Tangible reality is when there is this movement or vibration, and when movement ceases, matter and solid reality become diffused and disappears.

Bentove extrapolates that when we meditate, the mind enters a state of being when infinity is perceived in a flash of cosmic illumination. This causes great shifts in perception. This principle of motion and rest in the movement of the pendulum (oscillation between motion and rest) is the runic principle that we tap to render things invisible when we work with Dagaz.

We need to examine the form of Dagaz. Every Rune has three principles: esoteric meaning, sound and form. The form or shape of Dagaz represents this swinging motion of the pendulum. It is at this point, in the center of the Dagaz form, between its two

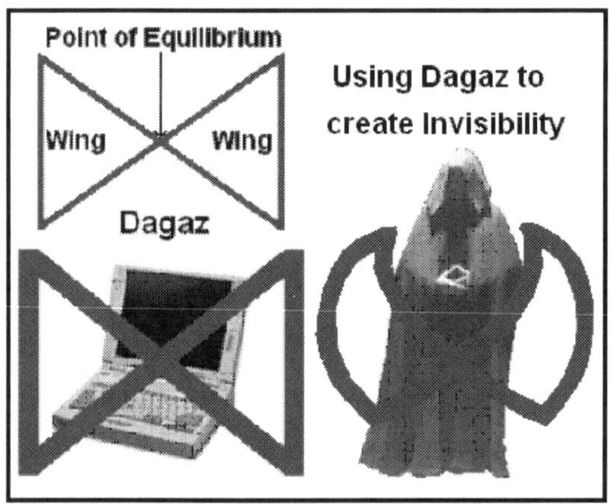

wings, where the point of equilibrium exist. It is akin to the point of rest or "blink" within the swing of the pendulum. Here, a state of absolute stillness, or non-movement, is reached. It is here that there is no vibration. It is at this point that we can assume that *everything that does not vibrate has no perceptible reality.*

Within this parameter, you should, with enough practice, be able to render anything invisible through the "dampening" effect of the runic energies that exist at the center of the shape of Dagaz. Like the center of a Black Hole, the energy here causes vibrations to cease, but the effect of contraction (the runic energy of Isa exists within this point of Dagaz) can actually bend light. Remember that Dagaz represents daylight, or just light. By bending light you can render something invisible. With Dagaz, or the center point of Dagaz, you are bending the vibrational rate of the conscious mind so that it does not notice whatever you have wrapped Dagaz around. The object is still there and in view, but the mind of persons do not notice it because the conscious mind is directed toward other objects whose vibrational rates are in tone with the vibrational rates that exist within Midgard.

The ability to render something invisible has two purposes. The first is mundane and practical. You can protect your possessions from theft. By encircling your possessions in Dagaz, they will become unnoticeable to other persons. The other purpose is to make yourself and our Folk communities inoffensive to the rest of society. Vrilology teaches that as Odinists, we can be mistaken as a threat to the established order, especially toward established fundamentalist religions and to political groups, especially with the Left, who might view anyone who displays or uses Runes as neo-Nazis.

You can harness this power of invisibility to make yourself appear both inoffensive and unnoticeable to anyone, including establishment entities, so that they will live you in peace to practice your faith undisturbed.

Invisibility Exercise:

1) Take several items in you house. One at a time, mentally visualize each object at the center of Dagaz. You can do whatever you think will help you to reinforce this image. If you want to draw a picture or photograph and draw a Dagaz over the item, with the center of Dagaz right on the center of the item, this should help you to reinforce the imagery. Another way is by drawing a Dagaz on the object itself.

2) You should then chant a Galdor chant over the image. You can make up your own chant. Here is an example:

I call on the runic energies of Dagaz
rendering my _________ invisible to others!

This will cause the object to be placed in the point of absolute stillness at the center of the Dagaz Rune. For this to work, you need to have a conscious understanding of how this process works. If you wish to learn more, and we encourage you to do so, you should read Bentov's book.

Another method you can use is to encase yourself in Dagaz to make yourself invisible. Visualize yourself standing in the center of a Dagaz that is wrapped around you like a shield. The center point should be located right before you. You can chant a Rune chant similar to the one given above, like this:

I call on the runic energies of Dagaz
Rendering myself invisible to others.

The ability to render yourself unnoticeable to your enemies or potential enemies is the ability to fly under the radar, or become stealthy. Stealth is a form of invincibility, for no one will target you as a potential threat to their social stability if they do not take notice of your existence. At worst, you will be considered a charming abnormality, much as the Amish are viewed.

Chapter Seventeen: A New Life Is Awaiting You–A Life of Order or Chaos–The Choice is Yours

By now you should have an understanding of the powers that dwell within you. You know now that you are made of energy–Vril, and that you have the potential to become a Vril Being. Vril is everywhere, and it cannot be created or destroyed. It exists everywhere in the universe, but it can be changed, shaped and used to transform your life and control your destiny. By now you understand that the universe emanates from your mind. You unconsciously create your reality and you can learn to consciously recreate it. You are now aware that the divine powers do not exist in some unseen heavenly realm, but within you. With your thoughts and feelings, you can awaken this power. You can communicate with them and especially, you can align yourself with them, working as allies in the task of giving order to the universe.

Balder Rising!

We discussed how in Norse mythology, Odin is the All-Father of the Gods, and his wife, Frigga, the All-Mother. Their twin sons are named Balder and Hoder. Balder is a beautiful God, representing love, peace and harmony and what is known as the Love Force. He is filled with the Light of Love and is the God of the Light represented by the Sun. His twin brother, Hoder, has a very different nature: dark and blind, representing ignorance. He is known as the God of Darkness. He is not evil, but his ignorance prevents him from knowing the Light that is his brother, and this is his weakness, which makes him an easy victim of the agent of Chaos, Loki.

It was revealed to Balder in a dream that he would die, and his death would herald the ultimate battle between the Gods (order) and the Giants (chaos). When he told his parents of his dream, his mother, Frigga, tried to prevent the inevitable by making everything in the universe take an oath never to harm her beloved son Balder, but overlooked one thing, Mistletoe. Mistletoe can be used to make a powerful poison.

One Loki tricked Frigga into revealing this secret and used it to killed Balder. He fashioned a poison dart from it and then tricked Hoder into using it to kill his brother, Balder. Hoder was punished by his half-brother, Vali, the Avenger, but Loki escaped, to eventually be hunted down by Heimdall and punished by the Gods.

Loki is Chaos. He uses the blindness of Hoder to stamp out the self-awareness that is Balder. If we remain blind to our true heritage, we become pawns, controlled by the forces of Chaos. Balder represents the self-aware Vril Being. As a Vril Being, in command of the power of Vril, nothing can harm you, and nothing stands in your way except for ignorance, personified by Balder's blind brother, Hoder. Ignorance will blind you to the truth about the universe, you and your heritage, your relationship with Odin and the Gods and secret power of Vril.

After Loki is captured, he is imprisoned, but eventually frees himself and leads an army of Giants in one all-out assault on the Gods. The final battle results in the destruction of the orderly universe, with both Gods and Giants destroying each other. But a new order rises from the Netherworld, the realm of the dead, where Balder is resting. Balder than leads the righteous in creating a new order, a golden age known as Gimli. In this new gold age, the Gods will be reborn and order reestablished in a new age of harmony, love, peace, order and honor.

This fable is not to be taken literally. This is no End-of-Times prediction, or a Heathen Revelation, but a tale filled with great knowledge–secret knowledge–to be discovered: That the Gods did not exactly die, but fell into a suspended state. They sleep within us, within each of our atoms, and through Vrilology you can cause the Gods to awaken within you. Through Vrilology, you will possess the knowledge of how to harness Vril, and use it to shape your future. Armed with Vrilology, you can call on Balder to rise from the Netherworld, (your subconscious) and establish his Golden Age of Gimli inside of you. This is what we mean by Balder Rising!

Once Balder has risen within you, you will become a Vril Being, and you will no longer be blind to the reality of the secret power of Vril that lies dormant with you. You will become aware that you possess the same powers as the Gods to harness and shape Vril into what you want. Up to now you have lived as one of Hoder's children, blinded by ignorance to your true heritage of being a Vril Being. You have lived in the realm of darkness, thinking you are a slave to the physical universe, and that you have had to struggle for everything you have achieved or still want. But once you have discovered your true heritage, that of being a Vril Being, with the power to shape and mold your future with your mind, you have called on the love, light and harmony that is Balder to arise within you and transform you into a being housing the Golden Age of Gimli.

How Do I Know I am a Vril Being?

Many religious traditions tell you that you are created in God's image. True. Whether you believe in one Supreme God, many Gods, or a Universal Intelligence, you are the Gods manifested in human form. The difference between you and the Gods is less than 1 percent. You are more than 99 percent Vril; the Gods, 100 percent. You are the Gods in physical form—a Vril Being possessing physical form, in a three dimensional reality—while the Gods exist on a higher planet of reality, perhaps with more than three dimensions. Quantum physics theorizes that there are up to eleven dimensions. Are the Gods beings with eleven dimensions, or even more? These are questions that we do not have the space to explore, but what you need to grasp is that you are made of the same divine essence as the Gods. You have the Gods' intelligence and wisdom. The only thing you lack is awareness of your true heritage because you possess a three dimensional physical body. Once you learn that you are not confined by this physical body, you will realize you are truly a Vril

Being. Your body will no longer be a prison. But how will you know when you have freed yourself of this physical enslavement and evolved into a true Vril entity? You will know by the transformation in your personality—by the way you look at the universe, life and yourself.

A Vril Being's perception of the universe and reality is not limited by five senses. He knows that he possesses other senses that can see beyond the physical reality that his physical body experiences in this material universe (Midgard). This is the meaning of Balder Rising.

A Vril Being knows he is not alone. He knows that he can become a partner with the divine forces giving shape to the universe, by aligning himself with the Gods and joining in this work. This is the meaning of Balder Rising.

A Vril Being is not concerned with external forces that stand in his way, but is confident of his personal powers to shape his own destiny. He knows he can evolve to a higher form of life, with a superior state of consciousness. He is free from anger, hostility and all negative emotions that would act like weights to hold him back. He is free from competition with others, and realizes he can transform his world through his mind. A Vril Being is aware of the great powers he possesses to manipulate the physical world into the image he wants for it through the power of his mind, filled with the power of Balder's love and not the blind ignorance of Hoder. This is the meaning of Balder Rising.

A Vril Being knows he is never totally separate from other beings and things, an island unto himself. He realizes he is connected to his Folk and family, and distantly, to all other life forms, and that he shares with them his physical and spiritual essence. He understands that all things are connected. Once he realizes that he is connected to others, the need for conflict and confrontation disappears. Once he has accepted this, he knows that he can live in respect and peace, not only with his brothers and sisters, but with those who seem totally alien to him and his kin. This is the meaning of Balder Rising.

A Vril Being understands the law of cause and effect, and that you attract more of what you think about. He understands that there is a higher power holding the universe together. We in the Folk Faith of Balder Rising refer to this higher power as the Gods, while others might refer to it as Go, or a Supreme Intelligence; but whatever image you believe in, you know that this higher power is behind the law of cause and effect. He knows that it is thoughts and feelings that will cause things to happen, and the return from one's thinking and feeling is the effect. He knows that this law is beyond the physical laws of material science. Your thoughts create your reality. This is the greatest example of cause and effect. You thoughts cause things to manifest themselves by transforming the flow of Vril, creating pathways into your future—the effect. This is the meaning of Balder Rising.

A Vril Being understands that true success in life is not dependent on the accumulation of material objects, but is dependent on your discovering your true purpose. He understands the difference between goals and purpose. If you are in business, he knows that increasing your wealth is a selfish goal that will never make you happy, but if your purpose is to be successful in business by ensuring that everyone benefits, including your customers and community through your entrepreneurship, then you will be creating a prosperous community for all, including yourself. You will be generating positive feelings on the part of your customers and those who live within your community, contributing to the creation of a happy and harmonious community. Once you have found your true purpose in life, you will be living a life that is ethically, morally and spiritually aligned with the Gods. This is the meaning of Balder Rising.

A Vril Being understands that we possess senses beyond the five physical senses. He understands that intuition is not just a "hunch," but your inner voice. It is your Vril soul guiding you as surely as your other five senses, and in truth, more surely and effectively than the other senses are capable of guiding. The Vril Being knows that these "hunches" are actually the voice of the Gods sending you messages. This is the meaning of Balder Rising.

A Vril Being is not concerned about fighting evil, for there is not evil in the universe. He does not spend his time opposing what he disagrees with, for by spending time, energy, thoughts and feelings on what he opposes, he is actually creating more of it. He understands that Vril does not receive negative thoughts, and reforms negativity into a positive affirmation of what should be created. If you are constantly opposing something, fighting it, you are actually creating more of it by focusing your thoughts and feelings on the subject.

The Vril Being understands that an idea can be defeated only by another idea. A Vril Being lives his life affirming what he wishes to manifest in the physical universe through positive thoughts and feelings, and knows his thoughts and feelings will bring about what he most desires.

A Vril Being spends his life working toward something, and not against things. A Vril Being is never against things. He is for things. This is the meaning of Balder Rising.

A Vril Being is aware of others who are connected with him, united in the knowledge of Vrilology. He realizes he is connected to kin and folk, and that Vril unites them all on a level beyond the physical. He cannot become truly successful without sharing his success with those he loves and shares a genetic lineage with, his kin and kindred. This is the meaning of Balder Rising.

A Vril Being is never preoccupied with revenge, or grudges or hostility. He knows that he can call on the higher powers to bring him justice in the physical world. He understands that by aligning himself with the Gods, order will be established in his life and this includes justice against those who wish to do him harm. This is the meaning of Balder Rising.

The Vril Being does not believe limitations on what he can achieve in this universe. He understands there is infinite abundance that he can draw on. What he can achieve in life is restricted only by his belief in limitations. A Vril Being knows he has the power to make miracles. This is the meaning of Balder Rising.

Let Wunjo Control What You Think

The use of Wunjo to fill your life with happiness and joy is one example of how you can use the Runes to help visualize and control your thoughts and feelings to create the proper pathways in your life. Runes are symbols with powerful esoteric meaning behind them. By understanding these meanings, your brain, which is geared to registering symbols, especially geometric symbols, will learn to gain greater control over your thoughts and feelings. We call this "Runic Thinking."

As we described, you can chant Wunjo to help fill yourself with joy, happiness and harmony, and to shape Vril to fulfill your wishes. Wunjo will help you to live in harmony with your environment. It runic energies will change the frequencies of everything around you so that resistence will be reduced. The power of Wunjo is to change the vibratory rates of all living things so that they work in synchronicity, so that you can glide through the day with as little resistance as possible.

There are hundreds of ways that the runic energies of Wunjo can change your life. When you spend time with your family or friends, do you enjoy yourself? I hope so. You would be surprised at how many people spend their time with friends and family arguing or discussing things that make them unhappy. When you are at work, do you consider your co-workers "idiots," "buffoons," or people that you are in competition with? Or do you enjoy their company? You have the choice in how others will treat you by the way you act toward others. Remember our discussion in of the mind games from Star Wars? You can get your way with most people you meet by being inoffensive, and by being pleasant, and friendly. If you consider this too much work, then you have problems—but problems are not something you should worry about. They are things that you can easily correct with the proper state of mind.

When you get up in the morning, just agree that you are going to be happy that day. No matter whom you come into contact with, no matter what happens to you on your way to work, or at work, you have got to just agree that you are going to remain happy about yourself and your life. Do the things that will bring you joy and make you happy. Be conscious of the joy you feel, and you will soon be aware of the power of Wunjo. You will discover that if you make Wunjo a major part of your life, you will be living in a state of bliss! Once you are living in a state of bliss, you are calling the abundance of the universe toward you. Enjoy life! Trust me that if you are able to be in a state of Wunjo, (joy) every day, all day long, people will notice. I know because I have noticed how people whom I've known for twenty years react differently toward me now. Many have commented on my "new and improved" demeanor. I have had people tell me, "Bob, you're always smiling. You always seem to be happy." They also want me to help them because they feel that I will seriously help. I am drawing them to me. Whether I am able to help them or not, they feel appreciated by my sincere effort to want to help them. And I have never had to ask twice when I needed these people to help me. I have created a Vril shield around me that causes people to act in accordance with what I desire in life. The reason for this is simple. I am thinking Wunjo all the time.

Try putting Wunjo in your life. Try thinking, meditating and chanting Wunjo every day. You will discover the power this single Rune, Wunjo, will fill you with. And you will notice that the more you draw on this power, the greater it will be for you to use. You will eventually reach a point when you will not have to consciously think Wunjo anymore, because you will be filled with its power and be radiating that power outward, transforming the world around you. This will happen because you will be thinking Wunjo. You will be thinking runically.

The Vril is With You

You now understand that through Vril, everything in the universe is connected, and that you can let go of all the negative influences from your past, and take control of your life. This can be done by your surrendering to the currents of Vril that are constantly flowing into you. Through total concentration, you can give shape to the Vril currents, which form the pathways (your

Wyrd) into your future. Those people who have abundance in their lives know, consciously or unconsciously, how to control this process. Their lives are not burdened with the tedious struggle of everyday existence. Instead, they live lives that seem blessed by Fortune's smiles. They move through life, not struggling against the flow of Vril, but moving along its currents, utilizing its powers to fill their lives with everything they desire. They have found their purpose in life, and once they have, they can ride the currents easily and effortlessly into the future. Once you have achieved this state, you will feel a kind of bliss communicating that you are working with the divine powers, the Gods, in giving order to the universe. Your life will then be orderly, free from strife and conflict. Once you have discovered your overriding purpose, your life will have meaning. You will have shifted the emphasis of your life to one of serving a greater purpose in the universe. Your mind will be closed to all distraction, and focused on your purpose. You will discover that once you have achieved your purpose, you can concentrate on this task with little effort. It will become second nature to you and you will eventually no longer have to think about it. You will be riding the currents of Vril into your future. You can do this through meditation, and with the use of the Runes. It really does not take much effort. Just two or three times a day for fifteen minutes, and you will soon learn that you can train your mind to act as a powerful tool to shape your life and the universe around you. You will be able to transform your physical reality, your physical body, and change your life forever.

You no longer have to be a slave to your senses, impulses and urges. You will discover that the world can work with you, instead of against you. You will discover that you need not struggle for everything you want. You have only to control your mind, and use your thoughts and feelings to draw them into your life through Vril. You need only align yourself with the flow of Vril and follow the pathways it creates for you. You no longer have to concern yourself with the results, the accolades, the outcome, the wealth, the success or the final destination. You need only send forth the thoughts, filled with joy, harmony and the love of life, and you will create the pathways that will be filled with everything you desire.

You need not strain to succeed in this process. The most difficult thing is to accept the reality of this process. You have been living a life dominated by the rational, logical, and reasonable left side of your brain. You need to rely more on the intuitive, psychic, and spiritual right side of your brain. Once you can achieve this, you will have achieved a state of bliss. You will know a type of ecstasy that will transform you forever. It will take you by surprise. One day, you will just know you have been transformed. You will just discover that you are no longer just a mundane human being—you will simply become aware that you have been transformed into a Vril Being.

Once you have become a Vril Being, new avenues of creativity will be at your disposal through the powers of Vril. You will be radiating Vrilic power. This is the natural state of those super achievers you hear about in the news. Most people don't even realize how they became super achievers. They have a natural ability to draw, increase, harness and shape Vrilic energy flowing into them. They were born that way. It is as natural for them as it is for a bird to fly, or a fish to swim. They never think about it—they just do it. But there is no reason you cannot become one of these super achievers. Find your purpose, learn to control your mind and use your thoughts and feelings to increase the flow of Vril to you, and mold it into what you desire. Once you can do this, you too will feel the bliss. You will then want more and more of this bliss. It will become effortless, and you will become more productive in everything you do. You will have transformed yourself into a Vril Being, possessing a Vril personality.

Through Vril, you can transform yourself, your physical well-being and your personality. You can awaken the divine powers that dwell within you, causing you to evolve into a higher state of being–a Vril Being. Your omnipotent mind will eliminate all doubts you might have about your faults and shortcomings. You can use the Runes to help transform yourself, train your mind into an instrument to harness Vril, so that you can transform all physical manifestations about yourself. Everything physical about you is a product of your mental process, and this process is powered by Vril. To change from a human being into a Vril Being, you need only to focus your thinking, calmly, confidently and constantly on the kind of person you wish to become. You can use individual Runes to symbolize each quality you wish to manifest, increase and strengthen about yourself. These thoughts are like seeds you are implanting into your being, causing you to evolve. They are also the seeds for transforming the world around you. They are also the thoughts that will create the pathways to the future you desire. Through your mind, you can control Vril, and reform the atoms, molecules and subatomic particles to reshape the physical around you to your desire.

You must learn to think positively and cease using terminology that affirms negativity. Stop worrying about the terrible things that are happening in the world. You will only be drawing more of these horrible things into your life. Let your mind reflect a conscious confidence. Think and talk about your unlimited ability to make anything you desire happen. Focus on your capacity to create whatever you desire most. Dwell on what you want to fill the world with, not on what you wish to eliminate. What you spend most of your time thinking and talking about will only get stronger and grow more powerful. Focus on what you are for, not on what you are against. Your mental powers will naturally draw more and more people into working toward those things that you are mentally focused on, so concentrate on what you want to manifest, not on what you wish to eliminate. If you do the latter, you will be drawing people into action to create the very things you want to eliminate, creating more and more of it. Create an image in your mind, through visualization, of the type of reality you wish. Tell yourself that you have divine powers radiating within that will create what it is you want. Think of yourself as a builder of the type of world you want to create, and not the destroyer of what you oppose. You will create a field of energy that will cause everyone you come into contact with to move according to the pathways that will cause them to work toward the creation of what you wish to manifest in the physical world.

Once you have accepted that your life has a purpose, you will never even have to think about it. You will be like a raft floating down a river on its currents. Your personality will reflect your purpose. You will feel blissful and the talents and abilities necessary to fulfill your purpose will manifest in you. You need only accept the reality that you are now a Vril Being, with a purposeful life, and all that is necessary in your personal characteristics will appear. Through the Runic forces of Nauthiz, necessity or Need-Fire, your evolution into a Vril Being, a God-human, will become a reality.

Once you know you have become a Vril Being, trust your newfound Vrilic powers. The divine powers, supreme intelligence, or whatever name you choose to identify the Gods, will speak to you intuitively. Trust your inner voice. Trust your instincts. It is the divine guidance communicating with you from deep within you. It is your way of knowing that you are never alone, that the Gods dwell within you. You have only to call to them, and they will answer you. You need only establish a link with their divine intelligence and you will be able to align yourself with their task of maintaining order in the universe, which will manifest in pathways filled with whatever you desire.

Begin right now to see yourself as a Vril Being. Begin to accept that you are 99 percent Vril, and that the godly powers that maintain order in the universe are within you. Know that you have the power, though your mind, to harness this divine force, Vril, and use it to shape and mold your life into whatever you desire. Once you have accepted this truth, you will discover that there is nothing you cannot do, nothing beyond your ability to achieve. You can do anything! Anything! Know that the secret is desire. If you can desire something, you can make it happen.

Learn to meditate regularly every day. Understand how slipping into Alpha and Theta states of consciousness is the means by which you can use your mind to send your thoughts into the Vril currents. Learn how to use the Runes to shape and mold the

Vril currents into pathways (your Wyrd) into the future filled with whatever you desire. Visualize what you want, and who you want to be. Master these techniques, and the possibilities are limitless!

Align Yourself With the Gods

You have a choice. You can abandon yourself to a life of chaos, chance and conflict, or you can consciously decide to align yourself with the Gods, the divine powers in the universe, and possess a life of order. You can begin by consciously affirming your decision not to submit to doubt. You have only to say to yourself every day: "I know that I am not alone. I can receive guidance if I maintain a positive attitude. I have within me the power to create miracles. I know there is nothing I cannot accomplish. I know the universe is infinite, and thus, there is nothing beyond my powers to make happen."

Once you have aligned yourself with the Gods, you can receive guidance by simply listening to that little voice inside of you, and you will know everything you need to. Every cell in your body is speaking to you. 99 percent of you is Vril, and the Gods are 100 percent Vril. You have only to listen to that 99 percent of you. To do so, you need only to accept this truth. You are made of atoms, each a universe possessing a universal intelligence. Nurture this intelligence. Trust it! Revere it! Treat it with the sacredness it deserves, and it will help you make the right decision.

Affirm to yourself that you have 99 percent in common with the Gods, and you will be on your way to evolving to a higher level of existence. You need only to challenge yourself to rise to a higher level of consciousness, and you will be amazed at what you can accomplish. You will soon discover that you no longer think of yourself as a victim of circumstances, but as a being with the power to transform the universe in accordance with your wishes. You will know that there is nothing you cannot do if you put your mind to it, and believe you can do it!

Learn to listen to and trust your body. Your body is 99 percent Vril. If you open your mind to it, you will receive guidance from your body on what you need to do to keep healthy and fit. Condition yourself to listen to your inner dictates. Don't be afraid to listen to those hunches and inner voices telling you what to avoid, what to do and not to do, whom to seek and whom to avoid, what to eat and not to eat, when to sleep and when to be active. Understand that Vril is the same Life Force the Gods possess. It is constantly flowing into every cell, every atom in your body, replenishing your life. But its flow will decrease over the years, because of the decisions you make according to the type of life you wish to lead. If you lead a life aligned with the Gods, you can maintain the proper flow of Vril and stay younger and healthier, and thus, live a longer and happier life. But if you align yourself with the forces of chaos, you will live a life that will block and decrease the flow of Vril, causing you to age more rapidly, become ill, and deteriorate faster. Learn to trust the Vril, your conduit to a higher, divine intelligence that flows through you. You need only tell yourself every day that you are more than a body possessing a soul, you are a soul possessing a body. Affirm the truth that you are a Vril Being and that your physical form is just one aspect of who and what you are, not the defining element of who and what you are!

Start right now and say to yourself, I will no longer doubt or fear. From now on, I know and trust the truth about myself! If you say this every day, as often as you can, then you will experience, at some time, an awakening—a moment when you say it and truly believe it! When this moment arrives, you will know it because it will be as if you suddenly walked into the light. Your eyes will be open for the first time and you will see the universe and yourself with a new understanding. You will be able to move forward in life with a new confidence, a new assurance. Your path into the future will appear bright and beautiful, free from fears and tribulations.

From this day forth, begin to readjust your vision of yourself, permitting your Vril self to hold a position of importance, and your physical self will follow. Understand that your physical body is part of your soul, and should not be viewed as separate from it. Keep a vision of what you want to manifest physically in your body, and then let the flow of Vril take over and make it so. Once your Vril self takes control, your physical body will no longer be in charge. It will no longer demand more of what you don't want and don't need. You will be able to control your eating habits, your craving for alcohol, your need for drugs, your susceptibility to illnesses and other "bad habits."

Do not ask for help in the physical world. Use the techniques to mentally assert your desire for whatever you need, and your thoughts and feelings will manifest it in the physical world. Your positive thoughts and feelings will form the flow of Vril to provide what you need in the physical realm, by creating pathways leading to those things, or leading those things to you. Once help arrives, accept it and be grateful, because it arrived as a result of your mental state creating a pathway that led it to you. Know that it happened on a realm of existence that is invisible to you in this physical reality.

Once you have aligned yourself with the Gods, your life will be transformed. The reason is simple: You will now be working with that Divine Intelligence that is giving shape to the universe, not against it. You will have replaced conflict with harmony, difficulties with ease, decline with growth. You will have unleashed great powers that reside within you but have been dormant. You will have awakened the Gods that dwell within you. This is what is meant by Balder Rising! You have begun to cultivate authentic powers that can create miracles. Authentic power resides not in the physical plane, but in the mind. It is through the power of your mind that you can control Vril, which makes up 99 percent of physical matter. Use your mind to control your physical self and your physical reality. This is truly what it means to become a Vril Being, and be aligned with the Gods.

You Have a Choice

Your mind is like a ship at sea in a storm. The storm is the chaos of the universe that will throw you about without direction. You can fight to stay afloat, but most of the time you will still be overwhelmed by the ferocity of the storm, and sink. That storm is the product of all the baggage stored in your Orlog, in your past.

The waves that come crashing into you are the negative things in your past that you obsess on. The thunder and lightning are the pain that these events cause you in the present. You are constantly being thrown about, off course, with the threat of sinking, by thoughts of your past. They caused you to sail into the storm in the first place. Your past thoughts, feelings and memories are leading you into a future reflecting their nature. They are causing you to act in a certain way in the present, making you think and feel certain things, and those thoughts and feelings are shaping the pathways into your future.

When you are aware of the power that resides within you, the power that your mind possesses, you suddenly take charge. When you are aware of the thoughts and feelings that are causing you to shape and form your future by what you are thinking and feeling in the present, you have control of your ship and you will be able to set sail on a course into calm and pleasant seas.

This entire book revolves around the single principle that what you create in the invisible world will manifest itself in the physical world. You, in the present, are always creating your future. The secret to a successful and happy future is the awareness that what you are thinking and feeling and how you are acting in the present is determined by those things in your past that have control over you. The real secret to this power is to know that you have it. Once you are aware of the power of Vril, and you make a habit of using it, you will find the answers to all your questions. You have only to ask the questions, and once you have aligned yourself with the Gods, the Universal Intelligence, or whatever you wish to call it, you will receive the answers to all your questions. The answers are all around you. They can appear in many forms. You have just got to be conscious of them. Don't be blinded by ignorance. This was the curse of Hoder, who was blind, and thus ignorant of the destructive nature of Loki, when Loki tricked him into killing his beloved brother, Balder. Once you accept ignorance, you become blinded to the truth. You then are that lost ship, being knocked about in the storm of a chaotic life.

Once you accept the truth of Vril, you are opening your eyes. You are no longer blinded by ignorance and you will be able to see the light of Balder rising and filling you with its power. You can then begin the task of evolving into a Vril Being, with a new personality–a Vril personality. To help you begin your new life, you can begin by using the Runes and try the few examples of how to use them in your meditation that we have provided for you in this book.

You can begin to transform yourself right now. Stop thinking about what you are, and begin seeing yourself as you wish yourself to be. Look at yourself in the mirror and see the new you. As soon as you close the covers of this book, after reading the last page, begin to see yourself acting at the new level of confidence that you wish to exhibit. Create in your mind the image of the new Vril Being that you have become. Know that this image can be transformed from a mental picture into a physical reality through the power of your mind. As soon as you know, and cease to doubt, that your mind has the power to manifest in the physical world what you are thinking and feeling, you will begin the process of transforming yourself. As soon as you know your purpose, your life will be changed. You will begin to trust in your power, and then there will be nothing that you cannot accomplish if you put your mind to it. You will become the Vril Being that will be a reflection of your marvelous new inner vision of yourself.

See this new Vril Being in possession of the new abilities and talents that you wish to possess. Know that your talents and abilities are a reflection of the invisible flow of Vril power into you and throughout your body. Know that you can be as intelligent as you wish. Know that your intelligence flows from Vril, that your brain is made of Vril. Every cell in your brain is made of Vril. Decide the type of personality you wish. You can begin right now to change those habits that lead you to defeat in everything you try to accomplish, and replace them with habits that will assure success in everything you set out to do. Know that once you become a Vril Being, you can cease to obsess over things you don’t want to focus on, and begin to concentrate on those thoughts and feelings that will empower you.

Know that you have the power to control the physical processes of your body. Once you become a Vril Being, you can begin to slow down the aging process. You will discover that you can increase the flow of Vril into you, filling and replenishing every cell, every gene, and every atom in your body with Vril. Once you can use your mind to control and increase the flow of Vril into you, you will be able to affect the aging process of every cell in your body.

Know that your thoughts create your feelings, and your feelings can affect the physical health of your body. You have the potential to use your emotions to create miracles. Your mind can produce emotions that will either hurt or help you. Stress can kill. But your body has the potential to create enough adrenalin to give you superhuman strength. Your thoughts can create physical manifestations that are experienced emotionally. All your emotions are the result of your mind's producing chemicals within your body, transforming your physical self. Know that it is through the power of the mind to harness Vril that these changes are created in your body. Your feelings are the physical manifestations in your body, created by the thoughts produced from your mind, powered by Vril. They are examples of how your mind can affect your physical form. Once you know that you are in command of which emotions you are producing, you can begin to be fully in control: a Vril Being.

Once you know you are a Vril Being, you will discover that you no longer doubt yourself. You will discover that you now love yourself. You might be surprised to discover that most people suffer from emotional and physical illnesses because they dislike who and what they are. But once you truly love yourself, you will be happy about your life. The happiness you exhibit will be manifested in a love of yourself and a love of life. When we don’t love ourselves, we lack self-esteem. This lack of self-esteem will manifest through your thoughts, creating paths into your future with more of the same. You will draw to you a lack of love and a lack of happiness. But once you truly love yourself, you will be attracting more love to you, more happiness and thus, success.

Your every want is the result of your loving something. Happiness, material wealth and possessions, a beautiful and loving relationship, fame and success—whatever you desire is a result of loving those things. But if you don't love yourself, you will not be creating pathways into a future filled with those things. You must truly love yourself and not focus on the world around you, or you will begin to hate what you see, and fill your thoughts with those feelings. If you focus on what you hate, you will never love yourself. Remember: you cannot feel happy when you are thinking about things that make you angry. If you are always thinking about things you are against, you will be filling your future with those things. You must begin to focus on those things you are for and want to fill your future pathways. Once you do, you will discover that you have complete control over your future.

You have a choice: to continue to be a victim of the chaotic forces that control the lives of most people, or take command of your destiny. You can decide what type of life you want, the nature of your future and what you fill it with. All you have to do is be conscious of your great potential. Know that the universe is made of Vril, and everything in it, including you, is made of Vril. Also understand that you can shape your future by what you think and feel. Realize that Vril, the source of all life, can be shaped and molded by the thoughts and feelings of your mind. But understand this. ***The process of evolving into a Vril Being does not happen overnight. This transformation can take your entire life, and even then you might never fully reach your full potential as a Vril Being. The reason lies hidden within your Orlog. In the book*** **A Christmas Carol** ***by Charles Dickens, Scrooge is visited by the ghost of his departed partner Marley. Marley is weighed down with an enormous chain that he tells Scrooge that "he forged in life." We are all weighed down by our individual chains, forged, not just in our individual life, but also in the lives of all our ancestors. The rate and progress of evolving into a Vril Being and gaining the powers described in this book is***

determined by the chain that weighs us down within our Orlog. It does not have to stop us from evolving, and this is why we emphasize the importance of learning to cleanse or bend what lies within your Orlog. What is in it will determine your success in your progress in evolving into a Vril Being.

You now know the secret of how to transform yourself from a human being into a Vril Being. Whether or not you take this step is entirely up to you. There are no limits to what you can do and become, there is only the desire to do it. Do you have that desire?

Made in the USA
Columbia, SC
08 August 2022

64861646R00295